Community Policing

International Patterns and Comparative Perspectives

Advances in Police Theory and Practice Series

Series Editor: Dilip K. Das

Policing and the Mentally Ill: International Perspectives
Duncan Chappell

Security Governance, Policing, and Local Capacity
Kam C. Wong

Policing in Hong Kong: History and Reform
Jan Froestad with Clifford D. Shearing

Police Performance Appraisals: A Comparative Perspective
Serdar Kenan Gul and Paul O'Connell

Police Reform in The New Democratic South Africa
Moses Montesh and Vinesh Basdeo

Los Angeles Police Department Meltdown: The Fall of the Professional-Reform Model of Policing
James Lasley

Financial Crimes: A Global Threat
Maximillian Edelbacher, Peter Kratcoski, and Michael Theil

Police Integrity Management in Australia: Global Lessons for Combating Police Misconduct
Louise Porter and Tim Prenzler

The Crime Numbers Game: Management by Manipulation
John A. Eterno and Eli B. Silverman

The International Trafficking of Human Organs: A Multidisciplinary Perspective
Leonard Territo and Rande Matteson

Police Reform in China
Kam C. Wong

Mission-Based Policing
John P. Crank, Dawn M. Irlbeck, Rebecca K. Murray, and Mark Sundermeier

The New Khaki: The Evolving Nature of Policing in India
Arvind Verma

Cold Cases: An Evaluation Model with Follow-up Strategies for Investigators
James M. Adcock and Sarah L. Stein

Policing Organized Crime: Intelligence Strategy Implementation
Petter Gottschalk

Security in Post-Conflict Africa: The Role of Nonstate Policing
Bruce Baker

Community Policing

International Patterns and Comparative Perspectives

Edited by
Dominique Wisler
Ihekwoaba D. Onwudiwe

CRC Press is an imprint of the
Taylor & Francis Group, an **informa** business

Top cover image: Copyright: Suzette Heald. Taken in 2005, the picture depicts the disciplining of a *sungu-sungu* by the iritongo for dereliction of duty. They - the *sungusungu* - had wandered off the night before and those held on remand had managed to escape from the "cell" by making a hole in the roof.

Bottom cover image: Copyright: Federal Police of Belgium

CRC Press
Taylor & Francis Group
6000 Broken Sound Parkway NW, Suite 300
Boca Raton, FL 33487-2742

First issued in paperback 2019

ISBN-13: 978-1-4200-9358-2 (hbk)
ISBN-13: 978-0-367-86603-7 (pbk)

Library of Congress Cataloging-in-Publication Data

Community policing : international patterns and comparative perspectives / editors, Dominique Wisler and Ihekwoaba D. Onwudiwe.
p. cm. -- (Advances in police theory and practice ; 2)
Includes bibliographical references and index.
ISBN 978-1-4200-9358-2
1. Community policing. I. Wisler, Dominique. II. Onwudiwe, Ihekwoaba D. III. Title. IV. Series.

HV7936.C83.C66 2009
363.2'3--dc22 2008052724

Visit the Taylor & Francis Web site at
http://www.taylorandfrancis.com

and the CRC Press Web site at
http://www.crcpress.com

Series Preface

While the literature on police and allied subjects is growing exponentially, its impact upon day-to-day policing remains small. The two worlds of research and practice of policing remain disconnected even though cooperation between the two is growing. A major reason is that the two groups speak in different languages. The research work is published in hard-to-access journals and presented in a manner that is difficult to comprehend for a lay person. On the other hand the police practitioners tend not to mix with researchers and remain secretive about their work. Consequently, there is little dialogue between the two and almost no attempt to learn from one another. Dialog across the globe, amongst researchers and practitioners situated in different continents, are of course even more limited.

I attempted to address this problem by starting the IPES, www.ipes.info, where a common platform has brought the two together. IPES is now in its 16th year. The annual meetings which constitute most major annual event of the organization have been hosted in all parts of the world. Several publications have come out of these deliberations and a new collaborative community of scholars and police officers has been created whose membership runs into several hundreds.

Another attempt was to begin a new journal, aptly called *Police Practice and Research: An International Journal*, PPR, that has opened the gate to practitioners to share their work and experiences. The journal has attempted to focus upon issues that help bring the two on a single platform. PPR is completing its 10 years in 2009. It is certainly an evidence of growing collaboration between police research and practice that PPR which began with 4 issues a year, expanded into 5 issues in its fourth year and, now, it is issued six times a year,

Clearly, these attempts, despite their success, remain limited. Conferences and journal publications do help create a body of knowledge and an association of police activists but cannot address substantial issues in depth. The limitations of time and space preclude larger discussions and more authoritative expositions that can provide stronger and broader linkages between the two worlds.

It is this realization of the increasing dialogue between police research and practice that has encouraged many of us- my close colleagues and myself connected closely with IPES and PPR across the world- to conceive and implement a new attempt in this direction. I am now embarking on a book series, Advances in Police Theory and Practice, that seeks to attract writers from all parts of the world. Further, the attempt is to find practitioner contributors. The objective is to make the series a serious contribution to our knowledge of the police as well as to improve police practices. The focus is not only in work that describes the best and successful police practices but also one that challenges current paradigms and breaks new ground to prepare a police for the twenty-first century. The series seeks for comparative analysis that highlights achievements in distant parts of the world as well as one that encourages an in-depth examination of specific problems confronting a particular police force.

It is hoped that through this series it will be possible to accelerate the process of building knowledge about policing and help bridge the gap between the two worlds-the world of police research and police practice. This is an invitation to police scholars and practitioners across the world to come and join in this venture.

Dilip K. Das Ph.D.
Founding President
International Police Executive Symposium, IPES, www.ipes.info
Founding Editor-in-Chief, Police Practice and Research:
An International Journal PPR, www.tandf.co.uk/journals

Table of Contents

Foreword

Community-oriented policing (COP) has achieved an enviable status in the practices of policing. The model and ideology has become the almost unchallenged definition of good and democratic policing. The terms *community* and *community policing*, and the many themes that these terms imply—partnership, working together, responsiveness, service, accountability, transparency—are now standard admonitions on how to practice effective, democratic, or, more generally, good and professional policing. COP norms have found their way into transnational regimes on what constitutes policing, which respects professional and democratic norms. COP is the ideological and policy model espoused in mission statements, police goals, and reform programs by practically all policing forces, and by the vast number of transnational police assistance programs delivered through intergovernmental organizations (IGOs), nongovernmental organizations (NGOs), and corporate and private consultancy firms (e.g., Caparini and Marenin, 2004; Friedman, 1992; Lab and Das, 2003; Neild, 2002; for a more critical assessment, see Brogden and Nijhar, 2005; Ellison, 2007). To be modern, in tune with current thinking, open to new ideas, aware of domestic and global developments in policing, and committed to professional standards means being able to speak the language of community policing, or, at the very least, be comfortable in talking about the need to have the community involved in policing practices.

As happens with "universal" solutions to policy problems, COP is in danger of becoming a meaningless phrase because it can be and has been interpreted differently by various countries and policing forces. The police of quite divergent countries claim to practice COP or are seeking to move toward that ideology and model. The flexibility and vagueness of the term, the inability to clearly define the almost mythical notion of "community," the ability to portray (in the official rhetoric of policing) many existing practices as examples of COP, and scholarly disagreements on how to conceptualize and measure whether a policing system practices COP should cause reformers, advocates, scholars, critics, and the police to step back to rethink what COP looks like when implemented. What really constitutes COP, in relation to the work of the police and their relations with civic society? One way is to analyze police practices undertaken in the name of COP in order to clarify the concept, to limit it to practices that clearly differentiate COP from other policing models, and thereby rescue the phrase from sinking into total ambiguity and vagueness.

The chapters in this book written by authors from different countries are an excellent start toward that rescue effort. The overall impression reached when reading these studies is that COP means whatever the police and political leaders wish to call their policing systems. The second impression is that policing, and attempts to change policing systems, does not occur in a political and social vacuum, but is heavily influenced by:

- Existing social and cultural traditions and structures.
- The conventional ways of doing policing.
- The cultural and ideological language and discourses that sustain those forms.
- The efforts and ability of entrepreneurs, including the police, to argue for or against new ways of doing policing.
- The social capital base found in civic society.

History and contexts will shape what policing systems can be developed, as they will with any major social policy agenda.

The third impression is that, no matter what the rhetoric says, the fundamental problem and goal for the state, the police, and civic society remains security, which is broadly conceived as less crime and more social order, more physical and mental safety, and confidence by people that they will be able to live and work knowing that they and their way of life will be protected. In the end, COP is still policing (a means for providing security) and when the police cannot do so because they lack resources, skills, effective organization, or commitment, engage in corruption or are subject to political influence, civic society (another "mythical" notion) and communities will turn to self-help forms of providing their own security. When the state and the state police cannot provide safety for individuals and communities, people will turn to other means, again influenced by the history and contexts in which they live. In the United States, that has meant, generally, arming oneself for protection; in Tanzania it means falling back or resurrecting forms of traditional social control; or in Nigeria, it is turning to vigilantism sponsored by economic groups (e.g., market associations) or ethnic segments of society to protect their real and perceived interests.

In short, there *is* no consensual model of community policing. The detailed analyses in the chapters from different countries make this absence of agreement perfectly clear. Instead, one finds various interpretations of what COP means and how it should be done to make it appropriate for the countries' political and cultural histories and contexts. At most, basic ideas and principles are used to justify changes or continuities in the policing systems of a country. However, the superiority of the COP model is not easily accepted and will be contested, and the model will be reshaped by political powers and informal influences into a security system people, the police, and the state can accept. There are numerous institutional mutations of COP, which begin to undermine the notion that COP is a different policing ideology and compared of other types of systems.

In Tanzania, according to Suzette Heald in Chapter 3, the state co-opted and helped legitimate *sungusungu* groups even against its own legal, judicial, and policing establishments. The state, or Julius Nyerere (former president of Tanzania), initially used the state divided against itself at the local levels to help sustain informal social control to deal with cattle thefts and the trade in guns. In response, the state police and courts, seeing their influence undermined, arrested and prosecuted *sungusungu* members. The chapter also raises some profound questions about the classic Weberian definition of the nature of the state—that is the organization entitled to the monopoly of legitimate force—and the role of legitimate control of coercion in defining the state.

Chapter 11 on India presents cases from eight villages in Tamil Nadu and how these were dealt with by the traditional *panchayat* (local council) system and the modern police. In some cases, the police and the councils cooperate; in others, the police work against the councils. There is no consistent pattern of police–community relations, and in each village these relations are conditioned and shaped by the still powerful influence of caste, culture, and economic control. Most of the cases described are about how formal and informal control interacts within traditional norms and contexts, and the influence of modernizing values. These are fascinating anthropological studies, but it is difficult to see these events as community policing, except in the broadest sense that the police and the local notables interact.

In contrast, the Nigeria Police Force (NPF) has officially adopted, with international assistance, COP as its model and has established police vigilante liaison officers to interact with vigilantes (which in Nigeria have a good reputation, generally speaking) to, at least, know what these groups are doing and advise them on their limited legal rights and powers. The NPF has told the northern states, which have adopted Sharia law, that their religious police cannot enforce Islamic norms against non-Muslims or to protect Islamic sentiments, such as trying to prevent the traversal of trucks delivering beer through Islamic neighborhoods. The police have either accommodated vigilante practices, which they know will be done in any case, or asserted that only they have policing authority and powers while communal and religious authorities do not, to protect their legal monopoly on force.

In South Africa, after the overthrow of the apartheid regime, community policing became the basic goal of much needed police reforms. The specifics of police reforms were heavily influenced by a plethora of international assistance programs offered by states and private consultants, resulting in numerous government white papers and pronouncements, a veritable "publication industry" (van der Spuy, 2007), and little progress. In the end, COP was overwhelmed by an exploding crime problem and the public's demand to get tough on criminals and foreigners.

Hugo Frühling's chapter (Chapter 12) on Latin America also stresses the international influences that promoted community policing as part of the larger democratization processes overtaking the authoritarian regimes of the region. He also writes of the specific and varied adaptations of the model in four cases studies in Brazil (two cases), Columbia, and Guatemala.

In Britain, the police have attempted to harness local community volunteers to enforce small violations of laws, local regulations, and public expectations by providing volunteers with limited legal powers, hence, protection from public complaints. In effect, the British police have attempted to shift, under the rhetoric of community policing, certain disagreeable and difficult to enforce decisions to the community, leaving them freer to concentrate on the "real policing stuff." In France, given the centralized history of the state and of the national police and the gendarmerie, efforts to promote locally controlled policing (city police) have been fragile, limited, and unsuccessful. There is very little foundation for the concept of COP in a society that is accustomed to being steered from the center. In Belgium, in similar fashion, attempts to promote proximity policing have faltered in the face of police, political, and community resistance, and the unstable political relationship between the two ethnic pillars of Belgian society. The chapter on Australia (Chapter 9), basically a case study of the Victoria police, depicts the changing conceptions of community policing held by the police as they struggle to adjust a managerialist language (consumers, service delivery) to the administration of a hierarchical bureaucracy and the rhetoric of professional norms that define their work. In the current incarnation, and the language of policy planners and consultants, the police have settled on a "fit for purpose" model of COP. Even within one local setting, exactly how to do COP has been organized differently over time, and continues to be subject to change.

In the United States, argue David Barlow and Melissa Barlow (Chapter 8), the basic functions of the police in a capitalist society—to protect those in power and control the threatening classes—has not changed. The introduction of community policing is a response to the crises of the postmodern capitalist system and state. Community policing has changed the rhetoric, is concerned with image control, and has achieved little of its rhetoric because policing in a capitalist society is not of that nature: to extend services and protection to those without power or influence.

The most interesting case is China (Chapter 10). In his fascinating chapter, K. C. Wong discusses how the Maoist notion of the mass line has become wedded to local community self control, in a synthesis of top-down and bottom-up social control that is *sui generis*. The chapter is a succinct introduction to cultural and legal traditions and thinking in China, not just to the police. Wang also argues that, for the public and the state, the police are a social resource to be used for one's own ends. What is interesting here is that he views the public as more powerful in activating the police for their own interests than most external observers would believe. Communist ideology was and still is (though its influence is slowly waning in policing ideologies) genuinely committed to empowering the people in those cases not touching on the security of the state or the ruling party.

In all cases, COP (or a related phrase) is the term used to describe what is being done, even though the specifics of policing practices and the interactions of formal and informal social control are unique and widely disparate from case to case. What to make of this?

The book, especially the introduction, raises a fundamental question: What should be the relationships between the police, who are employed by the state, and informal or self-help forms of providing security? The editors argue that COP can be viewed from the top-down as a state police-sponsored form of participation by communities that is controlled, steered, and guided (despite the rhetoric of partnership) by the police to protect and promote the goal and interests of the police. In contrast, COP from the bottom-up, includes all the civic society forms of providing security, be these community efforts, informal vigilantism, or even corporate and private security. Whether top-down or bottom-up, all of these are forms of policing and are based on various political justifications and influence. The question is this: How do these two basic categories meet, or how do the police deal with informal policing structures, and how does the community deal with the formal state police? Since informal policing exists everywhere, in forms that reflect history and contexts, top-down and bottom-up will always meet, clash, or cooperate, and have to be reconciled politically.

On a slightly critical note here, it is not clear that a bottom-up form of social control should be called policing. That widens the conception of what constitutes policing so broadly that policing itself becomes undefined. A more distinct language, which incorporates, but also differentiates, state-provided policing from informal social control, could use the language of security as a field of action populated by many actors having different powers, legal status, and goals.

The chapters as a whole provide extensive empirical analyses of the policing problems and changes faced within their case study countries, as well as sophisticated theoretical ruminations on the nature of this set of practices called "policing," of what constitutes "community," and what constitutes the "state." It is a solid contribution to the expanding, and now vast, literature on COP, as well as a useful and necessary corrective to the assumption that community policing can be understood in a general way without taking into account the contexts that shape how values, ideologies, and goals will transform patterns of policing.

Otwin Marenin

References

Brogden, M. & Nijhar, P. (2005). *Community policing: National and international models and approaches*. Cullompton, U.K.: Willan Publishing.

Caparini, M. & Marenin, O. (2004). *Transforming police in Central and Eastern Europe*. Munster, Germany: LIT Verlag; Geneva: Geneva Centre for the Democratic Control of Armed Forces (DCAF).

Ellison, G. (2007). Fostering a dependency culture: The commoditization of community policing in a global marketplace. In A. Goldsmith & J. Sheptycki (Eds.), *Crafting transnational policing: Police-capacity building and global police reform* (pp. 203–242). Oxford, U.K. and Portland, OR: Hart Publishing.

Friedman, R.R. (1992). *Community policing. Comparative perspectives and prospects*. New York: St. Martin's Press.

Lab, St. P. & Das, D.K. (2003). *International perspectives on community policing and crime prevention*. Upper Saddle River, NJ: Prentice Hall.

Neild, R. (2002). Community policing in themes and debates in public security reform. In *A manual for civil society* (pp. 4–20). Washington, D.C: Washington Office on Latin America.

Van der Spuy, E. (2007). Managerialist pathways to "good policing": Observations from South Africa. In A. Goldsmith & J. Sheptycki (Eds.), *Crafting transnational policing: Police capacity-building and global policing reform* (pp. 263–292). Portland, OR and Oxford, U.K.: Hart Publishing.

The Editors

Dominique Wisler, Ph.D., is senior consultant specializing in the internal security sector reform in transition states. He holds a "license" in philosophy (University of Fribourg, Switzerland), a master's degree in international relations (Graduate Institute for International Relations Studies, Geneva), and a doctorate from the University of Geneva, where he taught political science until 2002. He has been engaged in police reforms in Switzerland, Bosnia and Herzegovina, Mozambique, Sudan, and Iraq. His most recent publications are a comparative book on public order policing in Switzerland (*Protest and Police* [2007, Haupt Verlag, Bern], co-authored with Marco Tackenberg) and a history book on the republican adventure in Switzerland (*Geneva Democracy* [2008, Georg, Geneva]).

Ihekwoaba D. Onwudiwe, Ph.D., is a professor and interim director of the graduate programs in Administration of Justice at Texas Southern University, Houston. Dr. Onwudiwe's interests focus on issues of policing and terrorism, theoretical criminology, and African perspectives on crime and justice. He is the author of *The Globalization of Terrorism* (Ashgate Publishing, 2001). He earned his Ph.D. degree from the School of Criminology at Florida State University.

The Geneva Centre for the Democratic Control of Armed Forces

The Geneva Centre for the Democratic Control of Armed Forces (DCAF) is one of the world's leading institutions in the areas of security sector reform (SSR) and security sector governance (SSG). DCAF provides in-country advisory support and practical assistance programs, develops and promotes appropriate democratic norms at the international and national levels, advocates good practices and conducts policy-related research to make recommendations to ensure effective democratic governance of the security sector. DCAF's partners include governments, parliaments, civil society, international organizations and the range of security sector actors such as police, judiciary, intelligence agencies, border security services and the military.

Contributors

David E. Barlow
Professor and Dean of the College of Arts and Sciences
Fayetteville State University
Fayetteville, North Carolina

Melissa Hickman Barlow
Professor/Department of Criminal Justice
Director/Institute for Community Justice
Fayetteville State University
Fayetteville, North Carolina

John Casey
Associate Professor/School of Public Affairs
Baruch College, City University of New York
New York, New York

Hugo Frühling
Professor/Institute of Public Affairs
University of Chile
and
Director/Center for the Study of Citizen Security
Santiago, Chile

Suzette Heald
Senior Research Fellow
Crisis States Research Centre
London School of Economics
London, United Kingdom

Anita Kalunta-Crumpton
Associate Professor
Texas Southern University
Houston, Texas

Otwin Marenin
Professor
Political Science Department/Criminal Justice
Washington State University
Pullman, Washington

Anthony Minnaar
Professor of Criminal Justice Studies
Department of Security Risk Management
School of Criminal Justice, College of Law, University of South Africa
Pretoria, South Africa

Christian Mouhanna
Researcher
Centre for Research in the Sociology of Criminal Law
Paris, France

David Pike
Inspector
Victoria Police
Victoria, Australia
and
Doctoral Student
Charles Sturt University
Sydney, Australia

Sybille Smeets
Researcher/Asst. Professor
Centre of Criminological Researches/School of Criminology
Free University of Brussels
Brussel, Belgium

Carrol Tange
Researcher
Centre of Criminological Researches
Free University of Brussels
and
Professor
University of Mons-Hainaut
Wallonia, Belgium

Lynn Vincentnathan
Assistant Professor
Department of Criminal Justice and Department of Psychology and Anthropology
University of Texas–Pan American
Edinburg, Texas

S. George Vincentnathan
Professor and Chair
Department of Criminal Justice
University of Texas–Pan American
Edinburg, Texas

Kam C. Wong
Associate Professor
Xavier University
Cincinnati, Ohio

Rethinking Police and Society
Community Policing in Comparison

1

DOMINIQUE WISLER
IHEKWOABA D. ONWUDIWE

Contents

Introduction

The book reunites contributions of authors who are rarely encountered in the same workshops and conferences. The first are criminologists, lawyers, sometimes ex-cops (studying criminal justice processes), and police. The second are anthropologists, ethnologists, and social movements researchers focusing on informal ordering processes situated at community or civil society level. Both groups usually ignore each other despite the fact that they are quite often interested in the same issue: strategies of approaching security and crime.

The former group studies top-down policing. Core topics of their inquiries are legal and constitutional frameworks of policing and doctrines as well as police bureaucracies and their praxis in responding to crime and disorders. The latter group describes bottom-up communities' strategies mobilizing their own resources to deal with insecurity when the state appears distant, unresponsive, and sometimes partisan, inhospitable, and oppressive. Core topics of this group of researchers are culture, social networks and social movements, customary laws and justice systems, and informal strategies.

Where the nation-state is fully developed, as is the case in liberal democracies, criminologists find themselves quite at home. Informal strategies of communities seem to have largely vanished as a result of the progress of the state as well as the rule of law and social modernization. In the developing world and less institutionalized states, anthropologists are more at ease as their object of inquiries seems ubiquitous, popular, even though, at times, excessive. From a state-building point of view, bottom-up policing initiatives may appear to be anachronic interlopers in the modern world. From a community point of view, however, informal policing can prove quite popular and a rational response to growing insecurity and it always expresses a deep mistrust in the state.

The community policing movement, which started decades ago in liberal democracies and rapidly became a global movement, has rendered the dialog between the two groups much more likely than before and, as this book intends to demonstrate, this dialog is potentially fruitful. With the advent of what is labeled the "community policing era" in police history books, police and society have entered into a new intimate relationship calling for both groups of researchers to help redefine the relationship between the two. This dialog might be necessary to rescue community policing from becoming a marketing slogan rather than designating a fundamental paradigmatic change in the relationship between police and society.

From the police end, efforts have been undertaken to establish a bridge to communities. The doctrine of community policing in liberal democracies manifests the intention of closing the gap that had been created between police and society by the rise of the classical model of policing. In the United States at the end of the nineteenth century, so-called progressive leaders had erected an institutional wall between police and society as a means to insulate the police from corruption and political and other outside influence. Professionalization, bureaucratization, and the crystallization of the "classical" or "traditional" model of policing consolidated the trend. In this process, as discussed by Kam Wong (Chapter 10), the police response to demands for services became anonymous, generic, and fundamentally lost touch with the citizens' feelings and expectations. Calls for a rapprochement between the police and society grew louder in the 1970s after a decade of civil rights movement, social protest against the Vietnam War, and, more generally, the rise of new social movements. The formula of "community policing" carried the project of removing portions of the wall separating police and society or, rather, called for a radical transformation of the relationship between police and society. Community policing moved to the front burner of the police reform.

In the Anglo-Saxon world, opinion, ideas, and theories on how to transform this relationship started burgeoning in police and academic circles.

Local police departments and national police units embarked in highly publicized reforms that intended to reinvent the police–society relationship. The movement reached continental Europe in the 1980s and, with the wave of democratic transitions after the fall of the Berlin Wall, it became a slogan for the democratization of police forces around the globe and a tool for the reconciliation between police and society in former totalitarian or authoritarian regimes. The movement became so pervasive that even nondemocratic regimes today adopt the community policing rhetoric as an emblem of their capacity to respond to popular demands. Most powerful instruments of domination and coercion are thus wrapped up in a package seemingly beyond critics.

The elasticity of the community policing denomination and its recuperation at the opposite end of democratic regimes substantiates a thesis of Barlow and Barlow (Chapter 8) made in this volume that community policing is a public relations tool that "evokes positive images" with the ultimate aim of insulating the police from critical analysis. The appropriation of the community policing rhetoric by nondemocratic political regimes turns on its head the original project of bringing communities and police closer together. This development is not likely to benefit the community policing doctrine that, after a peak in the late 1990s, seems today to have lost its seduction capacity and, in many countries, is on the decline. Where the confusion and lack of clarity has not led community policing to implode at national level (as in South Africa, for instance), it has been a key factor in explaining how community policing has taken very different national paths, as we will see in the country analyses proposed in this book.

From the society end, community policing or, we should say, informal policing or self-policing is not something new. During the apartheid regime in South Africa, the lack of formal policing in black neighborhoods led many communities to police themselves. Self-policing was also promoted by the British colonial system (Deflem, 1994) in rural areas and, in India, as discussed in Chapter 11, customary institutions had the ability to reproduce order until the recent wave of social modernization. Informal policing might be vanishing in some countries, but is reappearing in others, such as Tanzania, South Africa, Nigeria, and Kenya. These initiatives seem to respond to a situation of growing insecurity, a weak and nonresponsive state, and may use opportunistically culture and traditional resources to strengthen their legitimacy. If Buerger (1994), reflecting recently on the history of community policing reforms in the United States, could rightly deplore the fact that community policing has often been mostly "a unilateral action of the police" promoting community self-rule, in these states the contrary is true. This is what anthropologists and sociologists are telling us and have substantiated with astonishing evidence and vivid analyses. The reports from these states underline the existence of new informal policing movements whose vigorousness contrasts sharply with the decline of community policing sometimes observed in the very same countries. Under conditions to be discussed in this book, imported top-down-style community policing might be less attractive, less legitimate, and less efficient for communities than bottom-up community policing. We believe that gaining a better grasp of informal policing initiatives, through a case study approach, and reflecting on their conditions of emergence, describing carefully the practices involved, as well as the modalities of interactions with the state and the insertion in local governance mechanisms, should open up the discussion and hopefully resuscitate community policing from an unexpected end.

Case Studies

The case studies proposed in this book will provide students of community policing with unique insight into national trajectories of community policing, whether top-down (state-led) or bottom-up (society-led). Country contributors discuss the rationales of the community policing reforms, their contents, how they developed and why, and what is left of the initial reform today. Each contribution deciphers—generally at national level, but sometimes at a more local level—what definition of community policing has been adopted and how the doctrine has been implemented empirically.

The states selected in this volume range from liberal democracies to the China of Mao, passing by developing and transitional states. Within the liberal democracies category, centralized and federal states were chosen to reflect upon the influence of state constitutional settings on community policing. For reasons that will be discussed, federal states are a more fertile ground for community policing initiatives than strongly centralized states. Liberal democracies are paradigmatic illustrations of a top-down community policing approach with communities left to play a small role. Tanzania and Nigeria were selected as examples of developing states where community-policing initiatives originate unilaterally from society. In both of these states, informal policing is highly popular. In Tanzania, village self-policing was promoted by the state ideology, while in Nigeria informal policing is an unwelcome appearance from the point of view of the central government. India, South Africa, and Latin America witness some coexistence of the two forms of community policing (state-led and society-led) in a context of social and political change and democratic transition. China, in this volume, occupies a specific position. The information on China offers more than an insightful view on the relationship between the people (the masses) and the state in Mao's doctrine of policing. The author of this chapter (Kam Wong) suggests a radically new theory of policing, which profoundly modifies our past understanding of the relationship between police and society.

The Ambiguity of Community Policing: The Issue of the "Model"

As deplored by Smeets and Tange in Chapter 6, there is no "model" of community policing or, to use Thomas Kuhn's precise vocabulary, "community policing has not reached the status of a univocal and coherent 'paradigm.'" A new paradigm, in Kuhn's view, implies a new ontology: it postulates "entities" or "things" and assigns them with specific "roles" (Kuhn, 1962). In the community policing literature, apart from the postulate that communities exist (see Kalunta-Crumpton's critical discussion in Chapter 7), competing views on the role that communities should perform in the policing framework have been coexisting and the lack of clarity on this issue has been responsible for misunderstanding, frustrations, and confusion when it came to implement community policing reforms concretely.

In one view, communities are understood as auxiliaries of the police and, in this role, can fulfill several functions. The "classical model" of policing has been criticized for its relative inefficiency in solving crimes as police officers are kept away from the main source of intelligence: social networks and local communities. Community policing, therefore, has often been understood as a new strategy of the police to produce better intelligence through, for instance, community forum, *îlotage* (or an officer based permanently in one neighborhood), *koban* (Japan-style police ministations in neighborhoods), and "sector policing" with the same patrols assigned in one neighborhood. The acclaimed problem-solving approach of Hermann Goldstein (1979) has staged communities in the role of potential partners in producing long-term solutions to the cause of public order incidents and crime. Goldstein's departure point is also the lack of productivity of the police. Instead of responding iteratively to the same incident, police should turn their attention to the problem at the origin of repeated incidents and, with the help of other stakeholders, identify permanent solutions to recurring problems. Problem-solving policing is a strategy of the police that might include communities in elaborating solutions for incidents as a means to reduce the workload of the police.

The other view of community policing assigns a very different role to communities. The arrow of the relationship points to the reverse direction. Communities, in this approach, are meant to have a normative say on how they are policed. Community policing is a philosophy of policing that opens up the police agenda locally to the influence of grassroot communities' expectations and priorities. Community policing is understood as a philosophy, not a strategy. Communities are not an "instrument" or an "auxiliary" to the police, but an end to which police are accountable. Community policing is about governance and accountability, not internal reorganization of police to increase productivity (Goldstein) or a democratic camouflage (Barlow and Barlow critical analysis [Chapter 8]).

The ambiguity of "community policing" and the fact that different groups had conflicting expectations when the community policing reform was initiated in South Africa led to dysfunctions, frustrations, and the progressive (unofficial) abandonment of the reform. Anthony Minnaar, in Chapter 2, shows that when community policing forums were established as an emblem of the democratic reform, communities expected the police to conform to the views of residents expressed in these forums, whereas the police interpreted these forums as an instrument for gaining better intelligence on neighborhood crimes. The competing views resulted in the subsequent disaffection of these forums by communities. Resisting the "democratic paradigm," the South African police called these forums a "necessary evil" as they helped legitimize the police action. As a sign of mistrust and a response to high insecurity, communities in poor black neighborhoods resorted to informal policing, using a form of self-policing that was common under the apartheid regime in townships. Community policing degenerated as simple "window dressing" and an empty democratic rhetoric.

Wong's theoretical essay, in Chapter 10, offers some fresh thoughts on how police and society could be reconciled. The bureaucratization of policing led historically to a transformation of people's problems into a universal administrative/legal language where the original individual meaning or intention of those who resorted to the police is often lost. Based on anthropological accounts of people calling the police, Wong doubts that the influential view of Egon Bittner (1970) of the role of the police as defined by their potential use of force is on target. Rather, he argues, police is seen as an agent in a position of authority to legitimate the "point of view" of the caller. A citizen-centered theory of the police would stage the police as a legitimizing resource of the people to solve their problems or conflicts. This might or might not involve the use of force. The author acknowledges the breakthrough of Goldstein who invited noncore classical activities into the police institution and repositioned police officers as problem solvers. However, Wong goes much farther and, indeed, turns Goldstein's theory on its head. While Goldstein maintains that problem solving is a strategy that would help the police in becoming a more efficient organization, Wong argues that solving the problems of the people is not a strategy, but the core mission of the police as a resource to the citizen.

Wong's pertinence might be illustrated by using opportunistically a case discussed by Mouhanna in Chapter 5 on France. Mouhanna reports on an incident involving guests in a Paris restaurant terrace calling the police to stop a young crowd from playing football next to them. To their surprise, the police arrested the youngsters rather than, simply, issuing a warning. Police had been called upon not for coercion, but for legitimating the point of view of the guests. This episode was followed by an altercation between the police and the guests infuriated by the disproportionate display of force.

The Lack of a Community-Policing Paradigm as a Handicap

There is no doubt that the ambiguity of community policing and the lack of consensus over the role of communities have been a handicap for the diffusion of the concept and, in some cases, a factor explaining its extinction. Smeets and Tange's contribution in Chapter 6 shows that the reform of the police in Belgium preceded the official formulation of a community policing doctrine. Key reform decisions, therefore, remained imprisoned in a classic view, which stages the police in the role of authority involving the potential use of force. Those activities, which did not imply a potential use of force (neighborhood policing, problem-solving activities), were discarded as nonessential and transferred to nonpolice services. What was pushed outside the field of police, in fact, was essential to community policing. Should community policing have been theorized better and earlier in Belgium, this might not have happened.

In the already much discussed case of South Africa in this introduction, the conflict and confusion over the concept led to the disaffection of community forums by frustrated communities. With this retreat of communities, the doctrine of community policing lost its substance and ended up being an empty shell. Officially, as discussed by Minnaar in Chapter 2, community policing was never abandoned in South Africa; in reality, there is not even a vestige of this doctrine in the current policing approach in the country (see also Burger, 2006).

Several contributions in this volume have identified internal organizational competition between police services or external competition with other security providers as a key element explaining the early stages of a community policing reform. Community policing, it is shown, has been historically promoted by national police agencies, sometimes even military-status police (gendarmerie), as a means to counteract the emergence of stronger municipal police forces (Belgium) or as a strategy to preempt the communalization of police (France). Auxiliary police (community support officers) were created in the United Kingdom to counteract the growing private policing industry (Kempa & Johnston, 2005).* However, in most instances, the threat proved short-lived. Municipal police—when they are allowed to grow—are often too small and lack the resources to innovate, experiment, and theorize. Given the

* Kempa and Johnston (2005).

lack of a preexisting coherent and robust community policing model, small municipal police forces have proven unable to innovate and to become the avant-garde of the community policing movement. These municipal police, as private security companies, aspire generally to resemble the national police and are readily keen to accept classical policing as the ultimate model.

Intermediaries and the State

Community policing is, in a sense, the story of the return of the subject (the citizen) in the constitution of policing. It is a bold attempt to socialize the state or, as such, it is more likely to be successful in some states than in others. In the French, strong state philosophy, and social characteristics, such as religion, gender, race or ethnicity, are discarded as anachronic remnants of ancient regimes and not allowed to disturb the direct and face-to-face relationship between the state and each individual citizen. To socialize this relationship implies the introduction of inequality, privileges, and distinctions. Mouhanna (Chapter 5) argues convincingly that this overall state philosophy has precluded a significant development of the community policing doctrine in the French police.

While community policing is essentially foreign to the French state, it seems burgeoning in the United Kingdom, the United States, and the Netherlands, where communities are legitimate parts of the state. Arendt Lijphard (1980, 1984) coined the term *sociological federalism* to describe a type of state, which not only recognizes social groups' legal existence, but also decentralizes policy decision-making or implementation to social groups rather than territories. In most of the twentieth century, the so-called "pillars" (socialists, secularists, and Christians) in the Netherlands have run their own state-sponsored schools, media, and insurance and pension systems. Sociological federalism, funded in communities, creates the legal constitutional space for community policing to flourish.

Federal (territorial) states might practice community policing more like the bourgeois gentlemen of Molière, who spoke in prose without being aware of it. They may be practicing community policing unintentionally. Federal Switzerland, Belgium, Germany, and the United States have a plethora of local police forces and the politics of the police is mostly decided at the local level. Some federal states are further decentralized and, as in a number of Swiss cantons and the United States, the police system is fragmented into a mosaic of municipal police forces. In Belgium, police districts are composed of one or an association of municipalities: the so-called ZIP or interpolice zones. All these police forces are inserted into a local system of governance with municipal authorities defining police priorities at the local level.

Not surprisingly, reformers in Belgium have designated these municipal police forces as the substratum of the new community policing philosophy while, as they understood, the federal police would have to concentrate on specialized and professional policing functions. Local municipal authorities and the police force they control are an interface between the national state and citizen allowing the politics of the police to be defined locally. The degree of autonomy of local police forces varies depending on the type of federal state. While in Belgium or in Germany, the federal level often defines the standards of policing countrywide, these standards are entirely defined at the local level in Switzerland with minimal or no influence from the federal level.

Political modernization is associated with the loss of political power of intermediaries and, often, the elimination of the latter by the rising state. In India, as shown by Vincentnathan and Vincentnathan (Chapter 11), political modernization is closely linked to social change and what the authors call "social modernization." Social modernization is defined as the advent of new egalitarian values (rejecting castes, classes, and social markers) in society—a phenomenon calling for political modernization and new governance structures. The traditional courts system, whose function was to reproduce an ancient and consensual order, lost its capacity to solve conflicts. With the growth of egalitarian values, traditional courts progressively disappeared in contemporary India. This process has left individuals directly facing a state under construction, still poorly institutionalized, and not necessarily able to respond unequivocally to new claims from society. While a layer of intermediaries disintegrated, the modern state had not gained the full authority, coherence, and legitimacy necessary to absorb social change. In an open attempt to fill the vacuum, the state has resorted to "pseudo" *panchayats* (traditional courts and ordering mechanism) taking the form of "friends of police" committees which, in the last analysis, proved to function more as information agents and early warning committees than as problem-solving and social control actors for their communities.

While the disintegration of the intermediary layer of the *panchayats* is a consequence of social modernization and, if we want, a bottom-up process, political modernization can take place too soon, be too ideological, precede social change, and provoke disorders. In Western Sudan, for instance, the poorly institutionalized and highly under-resourced central state removed traditional power structures during the Numeri era in the 1970s, but proved unable to replace them with functioning modern state institutions. This process created a vacuum of power. Bureaucrats did not replace traditional leaders. Informal or traditional institutions were not replaced by formal institutions. In a context of growing desertification, underdevelopment, marginalization, and changing patterns in the economy, groups' competition in Darfur increasingly took a violent turn in the vacuum of governance that had been created (Flint & de Waal, 2006).

Tanzania and Nigeria—to take two examples from the book—have tried to revive or create new intermediaries. Heald (2007) shows how villages in Tanzania and the Kuria region in Kenya, facing a surge of insecurity, organized themselves and took policing in their own hands. There is often a combination of the old and the new in the organizations created in these circumstances. Traditional leaders may play a role, but the initiative can also be taken by "new men." The Tanzanian *sungusungu* and its equivalent in Kenya are cases of production of new social intermediaries that have the trust of the communities and appear to be highly efficient in restoring security.

The Bakassi Boys in Nigeria and the Pagad in South Africa are new social movement organizations that have even less to do with traditional leaders than the *sungusungu* in Kenya and Tanzania. In short, they are the products of modern civil society rather than emanations of traditional society. The Bakassi Boys, for instance, were originally associated with traders' associations organizing themselves against violent theft and growing insecurity in market places. The tradition of self-policing predating colonization and promoted under the native administration in British colonies may play a role in the contemporary development of many of these movements in Africa, but more as a resource than a cause.* The Nigerian Bakassi Boys and similar formations should be conceptualized as social movement organizations (CSOs) responding rationally to a situation of insecurity and a vacuum of policing rather than as traditional organizations anchored in a premodern world.

Institutionalization of Informal Policing: Defining the Frontier

The frontier of competencies that separates policing intermediaries from the national police is constantly moving and the status of the intermediaries is often precarious. In highly decentralized Switzerland, the reforms of the past decade have resulted in successfully disbanding many municipal forces or reducing their competencies.† In highly centralized France, the trend is the reverse: municipal forces have grown significantly in the past 10 years and their claims for more policing competencies have been more vocal every year.

Recognition by the state is critical for informal policing, as the state is not likely to welcome the phenomenon and the police consider informal

* *Cf.* the concept of "frame resonance" of David Snow and Robert Benford (1988) discussed in the context of informal policing by Wisler and Onwudiwe (2008).

† In Zurich, for instance, the criminal municipal police was recently merged with the cantonal police; in the canton of Berne, municipal police were disbanded in exchange of the police to decentralize its services in four regions of the canton; in Vaud, the canton seems to progressively absorb municipal police.

policing groups as illegal competitors. Members of these groups might be prosecuted if something goes wrong. In the longer run, informal policing groups might lose steam if some retribution does not acknowledge the security services they provide to their communities. Some level of institutionalization might be sought and wished from both ends. When this happens, the frontier between the central state and society is redesigned.

Ideally, the institutionalization of the informal may take place in a process of decentralization. In Nigeria, decentralization is one of the main demands from states' governors who maintain local police forces without having the constitutional basis to do so. The advantage of decentralization is that policing is inserted in a readily available, functioning, and modern governance structure. This, we would say, is a top-down response to the question of institutionalization of informal policing. There are, however, other ways to harness informal policing into the rule of law framework. One may think of laws formalizing mechanisms of accountability as this is done, for instance, for the private security industry. This is the path that Tanzania has chosen to follow and it certainly provides for an alternative model to rule the informal. Traditional mechanisms of governance can be strengthened by the legislative framework and this path, we would argue, corresponds better to the bottom-up approach of informal policing. Finally, at the far end of the options, informal policing can be inserted in a framework of a legal pluralism as discussed by Heald for the second generation of the *sungusungu* movement (Chapter 3).

South Africa is a case of "state resilience" to informal policing even though the South African state's response to informal policing is rather selective, oscillating between repression and toleration depending on the group level of violence (Minnaar, 2001). While informal policing is strongly opposed by the police and academics, its survival in South Africa is largely due to a receptive African National Congress (ANC) party. More than anywhere else, informal policing in South Africa is linked to class issues and a high segmentation of society. Responding to insecurity, richer, often white, communities hire private security companies or sponsor the police in their neighborhoods (funding a police station, for instance), while the poor black neighborhoods resort to informal policing. Informal policing has tradition in South Africa, as black townships were systematically underpoliced during apartheid and people resorted to self-policing (Chabedi, 2005; Nina 2000).

Standing between the two opposite ends—institutionalization and repression—an informal *modus vivendi* is a third option. Heald (2007) shows that informal policing faces a rather tolerant state in parts of Kenya; at the beginning of the 2000s, the leaders of the *sungusungu* movement in the Mara region were able to reach an informal agreement with regional authorities that stated that thieves arrested by members of the *sungusungu* would be handed over to the police for prosecution. The *modus vivendi* helped to stabilize the situation of informal policing which, however, as in the early days in Tanzania, remains in a precarious equilibrium state. Institutionalization and, to a lesser extent, the *modus vivendi* option are platforms for negotiation with policing groups to eliminate the most controversial aspects of their practices.

The "grey" area in which informal groups can be maintained is not without danger for them. Meagher (2006) has discussed one case of instrumentalization by the political authorities. The Nigerian Bakassi Boys movement, she argues, was manipulated for political purposes. In exchange for toleration, the informal group was hijacked to fulfill the personal political ambitions of the state governor. Once this happened, the Bakassi Boys degenerated into a militia-type of movement and was even involved in political assassinations. Discussing the Kenyan case, in Chapter 3, Heald (2007) asserts that the *sungusungu* movement in the Mara region showed little interest in entering into negotiation with state authorities precisely to avoid any instrumentalization of their movement by the state.

The Risks of Informal Policing

Informal policing is believed to carry many risks. Researchers, the international community, public opinion, and leaders are divided when facing the reality of informal policing. South African criminologists are almost unanimous in denouncing informal policing as a threat to the rule of law, while Nigerian criminologists provide much more positive accounts of the phenomenon. Anthropologists are also less concerned with what is described as unacceptable by criminal justice researchers. Human rights advocates usually denounce the abuses of informal policing while development agencies start considering informal policing as an option. A 2004 United Nations Development Program report emphasized that people in Africa are more likely to resort to customary justice institutions than modern state formal courts (United Nations Development Program, 2004) and acknowledged the importance of traditional justice mechanisms in producing order and stability.*

The main issues at stake in this dispute are governance, rule of law, and human rights. Informal policing, argue the critics, moves essentially outside the framework of the rule of law and, often, is brutal, excessive, and fundamentally ignorant about basic human rights. Informal policing is associated with images of angry crowds beating to death suspects, summary executions, and all kind of human rights abuses and horrifying practices of "jungle justice." *Vigilantism* is the favorite term to depict these practices. Interestingly enough, the same criminologists who are appalled

* See also United Nations Habitat's positive account of the *Sungusungu* movement in Tanzania (United Nations-Habitat, 2000).

by informal policing are far less critical of private policing. Private policing is viewed as more orderly, legitimate, and easily regulated by law. While they see private policing as one key element of *nodal policing* (a term coined by Clifford Shearing (1997) underlining the fact that policing has ceased or should cease to be the monopoly of the police according to neoliberal views), they do not seem to acknowledge informal policing reemergence in societies as a rational response to insecurity problems by poor or traditional communities.

Another risk often associated with informal policing is radicalization. Radicalization can occur if the state represses informal policing. Terrorism, for instance, seems to have been the answer of the Pagad movement in South Africa (Dixon & Johns, 2001; Minnaar, 2001). Social movement researchers have amply discussed the relationship between repression and social movement violence finding that the relationship is curvilinear (see, for instance, Tilly, 1978).

Anthropologists have provided more positive and reassuring accounts of informal policing. The notion that informal policing occurs outside of governance structures can be disputed based on ethnological accounts of informal policing. In the cases discussed by Heald in Tanzania (Chapter 3) or in Kenya (2007) or the Igbo case in Nigeria as discussed by Okerafoezeke (2006), informal policing is well anchored in community-based governance structures. The *Iritongo* in Tanzania and Kenya is a general assembly of the village that gathers generally in times of crisis and function as village court for serious criminal cases. It is the *Iritongo* who decided the creation and control of the *sungusungu* in Kenya by, for instance, electing its "managing" committee. In India, village courts or *panchayats* were well anchored in cast-based society. Vincentnathan and Vincentnathan (Chapter 11) show how judgments are passed in the *panchayats* based on consensus in popular assemblies that are not dissimilar to the town meetings of the early days in America, the conseil général in Swiss cities, or the landsgemeinde of Alpine Swiss cantons (Wisler, 2008). Dramatic media images of angry and uncontrollable crowds contrast with the direct democratic nature of the Indian *panchayats* or the Kenyan *Iritongo*.

The account of Heald (2007) provides evidence that information gathering techniques employed by the *sungusungu* in the Kuria region of Kenya are poorly compatible with human rights standards: beating the suspect for extorting confession from him is a "normal" practice in the examples she provides. Heald notes *en passant* that excesses of informal policing have little to envy to the practices of the national police in Kenya who use the same means to extort confessions from suspects. Confession-based evidence methods—a widely spread practice in statutory policing around the globe—is known to entail the risks of abuses that only the development of a forensic science investigation is likely to reduce significantly. Punishment decided during the

Iritongo ranges from fine, restitution, banning, and, for thieves, *legeza*, which means locking the ankles of the thief so that he cannot run again. In the *Igbo* tradition in Nigeria, shaming and banning are regular practices to enforce traditional justice.

Importation of Models

If the type of policing mirrors the development and features of the state, importation in dissimilar state contexts might simply result in failure. As discussed earlier, even within the set of democracies, community policing does not seem to travel well from one state to another. The ambiguity of the community policing rhetoric and the lack of a coherent paradigm per se are, as Smeets and Tange rightly assert in Chapter 6, a handicap. But, more fundamentally, strong states, such as France, remain constitutionally impermeable to community policing while other states, such as federal states, are institutionally much more receptive to the doctrine.

The question of importation takes a new interesting twist with the emerging global doctrine of community policing as an essential component of democratic policing, a view carried out by development agencies and United Nations police missions when addressing the issue of restructuring police forces in transition and postconflict countries. This view has become even more important as United Nations missions are increasingly involved in "restructuring" police forces as per Security Council resolutions, and community policing is one key pillar of these reforms.

Minnaar in Chapter 2 shows that while community policing might have had a few advocates within the South African police at the beginning, the reform was driven mainly by outside democratic political forces importing Western ideas. In the case of South America, Frühling (Chapter 12) shows that the international community has played an important role in funding community policing pilot schemes. When external funding stopped, projects were often discontinued. One of the constraints faced by reformers in most importing countries has been the internal resistance found in the police organizations themselves. Frühling underlines that, in Latin America, lower rank officers have been less favorable to community policing than higher ranks, while, in South Africa, community policing has been viewed at best as a "necessary evil" (Minnaar, Chapter 2) and, more generally, as a failure by police management (see Burger, 2007).

Given the fundamental ambiguity of the rhetoric, community policing might be understood very differently and in irreconcilable ways by the various groups who promote the reform. The South African national police viewed community forums as a tool for intelligence gathering, while black neighborhoods hoped to gain through them a better control of the services delivered to them. Similarly, in India, "friends of police" committees have been established to provide the "modern" police with information on local developments while *panchayat* were reproducing a social order when it was consensual. The "friends of police" concept resulted in the creation of schools in Iraq and, in the summer of 2008, the city of Basra created, under the community-policing banner, its first "friends of police" committee, which was made up of personalities of the city. The committees—composed only by "friends"—are of delicate use and it remains to be seen whether they will be used as intelligence-gathering tools, instruments for mobilizing social support for the police, or tools for a better control of policing by communities in the neighborhoods. There is a high risk of misusing community forums for mobilizing society to become friends of the state rather than having the police become friends of the people. In deeply divided societies, community policing is a difficult thing to put in place. A key reason why Mozambique resisted efforts by the British to import community policing in the 1990s was the fear that community forums could be manipulated for partisan reasons. The government believed that the development of a professional police following the "classical" model of policing was necessary to avoid claims that, by being too close to the public, the police would follow partisan lines.*

Importation of community policing Western-style might fail for structural reasons or, in other words, for reasons that are not easily "fixable." Corrupt police officers will never be good community policing officers. When the state is distant, under-resourced, weak, corrupt, or partisan, police are likely to be a poor performer and the relationship with communities will be inherently irreconcilable with community policing. As a matter of fact, public opinion surveys usually identify police as one of the most vulnerable institutions to corruption in almost any state. In under-resourced states, corruption is rampant. In repressive states, police are used as an instrument of the state, not a service to the communities. What has been sometimes described as substitutes for community policing—auxiliary police in Uganda, Sudan, and many other states—are, in fact, tools of the state to better control society. The *shurta shabia* (or popular police: a voluntary local popular police force) in Sudan is more a militia serving the government than a resource to the communities (Salmon, 2007).

Suzette Heald is a pioneer in her claim that informal policing is superior to any top-down and state-initiated community policing projects in corrupt states: they have popular support, are inserted into local governance structures, and are more efficient than the statutory police. Because of the unfixable nature of the state, the importation of community policing top-down as promoted by the international community

* Observations collected in 2002 during a field mission in Mozambique by Dominique Wisler.

today is due to fail in these states. The strength of the *sungusungu* lies in the fact that thieves are sentenced by the community, whereas, in the past, "they were obliged to hand them over to the police and courts for sentencing, inviting the usual response, with the thieves simply bribing their way out. On their return to the community, they were once again in a position to terrorize, most especially those who had been brave enough to mount an accusation" (Heald, Chapter 3). Her claim is a strong call for a profound revision of the development agencies' agenda in the internal security sector.

References

Bittner, E. (1970). *The functions of police in modern society*. Bethesda, MD: National Institute of Mental Health. Reprinted in R.J. Lundman (Ed.), *Police behavior* (pp. 28–43). Oxford, U.K.: Oxford University Press.

Buerger, M.E. (1994). The limits of community. In D.P. Rosenbaum (Ed.), *The challenge of community policing. Testing the promises* (pp. 270–273). London: Sage.

Burger, J. (2006). Crime combating in perspective: A strategic approach to policing and the prevention of crime in South Africa. *Acta Criminologica, 192*, 105–118.

Burger, J. (2007). *Strategic perspectives on crime and policing in South Africa*. Pretoria: Van Schaik Publishers.

Chabedi, M. (2005). *Governing the ungovernable: Policing, vigilante justice, crime and everyday life in a post-apartheid city Soweto*. Paper presented at the IFRA conference, Nairobi, Kenya.

Deflem, M. (1994). Law enforcement in British Colonial Africa. A comparative analysis of imperial policing in Nyasaland, the Gold Coast, and Kenya. *Police Studies, 171*, 45–68.

Dixon, B., & Johns, L. (2001). Gangs, PAGAD and the state: Vigilantism and revenge violence in the Western Cape. In *Violence and transition series* (Vol. 2). Johannesburg, South Africa: Centre for the Study of Violence and Reconciliation.

Flint, J., & de Waal, A. (2006). *Darfur: A short history of a long war*. London: Zed Book..

Goldstein, H. (1979). *Problem-oriented policing*. New York: McGraw-Hill.

Heald, S. (2002). *Domesticating leviathan: Sungusungu in Tanzania*. Crisis States working paper (Series 1, No. 16). London: London School of Economics and Political Science.

Heald, S. (2007). Controlling crime and corruption from below: Sungusungu in Kenya.

International Relations, 21(2), 183–199.

Kempa, M., & Johnston, L. (2005). Challenges and prospects for the development of inclusive plural policing in Britain: Overcoming political and conceptual obstacles. *Australian and New Zealand Journal of Criminology, 382*, 181–191.

Kuhn, T. (1962). *The structure of scientific revolutions*. Chicago: University of Chicago Press.

Lijphart, A. (1980). From the politics of accommodation to adversarial politics in the Netherlands: A reassessment. In H. Daalder and G. A. Armin (Eds.), *Politics in the Netherlands: How much change?* (pp. 239–143). London: Cass.

Lijphart, A. (1984). *Democracies.* New Haven, CT: Yale University Press.

Meagher, K. (2006). Hijacking civil society: The inside story of the Bakassi Boys vigilante group of southeastern Nigeria. *Journal of Modern African Studies, 451*, 89–115.

Minnaar, A. (2001). *The new vigilantism in post April 1994 South Africa: Crime prevention or expression of lawlessness?* Johannesburg, South Africa: Institute for Human Rights and Criminal Justice Issues.

Nina, D. (2000). Dirty Harry is back: Vigilantism in South Africa—The reemergence of "good" and "bad" communities. *African Security Review, 91.* Institute for Security Studies, from http://www.iss.co.za/pubs/ASR/9No1/DirtyHarry.html (accessed April 29, 2008).

Okerafoezeke, N. (2006). Traditional social control in an ethnic society: Law enforcement in a Nigerian community. *Police Practice and Research, 41*, 21–33.

Salmon, J. (2007). *A paramilitary revolution: The popular defence forces.* Sudan Working papers Small Arms Survey, No. 10.

Shearing, C. (1997). Toward democratic policing: Rethinking strategies of transformation. In *Policing in emerging democracies* (pp. 29–38). Rockville, MD: National Criminal Justice Reference Service.

Snow, D.A., & Benford, R.D. (1988). Ideology, frame resonance and participant mobilization. *International Social Movement Research, 1*, 197–217.

Tilly, C. (1978). *From mobilization to revolution.* Reading, MA: Addison-Wesley.

United Nations–Habitat. (2000, August). *Crime and policing issues in Dar es Salaam. Community neighborhood watch groups: "Sungusungu."* Paper presented at the Conference of the International Association of Police Chiefs, Durban, South Africa.

United Nations Development Programme. (2004). *Access to justice. Practice note.* New York: United Nations.

Wisler, D. (2008). *La démocratie genevoise.* Geneva: Georg.

Wisler, D., & Onwudiwe, I.D. (2008) (to be published). Community policing in comparison. *Police Quarterly.*

Community Policing in a High Crime Transitional State

The Case of South Africa Since Democratization in 1994

2

ANTHONY MINNAAR

Contents

Introduction

In the negotiations for a peaceful transition of power prior to the April 1994 elections (which installed the first-ever black majority democratic government in South Africa), the drafters of the interim Constitution (1993) were well aware of the need to transform the South African Police (SAP). The emphasis in this transformation was firstly on changing the way that the South African public was policed (away from the previous apartheid[*] repressive and authoritarian policing style). Secondly, that previously underpoliced (in pure policing terms) communities were better policed with regard to service delivery and the allocation of resources. Thirdly, this policing strove to follow a more democratic and human rights oriented form of policing. To fulfill this new "vision for policing" in South Africa, the policy makers decided to make so-called Community Policing the core of this transformed policing approach in South Africa.

Early Forms of Community Self-Policing

While it can be said that South Africa had no real tradition of any form of formal Community Policing, in the days of political repression there were various forms of community self-policing that did occur. Here we think of the activities in the black townships of the anticrime street committees and the Peoples Courts,[†] which euphemistically self-administered "popular justice" in the townships in the late 1970s and 1980s. These were largely politicized struggle activities that were all but put an end to by 1988 with the then government's use of the Emergency Regulations powers to suppress all political dissent and public protest. However, a number continued to perpetrate anticrime vigilante acts in trying to self-police their neighborhoods in a covert manner.[‡] The subsequent massive increase in violent political protest all but halted formal policing in many areas with the exception where

[*] Apartheid is the term coined to describe white minority rule based not only on a physical geographic separation of races, but also on active discrimination in political, economic, and social spheres against black people in South Africa.

[†] During the 1980s, it has been estimated that about 400 People's Courts operated in various townships across South Africa (HRC, 2001, 12).

[‡] See Minnaar (2001) for more details on this vigilantism in South Africa.

shows of massive force were implemented—all in an effort to bring down the political violence rather than crime control initiatives. In addition, during the period up to 1994, the activities (political community control) of the so-called Self Defense Units (SDUs) aligned with the African National Congress (ANC), and the Self Protection Units (SPUs) aligned with the Inkatha Freedom Party (IFP), also formed part of this self-protection ethos in the townships.* Another factor in this self-policing was the activities of the so-called "warlords," particularly in the informal settlements (squatter shacklands) that proliferated around the major metropolitan areas of South Africa. These warlords would often set up their own community courts and their own "police force" of community guards, which were funded largely with forced household levies. These warlords exerted absolute political and economic control over the communities they controlled.†

However, this "self-policing" (what I prefer to call anticrime self-protection and crime prevention activities) became part of the problem in black communities' interpretation, involvement, and implementation of the new envisaged "community policing"‡ in South Africa. What the policy makers tried to formulate was not always in line with township community ideas of how they should be policed. Many thought that this new community policing was where citizens would police themselves merely under the supervision of the formal police agencies. It was also thought that the state police would provide the communities with resources to enable them to police themselves, prevent crime, patrol their neighborhoods (like the anticrime street committees), arrest criminals, and hand them over for prosecution by the criminal justice system. Furthermore, some communities thought that Community Policing would be a logical extension to the People's Courts structures of the civic organizations in the townships. In other words, that it would legitimize their activities by bringing down criminal justice structures to community level where they would be directly involved in the whole process—be their own community police, court officers, and even judges of these community courts in their midst. Many thought that these ideas would be accommodated by the insertion in the interim Constitution of the establishment

* See Minnaar (1996) for more details on these.

† For more details on the activities of the warlords, see Minnaar (1992).

‡ Recognizing the force control aspects of "saturation" policing in high conflict areas, the SAP in March 1991 had taken the first step toward some form of community policing by introducing so-called Police-Community Liaison Forums in black townships to deal with issues of crime control (as opposed to suppressing the political violence). However, these failed (on perceptions of police bias, involvement in covert operations, and fanning the political violence with support for hit squads and IFP SPUs) and this particular initiative came to an end with the signing of the National Peace Accord (NPA) in September 1991 and the start of the CODESA negotiations (see Scharf, 1991).

of Community Police Forums (CPFs).* Moreover, these perceptions were a direct result of the poor policing that most black communities had suffered from for years at the hands of the SAP.

Moreover, as Mistry (1997, p. 40) put it, the "adoption of community policing has to be understood against the background of the massive shortcomings of the 'old' (pre-1994) policing system" (some of which have been outlined above). By the mid-1990s, policing in South Africa was characterized not only by exceptionally high crime levels† (by any international standards), but also by an almost total lack of trust, which in turn led to low levels of actual reporting of crime. If any policing was being experienced by these traditionally underpoliced communities, it was purely reactive and of the so-called "fire engine"‡ type whereby members of the police (often fearing for their own safety§ and well aware of the strong antagonism of ordinary members of the public toward them) merely responded to crime (if they responded at all or at the best a delayed response) with a quick "in-and-out" approach to policing of any crime (if it was reported). By 1994, any patrolling or forms of "visible" policing had all but ceased to be performed by the police, with policing in most black townships being merely reactive.

It was no wonder then that the newly renamed South African Police Services (SAPS), being ordered by the policy makers and politicians to "police in a more humane and sensitive way to the needs of communities manner," went searching for models for community policing, not having any tradition or background in this form of policing at all. Moreover, community policing in South Africa was initially more concerned with political rather than policing issues.

Problems Impacting on Formulating a Community Policing Model

South Africa, in transforming its whole approach to policing, was also faced with a number of specific, almost unique, problems as well as its population

* As early as end of March 1992, Deputy Minister of Law and Order, J. Scheepers, had announced that consultative community forums would be established on a national level in order to "implement the principle of community involvement, and thus provide the community *a say in police matters*" [italics for emphasis] (Scheepers, 1992).

† See Annexure A for a look at the extent and rates per 100,000 of the population for reported violent crime in South Africa for the years 1994 to 2007.

‡ A phrase coined to describe them merely "dropping in to put out the metaphorical fire (crime) and then leave immediately."

§ From 1990 to 2000, police members were murdered at a rate of more than 200 per year; one of the highest per 100,000 of the population in the world. For detail of how and reasons for these killings of police, see Minnaar (2003).

race mix,[*] high wealth gap (the Gini coefficient), inequalities in the justice system, uneven distribution of policing services with poorer areas, i.e., generally the largely black-inhabited townships and informal (squatter) settlements, suffering from neglect in terms of resources and police personnel in contrast to the level received by the wealthy more affluent (traditionally white) suburbs, which made up only 20% of urban area households,[†] and overcoming the consequences of years of political repression against only certain sections of the population.

Moreover, there were also a number of structural problems facing the South African Police (SAP), among which was the militaristic-type of training they received: top-heavy management structures staffed largely by white officers, overcoming public perceptions of them being used by the previous (pre-1994) regime largely for political repression, and the forceful suppression of township protest actions (as the tool of oppression by the apartheid white government). Prior to 1994, policing in South Africa was traditionally highly centralized, paramilitary, and authoritarian. While these characteristics ensured that the police were effective under the pre-1994 apartheid government in suppressing political protest and opposition to white rule, it also meant that they were poorly equipped for crime control and prevention in the newly democratic South Africa. Under apartheid rule, the police force (SAP) lacked legitimacy and functioned as an instrument of control rather than as a police service dedicated to ensuring the safety of all citizens. In essence, such authoritarian policing has few (if any) systems of accountability and oversight and does not require public legitimacy in order to be effective. Thus, with the advent of democracy in South Africa, systems of police accountability and oversight were not present. Furthermore, the new SAPS had a poorly developed (historically disadvantaged) criminal detection capability (unlike the police in other democratic societies) because of the previous apartheid form of policing. The collection, collation, and presentation of evidence to secure the prosecution of criminals was underdeveloped. This was reflected by, among other indicators, the training levels and experience of the detective component of the new SAPS.[‡] The problems of criminal detection were also mirrored in the area of crime intelligence. Intelligence-gathering

[*] In mid-2007, the estimated population of South Africa was nearly 48 million, with 80% regarded as of African origin (Black) while just over 9.1% are categorized as White, 8.8% as of mixed race (so-called Colored) origin, and 2.4% as Asian (largely of Indian extraction).

[†] In 1994, 74% of South Africa's police stations were situated in white suburbs or business districts (Dept. of Safety and Security White Paper, 1998, p. 4).

[‡] In 1994, only about 26% of detectives had been on a formal investigation training course, while only 13% of detectives had over six years' experience. In any event, those detective skills present in the police before 1994 were concentrated largely in white areas (Dept. of Safety and Security White Paper, 1998, p. 13).

structures prior to 1994 were also orientated toward the covert surveillance of political opponents of the apartheid state (Dept. of Safety and Security White Paper, 1998, p. 4).

All of this impacted severely on perceptions about their legitimacy and led to high levels of distrust, which in turn led to ordinary township citizens being reluctant to report crime to the police (often in desperation against the depredations of criminals turning to vigilante actions through people's courts or simply violent mob justice).[*] A further drawback was the need to amalgamate 11 different policing agencies in South Africa. While the SAPS were national and by far the biggest, best trained, and resourced, the others (from the so-called independent Bantustans[†] and before self-governing territories, also known as tribal homelands)[‡] had less of everything: numbers, quality and level of training, experienced officers, facilities, equipment, and lacked organizational sophistication and professionalism. In addition, in leading up to the 1994 elections, these smaller agencies had often promoted wholesale members to higher officer ranks without the requisite officer and management training. This, in turn, created a number of personnel problems with the placement of these positions in the new national amalgamated policing service.

To give structure and form to this envisaged new form of policing in South Africa, policy advisors to the political parties/groupings negotiating the peaceful transfer of power at the Convention for Democratic South Africa (CODESA)[§] negotiations made various study trips overseas to look at numerous forms of Community Policing. One of the results of this was the formulation and insertion into the interim Constitution of the concept of Community Police Forums, which were designed to be the link between communities and the new SAPS in order to oversee the implementation of the new model of community policing.[¶]

[*] See Minnaar (2002b) for more details on this aspect.

[†] The so-called TBVC (Transkei, Bophuthatswana, Venda, and Ciskei) states.

[‡] These were the Qwaqwa, Gazankulu, KwaZulu, KwaNdebele, Lebowa, and KaNgwane territories.

[§] The Convention for a Democratic South Africa (CODESA) was a series of negotiations between December 1991 and 1993 between all political groupings including leaders of the tribal homelands (Bantustans) (with the exception of the right-wing white Conservative Party and the left-wing Pan Africanist Congress who both boycotted CODESA), under the chairmanship of the judges Michael Corbett, Petrus Shabort, and Ismail Mahomed, which basically negotiated the end of apartheid. The first plenary on December 20, 1991 set up working groups to deal with specific issues, as well as the transformation of policing. Finally, there was the writing of an interim Constitution.

[¶] Initial impetus to these policy formulations had come from the National Peace Accord (NPA) of 1991, which committed the police to a new type of accountability that emphasized better communication and consultation with communities by the SAP through the setting up of NPA Local Dispute Resolution Committees (see Scharf, 1992).

Community Policing Forums

In South Africa a Community Police Forum (CPF) is a legally recognized entity that represents the policing interests of the local community. CPFs were also intended to exert civilian oversight over the police at various levels, in particular at the local police station level.

CPFs were provided for in the Interim Constitution, Act 200 of 1993 (Section 221[1]) and their establishment by way of an Act of Parliament. The function of CPFs as stipulated in s221(2) was, among other things, to facilitate the accountability of police to the communities they served, monitor the efficiency and effectiveness of the services provided by the police, as well as advise the police on local policing priorities. In addition, the interim Constitution was explicit on the role of CPFs in respect of evaluating visible policing. This would entail assessing "the provision, fitting and staffing of police stations, the reception and processing of complaints, the provision of protective services at gatherings, patrolling residential and business areas and the prosecution of offenders" (s221[2]). The interim Constitution clearly saw CPFs as a mechanism through which communities, in particular black communities, could build a relationship with the police, given the way these communities in South Africa had been policed in the past. Essentially, CPFs were meant to provide some sort of civilian oversight of the police at the local level, supplementing the role performed by the National and Provincial Secretariats for Safety & Security and the Independent Complaints Directorate (ICD)* at the national level.

Developing a Policy Framework

As early as the end of 1994 and building on the interim Constitution, a Green Paper on Safety and Security (Dept. of Safety and Security Green Paper, 1994) was issued as a policy guide for policing in the "new democratic" South Africa. This outlined principles, such as community policing, democratic control, and accountability, as well as introducing a new style of policing that required a demilitarized approach whereby civilian values would imbue every aspect of the new policing services. This latter point was an important concept within the context of the past way of policing (pre-1994) in South Africa.

* The ICD was established in 1996 (operations began in April 1997) and mandated to investigate any complaints against the police, as well as of the service shortcomings, dereliction of duties, mistreatment of the public, misconduct, excessive use of force, deaths in detention, and to hand over such cases (if warranted) for criminal prosecution. This was the first time in South Africa that such a policing monitoring body, accountable directly to Parliament, was set up. (More details on the workings of the ICD, statistics on numbers of complaints, deaths in custody, and prosecutions can be found on their Web site: www.icd.gov.za)

Furthermore, an immediate start was made in drafting a new piece of legislation to restructure the amalgamated policing agencies. This new piece of legislation, The SAPS Act No. 68 of 1995, was passed early that year. The Act (which also tried to give structure to some of the principles and guidelines for a new South African democracy inserted in the interim Constitution) was a comprehensive attempt at defining and setting up a "new look" policing service for South Africa, with a new approach to crime prevention, crime reduction, and combating of crime. The Act provided for an accountable, impartial, transparent, community-oriented, and cost-effective police service. The Act also provided for a civilian ministerial secretariat, community police forums (CPFs), an independent complaints directorate (ICD) (all issues inserted into the interim Constitution), and the institution of the National Secretariat for Safety & Security largely staffed with civilians (academics and practitioners from other branches of the criminal justice system). The National Secretariat resided directly under the Minister of Safety and Security, i.e., did not report to the new National Commissioner of SAPS. They were tasked to undertake policy formulation and provision of management information and advice to the minister. This task included (as per the new Act) the evaluation (this term was used as opposed to monitoring, which implied some sort of administrative control) of service delivery and performance of the police as well as to promote democratic accountability and transparency in the new Police Service. Other changes looked at such aspects as training, which was adapted to reflect a nonmilitary style of policing; different policing styles or approaches, such as "community policing"; and even a brief flirtation with "zero tolerance."*

Review of Policies, Legislation, and Guidelines

There was a quick recognition by top management of the new SAPS and the National Secretariat that an urgent look at policies, legislation, and guidelines for a new way of policing in South Africa was needed. Work began in 1995 on a more comprehensive (than the Green Paper) document, the National Crime Prevention Strategy (NCPS). The NCPS document was approved by Cabinet in May 1996 and represented the first time ever that South Africa had formulated such a national policy or strategy, which clearly identified crime prevention as a national priority. The NCPS motivated for a change from the previous exclusive focus on law enforcement to now include "crime prevention" (i.e., away from a narrow "crime control" focus). Other important

* Commissioner William Bratten of the New York Police Department and the main architect of the operationalization of "zero tolerance" and "broken windows" policing principles came to South Africa in 1997 and conducted a series of workshops on this form of policing, mainly to SAPS officials at management levels (author attended one of these).

changes envisaged in the NCPS that impacted extensively on the future way of policing in South Africa were looking at crime as a "social issue" and that responsibility for dealing with it be shared by all agencies; a movement away from the emphasis on a state-centered criminal justice system to that of a victim-centered restorative justice system. Although the NCPS was of necessity wide-ranging covering the entire criminal justice system,* many of the issues raised in this document focused more on the role of the police in operationalizing these needs in fighting crime than on operational aspects of Community Policing.

The White Paper (1998)

The Green Paper (1994), the SAPS Act of 1995, and the NCPS (1996) in advocating a new approach to police practices made an important policy or paradigm shift by strongly advocating that policing be made more community-oriented. To ensure that these principles were implemented in actual policing and building on the impetus given by the policy acceptance of the NCPS (and the Green Paper), the Minister of Safety and Security approved the development of a White Paper in June 1997, with the main aim of reviewing existing policies and programs and finally to set the policy framework for the next five years.

Prior to the actual release of the White Paper in 1998, the Department for Safety and Security had released a detailed document titled: *Policy Framework and Guidelines for Community Policing,* in April 1997. As a consequence, the White Paper made little operational reference to Community Policing per se other than to mention that the SAPS policing approach continued to be "underpinned by the philosophy of community policing" and that this focus was "directly in line with international trends in policing,

* The NCPS started with 14 initial projects, some focusing on areas that were in need of immediate attention, such as the Integrated Justice System (IJS) (information systems to be shared), while others addressed specific areas of crime prevention, such as victim empowerment. Other initial projects included border control, an integrated security system, environmental design, vehicle crime, and corruption. Many of these projects also had identified subissues. For example, the border control project with 19 ongoing activities, while the project on streamlining the IJS encompasses victim empowerment, organized crime, corruption, commercial crime, gangsterism, and domestic violence. Other new projects envisaged by the NCPS centered on what was called "social crime and situational crime prevention." Social crime prevention was to focus on the cycle of violence that begins with young children and continues into adulthood. Efforts to develop projects in conjunction with the departments of Health and Education were outlined in the document, which intended to reach young children in schools and at home. Situational crime prevention also involved the planning of safer areas through, among other things, improved access and lighting, in essence Crime Prevention through Environmental Design (CPTED), which was a fairly new concept in South Africa (outside of purely academic circles).

which demonstrated that the participation of communities and community policing form the bedrock of effective law enforcement" (Dept. Safety and Security White Paper, 1998, 3 & 10).

However, in the White Paper the emphasis had shifted toward improved service delivery, at the heart of which was the principle that "a partnership between the police and communities is essential to effective service delivery" (p. 3). Therefore the White Paper went on to propose certain interventions for "a safer and more secure society" in two main areas, namely law enforcement and social crime prevention (p. 19). In the latter, implied was problem-oriented partnership strategies (again drawing from international trends) (p. 40). In addition, the Department of Safety and Security's (and SAPS) view then of serving the community better (i.e., Community Policing) would also involve more effective management of both direct and indirect victims and witnesses of crime as a vital part of successful police investigations. This, in itself, was integral to the accepted community policing philosophy (that the SAPS subscribed to in the guidelines document), which seeks to build relationships between the police and local communities. There was, thus, a further acceptance of the link between victim support and successful investigations being critical to improving service delivery and, therefore, to enhancing public confidence in the police (p. 24).

Social Crime Prevention

While the 1998 White Paper of the Department for Safety and Security emphasizes the role and involvement of other new role players outside of the SAPS within a framework of social crime prevention programs,* (p. 5), this White Paper did not spell out how this would be implemented in practical terms for these other role players (e.g., private security industry) in South Africa. In terms of partnerships, the White Paper merely states that, with reference to visible policing, the "capacity to implement visible policing be augmented through *partnerships* with local government" (p. 13) [italics for emphasis]. The implication here is that this would be done in conjunction with the proposed metropolitan or municipal policing structures.

* The White Paper, for the first time officially made use of the term *social crime prevention*. Implied here was where the community at large is involved in initiatives or projects run by those that aim to prevent crime in their own neighborhoods. These typically involves volunteer neighborhood watches that patrol certain residential areas, or being the "eyes and ears" of the police, such as in "e-block watches" where private citizens organize themselves in "blocks" and report any suspicious activities either to each other or directly to the local police by cell phone (or other means).

Private-Public Policing Partnerships

Furthermore, the White Paper does not provide a practical guide to private–public policing even though it explicitly mentions the private security industry in terms of being a "partner" against crime:

> Another important element of safety and security in democratic South Africa is the necessity to enhance the spirit of voluntarism in the country. There are many important *partners in the fight against crime.* These include, among others, organizations of civil society, particularly business and community organizations, citizens who volunteer for service as Police Reservists, as well as the private security industry, which performs a useful role. The role of such players is, in principle, one of partnership with the State. For this reason, greater attention will be paid to their role in the safety and security environment in future policy processes (p. 7) [italics for emphasis].

Finally, the White Paper refers only to areas of intervention to ensure effective crime prevention by way of Community Crime Prevention where:

> These interventions involve communities taking responsibility for crime prevention in their own neighborhoods. Such interventions involve localized programs, which mobilize a range of interest groups to address crime prevention on a town or city basis. Projects could include improving surveillance through schemes, such as car guards or community marshals .... (p. 17)

The Private Security Industry and Public Policing

It would appear then that the above created some sort of opportunity for the private security industry to engage in crime prevention exercises at a community level. However, as in the past, no legal or regulated framework for such initiatives was established or proposed at all. The implication within this omission is that any such action would actually occur in a legal and practical vacuum. According to Julie Berg (2004b):

> Government policy in terms of the National Crime Prevention Strategy, 1996, and White Paper of Safety and Security, 1998, refer to the partnering of the community and the responsibility of communities to respond to the crime threat. However, the nature of this proposed partnership is never detailed in terms of resource—use, policing powers, competition and the profit motive, community interest, forms of policing and how these should be regulated and held accountable, and in broad terms the role of the state versus the role of private initiatives—whether for-profit or not-for-profit (Berg 2004b, p. 3).

In addition, there remains uncertainty in a number of quarters on precisely what kind of support/cooperation or service would be provided by the security industry to the police. Moreover, the wide diversity of services provided by the general private security industry in South Africa further complicates the matter. Although a number of so-called joint or cooperative partnership initiatives have already been launched between certain companies/individuals and police stations at a local level, these have proceeded without the formal recognition or approval by the South African Police Services management and also without due acknowledgement to the legal implications* of such actions.

There is, in fact, no formal national cooperation agreement in existence between the SAPS and the Private Security Industry.† Accordingly, the outsourcing of some of the operational functions of the SAPS is at best problematic.‡ There is also no mandate from the South African Police Service that supports or gives any proposed guidelines regarding the expected standard service delivery in terms of outsourcing any policing functions to the private security industry. Moreover, there are no clear guidelines regarding the role of the security industry and the police or any clear-cut instructions defining the exact relationship between these two entities.

Implementation of Community Policing

What then of the accepted philosophy of "Community Policing" by the SAPS? As part of the policy changes (Green Paper, Police Act, NCPS, and the later the White Paper) in formulating a new way of policing the SAPS had officially adopted Community Policing as the way to go. *The Community Policing Policy Framework and Guidelines* (CPPFG), released in April 1997, was intended to serve as guidelines for implementing this official policing style in South Africa.

The Community Policing Model

The Community Policing Model as outlined in the policy framework was largely an adaptation of traditional Western European and American principles, as well as the emphasis on establishing police–community partnerships within a problem-solving approach responsive to the needs of the community (SAPS, 1997, p. 1). The CPPFG further accepted the following broad concepts

* Briefly, these legal implications refer to civil and public liability, as well as "peace officer powers." For the private sector to provide assistance to the police beyond just the provision of information or being the eyes and ears for local police is still legally guided by the existing powers extended to members of the public, i.e., they have no additional powers legislated specifically for this industry. For a more detailed discussion of these issues, see Minnaar (1997).

† There are, however, ad hoc agreements for cooperation between individual companies and the SAPS. A notable example is that of some vehicle tracker recovery companies.

‡ See Minnaar & Mistry (2004) for more details on outsourcing of policing activities.

of: (1) service orientation (community being the client and SAPS the service provider); (2) partnerships (cooperative effort to facilitate a process of problem solving); (3) problem solving (joint identification and analysis of the actual and potential causes of crime within communities); (4) empowerment (creation of sense of joint responsibility—joint capacity for addressing crime and service delivery); and (5) accountability (mechanisms for making police answerable for addressing needs and concerns of communities) (pp. 2–3).

The policy document itself gave detailed guidelines for the establishment of CPFs in every policing precinct; every police station commissioner was instructed to be "responsible for the establishment of Community Police Forums in their respective areas" (p. 5). Furthermore, they were delegated to undertake "the identification and mobilization, through consultation, of community resources and organizations that may assist in combating and preventing crime and the constant development of this capacity" (p. 4). Moreover, all police members were tasked (in the policy guidelines) "to develop new skills through training, which incorporates problem solving, networking, mediation, facilitation, conflict resolution. and community involvement" (p. 4). This in itself was a tall order for the SAPS—undertrained, underskilled, poorly resourced, and almost overwhelmed by the high workload and persistent high levels of crime they faced, without even mentioning the other socioeconomic problems facing an emerging democratic and developing country like South Africa.

Obviously, like all policy documents, it tended to veer toward idealistic best practices models culled from other international law enforcement jurisdictions. The real test in South Africa would be its practical implementation, and what structures would be implemented to support this philosophy.

At police station level, the police members were tasked to establish, within each precinct, a SAPS Implementation Committee, whose first task was to conduct an internal audit of current strategies, existing structures, (police) culture, and available resources. Then, to determine shortcomings and areas where changes needed to be made and adaptations undertaken. Furthermore, an analysis of each particular police station's response to calls for service from the community they were serving was also to be completed. In addition, an audit was to be instituted of community initiatives (which had to relate to crime and other policing-related problems, such as poor standard of service delivery, poor community relations experienced by the community, etc.) and community crime prevention programs (such as Neighborhood Watch) were operational and functioning in the precinct area. Finally, a change in management style was required, from paramilitaristic bureaucratic style to a more participative and strategic management style that emphasized not only accountability, but also a more proactive responsive form of policing (pp. 25–28). On the basis of the reported audit findings (list of strategic and critical issues), each police station, because of their community and station uniqueness, had to develop a comprehensive Action Plan (p. 36). Furthermore, part of this Action Plan was the compiling of a community profile* (external dimension) in order to facilitate consultations, forming partnerships, and engaging in joint problem solving with each specific community (p. 37).

Institutionalizing Community Policy Initiatives

All of these new community policing initiatives required skills that the SAPS did not have or which were simply in short supply. It was no wonder then that it took more than five years before it could be said that the South African style of Community Policing could claim to be fully operational.

Accordingly, various endeavors were embarked upon to institutionalize community policing. As from the beginning of 1998, a comprehensive program was launched within the SAPS to train all members in the philosophy, values, and principles of community policing.† It must be remembered that the old SAP certainly did not have the ethos or culture of following such a type of "softer" policing (as opposed to the more "hard" militaristic and forceful style of the past). In the South African context, this policing style was based on the premise that a community and its police service are equal partners with shared responsibilities in ensuring safety and security. However, as Mistry put it in her review of the implementation of Community Policing:

> When community policing was introduced, police feared that members of the community would take over their police stations and tell them what to do. The introduction of mechanisms enforcing transparency are breaking down old-style, "rules-based" policing. However ... [t]he rapid transformation of the SAPS resulted in confusion, misconceptions, and resistance to community policing and CPFs (Mistry, 1997, p. 47).

Establishing CPFs and CPF Area Boards

The Community Policing document also focused on the establishment of CPFs and CPF Area Boards as official structures to coordinate partnership

* Community profiles are to be inclusive of a demographic, unemployment, and crime analysis in each area. This profile is to be compiled by means of surveys to determine community perceptions as well as on the crime problem in general, relative seriousness of specific crimes, police-community relations, legitimacy and credibility of police, and standard of police service, as well as identifying the causes of crime,the nature and extent of community fears, and the nature of other community needs (SAPS, 1998, p. 38). Such surveys obviously required survey research skills (questionnaire formulation and data analysis) in addition to resources and funding and organizational skills that were beyond most individual police station's capabilities or previous experience. Those that were initially done were not standardized across the board nor implemented on a regular let alone annual basis.

† See Mistry (1997) for detail of this training.

policing initiatives at community level, while the White Paper provided for a supplementary role for local government in CPF activities by directing the CPFs toward a more cooperative relationship with municipalities and metropolitan councils in what was termed *social crime prevention,* thus shifting the CPFs' community role to one of community mobilization in order to address priority crimes in each community by maximizing civil participation in crime-prevention initiatives (Smit & Schnetler, 2004, p. 14).

As Scharf (1992, pp. 22–23) put it:

> If the police are using community policing merely as a legitimating buzz word while still continuing with orthodox policing as the[ir] main guiding philosophy, then the chances of changing on the ground relations with progressive communities are [...] low. [Furthermore], despite the considerable shift in the policing rhetoric of politicians, the police personnel have shown little, if any, change in their accustomed top-down attitude to civil society.

But according to Brogden and Nijhar (2005, p. 138), "From a police point of view, community policing assumed an intelligence gathering character in which the community would hopefully became a police resource." A survey of police officers in Gauteng Province revealed that the introduction of community policing simply meant to them that the community should help them in fighting crime (Mistry, 1997). This was diametrically opposed to by communities, especially those who had suffered at the hands of the old apartheid police where repression and oppression were the order of the day. Most communities viewed the new form of (community) policing as an opportunity to change the balance of power in their communities and make the police accountable to community needs and structures (via the new CPFs). Accordingly, especially in the poorer and largely black communities (townships), community policing "was about the control of the police and much less about preventing crime" (Brogden & Nijhar, 2005, p. 138).

At the beginning of 1999, the Gauteng provincial government tried to harness widespread public anger and outrage against perceived escalating crime by launching a public campaign to set up 1980s-era-style street committees in an effort to constructively engage communities in the fight against crime. The then Gauteng provincial Member of the Executive Committee (MEC) for Safety and Community Liaison, Paul Mashatile, was a strong proponent of setting up street and block committees because he felt that this would be the only means of getting the community involved by way of small units to really reach the people on the ground in order to achieve any sort of success in a provincial anticrime campaign. The difference for Mashatile of the apartheid-era committees and the present envisaged ones was that "then it was an alternative to the state machinery, while today it will be complementary to the criminal justice system. The focus today… will be the elimination of crime." The old M-Plan of the ANC consisted of command structures that in the past stretched from the local civic association that had representatives of block committees, who in turn consisted of representatives of street committees. The new street committees in the Gauteng model envisaged the Community Policing Forum (CPF) on top, followed by area subforums, block communities, and, eventually, street communities at the lowest level. The Gauteng Secretariat for Safety and Community Liaison planned to assist their establishment in each community so that they would not mushroom on their own in an uncontrolled manner. The structures were then to be monitored by the secretariat on an ongoing basis. A further major safeguarding mechanism built into the new model was that the police would be involved and informed of what the committees were up to. The first such street committee model was implemented in Ivory Park* (the scene of one of the post-1994 vigilante killings in early January 1999). The Ivory Park CPF was divided into eight zones, each under a subforum, and, in turn, the local police station dedicated one policeman to liaise with every two subforums as a link between the police and community. Furthermore, to promote this new concept of community policing, to coordinate crime prevention, and to deal with vigilantism, the Gauteng government declared the month of March 1999 as Safety and Security month during which Mashatile and the then Gauteng Premier Mothale Motshekga toured the province promoting the street committee system (Masipa, 1999). At a series of "Don't Do Crime" rallies, the new street committee/CPF model was strongly punted by Mashatile. However, in encouraging communities to fight crime, individuals were still inclined toward taking the law into their own hands, and in their eyes, quite justifiably so as part of their efforts to combat crime because the authorities were still perceived as being totally ineffective in dealing with crime in their neighborhoods. Therein lay the crux of the problem, since, after the initial burst of enthusiasm, as it became apparent that no real improvement in policing, let alone in the full implementation of community policing, was occurring, communities in black townships fell back into their old ways of either vigilantism or apathy, with the CPFs becoming either nonactive, dysfunctional, or merely a police-controlled "talk shop."

From the SAPS and the government side, in this roll-out of CPFs and community policing, the most important thing in this situation was for the authorities to formalize the whole system of "informal vigilante" justice by channeling these anticrime activities into a more formal structure, i.e., the new CPF/street committees in liaison with the local police structures. However, with the implementation of CPFs (as the foundation of the

* Ivory Park is an informal settlement in Midrand (a new growing urban area midway between the cities of Johannesburg and Pretoria).

new community policing), there very quickly arose disputes between forum members and local police station members, particularly over the operational independence of the SAPS themselves, and clashes erupted over CPF community crime priorities and the official SAPS priorities, which were set at national level* (Shaw, 2002).

Moving Away from 'Pure' Community Policing

In fact, it took only a little more than five years after the initial community police policy document for the new community policing style to largely become abandoned (or at best simply ignored or disregarded in terms of operational planning) in all but name throughout the SAPS. This "abandonment" (with SAPS personnel strongly believing it to be "too soft" for the tough crime conditions in South African townships) was also due in part to a number of inherent constraints. One of these being that at the time of its inception the personnel of the SAPS were still largely undertrained and underskilled, with estimates that almost 25% of its 128,000 members were considered to be functionally illiterate (Pelser, 1999). Even more members had never received formal training in the actual methodology of community policing. Initially the SAPS members had also tended to ignore the local CPFs or alternately took the initiative in setting up, in other words, coopting members from the community onto the CPFs, which were in any case administered (had their meetings at and resourced from local police stations) by the local police station commissioner. CPFs doing their critical monitoring role and advising police on priority crimes in their areas or even what crime prevention programs should be implemented (theoretically in partnership with communities) were few and far between. Moreover, in the more affluent predominantly white areas, the tendency was for the local CPF to turn itself into a Section 21 Company (not-for-profit) and then to contribute money toward the purchase of equipment and vehicles for the use by the police station in their area, so as to ensure that the type of quality policing previously received (in the apartheid era) from a well-resourced police station would continue to be received by its residents (Pelser, 1999).

This was a very deliberate response to what was perceived as the siphoning-off of resources to the under-resourced and poorly policed areas in the black townships. Therefore, inequalities in levels of policing continued (albeit, unintended) to be perpetuated because CPFs in poorer areas could not afford to equip their local police station at all. The entire effectiveness of CPFs was being questioned, particularly because they ended up being unelected, i.e., coopted by the local police station commissioner (community elections were tried, but

* National SAPS priorities of responding to murder, armed robbery, and other violent crime did not accommodate CPF/community priorities, such as dealing with rape, domestic violence, and child molestation.

became a waste of time because very few community members turned up for voting at community meetings; particular interest groups, such as minibus taxi associations, got their members voted onto a local CPF thereby dominating proceedings with their narrow crime concerns; or even criminals infiltrated and became privy to policing activities in their areas of operation) or consisted of local individuals who had a specific interest in improving police performance. Within the SAPS itself they were treated with disdain and regarded "as a necessary evil" required by law to bring members of the public into contact with the police. CPFs ended up having little impact or say on the day-to-day conduct of the police. In addition, this situation led to disputes arising between CPF members and the SAPS as to the latter's operational independence and eventually those CPFs (other than the ones who merely funded additional equipment and vehicles) were sidelined and ignored (Shaw, 2001).

In a study conducted by Pelser, Schnetler, and Louw in 2002, it was found that essentially community policing and CPFs appeared to have been subtly downgraded (operationally as well as a guiding policing philosophy) by the Ministry and the SAPS, as far as policies, regulations, and funding were concerned, while communities had also (through apathy and disinterest) abrogated any involvement in community policing, viewing crime prevention, reduction, and control as solely "police business" (Pelser et al., 2002, pp. 26–27, 64).

Community Policing Becomes Subordinate to Other Forms of Policing

Community policing in South Africa, as originally intended as an alternative policing model to assist the police to prevent crime in communities, soon came to be subsumed into other forms of policing. Although not initially apparent, while still paying lip service to a community-oriented approach (using all the appropriate terminology), the SAPS, as early as the launch of the Community Safety Plan in 1995, had already demonstrated—if one carefully read between the lines and observed the special operations launched as part of this plan—"their intention to revert to more traditional methods to combat crime" (Burger, 2007, p. 136). In addition, all pretence to community policing was in fact abandoned with the more formal Policing Priorities and Objectives (otherwise known as the Police Plan) of 1996/1997 and the implementation of Operation Sword and Shield with its "return to basics" policing approach.*

* This operation went back to using the more traditional policing methods of visible and targeted patrols (vehicle, foot, and horse); high-density (flooding) operations with numerous cordon-and-search, stop-and-search, and roadblock operations; and air-supported operations in the identified high risk (priority hotspot) areas in selected communities (Burger, 2007, p. 137).

So, in essence, Community Policing by itself faded into the background, and other forms of policing (such as visible and sector policing) were pushed forward by the SAPS, ostensibly in support of Community Policing, but all the more designed to improve the SAPS' operational effectiveness in fighting crime rather than dealing directly with community sensitivities and needs to be policed in a more considerate, sympathetic, compassionate, and sensitive manner.

Visible Policing

The 1998 White Paper had set out to emphasize the implementation of more "visible policing" linked to better service delivery to victims as well as coordinating an integrated criminal justice system. The White Paper advocated a dual approach to safety and security: effective and efficient law enforcement and the provision of crime prevention programs to reduce the occurrence of crime. Furthermore, the White Paper set out priority law enforcement focus areas on: improving criminal investigations by expanding and retraining investigative capacity in the SAPS and implementing targeted (active) visible policing and service to victims by meeting the needs of victims through adequate service delivery. Visible Policing was designed to fill the gap between operational crime combating activities and Community Policing by "providing a proactive and responsive policing service that will prevent the priority crimes rate from increasing" (SAPS Annual Report, 2007, p. 31). The emphasis was, however, on specialized crime prevention operations.*

Core to the visible policing approach was the following three phases as outlined in the White Paper:

1. *Preventive patrol:* This consists of a constant uniformed police presence in an area targeted on the basis of analysis of crime patterns. Officers on patrol activities can also respond to incidents reported by the public, the immediacy of the response being determined by the seriousness of the incident. This type of patrol has been found to be most effective in major urban areas. Municipal police services have an important role to play in this regard (see White Paper, 1998, section V).
2. *Directed patrol:* This involves the assignment of patrol officers to provide a visible presence in a specific location for a limited period and

* Also, these in practical terms were the institution of roadblocks, cordons and searches, searching of premises and vehicles, vehicle patrols, visits to schools, farms, and private homes—all in an effort to make communities feel safer and more secure, i.e., community policing.

for a particular purpose. Directed patrol relies on crime analysis to provide timely information on crime patterns in any area.

3. *Sector policing:* This entails the division of areas into smaller managerial sectors and the assignment of police officers to these areas on a full time basis. These police officers regularly patrol their own sector and are able to identify problems and seek appropriate solutions. Sector policing encourages constant contact with members of local communities. (White Paper, 1998, p. 6)

Of the three forms of visible policing outlined above, Sector Policing became the most important of the new initiatives with reference to the implementation of Community Policing. However, this required an unprecedented change, not only in training, but also in the thinking of ordinary policemen and women on the ground. The overloading of police officers and detectives within the context of the continued high crime levels* made it virtually impossible to implement meaningful training programs across the board. Members simply could not be spared to go off on training courses for weeks on end.

So, while the policy changes seemed to be on the right track in practical terms, policing in South Africa still continued to suffer from ineffectiveness and failed to significantly reduce and bring down crime (as reflected in the official crime statistics).

Further Additions to Policy Structures

Thus, by the turn of the century (six years after democratization), there still remained huge structural and operational problems facing a transformation of SAPS. With the realization that much of the intended changes were simply not being properly or adequately put into operation, the new Minister of Safety and Security, Steve Tshwete, initiated a review of the NCPS and in September 1999 a Strategic Implementation Plan was approved by the Cabinet in September. In addition, a Justice, Crime Prevention, and Security Cluster (JCPS), made up of the departments of Justice, Correctional Services, Safety and Security, Constitutional Development, Defense, Social Development, Finance, Foreign Affairs, Home Affairs, South African Revenue Services, National Intelligence Agency, and the National Directorate of Public Prosecution, was established in order to focus on addressing the incidence of crime and public disorder while improving the efficiency of the criminal justice system (Smit & Schnetler, 2004, pp, 15–16). The JCPS developed

* See Table 2.1. The full crime statistics from 1994 to 2007 can be viewed in detail (with totals and rates per 100,000) on the SAPS Web site: www.saps.org.za.

a National Security Policy (NSP) aimed at integrating crime prevention and crime-combating activities with a socioeconomic upliftment process.

As part of implementing the priorities of the JCPS cluster, the SAPS developed its own National Crime Combating Strategy (NCCS)* (launched on April 1, 2000) (as outlined in the SAPS Strategic Plan: 2002–2005) (Smit & Schnetler, 2004, p. 17; SAPS Strategic Plan, 2000).

Sector Policing

As part of the NCCS, the SAPS also launched (as envisaged in the White Paper of 1998) an intensive policing and patrol strategy known as sector policing. This approach basically meant that each police station area (precinct) was divided into smaller, more manageable areas. Police resources were then directed to those specific high-crime identified areas within the precinct in order to increase police visibility, improve community involvement by building trust and getting the public to report all crime and any suspicious activities in their neighborhood, and to try to address the causes of crime and the fear of crime (Smit & Schnetler, 2004, p. 17).† Better visible and sector policing was based on the premise that, if crime levels could be brought down, communities would feel safer, trust the police more, and as a consequence better report crime to the police, etc. Hence, operational improvements and increased policing effectiveness would then indirectly support and grow Community Policing.

Further changes implemented via the new NCCS included the restructuring of the detective division in the SAPS. Allied to this restructuring was the roll out of so-called visible policing with its subcomponent sector policing. The SAPS' Division for Crime Prevention was tasked to "reduce opportunities to commit crime by optimizing visible policing" (SAPS Annual Report, 2002/2003). In addition, as part of the commitment to extend and make Community Policing more effective, this division was also responsible for victim support programs.

* The NCPS, while having inputs from SAPS management, was almost entirely drafted and formulated by the civilians and academic consultants attached to the National Secretariat. With the NCCS, it was an entirely SAPS exercise and effort.

† Through such a geographic approach, the NCCS began to focus on 145 of the 1,130 police stations in South Africa, which generate more than 50% of the reports on crime in South Africa. During 2000 and 2001, all of the 145 identified high-crime risk police stations were provided with a Geographic Information System (GIS) and the appointment of crime analysts in order to analyze the crime on a daily basis in these specific precincts. The identified stations were also instructed to focus all policing activities and scarce resources (special operations, patrols, roadblocks, surveillance actions, etc.) on reducing the high crime levels in their precinct areas (Smit & Schnetler, 2004, 17).

Rollout of Sector Policing

Sector policing as one of the prioritized focus areas in the SAPS Strategic Plan (2002–2005) was officially launched in 2001 with a pilot project in the Johannesburg area. Sector policing was seen as the final practical manifestation of community policing. The basic concept of Sector Policing as exhibited in the South African context consisted of at least one police official being allocated on a full-time basis to a sector (i.e., geographically manageable area within a police precinct) for which he/she is responsible to enhance safety and security).

Crucial to the successful implementation of this concept is the involvement of all role players in identifying the policing needs in that particular sector and in addressing the root causes of crime as well as the enabling and contributing factors. The responsibilities of the sector police official also included the determining on a continuous basis (in cooperation with nonpolice role players) policing needs, and identifying crime problems, tendencies, crime, hot spots, criminals, etc. In addition, their role included the initiating and co-coordination of policing projects (e.g., special patrols) and other safety and security initiatives. They would also be responsible for overseeing the activation of other role players (e.g., municipalities, government departments, and nongovernmental organizations [NGOs]). Underlying these actions would be initially to establish direct communication with community members (often via CPFs, if there was a functioning one in the area). Alternately, sector police officers would usually start off with a public awareness campaign sometimes involving "knock-and-drop-off" (of information sheets and pamphlets)* actions and the holding of monthly crime discussion meetings with community members. Essentially, the "new" sector policing initiative looked at addressing local crime problems and, where possible, the root cause of crime.

According to Dixon and Rauch (2004, p. 1), the most important aspects of sector policing are its "local geographic focus, problem-solving methodologies, and community consultations." At the end of 2003, the SAPS had sent out a directive to police stations across the country to start implementing Sector Policing (on the basis of the positive results from the Johannesburg pilot project). According to Jonny Steinberg, the aim of Sector Policing was to "improve neighborhood policing, which the police had been struggling to accomplish for the past decade. The idea is that grassroots cops will begin to understand microlevel crime patterns and tackle them with creative problem-solving techniques; this will draw police into constant communication with their constituents and help them understand the public as clients and themselves as service providers" (Steinberg, 2004).

* By the end of the 2006/2007 reporting year, the Sector Policing rollout had involved the SAPS in distributing 15,000 learner manuals on sector policing, 2,500 booklets on community safety, 16,000 posters on sector policing, and 300,000 flyers on sector policing in five African languages (SAPS Annual Report, 2007, p. 61).

In essence, Sector Policing is an amalgam of past policing initiatives drawing on elements of CPF structures, community policing, visible policing, special operations, crime analysis, and intelligence-led policing. It also creates a perfect platform for the involvement and integration and coordination of the policing activities of certain sectors of the private security industry. Accordingly, within all of these policy changes there were persistent calls by the private security industry to be allowed to play a larger role in assisting the police to combat and prevent crime or at least to outsource certain services still being provided by the SAPS, which could very easily be outsourced without compromising any strictly policing functions of the SAPS. (See later section on the president and minister's call for better use of private security industry in policing.)

Special Operations and Other Crime-Combating Support Mechanisms

Allied to Sector Policing and in support of this form of Community Policing, from the end of 2002, crime-combating mechanisms were established that included Crime Combating and Response units (increasing roadblocks and searches and impacting on gang violence, taxi violence, faction fighting, and bank and cash-in-transit robberies), as well as the establishment and deployment of 50 Sector Policing units (assisted by metropolitan police) as roaming units in those areas inflicted with the highest crime (mostly in the aforementioned 145 police station precincts).

Special projects and special operations were launched, which included the arresting of wanted persons, addressing cell phone theft, addressing the influence of illicit drugs, improving border control, reducing case backlogs (rollout of the Court Centre Project), and reducing overcrowding in prisons and the proliferation of firearms.[*] Some observers were skeptic regarding the "Special Operations" in policing terms. In essence, these were nothing more than high-density, high-visibility operations.[†]

[*] In this regard one of the most successful of the special operations was Operation Rachel (implemented annually since 1995), a joint crossborder operation with Mozambique specifically aimed at dealing with the supply of illegal guns from external sources, namely that which was being smuggled in from neighboring countries. The main purpose of this operation was to find and destroy weapons caches within Mozambique. (For more detail on this operation, see Minnaar, 2007).

[†] The special operations like Operation Crackdown were premised on the fact that more than 50% of crime occurred within the policing areas of about 12% of South Africa's police stations (145 out of 1,136 stations). The idea behind Operation Crackdown and the more recent Operation Tshipa was to assemble a massive national task force and saturate these identified crime hot spot areas with large numbers of visible police in order to carry out frequent roadblocks, cordon-and-search operations, and vehicle and premise searches.

However, underpinning the rollout of increased and improved policing services at the individual police station/community level, a detailed Performance Management System was developed and implemented with specific performance indicators (e.g., reducing crime in precinct by X%). However, having learned from the pilot project launched in 1998, target setting (e.g., reduce a specific crime each year by 5%) was left up to each station commissioner's operational team based on the analysis of trends and prioritizing of specific crimes at each station. An adjunct to the Performance Management System was the use of Client Satisfaction Surveys to also establish whether service delivery was improving, if the new policing initiatives were successful, where improvements could be done, identifying community needs, etc.

As can be seen from the above analysis, an integrated system of crime combating and crime reduction based on the policy frameworks outlined in the Interim Constitution (1993), Green Paper (1994), NCPS (1996), White Paper (1998), and the NCCS (2000) was slowly being implemented and put into operation by a restructured, transformed (in its policing approach and policing culture), and reengineered (operational changes) SAPS. Unfortunately, with this new operational policing emphasis (and the fact that the NCCS was formulated entirely by police officers), the philosophy of Community Policing increasingly became "lost with it," merely being paid lip service as a separate policing form in the South African context. However, officially it was being stated that Community Policing was being supported and served in practical terms by the rollout of the new operational forms of visible and sector policing. But, the rollout of sector policing was a slow process. After the Johannesburg Pilot Project in 2001, Sector Policing was formally introduced countrywide in 2002 and 2003 in order to "increase police visibility and accessibility," particularly in areas having limited infrastructure and high levels of crime. By the end of the 2003/2004 reporting year (April 1 to March 31), it had been introduced at 47 priority and 14 presidential* stations and, in 2005, further rollout occurred to 169 high-contact crime (including the priority and presidential) police stations. However, by the end of the 2006/2007 reporting year, Sector Policing, as a crime prevention strategy (and, by implication, a Community Policing intervention), had only been implemented in a total of 76% of the sectors at these 169 high-contact crime police stations (out of the approximately 1,200 police stations in South Africa) (SAPS Annual Report, 2007, pp. 2–3).

* These were specific police stations identified as high risk lacking infrastructure and adequate resources and having high levels of crime in their precinct areas, which were made Presidential Stations in terms of being prioritized for additional allocations of resources, manpower, and funding.

Social Crime Prevention Programs

Within the context of more visible policing under the program of Social Crime Prevention, SAPS tried to implement specific community policing-oriented strategies or programs among:

- Antirape strategy involving community awareness campaigns (additionally with active involvement of police personnel in the annual national "16 Days of Activism" week (the last week in November).
- Further implementation and training around the Domestic Violence Act (under the 2006 revised SAPS Domestic Violence Learning Program).
- Participation in the National Action Plan for 365 days to end Violence- and Gender-based Violence.
- The Youth Crime Prevention Capacity Building Program (e.g., Safe Schools Program, Drug Reduction Program (for youth) and Child Protection Program).
- The rollout of the National Victim Empowerment Program.

Participation in all of these was designed to grow and extend the "human" face of the SAPS and build trust and faith in the police throughout communities (a central tenet of the philosophy of community policing).

But, one of the accepted tenets of Community Policing in the South African context had been the aim of the "establishment of active partnerships between the police and the public through which crime and community safety issues can be jointly addressed." In South Africa, these "partnerships" were largely structured through the CPFs and under the premise of fulfilling the Community Policing approach of recognizing "the interdependence and shared responsibility of the police and the community in establishing safety and security" (SAPS Annual Report, 2007, p. 50). This was fine where there were effective and properly functioning CPFs, but real crime prevention partnerships, other than commercial and for-profit ventures, such as private security operations, were few and far between.

Although by the 2006/2007 reporting year, there were officially 1,064 CPFs established at police stations around the country—many operating under varying degrees of success or inadequately fulfilling their legislated mandate. In 2007, the SAPS and parliamentary policy makers entered into discussions to change the legislation governing CPF activities to allow the CPFs to act to a greater extent on behalf of the communities they were supposed to represent. Part of these envisaged changes would be greater interaction (in terms of identifying and setting) with each police station's crime and policing priorities and performance targets, and the drawing up of a policing program for each precinct that would be co-owned by both parties.

Furthermore, formal regular feedbacks were to be provided by station commissioners to the local CPF and then back to communities on crime trends and progress in dealing with them. In turn, the communities were to be actively involved in assessing police performance at the local police station based on the policing priorities and targets set in the jointly formulated policing program for that police station (SAPS Annual Report, 2007, p. 51). One of the implications of these changes would be better funding and the provision of resources to CPFs, but these changes were to date still at the policy formulation stage. The Minister of Safety and Security had also in 2007 indicated his intention of investigating the expansion of the role of CPFs by transforming them into Integrated Community Safety Centers, with the obvious implications of funding resources and infrastructure to better serve communities.*

Other initiatives (again SAPS led) were the reintroduction in November 2006 of the National Community Policing Consultative Forum (NCPCF).† One of the first initiatives of the reconstituted NCPCF was the drafting of a Uniform Constitution for CPFs (whose finalization had to await the changes in the CPF legislation and the SAPS Act currently under discussion in Parliament). A task team to draft a Community Policing Training Manual was also established by the NCPCF, but this too awaits final approval before being released to all CPFs.

Some Concluding Remarks

While all of these policing changes (theoretically in support of the overall philosophy of Community Policing) have and are being made, it is a moot point on how successful they were and currently are. If one looks merely at the crime statistics,‡ it is apparent that most crime categories have merely "stabilized," i.e., remained at unacceptably (by any international standards) high levels, with at best a marginal percentage reduction. While some categories (e.g., murder—reduced from a high of approximately 24,000 in 1994 to a low of just over 18,000 in 2006, an overall reduction of 25%, but in any society, such a high number of murders would be totally unacceptable)§ have recorded slight percentage reductions every year, others have fluctuated annually with increases

* These centers incorporated victim counseling rooms and other victim empowerment services, advice/information service, and to basically evolve into crime prevention community resource centers with a host of other criminal justice services located there, i.e. "one-stop" criminal justice centers dealing with other services like witness and court services, parolee (probation) services, community sentencing management, etc.

† The forum represents role players from the SAPS, the National Secretariat for Safety & Security, and the provincial chairpersons of CPFs.

‡ See www.saps.org.za, for all crime statistics.

§ The United Kingdom has about 800 murders a year on a higher population ratio, while Australia is even lower at just over 100 per annum for the past 10 years.

being recorded recently in some of the violent crime categories* (e.g., house robbery†). These would indicate that while the SAPS is successful in certain areas, overall they are seen and perceived to be failing in their primary crime reduction and in protecting the public responsibilities (Table 2.1).

A number of public surveys (on victims of crime, feelings of safety and security, satisfaction with police services, etc.) have graphically demonstrated that the general public places high crime levels as their number 1 concern with high levels of insecurity being exhibited. Furthermore, some surveys have recorded the SAPS (together with the Department of Home Affairs) as the worst-performing government department as well as being perceived to be the most corrupt.

Crime seems to have become a national obsession in South Africa and many public debates rage around the issue. Every time a homeowner is murdered during a house robbery or a child shot during a vehicle hijacking, a public outcry ensues, often linked to a letter campaign in the media or directly to the president of the country. Crime has also impacted on perceptions by international companies and financiers of whether to invest in the economic growth of the country.

What has also happened in South Africa since 1994 is the significant growth in the size and number of the private security industry.‡ There was also the concomitant infiltration of private policing services into the terrain of the traditional public police areas, such as responding to alarms, patroling areas, and even investigating crimes. Much of this growth was because of public perceptions at the poor service delivery and virtual absence of visible policing in many suburban areas§ (one of the main reasons for the implementation of the policy of visible and sector policing). Those who could afford it hired armed response companies to protect their homes and businesses and installed sophisticated surveillance and alarm systems.¶ Other phenomena

* Crime statistics released in July 2007 revealed that, while overall crime had decreased 2.6% compared to the previous year, crimes most likely to be reported to the SAPS (murder, robbery with aggravated circumstances, and robbery and burglary of residential premises) all showed increases.

† A house robbery is when burglars break into a residence while the occupants are inside and then intimidate, threaten (usually with a firearm), and most often use force (sometimes murdering them) to rob them.

‡ By the end of March 2007, the whole private security industry had approximately 900,000 persons registered with the Private Security Industry Authority (PSIRA) of which only 301,584 were termed *active security officers* with 4,833 service providers (companies) registered (www.sira.co.za). (See Minnaar (2005) for details on this growth and reasons for it. At the same time, the numbers of the SAPS stood at approximately 128,000.

§ For more details on this aspect of the growth of private policing, see Minnaar (2005).

¶ In Johannesburg, one scheme to harness cell phone technology was launched in 2001 and called eBlockWatch whereby a network system using cellular telephones can send crime alerts via SMS to signed up members' cell phones. These crime alerts are everything from attempted hijackings to burglaries. Its founder, Andre Snyman, stated that he wanted to use the system as a "crime fighting" tool. (See www.eblockwatch.co.za for more details on this community initiative.)

Table 2.1 Reported Violent Crime in South Africa: 1994/1995 to 2007/2008[a] (Rate per 100,000 of population)

Crime Category	1994/95	1995/96	1996/97	1997/98	1998/99	1999/2000	2000/01	2001/02	2002/03	2003/04	2004/05	2005/06	2006/07	2007/08
Murder	25,965	26,877	25,470	24,486	25,127	22,604	21,758	21,405	21,553	19,824	18,793	18,545	19,202	18,487
Rate/100,000	66.9	67.9	62.8	59.5	59.8	52.5	49.8	47.8	47.4	42.7	40.3	39.5	40.5	38.6
Attempted murder	26,806	26,876	28,576	28,145	29,545	28,179	28,128	31,293	35,861	30,076	24,516	20,553	20,142	18,795
Rate/100,000	69.1	67.9	70.4	68.4	70.4	65.4	64.4	69.8	78.9	64.8	52.6	43.9	42.5	39.3
Robbery with aggravating circumstances	84,785	77,167	66,163	73,053	92,630	98,813	113,716	116,736	126,905	133,658	126,789	119,726	126,558	118,312
Rate/100,000	218.5	195.0	163.0	177.5	220.6	229.5	260.3	260.5	279.2	288.1	272.2	255.3	267.1	247.3
Other robbery	32,659	45,683	50,676	54,932	64,978	74,711	90,215	90,205	101,537	95,551	90,825	74,723	71,156	64,985
Rate/100,000	84.2	115.4	124.9	133.4	154.7	173.5	206.5	201.3	223.4	206.0	195.0	159.4	150.1	135.8
Rape	44,751	49,813	51,435	51,959	49,679	52,891	52,872	54,293	52,425	52,733	55,114	54,926	52,617	36,190
Rate/100,000	115.3	125.9	126.7	126.2	118.3	122.8	121.0	121.1	115.3	113.7	118.3	117.1	111.0	75.6
Indecent assault	4,009	5,127	5,224	4,920	4,968	6,106	6,652	7,683	8,815	9,302	10,123	9,805	9,367	6,763
Rate/100,000	10.3	13.2	12.8	11.9	11.8	14.1	15.2	17.1	19.4	20.7	21.7	20.9	19.8	14.1
Assault (GBH)[b]	215,671	223,097	231,497	234,819	237,818	261,804	275,289	264,012	266,321	260,082	249,369	226,942	218,030	210,104
Rate/100,000	555.8	563.7	570.4	570.4	566.3	608.1	630.2	589.1	585.9	560.7	535.3	484.0	460.1	439.1
Common assault	200,248	206,006	203,023	201,317	203,678	232,024	248,862	261,886	282,526	280,942	267,857	227,553	210,057	198,049
Rate/100,000	516.0	520.5	500.3	489.0	485.0	538.9	569.7	584.3	621.6	605.7	575.0	485.3	443.2	413.9
Burglary at business premises	87,600	87,377	87,153	90,294	94,273	93,077	91,445	87,114	73,975	64,629	56,048	54,367	58,438	62,995
Rate/100,000	225.7	220.8	214.7	219.3	224.5	216.2	209.3	194.4	162.8	139.3	120.3	116.0	123.3	131.7
Burglary at residential premises	231,355	248,903	244,665	251,579	274,081	289,921	303,162	302,657	319,984	299,290	276,164	262,535	249,665	237,853
Rate/100,000	596.2	628.9	602.9	611.1	652.7	673.4	694.0	675.3	704.0	645.2	592.8	559.9	526.8	497.1
Theft of motor vehicle and motorcycle	105,867	98,669	97,332	102,571	107,448	103,041	100,030	96,859	93,133	88,144	83,857	85,964	86,298	80,226
Rate/100,000	272.8	249.3	239.8	249.2	255.9	239.3	229.0	216.1	204.9	190.0	180.0	183.3	182.1	167.7

Firearms														
Illegal possession of firearms and ammunition	10,999	12,336	12,750	13,836	14,714	15,387	14,770	15,494	15,839	16,839	15,497	13,453	14,354	13,476
Rate/100,000	28.3	31.2	31.4	32.5	35.0	35.7	33.8	34.6	34.8	36.3	33.3	28.7	30.3	28.2
Subcategories (already accounted for under robbery with aggravating circumstances)														
Carjacking[d]	–	–	12,912	13,052	15,773	15,172	14,930	15,846	14,691	13,793	12,434	12,825	13,599	14,201
Truck hijacking	–	–	3,732	4,657	6,134	5,088	4,548	3,333	986	901	930	829	892	1,245
Robbery of cash-in-transit	–	–	359	236	223	226	196	238	374	192	220	385	467	395
Bank robbery	–	–	561	463	493	450	469	356	127	54	58	59	129	144
ATM bombings	–	–	–	–	–	–	–	–	–	–	–	–	–	460
House robbery[c]		–	–	–	–	–	–	–	9,063	9,351	9,391	10,173	12,761	14,481
Business robbery	–	–	–	–	–	–	–	–	5,498	3,677	3,320	4,387	6,689	9,862

Note: The implementation of the Criminal Law (Sexual offences and Related Matters) Amendment Act, Act 32 of 2007 on December 16, 2007, resulted in changes to the definitions of certain sexual offences (among which was providing for male rape, which was previously recorded under indecent assault). This has an impact on the statistics pertaining to sexual offences. The statistics reflected in the table above with regard to rape and indecent assault thus only have bearing on the period April to December of the different financial years under review to allow for some sort of comparison

[a] For financial year period of April 1 to March 31. Top figure refers to actual numbers of reported crime to SAPS, bottom figure is the rate per 100,000 of the population. Rate is calculated not only on the Census data, but is updated every year using StatsSA mid-year population estimates figures.

[b] GBH = with the intent to inflict grievous bodily harm.

[c] "House robbery" is the unofficial term used by SAPS and first used as a subcategory crime code in 2001 to describe robbery where the perpetrators overpower, detain, and rob residents of a residential premise, most often resorting to threats, intimidation, and violence (sometimes murder and rape), usually with a firearm to achieve their aims.

[d] The robbery of a vehicle or truck is commonly known in South Africa as hijacking, which denotes the stealing (with use of force) of a vehicle having the occupants inside while this crime is being perpetrated.

were the proliferation* of so-called "security villages" as well as the institution of "gated neighborhoods"—the installation of boom gates ("booming off") of suburbs with access control and closed-circuit television (CCTV) surveillance systems.†

The Private Security Industry and Cooperative Policing

The increasing role of the private security industry in policing and crime prevention led to the revival of interest in so-called "partnership" or "cooperative" policing.‡ In his State of the Nation Address to a joint sitting of Parliament on February 9, 2007, President Thabo Mbeki made mention of a possible role for the South African private security industry in working together with the SAPS in order to, as he stated, "create an environment in which the security expectations of the public are actually met" (South African Parliament, 2007a)—this remark being in the context of the increase in the incidence of particular crimes during the security workers' strike of early 2006. This sentiment was reinforced by the Minister of Safety and Security, Charles Nqakula, in his departmental budget speech on May 22 where he clearly indicated that the private security industry had been drawn into the "loop of partners" in the fight against crime and that talks with them had already been initiated on aspects of so-called "partnership policing." The minister very explicitly stated that such a partnership between the private security sector and the SAPS would need to be based on a sharing of information and resources. Moreover, he called for the "alignment of private security with SAPS operations," by enhancing their own information gathering and sharing capabilities among themselves and then sharing the collected information directly with the government (SAPS) (South African Parliament, 2007b).

* Again, this growth has partly been attributed to public perceptions about the failure not only of effective policing, but also to that of any form of Community Policing, with those who can afford to pay for private security while communities not able to afford it have tried to institute more self-policing activities within their own community and street committee patrols, e-block, or neighborhood watch systems. These typically involve volunteer neighborhood watches that patrol certain residential areas, or being the eyes and ears of the police like in e-block watches where private citizens would organize themselves in blocks and report any suspicious activities either to each other or directly to the local police by cell phone (or other means). Another danger of these perceptions has been the regular and frequent use of anti-crime vigilante actions (mob justice) by highly frustrated and angry communities tired of the depredations of criminals and perceptions that such criminals act with impunity and are not afraid of ever being arrested by absent or ineffective police and ever being prosecuted by the courts.

† For the implementation of public CCTV surveillance systems, see Minnaar (2007).

‡ A report for the SAPS was written as early as 1997 outlining the problems and issues involved in any partnership policing between the SAPS and the South African private security industry (see Minnaar, 1997).

In practical terms, cooperation has occurred, but usually on an ad hoc basis and in areas of mutual interest and benefit, e.g., cash-in-transit heists. In some of the City or Business Improvement Districts (CIDs) set up in the major cities, in particular Cape Town, where private security companies have been contracted to provide security services, such as CCTV surveillance, access control, and street patrolling, security officers have been at the forefront of dealing with crime, but only on the level of petty street crime by means of crime deterrence (their presence) or first response to a crime in progress—simply because they are closest to the action—and then detaining offenders and handing them over to the SAPS.* The more formal aspects of public or state policing, such as crime scene handling, collecting of evidence, and further crime investigation, do not strictly fall within the scope of such "private" policing activities.

This "private" policing situation is further complicated by the absence of any official cooperative and regulatory framework between the SAPS and private security companies. Most private policing has occurred or ends up as being ad hoc or small local initiatives, and certainly does not fulfill the traditional aims of Community Policing, serving as it does private individual or sectoral specific interests (home or business security) with Community Policing only occurring where crime is prevented in public spaces by their paid-for patrols and access control activities, etc. Within this situation then there have consistently arisen issues around control and reporting lines: Who has ultimate authority over actions of private security officers involved in policing actions—the company owner, the local police station, the client (and, in the case of the CIDs, the local committee contracting their services)? Ultimately to whom are they accountable—client or local public police and certainly not to any representative of the community? All of these questions are very vexing, especially when there is such a need for all parties (inclusive of communities per se) to cooperate, work together, and coordinate activities in the wider fight against crime. Again, at ground level, there has occurred, and still occurs, a great lack of coordination of activities between public and private policing entities.

It must further be noted that the reengineering of community policing and its implementation in South Africa occurred in drastically different social, environmental, economic, political, and societal conditions than that in established countries, such as the United States, Canada, United Kingdom, The Netherlands, and Belgium (from whose models many of the guidelines were culled). Besides the difficulties in changing the police culture and attitude toward community policing within the new SAPS from the side of the communities, there was also other ingrained obstacles to establishing trust

* For more details on partnerships in CIDs in Cape Town, see Berg (2004a).

and cooperative relations as well as the longstanding absence of censure (and reporting) of those who participated in criminal activities within their communities, often because many community members in the poorer townships actively benefited from the proceeds of crime by providing a ready market for stolen goods, household and electronic appliances, and motor vehicles.*

Community Police Failing Communities and the Continuation of Vigilante Activities

Essentially the failure† in black townships of not only CPFs, but the wider concept of community policing, has foundered on such very real issues as public apathy‡ and disinterest, continuing lack of trust in the police, and reluctance to cooperate or work together with them. This is driven by perceptions of police failure to effectively deal with or adequately solve (poor success and low conviction rate)§ local crime because "they [police] don't do anything about reported crime anyway, so why report or co-operate with them" (Vujovic, 2001, p. 13). This attitude is compounded by the condonation or tolerance of criminal activity in their midst by many, but also by such issues of ordinary citizens' vulnerability to report crime because of intimidation by gangsters, fear of retribution by them of witnesses, a poorly functioning witness protection system,¶ a clogged criminal justice system (slow processing), and reluctance to get actively involved and give evidence in court against arrested criminals. One upshot of this situation has been the continuation of other self-policing methods of the past, especially in the poorest sections of black townships, such as the informal shack settlements, of vigilante activity. In these areas, not a week goes by without a report that members of the public have caught a suspected criminal and meted

* The conspicuous exception to this lack of censure was the reporting and informing on murder and sexual violence against children.

† This is not to say that there were not a number of well functioning CPFs in a number of areas, but these were again largely confined to the more affluent neighborhoods, and, as mentioned previously, where they have sometimes turned themselves into Section 21 Companies, are better funded and set up with the full cooperation and participation of volunteer residents from the area.

‡ It has also been argued (see Schonteich and Louw, 2001) that this "apathy" stems from the very high levels of crime, often violent crime, in many townships that has sanitized or inured residents to the effects of crime in their midst. In other words, it is of such frequent occurrence that they have become accustomed (hardened) to its frequency and are no longer concerned about it. It is only when a particularly brutal crime occurs (e.g., the rape and murder of a young girl, Sheldean Human, in March 2007, in a Pretoria North suburb) that communities are for a period of time briefly galvanized into action and often try to restart defunct or nonfunctioning CPFs (Bateman, 2007).

§ According to the SAPS *Annual Report 2007/08*, tabled in Parliament in September 2008, they had, by their own recognition, only secured a pitiful 12.6% conviction rate for murders, while, overall, the conviction rate for contact crimes was 19% (www.saps.org.za, accessed September 19, 2008).

¶ See Minnaar (2002a) for more details on South Africa's witness protection program.

out their own rough justice (a beating so severe that the victim either later dies or lands up in the hospital with serious injuries—many of those victims who do survive such vigilante action only do so because they were luckily "rescued" by the police's timely arrival on the scene). The public, in these cases, does not bother to merely detain the suspect and then hand him over to the police, which would require citizens' involvement as witnesses in a subsequent case and the provision of hard evidence of the suspect's wrongdoing. This "taking of the law into own hands" action, so reminiscent of pre-1994 days, is redolent of all the old sentiments of "police do nothing against criminals," "we have to protect ourselves from the depredations of criminals," the "criminal justice system does not punish criminals, so we have to punish them ourselves," and "take back control of our communities" (see Minar, 2001 for details on vigilantism activities in the townships). This vigilante action is also a self-protection response because of individual fears of retribution by gangsters; mob (crowd) vigilantism is used and seen as a subtle form of protecting their identities (recognition) through the anonymity of crowd action, and, therefore, an opportunity to strike a community blow against criminal depredations in their communities.

The Reinstitution of Street Committees

The recognition of the "failure" of any real form of community policing in black communities led to the National Conference of the ruling ANC, held in December 2007, in Polokwane, Limpopo, passing a resolution for the reinstatement of street committees at the local level to replace or assist the operations of CPFs as part of the ANC's revised policy on fighting crime. At the beginning of 2008, the new ANC president, Jacob Zuma, had toured a number of communities with the message that communities must not wait for the government or the SAPS to set up these street committees. Instead, Zuma encouraged ANC party structures in the townships to take the initiative and establish their own street committees to fight against crime in order to "take back the streets," i.e. to wrest control of their neighborhoods away from criminals. This response to the nonfunctioning of CPFs and community policing was again couched in such terms as *community vigilance* and being "tough on criminals."* Although Zuma had been careful to emphasize

* In his various tours around the country launching street committees, Zuma had stressed the importance of not being soft on criminals. "I warn you not to be lenient with criminals because they do not respect lives. These street committees must not be user-friendly to criminals, but that does not mean that you must kill. Just catch the criminals and hand them over to the police." He had also stated that police should not ask too many questions when the committees bring captured criminals to the local police station. He also clearly stated that the setting up of the street committees was because the ANC wanted to help communities to "get rid (from their areas) of drug traffickers, rapists, and other criminals" (SAPA, 2008).

that the creation of these new street committees was "not a vote of no confidence in the police, nor ... an endorsement of vigilante justice in the fight against crime" (Quintal, 2008) (see also Mbanjwa, 2008; and South Africa Press Association (SAPA), 2008), this establishment of new street committees and CPFs (or kick starting moribund CPFs back into life) was conspicuous for its absence of use of any community policing terminology.

Community Initiatives to Restart Own CPFs

Some of the CPFs, in response to high crime levels, started up again without any reference to local police structures or talk of cooperation or partnership with the SAPS. Many of them were based on concerned residents getting together informally, electing a street committee or area CPF, then going about setting up neighborhood watch-type patrols. When they were better organized, they would get funding for the payment of private security company patrols in their neighborhoods supported by linked cell phone incident reporting systems, together with the contracted private security company control room operations. All in all, these developments were again in the realm of self-policing and crime prevention/protection rather than in formal community policing structures under the control of the SAPS.

A final comment on Community Policing in South Africa would be that while the policy framework makes provision for its wider implementation through such initiatives as social crime prevention, CPFs, and is supported by the activities of visible and sector policing, it has only been accepted as a wider philosophical guideline without real community implementation and participation in its envisaged form. Furthermore, since its official acceptance in 1994, it has only become accepted through other, largely police operational, structures with the communities having limited say in the evolvement of an adapted South African model. Most community policing initiatives appear to be led and managed by SAPS structures (all the way down to the police station level). The usual order of business is that CPFs are called to a monthly meeting at the police station and then informed of various police actions and crime trends with very little, if any, input from their side or self-initiated community crime prevention activities.

Ultimately, as Burger (2007, p. 102) put it, in South Africa, "the role of community policing, and specifically of community policing forums (CPFs), was much more focused on the monitoring of the police than on solving community problems." But more than that Burger considers it, in South Africa, to be "a failed strategy because it had little or no positive (reductive) impact on crime." Although Burger does concede that it had a positive contribution "in its real or potential ability to improve the legitimacy of the [South African] police."

In the early years of South African democracy, community policing had been launched with great expectations of not only being the answer and solution to the high (and continuing) crime levels, but would also facilitate the transformation of the SAPS. However, its failure to fulfill community expectations of a "more humane" and community needs-oriented form of policing in their communities, and to better combat crime itself, the SAPS had soon increasingly reverted to more traditional methods of policing, such as visible and sector policing, in an effort to improve service delivery and operational effectiveness with its unofficial abandonment of any pretence of following a Community Policing approach at all.

References

Bateman, B. (2007, April 2). Praise for community in suburb's fight against crime. *Pretoria News*, http://www.pretorianews.co.za/index.php?fArticleId=3761996.

Berg, J. (2004a). Challenges to a formal private security industry–SAPS partnership: Lessons from the Western Cape. *Society in Transition, 35*(1), 1–20.

Berg, J. (2004b). *Suspension of crime watch patrols in Cape Town areas*. Cape Town: University of Cape Town, Institute of Criminology.

Brogden, M. & Nijhar, P. (2005). *Community policing: National and international models and approaches*. Uffculme, U.K.: Willan Publishing.

Burger, J. (2007). *Strategic perspectives on crime and policing in South Africa*. Pretoria: Van Schaik Publishers.

Department of Safety and Security. (1994). Green Paper on Safety and Security. Pretoria: Department of Safety and Security.

Department of Safety and Security. (1996). Draft policy document on the philosophy of community policing. Pretoria: Department of Safety and Security.

Department of Safety and Security. (1998). *In service of safety — 1999-2004*. White Paper on Safety and Security. Pretoria: Department of Safety and Security.

Dixon, B. & Rauch, J. (2004, March). *Sector policing: Origins and prospects* [ISS Monograph No. 97]. Pretoria: Institute for Security Studies.

Human Rights Committee of South Africa (HRC). (2001, January). Popular justice. *HRC Quarterly Review*, 1–32.

Interim Constitution of South Africa. (1994, April). Act No. 200 of 1993. *Government Gazette*.

Masipa, M. (1999, February 17). Street committees returning to cut crime. *The Star*.

Mbanjwa, X. (2008, May 18). Zuma talks tough on crime — again. *Pretoria News*. http://www.pretorianews.co.za/index.php?fArticleId=4408808.

Ministry of Safety and Security. (2007, May 10). Justice crime prevention and security (JCPS) cluster media briefing: First cycle of 2007. Pretoria.

Minnaar, A. (1992). "Undisputed kings": Warlordism in Natal. In A. Minnaar (Ed.), *Patterns of violence: Case studies of conflict in Natal* (pp. 61–94). Pretoria: Human Sciences Research Council (HSRC).

Minnaar, A. (1996, October 10–11). *Self-defence units (SDUs): Post-April 1994 — What role in community policing?* Paper presented at the South African Political Studies Association (SAPSA) Biennial Research Colloquium: Rustenburg, South Africa.

Minnaar, A. (1997, June). *Partnership policing between the South African Police Service and the South African private security industry* (information document). National Policy and Strategy, Management Services Division, SAPS. Pretoria: SAPS Research Centre.

Minnaar, A. (2001, June). *The "new" vigilantism in Post-April 1994 South Africa: Crime prevention or an expression of lawlessness?* Technikon SA: Institute for Human Rights and Criminal Justice Studies.

Minnaar, A. (2002a). Witness protection programmes — Some lessons from the South African experience. *Acta Criminologica: Southern African Journal of Criminology, 15*(3), 118–133.

Minnaar, A. (2002b). The "new" vigilantism in Post-April 1994 South Africa: Searching for explanations. In D. Feenan (Ed.), *Informal Criminal Justice* (pp. 117–134). *Advances in Criminology* series. Aldershot, U.K.: Dartmouth/Ashgate Publishing.

Minnaar, A. (2003). The murder of members of the South African Police Service: Some findings on common causes and practical preventative steps. *Acta Criminologica: Southern African Journal of Criminology, 16*(3), 1–23.

Minnaar, A. (2005). Private-public partnerships: Private security, crime prevention and policing in South Africa. *Acta Criminologica: Southern African Journal of Criminology, 18*(1), 85–114.

Minnaar, A. (2007). The implementation and impact of crime prevention/crime control open street closed-circuit television surveillance in South African Central Business Districts. *Surveillance & Society eJournal* (special issue on Surveillance and Criminal Justice), Part 1, 4(3), 174–207. (http://www.surveillance-and-society.org).

Minnaar, A. & Mistry, D. (2004). Outsourcing and the South African Police Service. In M. Schönteich, A. Minnaar, D. Mistry, & K.C. Goyer (Eds.), *Private muscle: Outsourcing the provision of Criminal Justice Services* (pp. 38–54). [ISS Monograph Series No. 93] Brooklyn, NY: Institute for Security Studies.

Minnaar, A. & Ngoveni, P. (2004). The relationship between the South African Police Service and the private security industry: Any role for outsourcing in the prevention of crime? *Acta Criminologica: Southern African Journal of Criminology,* 17(1), 42–65.

Mistry, D. (1997). A review of community policing. In M. Shaw, L. Camerer, D. Mistry, S. Oppler, & L. Muntingh (Eds.), *Policing the transformation: Further issues in South Africa's crime debate* (pp. 40–49). [ISS Monograph No. 12]. Pretoria: Institute for Security Studies.

Pelser, E. (1999, September). *The challenges of community policing in South Africa.* (Paper No. 42). Pretoria: Institute for Security Studies.

Pelser, E., Schnetler, J., and Louw, A. (2002). *Not everybody's business: Community policing in the SAPS' priority areas.* [ISS Monograph No. 71]. Pretoria: Institute for Security Studies.

Quintal, A. (2008, May 1). Everyone must fight crime, says Zuma. *Pretoria News.* http://www.pretorianews.co.za/index.php?fArticleId=4382737.

Scharf, W. (1991, November). *Transforming community policing in black townships in the new South Africa*. Paper presented to the American Society of Criminology Conference, San Francisco, CA, USA.

Scharf, W. (1992, June 21–27). *Community policing in post-apartheid South Africa: The views of some black township civic associations in Cape Town*. Paper presented at the Conference on International Perspectives: Crime, Justice and Public Order, St. Petersburg State University/John Jay College of Criminal Justice, City University of New York (CUNY).

Scheepers, J.H.L. (1992, May 14). Speech during the Law and Order Budget Vote. Cape Town: Hansard, Parliament.

Schonteich, M. & Louw, A. (2001). *Crime in South Africa: A country and cities profile*. [ISS occasional Paper No. 49]. Pretoria: Institute for Security Studies.

Shaw, M. (2001). *Marching to a different tune: Political change and police transformation in South Africa and Northern Ireland*. Johannesburg: South African Institute of International Affairs.

Shaw, M. (2002). *Crime and policing in post-apartheid South Africa: Transforming under fire*. Bloomington: Indiana University Press.

Shaw, M., Camerer, L., Mistry, D., Oppler, S., & Muntingh, L. (1997). *Policing the transformation: Further issues in South Africa's crime debate*. [ISS Monograph No. 12]. Pretoria: Institute for Security Studies.

Shaw, M. & Shearing, C. (1998). Reshaping security: An examination of the governance of Security in South Africa. *African Security Review, 7*(3), 3–12.

Singh, A-M. (1997). *National crime prevention strategy: Changing the face of crime in South Africa* [Paper series]. Cape Town: The Institute of Criminology, University of Cape Town.

Smit, J. & Schnetler, J. (2004). Policies guiding the police and policing. In J. Smit, Minnaar, A., & Schnetler, J. (Eds.), *Smart policing for law-enforcement official* (pp. 10–24). Claremont, South Africa: New Africa Education.

South African Parliament. (2007a, February 9). State of the Nation Address of the president of South Africa, Thabo Mbeki: Joint Sitting of Parliament. www.parliament.gov.za.

South African Parliament. (2007b, May 22). Budget vote speech delivered by Minister for Safety and Security Charles Nqakula, MP, Ministry for Safety and Security, National Assembly. www.parliament.gov.za.

South African Police Service (SAPS). (1995, October 15). Act No. 68 of 1995. *Government Gazette*.

South African Police Service. (1997). *The Community Policing policy framework and guidelines*. Pretoria: Government Printer/SAPS.

South African Police Service. (1998). *Manual on community policing (policy, framework and guidelines)*. Pretoria: Government Printers.

South African Police Service. (2000). *Strategic plan for the South African police service: 2002–2005*. Pretoria: Strategic Management, SAPS HQ.

South African Police Service. (2000–2007). Annual report of the South African Police Service. Pretoria: Government Printer/SAPS (all reports are available on the SAPS Web site: www.saps.org.za).

South Africa Press Association (SAPA). (2008, August 10). Zuma launches committees to help fight crime scourge. *Pretoria News*. http://www.pretorianews.co.za/index.php?fArticleId=4552363.

Statistics South Africa. (2007). *Mid-year population estimates 2007. Statistics South Africa*. Pretoria. Available at: www.statssa.gov.za (accessed on February 24, 2008).

Steinberg, J. (2004, August 26). Holding ground means losing ground when it comes to policing. *Business Day*.

Vujovic, M. (2001). *Popular justice: A case study in Diepsloot*. Unpublished research report. Technikon SA: Institute for Human Rights & Criminal Justice Studies.

Reforming Community, Reclaiming the State

The Development of Sungusungu in Northern Tanzania

3

SUZETTE HEALD

Contents

Introduction

In the 1980s, a Kuria village in the far northwestern region of Tanzania, near the Kenya border, declared its secession from the state and hoisted the skin of its totem animal, the leopard, as a flag.* This act of defiance remains emblematic. Yet, it is remembered not as a time when the state was overthrown, but as a time when the thieves "ruled." This was no peasant rebellion in the normal sense, but the outcome of simple plunder, fueled by the returning militias after the Tanzania/Uganda war of 1979. The violence that was then set in train did, however, prompt peasant reaction and the formation of

* I am very grateful to the Republic of Tanzania for giving me research clearance. I would also like to thank Dr. Masanja of the University of Dar es Salaam and Dr. D. Ndagala of the Ministry of Culture for their help and advice. I am also extremely indebted to the many people in the regional and district administrations of Shinyanga, Mwanza, and Mara who facilitated the research, as well as many other individuals and *sungusungu* committees who agreed to be interviewed in the course of the research in 2002. I would also like to gratefully acknowledge the Crisis States Program of the London School of Economics (LSE) who funded the research. An earlier version of this essay was published as *Domesticating Leviathan: Sungusungu in Tanzania*. LSE: Crisis States working paper, series 1, no. 16. 2002: www.crisisstates.com and a shorter version as: State, law, and vigilantism in Northern Tanzania. *African Affairs 105*, 265–283, 2006.

a movement, which was to have long-term consequences. From 1982 onward in central Tanzania, Sukuma, and Nyamwesi, villagers began to organize their own form of community policing, which became known throughout Tanzania as *sungusungu*. Over time, these groups, which initially bypassed the official organs of state, far from being rejected, became an integral part of the administrative structures of vast areas of rural Tanzania.

The emergence of *sungusungu* in central Tanzania has been the subject of considerable academic discussion (Abrahams, 1987, 1989, 1998; Abrahams and Bukurura, 1993; Bukurura, 1994a, 1994b, 1994c, 1995; Campbell, 1989; Masanja, 1992; Heald, 2002). This chapter will concentrate on Kuria of Mara Region in the north, a region bordered by Lake Victoria to the west, Kenya to the north, and the Serengeti National Park to the east. Here, effective *sungusungu* organization was not to emerge until the mid-1990s. And, then, it took its own form, adapted to the particular cultural repertoire of the area as well as to developments on the national and regional political scene. The lateness of the development raises particular questions as this area was one of the worst hit by the state of lawlessness into which Tanzania was plunged following the war with Uganda. Further, when it did emerge, it was with strong state support, with the administration in effect mandating local communities to codify their own laws and impose their own punishments, bypassing the official agents of the state in the form of the police and, most particularly, the judiciary.

This raises questions about the nature of the postcolonial state in Africa. Bayart et al. (1999) have talked of the visible state as opposed to the invisible; the visible being little more than a legal edifice, while the invisible represents the real state of the polity, riddled by corruption from top to bottom, an indication of *la politique du ventre*. Certainly, external observers, Human Rights Commissions, Amnesty International, and so on, tend to regard the emergence of these unofficial police forces as "vigilantes" and, yet, another index of the abuse of human rights. So do lawyers in Tanzania. Yet, at the community level, they receive little but praise when they are deemed to be working well; that is, enforcing a regularity of norm and sanction, defined by and adapted to local needs. At this level, they represent the righteousness of the ordinary citizen, a response to the criminals within, and a guard against the corruption without in the form of state officialdom. And, the political wing of government largely concurs in this judgment and supports them. In doing so, it has opened up a chasm between different branches of the state apparatus, between the political/administrative and the police and judiciary. The state, far from being a unitary enterprise, is shown to be at war with itself.

The implication of state sponsorship of *sungusungu* is an issue that will be returned to in the concluding discussion. The main body of this paper deals with the crisis which prompted the formation of *sungusungu* groups in the Tarime and Serengeti Districts of the Mara Region.

War Without to War Within

Demobilization of armies always poses problems and, in Tanzania, following the successful invasion of Uganda, these were acute.* Tanzania had been able to enlist a large number of recruits to its army in a very short period of time, mainly because of the state's emphasis on military preparedness.† Arms training was almost universal in schools, and enhanced for those who volunteered for the Youth Service Program or People's Militias, both of which served as adjuncts to the police and security forces in rural areas. Demobilization was equally rapid, with the recruits from the militias dispersed back to their mainly rural homes. However, the soldiers, known for their discipline during the war, also had in Uganda learned of the value of arms in banditry and raiding. Rather than returning to a life of toil and poverty in their home areas, many, it now appears, took to the freebooting life of the gangster. The war without, in effect, was turned into a war within. Tanzania was hit by an unprecedented wave of violence. In 1980, there were reports of banditry all over the country. Nor did these die away, for the 1980s were to see an escalation of armed raiding over much of the country. In the urban areas, the targets were shops, bars, banks as well as residential buildings. In the rural areas, the crime wave and the mayhem that ensued took the apparently traditional form of cattle rustling.

Government attempts to counter this situation proved largely ineffectual. The "problem" was not restricted to a few men of violence. Crime and the perennial one of corruption went together so that people at all levels of society, from the highest to the lowest, profited in it. The war had drained Tanzania's meager treasury fueling inflationary pressures. Indeed, as the economy sank farther into insolvency, with successive devaluations of the Tanzanian shilling, corruption of all kinds became the order of the day. President Julius Nyerere‡ responded by launching a fight against "economic sabotage"—a broad category that included all forms of corruption from profiteering, smuggling, and illegal currency transactions to banditry and cattle raiding. In May 1983, he gave presidential consent to a new law to set up tribunals to deal with economic saboteurs. Arrests were immediately made countrywide and a National Antieconomic Sabotage Tribunal was set up to expedite trials. Details, where these are given, of those arrested made clear the

* In October 1978, Uganda occupied an area of NW Tanzania. Tanzania retaliated in 1979, retaking its territory and going on to occupy most of Uganda and ousting the regime of Idi Amin. Amin, an army general, had taken the presidency from Milton Obote in 1971 in an army coup.

† This was prompted partly by Nyerere's socialist state's concern for protection against its neighbors and partly to provide some insurance against the type of military coup that had occurred in Uganda.

‡ Julius Nyerere was president from independence in 1961 until his retirement in 1985.

nature and extent of the problem. In Mara Region, bordering Lake Victoria to the west and Kenya to the north, for example, it is reported that over 1,000 people, including government leaders, were arrested. These arrests included notorious cattle raiders, but also the regional police commander, who had his livestock and seven houses impounded, as well as half a dozen other named police officers. The People's Militia adviser in the region was also arrested for "sabotaging" the Tanzanian Peoples Defense Force by buying and selling the cattle confiscated under the presidential directive.* The very government forces enlisted to fight crime were also the ones profiting from it.

The tribunals continued until April 1985. They heard 2,859 cases† but, apart from publicizing the extent of the problem, they had done little in themselves to quell the unrest. Banditry went on, if anything, on a larger scale.‡ Nor did other government measures provide more than a temporary salve to the problems. The "solution" when it came was to be unofficial and to emerge from the Sukuma and Nyamwesi areas of central Tanzania.

The central areas of Tanzania, from the Kenyan border in the north stretching down to that with Zambia in the south are dominated by agropastoralist and pastoralist peoples, for whom movement and migration are as much part of their history as the claims they have to the particular tracks of land they currently occupy. Relationships between such groups may be peaceful, but they also, very typically, are played out through reciprocal cattle raiding. The coming of guns in the 1980s, in the aftermath of the Tanzania/Uganda war, and the subsequent development of large gangs of thieves who operated over wide areas, inflamed such interethnic hostilities to the point where they threatened, in some instances, full-scale tribal wars. Ndagala (1991) explains how the thieves deliberately contrived such conflict, to both camouflage and justify their own activities. Quite typically, the thieves dressed as members of a hostile tribe—as Sukuma when raiding Datoga, as Datoga or Maasai when raiding Sukuma, and so on. One result of the tension this created was a particularly bloody battle between the Sukuma and Datoga in May 1984, in which 48 Sukuma, who were members of *basalama*§ groups, were killed (Ndagala, 1991).¶ There is no firm evidence that the cattle thefts that both sides had

* *Tanzania Daily News*, May 6, 1983.

† *Tanzania Daily News*, April 3, 1985.

‡ For further details, see Heald (2002).

§ *Basalama*, meaning "people of peace," is the Sukuma word often used interchangeably with *sungusungu* to refer to groups in the area. The derivation of *sungusungu* is subject to some dispute, but these days most relate it to the KiSwahili term for black safari ants.

¶ Ndagala was a member of the CCM commission of inquiry, which was sent to the area to investigate this incident. CCM (Chama cha Mapinduzi or revolutionary party) was formed by a merger between TANU, the party that had led Tanganika into Independence in 1961 and the main Zanzibar party, ASP, after the two countries merged in 1964. It has been the ruling party ever since.

recently suffered were the work of the other. Ndagala gave another example from this same general area where the police followed a gang of thieves and a running battle ensued, during which some of the thieves were killed and others later arrested. This gang was obviously prepared to camp out for a considerable time, having 65 donkeys carrying arms and food for several weeks as well as the cattle it had captured. It appears that the leader's name was Chacha, indicating that he was probably a Kuria from the Mara Region in the north.*

I now turn to what was happening in the Mara Region. According to sources in the area, there were three major gangs who were linked together operating at this time. One in the south was wreaking havoc among the Sukuma in Bariadi, Ramadi, and Shinyanga districts. Another, in Serengeti District, was dominated by Kuria, but with accomplices in other groups. The third group was operating from Maasailand but it was again a Kuria gang. Indeed, in Tarime and Serengeti Districts of Mara (as well as in Maasailand in the Arusha Region), throughout this period, the fighting and raiding was dominated by Kuria, just one of the 28 tribes represented in Mara. In the course of the 1980s, the entire region was drawn into the resulting turmoil.

Tradition has it that the Kuria migrated down from Kenya into Tanzania at the beginning of the nineteenth century (Ruel, 1959; Kjerland, 1995). At the beginning of this century, they began returning to Kenya, reclaiming their former lands just over the border and extending their settlement into areas, which had been claimed by the Maasai. Some of these areas were not fully settled until the 1950s. By that time, some of the Kenyan residents had already begun moving south again into Tanzania to establish settlement not only in their home district of Tarime, but farther afield into what was to become the Serengeti District. Migration gained in momentum throughout the 1960s and 1970s, with the different Kurian clans setting up distinctive zones for settlement, where their fellow clansmen joined them. Kjerland quotes an estimate of nearly 100,000 people having moved from Kenya into Tanzania by 1969 (1995). The once empty plains were becoming populated, as many Kuria capitalized on the two halves of their agro–pastoralist life, keeping one wife in the more fertile zones of Kenya or Tarime Highlands of Tanzania and setting up a second household in the dryland plains more suited to cattle. Two of the four sections represented in Kenya dominated in this movement: the Kira and the Nyabasi/Timbaru, joined by their fellow clansmen from Tanzania.† The Nyabasi, together with the Irege, simultaneously were pushing westward

* Ndagala, personal communication, January 16, 2002.

† There is a problem in naming these Kuria sections because of the different practices of the administration in Kenya and Tanzania. In Kenya, administrative divisions are known by the section name. In Tanzania, they are named after the totems of such groups and in both cases these have become the most commonly used nomenclature by Kuria living in the two countries, respectively. In this chapter, I am following the Kenyan practice.

into the Rift Valley of Trans-Mara in Kenya, sandwiched between the Kuria district and the Maasai Mara National Park. All of this movement was punctuated by raiding, as the Kuria pushed against the Ngoreme in Serengeti and against the Maasai and Kipsigis in the Rift Valley of Kenya.

Yet, what is distinctive about the Kuria and what makes the Tarime and Serengeti districts, as the District Commissioner Tarime put it in 2002, "the most difficult to administer in the whole of Tanzania," is not the ferocity of the raiding they pursue with others, but that which they pursue among themselves. This makes them distinct among other raiding groups because the focus of the Kuria conflict is as much or more internal than external. Further, when raiding into surrounding areas dominated by other groups, attitudes are more accommodating and less commonly escalate into war. As Tobisson (1986) writes, "Being a Kuria, in fact, designates little beyond the vague recognition of a common cultural identity, while belonging to one of the … Kuria clans (pl. *ibiaro*, sing. *ikiaro*) has always been of superior significance" (1985).* I am translating this basic political unit among the Kuria as *section* or *clan*. It has a common name and totem, and recognition of common ancestry. In Kenya and in Tarime District these sections also form territorially discrete blocks, with newer outlying territories, particularly as mentioned in the Serengeti District, though groups are found throughout the Mara Region.†

Stock raiding among these groups is a perennial part of the local scene, sometimes escalating into wars, as raiding intensifies prompting even more extreme retaliation (Heald, 2000; Fleisher, 1997, 2000a, 2000b). In fact, war is marked by a gradual hardening of attitudes, a series of graduated steps. In normal situations, people are simply wary of being in other clan territories, but may do so freely to attend markets or to visit relatives. The odd raid is expected, however, as these become more frequent, anxiety rises and attitudes harden; visitors come under suspicion as possible spies. Violence now begins to accompany raids and people defer visits to other territories. In "normal" raiding, it is not expected that the raiding force have come to kill the owners, though if they put up a defense and in any attempt to pursue the raiders and recapture the cattle, there may be deaths on both sides. In full-scale war, however, the raiders may deliberately kill. Large parties now accompany the

* It is indeed a moot point as to which groups count as Kuria. A common distinction is between "peoples of the sunrise," that is the East and "peoples of the lake," the West, with the Kuria being those of the sunrise. However, many of the "lake people" speak closely related Bantu languages and may be regarded as Kuria by some. Other groups elsewhere in Mara speak languages closely related to KiKuria.

† Four such sections are represented in Kenya; from west to east: Gumbe, Kira, Nyabasi, and Irege, each extending into Tanzania, where there are, in addition: Renchoka (closely allied to the Gumbe), Nchari, Sweta, Timbaru (closely linked to Nyabasi), and Nyamongo, who are totemically linked to Irege.

trackers pursuing stolen cattle and are met at the borders of their territory with equally large parties of opposing clansmen to prevent entry. Fighting might then go on for days or even weeks and in the extreme situations, years. But, even in "normal" situations, following the tracks of stolen cattle into the territory of the enemy is a precarious business and subject to resistance.

Warfare, then, was a regular feature of the local scene, and there have been major disturbances in each of the decades of memory. But, those wars pale in insignificance in comparison with what was to happen in the 1980s in the aftermath of the Tanzania/Uganda war. As Fleisher (2000a, 2000b) argues, Kuria were extremely well-placed to take advantage of the upsurge in cattle rustling that engulfed the pastoral and agropastoral peoples of Tanzania. Firstly, as indicated above, raiding was an entrenched part of Kurian life. Secondly, military service had long been a favored occupation for Kuria in Tanzania and they were regarded as especially good soldiering material. With the mass recruitment into the army for the invasion of Uganda in 1979, they were heavily over-represented. Fleisher (2000b) gives an estimate as high as 50% of this army, as regular soldiers were swelled by recruits from the People's Militia (*mugambo*).[*] While this is probably an over-estimate, it gives some idea of the disproportionate number of recruits that came from Kuria, a group who represent less than 1% of the national population. Further, raiding, as elsewhere, had long had a commercial aspect, yielding a form of wealth that could be translated both into traditional means of accumulation (cattle and wives) and into money and lifestyle. Of relevance in this context is the fact that the value of stock throughout the 1980s remained high. The price of cattle more than kept pace with the rampant inflation in Tanzania at this time and prices were also kept buoyant due to the sale of much of this herd over the Ugandan and Kenyan borders (Ndagala, 1991). With Kurian sections represented on both sides of the international border, they were well placed to facilitate the movement of stolen stock from Tanzania to markets in Kenya. Ndagala (1991) talks of a "stock raider corridor" stretching up from the south through the sparsely populated land of the Serengeti plains to the Kenyan border.[†]

In short, Kuria had the manpower in the form of highly trained fighters, the means in the form of guns, and the motivation to pursue raiding on a new footing, which had its roots in the past, but was equally shaped by the realities of the present. Initially, guns were said to have come from those smuggled back by the returning soldiers in the aftermath of the war. Wry stories are told of how people stood solemnly at attention saluting the coffins

[*] Fleisher also reports that there were more Kuria army officers in the Tanzanian army in 1995 than from any other tribe and more retired officers living in Mara than any other region of Tanzania (2000b, p. 82).

[†] Another route for stolen cattle went west across to Uganda.

as they passed along the road, unaware that these contained not the heroic dead but AK47s finding their way into the rural hinterland. Yet, the guns did not only originate from the war itself and from the vast stockpiles of weapons captured from Amin's troops. Contacts made while serving in the army provided a continuing supply of weaponry and bullets, and was also facilitated by links with gangs operating elsewhere. Kuria was awash with arms. Indeed, from accounts of that time, it appears that in the end almost everyone had a gun for protection, while notorious raiders were brazen enough to carry theirs openly during the day. When the fighting began it was ferocious—characterized by the bravado of exultant killers.

Serious fighting appears to have begun between the Nyabasi/Timbaru and Kira living in the Mugumu area of the Serengeti District. From there it spilled over to engulf everyone in the entire region, as Kuria went on the attack: first to Ngoreme and then farther south to Fort Igoma and from there to the Watatiro and over to the east to Banata and Ikizo at Nyamuswa. As the raiding escalated into war, it became solidified along section lines. The gangs that had initially been mixed (formed of alliances of thieves from rival sections) now split to oppose each other along section lines. The gangs were very large at this time and, because leaders, now on opposing sides, had previously raided together, they knew each other well, and their tactics and routines. The gangs threw down challenges to fight. Many people described how letters would be written to targets, informing them of the day and hour when they would be coming "to collect the cattle." Effectively, shootouts were announced in advance and the death toll was huge. In January 1985, the District Party secretary of Tarime District in Mara Region gave figures of 43 people killed between 1982 and 1984 and 25,606 head of cattle stolen.* In October 1986, *Tanzania Daily News* reported that between January and August 1986, over 25,000 head of stock were stolen in the Serengeti District and more than 100 people were killed.†

Most raiding at this time, it is said, was in broad daylight with the gangs organized along military lines, with two leaders, one at the fore and one at the rear, and a series of ranks as in the army. There were many heroes. The following excerpted account‡ from Mathias Mwita, a Kira, recounts the death of the famed Nyabasi warlord, Musubi:

> In [19]86, Musubi was killed in Kibanchebanche (a hill village, some 15 k[ilometers] to the northwest of Mugumu town, the headquarters of Serengeti District). He was killed by Mogaya of the Kira, his *seemo*! Chacha Nsabi was also killed later that morning. The Nyabasi came to raid the village, but Kira

* *Tanzania Daily News*, January 28, 1985.

† Cited by Kjerland (1995, p. 255).

‡ Interview, February 13, 2002, Bukira, Kenya.

> were waiting as they were meeting to prepare an attack on Nyabasi the next day. I was then in Form 1 at Isibania (on the Kenyan border) and heard the news the next morning. The *inchaama* (the conclave of ritual elders) are said to have mutilated the body, taking the tongue and penis. The body was never found. The Kira celebrated and there were songs, which memorialized the deed. Four others were also killed at the same time, as jubilant Kira followed the Nyabasi back to their villages and killed them … Even the women went from Kibanchebanche — and the Nyabasi fled north across the Mara river, from Nyansurura back to Tarime and were dispersed and much weakened.
>
> After this, Kira went to conquer other groups to the south. In one raid, they went to Ikoma and got 200 cattle, killing 13 Isenye and Bakoma. In response, the government launched a punitive expedition and went to Musati and confiscated all their cattle and goats. My grandfather died at this time, in trying to rescue his cattle from the police lorry. Thus, the Kira became poor. But, that was not for long. This happened at the end of [19]86 and they still had their guns. They started raiding the Maasai in Arusha Region. Gibewa, my father's brother, had three guns and formed a gang, which raided in Irondo in Maasai. They went on long expeditions, taking their own food, and attacked the Maasai while they were out grazing. The gang had more than 50 men and 15 guns. Once they had captured the cattle, they split into smaller groups to take the cattle back. Many game wardens were killed, together with Maasai, as they attempted to stop them. In the process, the Kira captured yet more guns. They had superior firepower.
>
> With this, the Nyabasi made friends again with the Kira and raided the Maasai with them and the Maasai got poor. Gibewa however, got rich and married 21 wives. All this went on until Kubiha came.

This account not only gives testimony to the intensity of the raiding, but also to the shifting nature of alliances between Kuria groups. Musubi and Mogaya were *seemo*, i.e., they had married sisters and were bound by special bonds of friendship. Previously, they had raided together when they were fighting the Ngureme. But, Mogaya eventually killed Musubi to great jubilation among the Kira. The mutilation of the body by the *inchaama* is said to provide them with the materials for counter-magic against their opponents.* Indeed, almost all of these heroes died in the period of intense warfare up until 1990, though they were soon to be replaced by others.

Others were fleeing, with many Kenyan migrants returning to their home areas in Kenya. There, the 1982 war between Kira and Nyabasi had also flared up. Again, guns were freely used and, as hostilities intensified, raiders did not hesitate to kill. Life became centered on survival; a time that, as many people described, when on going to bed at night, you did not know whether

* As described, one such form of magic involves roasting the body parts to cinders, which are then mixed with snuff to be sold back to the opposing side, who thus unwittingly commit acts of endocannibalism.

you would be alive the next morning. People put their cattle out with others living farther from the more dangerous border zones and, abandoning their own homesteads, took refuge each night in well-fortified homes of neighbors. This fighting was cooled in some measure by the Kenyan government sending in a force of the paramilitary General Service Unit in 1984 to establish a camp in Kuria. It was further cooled in 1985 by a guns amnesty initiated by Kenya's president, Daniel Arap Moi, in July and August of that year. Many guns were collected during this time, mainly by using the traditional instruments of the *iritongo* (assembly) and the *inchaama*, the conclave of ritual elders who put suspects to the oath to extract the guns. The war shifted onto a cold rather than hot war footing throughout the rest of the decade. But despite such measures, the raiding went on, tending to wax and wane, but with growing intensity throughout the 1990s.

In Tanzania, in the 1980s, there was no such guns amnesty; instead the government responded with "special operations" of the police and military. There were between 8 and 11 of these during the period 1982 to 1988.[*] In addition, over 200 rustlers were deported from the Mara Region to Lindi and Mtwara where there were no cattle.[†] Even apparent victories by the administration turned to dust. In September 1988, the Mara regional commissioner celebrated a peace pact between the warring factions by erecting a monument at Kenyana on the borders of Ngureme and Kira in Serengeti, close to the Tarime District. He had called together the elders of all the communities and persuaded them to shake hands. The president came later to add his weight to the peace; however, to no avail. The war broke out again a few months later, in what appears to be an all-out offensive by the thieves in the district, who staged outrages particularly at times that official visits were planned. Their general bravado, not to say cheek, is evident from the occasion when they surrounded the police station at Mugumu, forcing the police to flee for their lives.[‡]

Kubiha: Man and Myth

The decisive event for all in Serengeti and Tarime Districts was the coming of Kubiha, who is attributed with breaking the terror of the guns and ushering in a new era of peace. He is as much myth as a man because few people know anything about him apart from the fact that he was an army officer.

[*] The first figure was given by the district commissioner, Serengeti, Ole Sabaya, and the second by the divisional officer, Paulo Wambura Shanyangi.

[†] *Daily Nation*, February 14, 1985, in a report from the Regional Development Director. Reports that the government spent 20 million shillings in fighting rustling in just one district (*Daily Nation*, April 20, 1985)

[‡] Fleisher (2000b, p. 92) gives 1990 as the date of that event.

No one is sure either where he came from; some say the "South," others hazard that it was "Zanzibar." The stories of the methods he used to collect the guns are fairly similar between different accounts. Dating his visit proved more difficult. For all, it was synonymous with the beginnings of the second "*iritongo*" and the coming of peace, and this probably explains at least some of the variation. The most authoritative source, the district administrative secretary in Serengeti, who had welcomed him to the district, put it as June and July 1990. According to him, following the abortive peace of 1988, the president decided to take a new line in dealing with the continuing disorder in Serengeti. He put the task in the hands of an army officer, Kubiha, who had control of his own independent force and was answerable only and directly to the president.

Kubiha is said to have sent an undercover investigative team to Serengeti, mandated to get the names of those with guns and to effectively do anthropological work among the Kuria in order to find a way to break the terror. Kubiha followed this up by arriving in June 1990 and setting up camp with a special force of 200 at Mara Somochi. He is said to have used a variety of methods, some even draconian. But there were significant differences with the brutality associated with previous swoops by field force units.* Emphasized was the honor he paid to Kurian values, on how he used their assemblies, and his insistence on public confession by the thieves. There were none of the collective punishments, confiscations, and random beatings so associated with previous punitive expeditions. Rather, the thieves were identified, interrogated to identify their accomplices, and urged to hand in their guns. Where they did so, together with other elders in the community who cooperated, they were feted by Kubiha and rewarded with gifts. Gibewa, mentioned in the account above, handed in his gun and was invited to a celebration feast in Mugumu, the Serengeti District headquarters.

This then was a punitive expedition with a difference, based on knowledge of Kurian values and which granted rewards as well as rough justice. In addition, he was seen to be independent. Answerable only to the president, he was not seen as being influenced by the pervasive corruption that surrounded the local police and the district and regional administrations of that time. Most significant, perhaps, was his utilization of the *iritongo*, the Kurian assembly, for the interrogation and punishment of thieves. It was also effective. In two months, Kubiha is said to have collected hundreds of guns: army issue machine guns, rifles, pistols as well as many of the homemade variety. The number is usually put at 600. Without the guns, the community could not be terrorized in the same way. This was clearly a major step in initiating a peace and it has given Kubiha the status of a hero. Universally respected,

* Fleisher (2000a; 2000b) gives graphic descriptions of these.

it was commonly said in 2002 that were he to return he would be elected to Parliament immediately.

It is Kubiha who, for Kuria in Serengeti and Tarime Districts, is credited with the inauguration of the new-style *iritongo*. In breaking the rule of the guns, he gave people new ideas as to the power the *iritongo* could wield. However, it was not just the Kuria he impressed. The regional administration also took to heart the lessons from his visit and in 1995 encouraged the development of a new form of *sungusungu* in the region. This spread throughout Serengeti and Tarime Districts (and indeed to other districts in the region) and then into Kenya's Kuria District in 1998. In the process, the older impediments to catching the thieves have, to a considerable extent, been overcome as *sungusungu* cooperated with others in different divisions and even over the national boundary. It became possible to follow the tracks of stolen cattle over clan borders and there enlist the help of the *sungusungu* of that territory to track down both thieves and cattle, with some hope of getting the cattle returned. As important, the thieves have nowhere to run as they are liable, once apprehended, to be handed back to their areas of origin. This is always a controversial process as thieves often have charges to answer in many areas. But, because these invariably include their own home area—the old rule about raiding outside the section being long since honored only in the breach—there is usually agreement that this is the place where they should be finally tried and punished. Nor does this mean that the punishments are necessarily more lenient; the anger of a home community against a thief who has robbed them for years may well exceed that of a stranger community.

There remains the question of why it took so long for *sungusungu* to be established and to become effective in this area. This is probably answerable in terms of the remoteness of the region, its militaristic culture, and perhaps the sheer volume of guns. The thieves, as people said, were the "rulers" and the few who were not in their pockets dared not oppose them. It needed the example of Kubiha plus strong government encouragement. In this, Kuria contrasts with the Sukuma and Nyamwesi, where *sungusungu* had emerged as a spontaneous initiative in the early 1980s to counter the thieves and bandits. At its inception, the movement owed little to the forces of the state, and, indeed, the administration was initially wary of it, fearing in its use of traditional regalia and symbolism a return to ethnic-based loyalties (Abrahams, 1987). But, if regional administrations were initially worried, this was quickly countered by the response from the top, where the ruling CCM rapidly endorsed this revolution in village defense (Masanja, 1992). From 1985 to 1995, using an almost uniform template, the development of *sungusungu* groups became official state policy throughout the country in urban as well as rural areas. During this period, the People's Militias and Youth Service Groups, which had previously been charged with rural defense, went into a general decline, for the most part due to financial stringency.* *Sungusungu* became the ready-made alternative and one that required no financial support from the state for their leadership was unpaid and all members of the community were required to render service. Organized by local administrations, demanding compulsory service from members of the community (most especially in the form of assistance with night patrols), it became another instrument of state coercion. Not surprisingly, not all of these groups were equally effective nor were they necessarily popular.†

Sungusungu in this form, organized by village administrative and ward secretaries, was also promoted in Kuria during this period, most particularly after 1990, with villagers electing their own *sungusungu* committees. According to Fleisher, who witnessed a *sungusungu* crackdown in Tarime District early in 1995, they were intermittently effective, tending to wax and wane. Though all villagers were pledged to help in the tracking of thieves after an alarm, the organization and trials seemed to be almost entirely in the hands of the *sungusungu* committees attended by about 15 people, including administrative officers (2000a). The raiding went on. However, by 1995, the administration seems to have had a change of heart and authorized the formation of new a kind of *sungusungu*, giving more power to local communities. While the movement was allowed to decline in many areas, it was effectively relaunched in areas such as Kuria with people now encouraged to take more control over their own security and to codify their own rules and punishments.

The Second Iritongo: "We Have Found the Medicine for Thieves"

The new organization of *sungusungu* spread through Tarime District in 1995. Most informants made a big distinction between this version of *walinzi wa jadi* (Kiswahili, traditional guards), the name used by the administration, or *serikali wa jadi* (Kiswahili, traditional government), which they are also sometimes called, and that which went before. Now, it is more commonly

* The exception here was in Kuria where the People's Militia was abolished as early as 1985 after evidence that they were actively participating in the raiding.

† As the administration gained control over these groups in Sukumaland, the older symbols of the *basalama* were expunged and limits set to their powers, most particularly with regard to the trying of witchcraft cases. Witch killing among the Sukuma has long been an embarrassment to the Tanzanian Government, predating the development of *sungusungu*. The first *basalama* groups tried witches as well as thieves, but this was suppressed by the administration and none of the groups I spoke to in 2002 claimed to try witches. However, this has not affected the incidence of such killings, which are usually attributed to hired thugs. Witches are not killed among the Kuria and never tried by the *sungusungu*.

referred to simply as the *iritongo*, the assembly or community. As this indicates, the current version has been more fully incorporated into the structure of the *iritongo* to which the committee and the guards answer.

Such *iritongo* (pl. *amatongo*) in Kuria may occur at any level, from that of a family cluster to that of the main political unit, the village, ward, or division in Tanzania, the sublocation or location in Kenya. They can be spontaneous gatherings, as for example, when suspected thieves have been apprehended and a crowd gathers to interrogate them, or they might be more formal meetings called by the elders or government officials to discuss issues of pressing concern, again, particularly the rising levels of raiding. They are essentially democratic assemblies where all adult men have a right to speak, led by members of the "ruling" generation.* Generation is also important in the way the *iritongo* constitutes itself in a semicircle, with the older men taking up positions (when seen from the chair) to the right and younger men to the left, where they are joined by women, who rarely, however, play an active role. Age set organization may also be apparent, with members of an age set sitting together and, as they have the prime responsibility for disciplining their members, they may also meet in separate groups prior to a full-scale *iritongo*.

Behind the *iritongo*, but rarely playing an active role in the meetings, is the *inchaama*, the conclave of ritual elders. They usually meet in secret and are responsible for the ritual well being of the people, setting the dates of the initiation ceremonies, and ruling on other issues that affect the community as a whole. Many regard them as the "real government" of the Kuria, and this is acknowledged by the members of administration who find it difficult to push through reforms of any nature if they are opposed by the people and *inchaama*. As the Tarime district commissioner emphasized to me, the only the district commissioners who have been successful in Kuria have been those who have been prepared to work with them rather than against them. This is especially true with respect to raiding and warfare. While the *inchaama* might well, in circumstances where their side is seen to be suffering unduly, encourage raiding and offer magical protection to the raiders, they are more often important as peacekeepers, advising against war. Such counsel is backed by sanctions, as they have the power to curse thieves and their lines, or, where a thief refuses to confess, put him through the *ekehore*, the oath or ordeal. Today, this is often seen as their most important function, with the *inchaama* being described as a "high court" or "court of final appeal." The *ekehore* itself takes a variety of forms, depending on the area, but it is believed that a man who falsely swears when going through the ordeal will reap a speedy punishment in the death and destruction of himself

* The Kuria have a generation class system as well as an age set system. In the past, there were regular ceremonies to signal the handover of power from one generation class to the next. These were revived in the 1990s in two areas: Bwirege and Nyabasi.

and his family. Though many thieves, in bluster, offer to take the *ekehore*, it is believed in many areas of Kuria that no guilty man will go through it, and few are said to actually dare to take it.*

Sungusungu is now an integral part of the *iritongo*. An example can be taken from the group, which claims it was the first to be established in the Tarime District, in 1995. An *iritongo* was first called consisting of all the people in the two Kira wards of Sirari and Pemba of Nchugu Division. This elected the first committee, thereafter succeeded by others, in February 2002, numbered 22, with two members elected from each of the 11 villages (two of which are women, which is in line with government directives). The committee has a chairman, vice-chairman, secretary, and treasurer. It also has an "adviser," a senior man whose role is to counsel. In this case, he is an exCID (city/business improvement district) officer. The chief commanders of the guards also sit on the committee. Here, though, there is a single committee and two branches of guards, each covering one ward. In all, the guards number 32, again drawn from all villages, with each ward electing its own *komanda mkuu* (chief commander). This policing arm of the committee is referred to as the *ulinzi wa jadi* (traditional guards) or *sungusungu* or simply as the *jadi*. These expressions can be used to refer to the whole organization or just to its police force. The development of its own cadre of guards signals a difference in the nature of the *sungusungu,* as does their ultimate responsibility to both the committee and to the *iritongo* as a whole. The links with the administration remain strong and minutes and reports are regularly filed with the divisional and district administrative secretaries. Such administrative officers do not, however, normally attend either the committee meetings or the *iritongo* unless they have administrative announcements to make, in which case their participation is usually limited to these.

Although cases are first heard by the committee, full trials are now held weekly or biweekly before the entire *iritongo*. These are people's tribunals in the full sense, and the judgment is a community judgment, which all see and endorse. In the old system, according to Fleisher (2000a), the accusers were never called to the committee trials. Now they must stand to give evidence, as must other witnesses. The *iritongo* are also wary of coming to a judgment before all the accused in a particular case are made to appear and answer. This guards against malicious accusations on the part of an accuser, witness, or, indeed, a thief or who might falsely name others as accomplices and confederates. Trials, in effect, are inquisitional and guided by procedural norms, which have developed over time. Further, the accused must in the

* The *inchaama* continue to have considerable power in Tanzania. In Kenya, its influence is felt more in the eastern regions and there is much less respect for the institution in Bukira and Bugumbe.

end confess before a punishment is decided, a confession which is frequently preceded by whippings or *legeza*.

Punishments are now much tougher. Fleisher (2000a, 2000b) mentions whips of hippopotamus hide used to elicit confession, and heavy fines as punishment. With this new *iritongo*, there are more severe punishments, with beatings with sticks sometimes leading to the death of thieves. *Legeza* (KiSwahili) is key to this process and means literally "unlocking." It refers both to the unlocking of evidence, that is, a confession, and to the means used to achieve this, most typically by "unlocking the ankles," that is, breaking them. This is said to be a traditional punishment for theft, though, if so, it had not been used for a considerable time before the coming of this new form of *sungusungu*, and its KiSwahili origin would tend to belie such a claim. However, its rationale is that it prevents a thief from ever running after cattle again, though most are said to heal sufficiently to cultivate and walk and some recover completely from this laming. However, that depends in part on the severity of the original beating. Where the desire is to really punish the thief, the beating might be extreme, and his knees and elbows might be broken as well. Such a thief will also be fined.

Fines are imposed above that needed to compensate the victim of a raid. These create a pool of money, some of which is used to finance community projects and the rest to finance the work of the *sungusungu*. Though they all claim to be unpaid, this is not strictly true and the administration sanctions a split of such money, usually along 60:40 lines, the former regarded as an allowance for the time and work of the guards and officials, and the latter going into a community pool to finance development projects. Such payment can hardly be considered unfair as both the committee and guards effectively undertake full-time policing jobs. The work they do is extensive, including: answering alarms and tracking stolen cattle, detailed investigation of cases, arresting suspects, bringing them to trial, ensuring the attendance of witnesses, arranging for the repayment of stolen property, liaison with other groups, and keeping records. In addition, they undertake a host of day-to-day surveillance activities, for example, checking on cattle slaughtered at local butcheries and on those offered for sale in the markets.

Other punishments include shunning and finally banishment. Shunning—which is widely used among the Sukuma—is a very severe form of punishment in Tanzania, as it not only implies total ostracism, but denies access to all village services. Many of those ostracized are effectively forced to migrate away. But direct banishment is also an option. It is used only for the most serious cases in Kuria, for the recalcitrant thief or one who has killed many people. The severity of the punishments meted out is deemed critical to the success of the *sungusungu* and a measure of a "strong" group. This is certainly tough justice and the question must be posed as to whether it is also rough justice. No system is perfect. To be tried by an assembly in which you are well known and where your relatives and friends can as easily pack the meeting as those of the accusers is not a kangaroo court. This is emphatically not the kind of lynch law so often associated with vigilantism. Though crowds can be manipulated and the *jadi* overstep the mark, for most people such abuses are deemed of lesser consequence than the alternative in the form of the official court system. The relative lack of success of the earlier administrative *sungusungu* is often said to lie in the fact that once they had arrested thieves, apart from lashings, they were obliged to hand them over to the police and courts for sentencing, inviting the usual response, with the thieves simply bribing their way out. On their return to the community, they were once again in a position to terrorize, most especially those who had been brave enough to mount an accusation.

The strength of groups throughout Kuria varies, but many still have the vigor of recent converts. Indeed, the actions now taken against thieves signal far-reaching changes in Kurian attitudes to theft (Heald, 1999). They no longer say, with some pride as well as a little ruefulness, that they are a "nation of thieves" (Heald, 2000). The moral economy has undergone a major shift. It might be tempting to describe the old warlords as social bandits because of the way they challenged the forces of the state, if they had not, as indicated earlier, also entered into alliances with such forces. They were never peasant social rebels in the sense defined by Hobsbawn (1959, 1969), though, as Fleisher (2000a, 2000b) has argued, their defiance might be seen as one against the extreme poverty that was otherwise their lot. Their victims, however, were peasant tribesmen like themselves. And, while the thieves' plunder was shared among their own group to an extent, attitudes to such thieves had long been equivocal, as social interest, their role as champions of their groups was combined with self-interest with a definite commercial bent. They stood on the cusp of hero/criminal even within their own group as their raiding invited retaliatory vengeance (Heald, 2000). One man's booty led to another man's loss. It is only by taking heed of this ambivalent attitude that one can begin to comprehend the dramatic revolution that *sungusungu* signaled.

By 2000, these groups had had a profound effect on Kuria life, and a tangible effect on security. Kuria is now deemed "safe"; cattle can be tethered in their pasturage without a watch during the day and moving around at night no longer carries the risks that it once did. In Kenya, the General Service Unit camp, which had been set up in 1984, was finally removed in 2000 when the establishment of *sungusungu* on the Kenyan side rendered its presence unnecessary. But, if the terror of the guns and the thieves has to a large degree been broken, this does not mean that these threats have completely disappeared. Just as it is often said that "there will always be theft," so too it seems will there always be guns. While relatively minor cases of theft provide the bulk of the work of *sungusungu* groups, they still have to deal with armed raiding and banditry. Though there are fewer modern weapons around, there are many skilled gunsmiths turning out guns whose barrels are fashioned to the caliber of available bullets. On my last day in Tanzania in February 2002, while waiting at a divisional headquarters near the Kenyan border, the local *sungusungu* leadership arrived with two such handmade guns, which they had just confiscated. They were on their way to an *iritongo* to try the thieves.

The Quiet Revolution

In retrospect, one could say that the *sungugungu* movement was hijacked by the state partly for instrumental reasons, given its difficulty in maintaining any semblance of law and order in the rural hinterland. But, if necessity here was turned into virtue given the penury of the Tanzanian state, it was also, one suspects, because the *sungusungu* represented for those at the socialist center a vibrant grassroots organizing power, which Nyerere's vision had demanded, but which the party had been so unsuccessful in actually developing (Abrahams, 1989; Masanja, 1992; Feierman, 1990; Ingle, 1972; Nellis, 1972). It happily chimed with both necessity and ideology. Nevertheless, there is a huge irony in this development. A quiet revolution has been effected, reversing, by this sanctioning of diversity, the initial project of the postcolonial state.

The administrative structure of the Tanzanian state was monolithic and top-down. The division between the executive and political arm of government, inherited on the British model at Independence in 1961, was dissolved when the country was declared a Republic in 1962. TANU (Tanganika African National Union) then became the only recognized party and there was a general politicization of all institutions, particularly the administration in an effort to instill a general sense of unity and to counteract tribal loyalties. As Feierman reports, "Every regional commissioner, appointed by the president, was *ex officio* the TANU regional secretary, a member of parliament, and a member of the party's National Executive Committee" (1990). Thus, party and administration spoke with one voice and this voice extended down into the districts, divisions, wards, and villages where officials were all government appointees for whom party membership was a prerequisite for office. Although ten-house leaders (*balozi*) were elected from the local party membership and formed the village council, with an elected chairman, the main link to the administration was through the appointed village administrative secretary.

Nor, at one level, has much changed in the formal administrative structure, despite the radical reforms introduced in the 1990s. In 1985, President Nyerere stood down in order to allow his successor, Ali Hassan Mwinyi, to renegotiate the country's relationship with the international community, particularly the International Monetary Fund (IMF) and World Bank. The new ideas of "good governance" were put into effect; most particularly, the demand that economic aid be tied to the processes of democratization, liberalization of the economy, and effective controls over corruption. Nevertheless, since the same party CCM, the successor to TANU after the merger with Zanzibar in 1964, has managed to keep control in both first two democratic elections of 1995 and 2000, the administrative structure remains largely the same. At the bottom, ten house leaders have been replaced by subvillage headmen, with party membership no longer a prerequisite for office. However, at the top, the regional and district commissioners still tend to be members of the National Executive Committee of the party and, thus, represent the interests of both party and state.

As Masanja has noted, "... the involvement of the ordinary villager in such a structural setup tends to be limited" (1992). The bureaucratization of the state led, as Feierman (1990) puts it, to the ascendancy of the "clerks," of the young and educated, who were recruited into the machinery of the government. Older generations of leaders were left behind in such a move and there was a clear schism between the new men and the old. And, it could be argued that it is the "old" who reclaimed power with the development of *sungusungu*. Among the Sukuma, every villager was a member and the leadership was directly accountable to the village assembly. The same is also true of Kuria. The qualification for election to the committee is to be of known good character, and education is only important for the top officials who must be literate in order to carry out their duties and liaise with the local administration. The only people effectively excluded from office are those with professional or business occupations which preclude them attending the assemblies or of taking up the onerous duties of office. This might be said to highlight a distinction between villager and professional elite at the local level. Retired professionals are, however, found on the committees, and there is many a reformed thief among the guards.

The emergence of *sungusungu* as a new form of local assertion and autonomy, legitimized by the state, could be said to dramatically undercut the "centralized despotism" Mamdani (1996) discerns in Tanzanian state formation. Nevertheless, he argues that the significance of the *sungusungu* was both limited and temporary on the grounds that they did not alter either productive relations or the nature of central state power. By being incorporated into state administration, he argues that they "became the custodians of the very order that they had originally organized against" (1996). There are several issues needing discussion here. First of all, there is the question of the extent to which they were—even initially—organized *against* the state. There is little evidence that that is so.* Rather, it appears that the early *sungusungu* groups in Sukumaland had the primary objective of controlling theft and organized not against state power, but into its vacuum. If the leaders of the movement asserted an older template of community leadership, it was one that was not in essence oppositional, but all-inclusive, as their cooperation with the party and administration early on showed.† In turn, the speedy response of the state in recognizing these groups might well have preempted any potentiality *sungusungu* had to develop as a more far-reaching protest movement. But, there is no evidence that this would have been its trajectory. As likely would have been its degeneration into an ephemeral vigilante movement. What was achieved by the alliance with the state was considerable and it has radically modified the nature of state power by ceding much of it back to local communities.

However, this opens up the issue of how exactly one should conceive of the state and state power? Conventionally, the state is seen after Weber as having a monopoly on the use of legitimate force. This assumes that the state is a unified entity, a single leviathan. But, modern democratic states are anything but monolithic; they have multiple specialized institutions, claiming different kinds of legitimacy as recognized from both within and without. And not all branches of the state were equally behind the movement. If the political and administrative arm of the government supported these groups—and continue to do so—it was largely otherwise with the police and the judiciary. Clearly, the actions of *sungusungu* groups constituted a "taking of the law into their own hands" and were in any event outside the law, challenging the powers the judiciary took as its own, of arrest, trial, and punishment. They directly undercut the very rationale of the official agents of the law. More cynically, it could be said with Fleisher (2000a) that both police and judiciary found not only their role preempted, but also the graft that accompanied it. They acted swiftly in attempts to suppress these groups through prosecutions. In the process, they demonstrated only further to the ordinary populace that they were not the enemies of crime, but in league with it. Local magistrates took up the cases of those who had been punished by *sungusungu* groups in order to indict the leadership and to return cattle, which the thieves claimed to have been wrongfully confiscated. Many groups were brought to a speedy halt by such prosecutions, at least for a time. The president has had to intervene on many occasions, in the last resort, by issuing special pardons, but often not before members of these groups have spent a considerable time in

* Unfortunately, little of the literature on the early years of the *sungusungu* movement in Sukuma gives much detail here. There is, for example, no indication of the role (or lack of such) of local ten-house leaders or low level administrations in the initial organization.

† They can only be said to have colluded with the state to defeat their own objectives if, with Mamdani, one takes a neo-Marxist teleological stance that the purpose of such a movement is already predefined.

prison or on remand. Bukurura (1994) records the earliest such presidential amnesty by Julius Nyerere as 1982. There were many in the years to follow as this has proved an enduring and intractable problem.

But there is a further issue here. The administration has allowed *sungusungu* groups to codify their own laws and set out their own punishments. In effect, the national penal code has been suspended—at least with respect to theft and offenses committed in association with theft, such as the possession of firearms and even murder. The government stands uneasy here, encouraging such codification, endorsing community action, and offering protection to *sungusungu* groups, but, ultimately, unable to flout its own judiciary by fully legalizing them. By amending the People's Militia laws, in both 1989 and 1997, the government did find an instrument to give some official recognition to these groups, bestowing upon them a quasilegal status. Through these measures, they gained similar powers of arrest to that of the militias and also the same kind of compensation if injured in the course of duty. But, since Nyerere pronounced in May 1986 that the law under which *sungusungu* leaders could be brought to book for returning stolen property to the original owners (Abrahams, 1987) was a "bad law" and should be changed, there have been continuing promises for a more thorough reform of the law. Succeeding presidents, under pressure from regional administrations, have made similar statements of intent. Discussion papers and proposals had in 2001 been submitted from the districts and regions, but there has been little feedback on progress at this level. Indeed, it is difficult to anticipate a resolution of a *de facto* situation of legal pluralism being made *de jure* in the face, not only of an established system of national law, backed by an independent judiciary, but also the current pressures from the international community for universal forms of accountability.

Meanwhile, the current situation leaves *sungusungu* groups in continuing danger of prosecution. In Mara, in 2000, the regional commissioner introduced new guidelines designed to head off malicious prosecutions by insisting that cases which dispute the rulings of the *sungusungu*, are referred initially to the divisional administrative secretary. The intention is to adjudicate such cases at that level before they reach the court system. To an extent, this provides some reassurance to *sungusungu* groups, but it is by no means a comprehensive answer. It does, however, provide for an interesting concatenation of checks and balances. In normal liberal thinking about the nature of democratic states, the independence of the judiciary is held of prime value, a necessary check on the abuse of executive power and a safeguard for human rights and justice. That presupposes a dedicated and honest judiciary. Local courts in Tanzania fall far short of such an ideal.* Instead, what has evolved is a system

* The corruption of the judiciary and police is detailed in the 1997 Report of the Warioba Commission.

where the administration protects the *sunsugungu* from the abuses of its own judiciary just as it is able to use the leverage it has on such groups to prevent abuses at that level. In the praxis of government in rural areas, the anomalous legality of *sungusungu* is by no means to the disadvantage of the administration. In turn, the community in making common cause with the local administration is able to make its voice heard, something by no means unimportant, especially since the advent of multipartism and democratic elections.

Thus, taking the longer-term view, it is certainly arguable, against Mamdani, that they have altered the nature of state power at the local level and initiated long term reforms. The *sungusungu* have come to operate in a distinctive space, co-opting government and, in turn, co-opted by it. Communities have taken back power, developed their own policing capacity and, in so doing, effectively reinvented themselves. With reformatory agendas, they have evolved new normative structures and modes of cooperation and organization, which both actually and potentially have far-reaching consequences for economic and social welfare. A new vision of community responsibility is heralded and held out as an ideal. In the same way, perhaps, they have reformed and reclaimed the state, with the administration demonstrating an increasing responsiveness to the priorities of local communities, and allowing them a greater degree of autonomy in the management of their own affairs.

References

Abrahams, R. (1987). Sungusungu: Village vigilante groups in Tanzania. *African Affairs, 86*, 179–90.

Abrahams, R. (1989). Law and order and the state in the Nyamwesi and Sukuma area of Tanzania. *Africa*, 59, 354–68.

Abrahams, R. (1998). *Vigilant citizens*. London: Polity.

Abrahams, R. and Bukurura, S. (1993). Party, bureaucracy and grassroots initiatives in asocial list state: The case of Sungusungu vigilantes in Tanzania. In C. Hann (Ed.), *Socialism: Ideals, ideologies and local practices* (pp. 92–101). London: Routledge.

Bayart, J-F., Ellis, S., and Hibou, B. (1999). *The Criminalisation of the State in Africa*. London: International African Institute.

Bukururu, S. (1994). Sungusungu and the banishment of suspected witches in Kahama, Tanzania. In R Abrahams (Ed.), *Witchcraft in contemporary Tanzania* (pp. 61–69). Cambridge, U.K.: African Studies Centre.

Bukururu, S. (1994). *Sungusungu: vigilantes in west-central Tanzania*. Unpublished doctoral dissertation, University of Cambridge, Cambridge, U.K.

Bukururu, S. (1994). The maintenance of law and order in rural Tanzania: The case of the sungusungu. *Journal of Legal Pluralism and Unofficial Law, 34*, 1–29.

Bukururu, S. (1995). Combating crime among the Nyamwezi. *Crime, Law and Social Change, 24*(3), 257–66.

Campbell, H. (1989). Popular resistance in Tanzania: Lessons from the sungusungu. *African Development, 14*(4), 5–43

Feierman, S. (1990). *Peasant intellectuals: Anthropology and history in Tanzania.* Madison: University of Wisconsin Press.

Fleisher, M. (1997). *Kuria cattle raiding: A case study in the capitalist transformation of an East African sociocultural institution.* Doctoral dissertation, University of Michigan, Ann Arbor.

Fleisher, M. (2000a). Sungusungu: State-sponsored village vigilante groups among the Kuria of Tanzania. *Africa, 70*(2), 209–28

Fleisher, M. (2000b). *Kuria cattle raiders: Violence and Vvgilantism on the Tanzania/Kenya frontier.* Ann Arbor: University of Michigan Press.

Heald, S. (1999). Agricultural intensification and the decline of pastoralism: A Kenyan case study. *Africa, 69*(2), 213–37.

Heald, S. (2000). Tolerating the intolerable: Cattle raiding among the Kuria. In G.Aijmer and J. Abbink (Eds.), *Meanings of violence* (pp. 101–121). Oxford, U.K.: Berg.

Heald, S. (2002). *Domesticating leviathan: Sungusungu groups in Tanzania.* Working Paper 16, Series 1. Crisis States Programme. www.crisisstates.com.

Heald, S. (2006). State, law and vigilantism in Northern Tanzania. *African Affairs, 105*, 265–283.

Hobsbawm, E.J. (1959). *Primitive rebels.* Manchester, U.K.: Manchester University Press.

Hobsbawm, E.J. (1969). *Bandits.* London: Weidenfeld and Nicolson.

Ingle, C. (1972). *From village to state in Tanzania: The politics of rural development.* Ithaca, NY, and London: Cornell University Press.

Kjerland, K. (1995). *Cattle breed, shillings don't: The belated incorporation of the aba-Kuria into modern Kenya.* Doctoral dissertation, University of Bergen, Bergen, Norway.

Mamdani, M. (1996). *Citizen and subject.* Princeton, NJ: Princeton University Press.

Masanja, P. (1992). Some notes on the sungusungu movement. In P. Forster and S. Maghimbi (Eds.), *The Tanzanian peasantry: Economy in crisis* (pp. 203–215). Aldershot, U.K.: Avebury.

Ndagala, D.K. (1991). The unmaking of the Datoga: Decreasing resources and increasing conflict. *Nomadic Peoples, 28*, 71–82.

Nellis, J. (1972). *A theory of ideology: The Tanzanian example.* Nairobi: Oxford University Press.

Ruel, M. (1959). *The social organisation of the Kuria: A fieldwork report.* Unpublished manuscript.

Tobisson, E. (1986). *Family dynamics among the Kuria.* Doctoral dissertation, Acta Universitatis Gothoburgensis, Sweden.

Community Policing
The Case of Informal Policing in Nigeria

4

IHEKWOABA D. ONWUDIWE

Contents

Introduction: Criminological Perspectives on Community Policing

While community policing (CP) generally may have gained worldwide acceptance in the past two decades as a philosophy, its definition has not generally received an intersubjective acceptability. There is a problem with defining the concept of CP. Its definition is still in limbo, pejorative, and rooted in various dictums and aphorisms. Despite the popularity of community policing, a universally acceptable definition has evaded law enforcement practitioners in the United States in particular, and the global society in general (Cheurprakobkit, 2002). Trojanowicz and Buequeroux (1990, p. 5) have provided a trendy definition as:

> Community policing is a new philosophy of policing, which emphasizes the working partnership between police officers and citizens in creative ways

> in order to solve community problems relating to crime, fear of crime, and neighborhood disorders.

The utilization of the term *philosophy* in CP definitions allows the concept to generate different ideas and meanings to different proponents of the CP style. The concept of CP philosophy connotes a set of values relating to individuals and civilizations, traditions, and customs (Cheurprakobkit, 2002). Indeed, attempts to follow the dicta in definitions result in different methods and strategies of CP programs, meaning that each culture adopting CP must adapt it to fit its local needs and traditions. According to the Community-Oriented Policing Services (COPS) office, CP can be defined as:

> A policing philosophy that promotes and supports organizational strategies to address the causes and reduce the fear of crime and social disorder through problem solving tactics and police–community partnerships (Newman, 2006).

Another oft-quoted definition of CP in the literature is provided by Cordner (1997), who identified in his definition four different dimensions of CP: philosophical, strategic, tactical, and organizational. Cordner's philosophical dimension includes three aspects:

1. Citizen input, which assumes that the police departments should seek and carefully consider citizen input when making policies and decisions that affect the community.
2. Broad police function, which refers to a broad view of the police function, such as order maintenance, social service, and general assistance duties instead of relying only on crime fighting and law enforcement.
3. Personal service, which is the idea of tailored policing based on local norms and values as well as individual needs. Officers are encouraged to "consider the will of the community" in decision making about policies, programs, and the type of laws to enforce.

The strategic dimension consists of the principal operational practices that convert the philosophy of CP into practical actions and programs by bringing officers closer to the communities that they police, encouraging less reliance on patrolling in police vehicles, and an emphasis on proaction policing. The tactical dimension focuses on positive interaction with citizens, partnership, and problem solving. The final dimension—organizational—highlights administrative practices, such as articulation of mission statements and CP values. The whole idea is to enhance strategic planning that includes the mentoring of officers, encouragement of officer's originality, and resourcefulness, rather than placing an overemphasis on stringent law enforcement (Cheurprakobkit, 2002).

It must be underscored that implementing a CP program successfully requires immense governmental and cultural approval and structural changes (Broeck, 2002). In Nigeria, for example, as we describe below, CP is still at its formative stage and conceptualization. It has not received organizational acceptance. To develop a CP strategy, it is essential to monitor, through training and practice, the contemporary and historical and the social and political context that is suitable for any model of CP such as problem-oriented policing (Goldstein, 1979; 1990), community-oriented policing (Bailey, 1991), and ecological community policing or the "broken windows" theory (Wilson & Kelling, 1997). Briefly, the problem-oriented policing strategy represents a major evolutionary stride in encouraging the police to perform intelligently, not inflexibly, in discharging their functions. According to Eck and Spelman (1989), this model of policing emphasizes analyzing clusters of incidents and locating solutions to community problems. The police seek solutions to problems by working hand-in-hand with the public agencies, private organizations, and individuals. They describe problem-oriented policing as:

> A department-wide strategy aimed at solving persistent community problems. Police identify, analyze, and respond to the underlying circumstances that create incidents (Eck & Spelman, 1989, p. 489).

Following Goldstein's original articulation of the subject, problem-oriented policing serves as an alternative to incident-driven policing. His view is that the police must not rely only on reacting to incidents, but should also endeavor to find permanent solutions to problems. While the philosophy of CP (or Community-Oriented Policing [COP] as referred to in the literature) emerged through the research conducted by the Police Foundation and the School of Criminal Justice at Michigan State University, problem-oriented policing has its genesis in the Police Executive Research Forum (Gaines, Kappeler, & Vaughn, 1994). CP, therefore, presupposes a range of issues in different regions; it focuses on innovative schema in which the police utilize a managerial plan that emphasizes fear-reduction and order-maintenance actions by involving citizens and by using problem-solving methods (Eck & Spelman, 1989; Gaines, Kappeler, & Vaughn, 1994; Cheurprakobkit, 2002; Goldstein, 1979, 1990; Greene & Pelfrey, 1997; Cordner, 1997).

In a 1982 classic article, Wilson and Kelling articulated the "broken windows" thesis in criminology. The authors, through historical analysis, examined the impact of reintroducing foot patrols in policing and suggested a return to order-maintenance policing. The broken windows theory refers to a metaphor in policing indicating the decay of an unattended neighborhood characterized by abandoned vehicles and buildings, trash, graffiti, and broken windows and lights. In addition to these physical deteriorations of the community, there are also problems of public drunkenness, prostitution, and vagrancy. These social and physical indicators of the community constitute symbols of rudeness that attract lawbreakers to the neglected communities. While Walker (1997) discredited the historical approach used by Wilson and Kelling by referring to it as a misuse of history, the essential point made by Wilson and Kelling remains important. In summary, the thesis argues for the police to be neighborhood-oriented, focuses on foot patrol, embraces some elements of team policing, places lesser emphasis on crime control, and focuses on citizens' needs. This paradigm shift in policing—label it CP, COP, or Broken Windows—offers divergent alternatives and models of policing. Obviously, an American innovation in policing is engulfing the global society, including the Nigerian police, who are looking at this phenomenon with ardent interest.

The Historical Context of the Nigerian Police

Historically, the Nigerian Police Force (NPF) emerged out of the crucible of colonial dominion. Like many of the African police systems under colonial administration, the police in Nigeria was primarily developed to serve the interests of the metropolis. It was developed as an instrument of coercion in order to maintain colonial control of the populace under subjugation (Tamuno, 1970). As a result of the nature of its development, the police relationship with the citizens of different geographic locations was characterized by violence and distrust (Alemika & Chukwuma, 2000; Adebayo, 2005). The Nigerian police establishment was created out of the yearning of the colonial authorities to control various regions of Nigeria and to protect the domestic interest of Britain in trade and governance. In his classic work on Nigerian police, Tamuno (1970) echoed the same sentiments by insisting that the police was originally created to serve as an instrument of social control by oppressing and suppressing opponents of regal management. It was not designed to serve the interests of the people; rather, the colonial police cemented the seed of discord between the public and police, a dire situation that remains today.

During colonial rule, the police were used to coerce, harass, intimidate, and violate the human rights of Nigerian opposition groups with utter impunity. Police relationship with the Nigerian citizens suffered. Local police were also utilized by local leaders to further their own political aspirations. Employment into the police force in some of the regions was characterized by the political patronage system (Marenin, 1985). Early policing in America suffered the same fate when the political machines and mayors in American cities controlled who got employed as police officers (Peak,

2009). Like in America, officers in Nigeria were hired by the local chiefs for political survival. The police were used to suppress opponents of political parties. These historical realities still permeates the country's thinking about developing democratic and community policing. It is still part of the memory reservoir in Nigerian police history that the local police were used as instruments of oppression and mischief. During this era, citizens resented and feared their local police, leading to poor police relations with members of the community.

Beginning with the 1966 coup and the subsequent military governance of Nigeria, the soldiers were determined to dislocate any aspiration of local police formations in the country (Marenin, 1985). The police were poorly paid, stripped of their power by military rulers, and alienated from the public. The intention was to maintain military rule. This meant that the chiefs and native authorities no longer possessed control of their police forces. The military clearly feared insurrections and resented police arsenals in the hands of the police and local authorities for fear of instability in the country (Adebayo, 2005). The Nigerian police essentially became a militarized unit forced into one central police command (Ekeh, 1997).

As deciphered from Marenin's apt analyses of the Nigerian police, there was fierce opposition by all the emirs and native authority posts against any form of unification of local police forces with the national police. In 1967, the Nigerian military administration appointed the Gobir Commission, which recommended that the police forces in the western region of Nigeria be integrated immediately, but opted for a slow unification of northern police forces into the NPF. Undoubtedly, the military adopted the Gobir's recommendations and integrated the western police forces in 1967 and the northern police forces in 1972 (Marenin, 1985).

Additionally, the issue of fusion was reinvented in 1979 during the draft of the Nigerian Constitution. The abolition of local police formations negated effective maintenance of order and tranquility in the communities. While the military achieved its objective of hiring, training, and posting officers to different areas of the federation, regardless of geographic and ethnic origin, the districts suffered primarily from the mayhem caused by thieves and armed robbers (Marenin, 1985; Dent, 1978). While the military no longer feared overthrow from the police and their local authorities (as they controlled the police), local authorities were unable to provide citizens with community protection. But, the issue of amalgamation of the levels of the police remained a perennial problem in Nigeria, and under the Constitution of the Federal Republic of Nigeria, the president and the inspector general of police were vested with the power and responsibility for preserving harmony, community security, and civic serenity. The Constitution mandated for one central police unit. It declares:

> There shall be a Police Force for Nigeria, which shall be styled [after] the Nigerian Police Force, and subject to the provisions of this section, no other Police Force shall be established for the Federation or any part therefore. (Constitution of the Federal Republic of Nigeria, 1989, p. 78)

This historical context has been provided to demonstrate that, despite colonial control, the original formation of the Nigerian Police Force was conceptualized to reflect community needs. Despite the misuse of the police by local authorities, community policing is not germane to the Nigerian situation. Indeed, as we have described, the emirs of the north fiercely agitated against police centralization. When the military knelled a final blow against local police formations in Nigeria, the local authorities were hindered in their efforts to protect citizens from lawbreakers. Citizens were further alienated from the top-down and from militarized police. They were not adequately protected from the colossal police command in Nigeria. To the extent that citizens feel unprotected from the havoc of criminals, states, local authorities, and citizen groups have formed informal policing structure (IPS) outlets for self-protection. The evolution of bottom-up policing in Nigeria today is reviewed below as methods of informal policing.

Methodology

This chapter is based on secondary analyses of published research on community policing and literature on IPS study in Nigeria. Currently, studies on community policing in Nigeria are scarce. As a result, the author utilized research conducted by Western criminologists to present the philosophy of CP. Given that CP establishment is seriously being considered in the country, this is important, especially if Nigerian readers and policy administrators are to have a scholarly review of the tenets of CP. Studies conducted by CLEEN (formerly known as Centre for Law Enforcement EducatioN) researchers were retrieved from their Internet database to illustrate the current state of IPS in Nigeria. These studies reveal that some aspects of IPS in Nigeria today take the shape of vigilantism due to their involvements in extrajudicial killings of offenders without due process. Based on these efforts, this chapter presents IPS in vogue in the Nigerian context.

Informal Policing Structure (IPS) and Social Control Mechanisms in Nigeria

As used here, informal policing connotes an aspect of policing that is in direct contrast to a formal police force in Nigeria. Informal policing mainly develops from the efforts of citizens' generated opposition to their government's failure to provide shelter for communities in the advent of rising crimes, inadequate security, protection from criminals, and the formal police failure to stop vices, such as armed robbery in the communities (Scharf, 2000; Shaw, 2000). Wisler and Onwudiwe (in print) have labeled this form of policing "bottom-up police structures" that have historically existed in various societies outside of official policing and, in some cases, developed because formal policing has failed to protect citizens from crimes and criminals. Informal policing became necessary in Nigeria when communities began to fear for their safety and security. Some Nigerian scholars have examined different aspects of plural law enforcement and social control mechanisms that have traditionally existed in Nigeria.

In his book, *Doing Justice Without the State*, Elechi (2006) identifies the existence and practice of an indigenous social control practice of Afikpo people in Igbo regions of Nigeria, which is rooted in traditional values and customs of the Igbo people. Elechi points out that these traditional methods of social control in Afikpo have been modified to accommodate the advent of Western law. He insists, however, that the traditional methods in Afikpo are not a static form of law, but rules and regulations that govern the behaviors of citizens with adherence to traditional legal principles. The Afikpo brand of justice allows for the inclusion of all members of the community in participatory decision making. Indeed, the findings indicate that the Afikpo form of justice is not only practical and professional, but distinctive and democratic. Elechi provides a surfeit of information addressing the impact of the offender's actions on the community and the victim. The justice system, under the Afikpo model, attempts to restore the emotional and material losses of the victim. Unlike this African justice model, Western European law relies on offenders and their illegal actions against the government and its laws, rather than focusing on restoration and reinstitution for the victims and their communities. Elechi's model is devoid of the government, which encourages both the accuser and the accused to live and function in communities together.

Prior to colonial occupation, African societies were not centralized, and they virtually developed systems of dispute-settling mechanisms in order to preserve domestic harmony. Naturally, the elders of the villages or towns, senior members of the disputing families, and appointed men of wisdom play significant roles in adjudicating matters. After this form of traditional settlement, disputing parties abide by the final judgment and accept it in order to live in peace.

Since Africa as a whole—and Nigeria in particular—is now confronted with high crime rates, scholars are focusing on the various traditional forms of informal policing and unofficial justice modalities in rural and urban environments in order to address the inability of the formal police structure to protect citizens from criminals (Okereaforezeke, 2002; Elechi, 2006; Heald, 2007; Alemika & Chukwuma, 2000; Ahhilomen, 2006). In Kenya, for example, Heald (2007) describes (see Chapter 3) the formation of a variance of Tanzanian *sungusungu* group adopted by the citizens of Kuria for self-protection from raging armed cattle thieves. Rural farmers in Kuria supported the development of the group, a form of community policing, independent of the government that is bestowed with the power to combat crime and avoid formal police complicity and harassment. Heald notes that formal Kenyan police authorities welcomed the development of the *sungusungu*, self-help informal policing group for Kuria, because thieves had taken control of the streets with the support of the formal police and local chiefs. In its formative beginning, membership in the policing arm of the *sungusungu* was required for adults and was predicated upon good character, although repented criminals were not excluded from membership.

In Nigeria, Elechi (2006) addressed a similar phenomenon in Afikpo town, where age-grades (groups of the same age and gender in a community or village) performed informal policing functions for the maintenance and preservation of peace in the community. Prior to colonial rule, the age-grades in Afikpo town were like the informal police of the community and were mobilized to combat crime as well as amassed to protect the town from external aggression. Their policing responsibilities in contemporary Igbo land included the enforcement of the native laws and collection of fines. Most importantly, they also imposed strict discipline on irritant members that were prone to misbehave and to violate compound regulations.

The age-grades finance their group by contributing money to a "pot" and, in turn, they lend that money to members for educational and professional apprenticeships or for family needs. As a highly disciplined group, they reject alcohol, narcotics, and profanity that may lead to verbal napalm. Respect for elders is expected from every age-grade member. The elders trace their power to the fortitude of their ancestors, which provides them with direction and security (Elechi, 2006).

In contemporary Nigerian policing, the NPF welcomes the establishment of informal policing groups, such as the age-grades, as long as these groups register with the police, submit to police screening, do not carry weapons, and avoid detaining suspects (Alemika & Chukwuma, 2004). In their study of IPS in four Nigerian states, Benue, Ekiti, Enugu, and Jigawa, CLEEN criminologists identified several community groups, such as the Olode (hunters) and Ndi-nche (community guards), that were developed to fight crime and provide safety and security.

Alemika and Chukwuma (2004) noted that groups, such as the Olode in the Jigawa state, are part of a long-standing traditional and cultural safety performance of hunters in Yoruba land that have historically provided guard services and protection to the people. In Igbo, represented by Enugu state in their investigation, the authors claim that groups such as the Ndi-nche, provide watch activities designed to apprehend and detect criminals. Like the age-grades discussed above, Ndi-nche consisted of community youths who are required to participate in community safeguard. Alemika and Chukwuma (2004, p. 30) write:

> The [...] young men are divided into groups by the elders and assigned different days as the day they will be on guard. At the appointed time, a wooden gong is sounded signaling when the group for that day is supposed to assemble. They are now assigned to different areas where undesirables are likely to be lurking around (for example) houses built by those who are still "abroad" [...] Their major weapon is a stick and torch light since the area is dark and there may be snakes and other reptiles around.

Based on the customs of the community, the elders supervise and administer the guard services of the youths, which are highly organized with the cardinal objective of identifying prospective offenders who may undergo a process of "shaming" after apprehension (Alemika & Chukwuma, 2004; Elechi, 2006; Okereaforezeke, 2002). Indeed, by publicly exposing and shaming the offenders for their transgressions, this procedure performs an important social control function: deterring future offenders who want to avoid both public humiliation and the residual effects that their family members might experience.

The next important informal police group historically rooted in Igbo land is the masquerade cult, revered due to its supernatural linkage. Alemika and Chukwuma (2004) indicate in their study that the masquerade cult, like the Ndi-Nche, implements sanctions imposed by community elders against offenders who have wronged community people. In the Afikpo model, the masquerades are not necessarily a permanent institution involved in dispute settling mechanics; however, Elechi (2006) points out that they are a regular part of Afikpo culture that performs important cultural rituals and activities. The masquerades perform three significant social control functions: Oteru, Okpa, and Okumkpo.

The Oteru and Okpa function as entertainers as well as rule enforcers. In Afikpo, the masquerades wear masks to place them in the sphere of the spirit world, which, in turn, imbues them with the reverence to quell riots and fights in the village by intervening with the threat of force. The mere sight of the masquerades was enough to disperse disputing crowds into orderly compliance and behavior. Individuals found guilty of felonious acts and who refuse to pay restitution to the community would have their properties confiscated by the masquerades. The Okumkpo, on the other hand, play a different role in social control. The Okumkpo uses the community theatre to denounce behaviors that are repugnant to the acceptable customs, norms, and traditions of the village. Through songs and acting displays, corruption and gluttony of the leaders would be manifested in public. Furthermore, individuals who commit "taboo" offenses (e.g., the killing of a family member) are exposed through songs and drama. The Okumkpo play an important law enforcement function by acting as investigative journalists and unofficial police detectives in dealing with difficult matters that otherwise would not have been uncovered by the formal police (Elechi, 2006).

In another significant study entitled *Law and Justice in Post-British Nigeria*, Nonso Okereaforezeke (2002) describes the functions of the masquerades when community rules against public security are violated. When lawbreakers commit offenses against "iwu nmmanwu" (masquerading rules), such as stealing and destruction of property, masquerades are empowered by the community council to seize property—usually goats—from the family of the perpetrators. Offenders are given ample time to pay fines and avoid confiscation of property. In cases of offenses against public morality—crimes that pollute the community—such as incest and homicides, offenders are meted with the more serious punishment of exile if they refuse to vacate the community for a period of seven years.

With regard to quality of life and the growth of communities, Alemika and Chukwuma (2004) found safety and security to be of paramount importance in the lives of Nigerian citizens. Research findings from the states they studied indicate that the poor in those states "expressed some fear of criminal victimization." This finding was articulated by participants in one of their study groups as:

> Safety and security are very important in our communities [...] It affects aspects of our health, family coexistence, and our lives and properties [...] It affects everything! Without safety and security, everything would get spoilt.

The study (Alemika & Chukwuma, 2004, p. 6) also noted that concerns for security and safety centered on the following factors for which citizens needed assistance from informal police groups:

- Personal safety from criminals, especially armed robbers
- Protection from harm associated with political thuggery
- Prevention of violent conflicts
- Eradication of police corruption
- Security of property from theft and destruction

Additionally, the study groups indicated that the IPS was helpful to them by responding rapidly to their needs when the formal NPF were reluctant to act, and because the IPS was closer to the people. According to the study, informal policing is predominantly utilized in Ekiti state (88.9%) and Jigawa (62.5%) more than in Benue (36.7%) and in Enugu state (38.1%). However, the informal police groups are not without some problems because they lack funding from the government, except in Ekiti state where the IPS received monthly wages. The IPS also is confronted by official police persecution and illegal threats in the performance of their duties. Finally, the authors reported that the IPS was not recognized by some of the local governments in the states studied, and they generally lacked essential operational apparatus, such as warm clothing, rain coats, boots, whistles, uniforms, and official identification.

Other obvious setbacks faced by the IPS development is rooted in inadequate management of some of the groups, gender discrimination in membership, closed membership as reflected with the age-grades and some hunter groups, screening of members, and accountability. Accountability is particularly important because some of the IPS groups possessed weapons in violation of established Nigerian laws (Alemika & Chukwuma, 2004). Membership in the traditionally based IPS (age-grades and hunting groups) is restricted to those responsible for the community's defense and residents of the community. However, registration fees are not required among the IPS groups, as individuals can become members by demonstrating their willingness to shield their communities from the members of the dangerous class.

A Typology of Informal Policing and Vigilantism in Nigeria

Unfortunately, some of the informal police structures in Nigeria are labeled vigilantes in some of the states studied by CLEEN criminologists (Chukwuma, 2002; Alemika & Chukwuma, 2004). In some cases, it was difficult for the researchers to distinguish vigilante groups from the cultural and traditional IPS groups because the people generally welcomed their establishments. However, the most important distinction between the two is that those groups identified as vigilantes by the communities carried weapons and engaged in extrajudicial killings of their captured suspects. It is essential to assert that most of the vigilante groups in Nigeria originally developed as community self-help guards before they were enticed by their respective governments. The groups were accepted by their communities as local and urban protectors from the havocs and raids of the criminals. Some Western scholars have frowned upon their methods of operation as constituting extreme forms of violence (Simonsen & Spindlove, 2007), while Nigerian scholars have intimated that the Bakassi Boys enforcement roles have been significant triumphs (Okereaforezeke, 2007), and others have described their extrajudicial killings as vigilantism (Elechi, 2003). Legal scholars tend to refer to vigilantism as extrajudicial self-help (Black, 1983), while philosophers (French, 2001) portray it as vengeance with ethical problems. Some scholars are seriously examining the concept and finding solutions to the dilemma of jungle justice (Chukwuma, 2000, 2002; Scharf, 2000; Shaw, 2000; Elechi, 2003; Okereaforezeke, 2007).

Nigerian criminologists have provided cogent rationale for the acceptance and existence of informal policing (Alemika & Chukwuma, 2004). The most important aspect of the CLEEN research is the development of the typology of informal policing structures in Nigeria. By identifying the types of bottom-up policing, CLEEN researchers have demonstrated the importance of these forms of unofficial and partially official CP in Nigeria. The term *partially official CP* is used to illustrate that some of the informal policing ideal types have the covert and overt patronage of the government. This means that states and local governments understand the need for citizens to be protected from hard-core criminals.

The CLEEN (2008b) researchers described the Nigerian type of vigilante groups as constituting a variance of informal policing structures, while insisting that some of the vigilante organizations in Nigeria "do not operate as a bunch of death squads that mete out jungle justice on their victims." They identified four typologies of vigilante or informal policing in Nigeria. These include religious, ethnic, state-sponsored, and neighborhood or community groups (Chukwuma, 2002). Alemika and Chukwuma (2004) make it apparent that these ideal types may contain elements of each other, that some of the structures may employ methods of "mob justice" and "crudity" in the performance of their tasks, and some types may function cooperatively with the formal authorities as illustrated below.

Holy Policing

According to Chukwuma's (2002) account, the Hisbah groups in Nigeria operate primarily in the northern Sharia regions of the country and represent a typical example of the religious angle of informal policing. Hisbah is used to refer to local religious groups, originally formed without state involvement to enforce the compulsion of the Sharia doctrines. However, for political reasons, Hisbah has been "hijacked" by their state governments. Hisbah is bestowed with the authority to reprimand, arrest, and, in some cases, use force to gain compliance from citizens in violation of the moral law. Drinking or distribution of alcohol, engaging in premarital intercourse, prostitution, or speaking against Sharia and Islam constitute punishable transgressions. Unfortunately, Hisbah is used today by corrupt politicians to engage in extrajudicial duties, such as inflicting punishments for transgressions without proper supervision by the judiciary (Chukwuma, 2002). In this way, the Hisbah group, while enforcing the moral principles, may adopt vigilante tactics in the enforcement of Sharia laws (Human Rights Watch, 2007).

Ethnic Policing

Ethnic policing refers to the groups bound together by their ethnic identity in Nigeria for law enforcement purposes, such as guard activities and other crime control tasks. Vigilante activities in Nigeria are entrenched in a range of social, historical, economic, and political curves. Nolte (2007) argues that although vigilantism may succeed in transforming political influence within a country, it cannot necessarily destabilize all spheres of state power. These groups may also engage in political violence that is predominantly framed by causes and issues related to ethnic pride and survival. In Chukwuma's analysis, the Odua'a Peoples Congress (OPC) in southwestern Nigeria represents a typical example of ethnic vigilantism. Founded in 1994 (Chukwuma, 2002), after the annulment of the 1993 presidential election of a Yoruba (Nolte, 2007), the OPC's main goal was to stop any perception of political marginalization of the Yoruba people in Nigeria. However, in 1999, the organization was transformed to engage in vigilante activities with a focus on combating crime (Nolte, 2007).

Additionally, the OPC activities were brutal in that its members used punitive punishment against suspects, tortured their captives, lynched armed robbers, and utilized methods of "necklessing" (setting people on fire) against their enemies. It has also been documented that the members of the OPC were also murdered by the formal police who were determined to erase its existence (Tersakian, 2003). In his fitting analysis of the OPC, Aderemi (2006) indicates that Nigeria experienced the proliferation of other cultural groups that did not consider the use of violence as a viable means to resolve conflicts.

Secondary State Policing

In Nigeria, some bottom-up policing groups operate with the understanding and cooperation of their governments and with the sole purpose of fighting crime, although these groups were originally developed independent of their respective state governments and for the protection of their rural and urban environments. Unlike the OPC, which was partly developed to seek autonomy for Yoruba, the Bakassi Boys' historical mission, as nongovernmental self-help guards, was to rid urban communities of the criminal underworld without an explicit political motive. Chukwuma (2002) suggests that the Bakassi Boys exemplify this typology of informal policing in Nigeria. They were originally established by traders in the Abia state to fight unbridled crimes in the major market towns of Aba, Onitsha in Anambra state, and lastly in the Imo state. In Anambra state, the Bakassi Boys were commandeered and legalized in 2000 through a special law adopted by the state legislature (Anambra State Law, 2000). It must also be underscored that the operations of the Bakassi Boys have also been outlawed (The Norwegian Directorate of Immigration,

2004) because the methods they used to carry out their unofficial policing functions were extremely cruel, callous, and capricious. Some citizens of these states were executed and mutilated in public without the rule of law, while thousands were tortured and detained without the opportunity to face the judicial bench (Human Rights Watch, 2007).

In a 1999 article published by the *Guardian Newspaper*, an Imo State Chief Judge noted that people who violated the law should be tried according to the established law, "not according to the matchet" (Ogugbuaja, 2002). However, communities accepted the Bakassi Boys because armed robbers ruled the streets and markets, and killed, robbed, and terrorized families without formal police protection. People were relieved with the presence and operation of the group because the areas in which they visited and operated witnessed a sharp decline in crime. While the group claimed that they targeted only armed robbers or criminals that threatened the safety and security of the people, innocent citizens were also victims; after all, in a democracy, even the guilty are afforded the inalienable rights to due process of law (Peak, 2009; Onwudiwe, 2000, 2001). The Bakassi Boys' existence can be traced to the village security tradition of the Igbo communities (Elechi, 2006; Okereaforezeke, 2002).

Village-Gate Policing

Indeed, village-gate policing in southeastern Nigeria, like much of America's common law tradition, may be similar to the English police heritage. Social control in early England was looked upon as both an individual and village responsibility. The frankpledge system of community surveillance was an early method of law enforcement that relied on self-help and mutual aid of extended families living in close proximity (Peak, 2009).

Chukwuma (2000) labels this typology of informal policing in Nigeria as "neighborhood or community" gatekeepers represented by the Olode, Ndi-Nche, and the age-grades. He described this typology as:

> These are groups of people that are organized by street associations in the cities or villages in the rural areas, to man street entrances or villages' gates as the case may be, at night. They also carry out foot patrols at night to reassure members of the community that some people are watching over their security. They do not carry weapons, but rather armed with whistles, which they use in arousing the neighborhoods if there are unwholesome "guests."

Often, most of these villages have physical gates and roadblocks to prevent unknown visitors from entering the villages at night. Keeping watch is rotational among members of the community. Human Rights Watch (2007) reports that because of police corruption and complicity, citizens feel obligated to establish local protection groups to protect them from armed robbers. This means that citizens no longer trust their police and vice versa. Tamuno (1970) understands this reality by noting that Nigeria has historically practiced a decentralized police system, which was dismantled by colonial Britain and the subsequent military rule. A return to local police devolutions in Nigeria, akin to the structure of the Nigerian judiciary, may be more palatable to unofficial community defense than the federal police focus as is currently practiced.

The Nexus between Informal Policing and Customary Courts

Historically, Nigeria has not always had a centralized police system (Marenin, 1985; Tamuno, 1970; Kayode, 1976; Ekpenyong, 1987; Iwarimie-Jaja, 1988; Onwudiwe, 2000; Ekeh, 1997). The current police force emerged after political independence in 1960 (Tamuno, 1970). Soon after, different regions of the country maintained autonomous police departments and community law enforcement units alongside the central command. This decentralized police mechanism, customized to fit local needs for the regions of the federation at the time, provided a sense of security and stability for the citizens and their local leaders (Onwudiwe, 2000).

In Nigeria, such decentralization is the case with the judiciary that has federal courts for federal cases and a separate court for state cases. Each state also has its own lower courts for the local government cases, such as the magistrate courts. Additionally, a separate court has been created for those Nigerians professing the Islamic faith (Ekeh, 1997). I label this excellent judicial system *the customization of the Nigerian judicature.* I argue, also, that, for many reasons, the same principle should be extended to the Nigerian police. According to Ekeh (1997), a reform of the Nigerian police must include decentralization of law enforcement functions that will reflect the character and cultures of the different layers of the government. The development of local and state community policing styles will allow the various units to prepare and control their own security needs. If this goal is achieved, the central police command, headquartered in Abuja, the Nigerian capital, will have “narrower and sharper” functions, leading to a more efficient and effective performance than is currently the case. Local police formations will be better equipped to work hand-in-hand with the traditional police structures than cooperation with the colossal police deriving its command from the federal government. The customary courts operate closer to the people, seeking justice, which is why it is still an important layer of the judicial structure in Nigeria.

The Nigerian customary courts exemplify the decentralization practice of the Nigerian judiciary. Okereaforezeke (2007, 2002) has demonstrated how individuals in Igbo land who are dissatisfied with community justice are allowed to appeal their cases to the formal courts, beginning with the customary courts. Kolajo (2000) provides a holistic meaning, characteristics, and applications of customary law in the Nigerian context. Indeed, customary or native laws are defined as traditional rules of conduct binding on a particular community. In Nigeria, each ethnic group has its own binding native laws based on time-honored customs and traditions, which constitute their own common law. Native law is the recognized natural law of the inhabitants of Nigeria rooted in customs and usage that preserve their unique existence and interactions with each other (Kolajo, 2000). Its validity is predicated on the consent of the indigenous members of the community. Usually, the judges of the customary courts are composed of local chiefs knowledgeable of native customs and traditions. While these judges are originally not trained in formal law, recent trends indicate that they have begun to receive training in modern law (Okereaforezeke, 2002).

Before the emergence of the contemporary Nigerian police, like the judiciary, ethnic groups in Nigeria had their acceptable machinery for the preservation of peace and quietude. Local chiefs and traditional rulers maintained peace and harmony within their respective communities. As indicated earlier, age-grades and masquerades were utilized in the preservation of customs, traditions, order, and law. Aside from their basic character, societies in ancient and modern times using these informal groups maintained and continue to keep peace and regulation. Because the majority of the populace has lost confidence in the official police, the performance of the IPS must be embraced by the formal police structure. After all, the judiciary has not abandoned local formations of judicial structures in the country.

Current State of Community Policing in Nigeria

In 2004, the former Speaker of the House of Assembly Alhaji Amino Bello Musa indicated that the National Assembly would promulgate legislation for the establishment of community policing. He indicated that the concept of community policing has gained global acceptability and that Nigeria has no option but to adopt it (ThisDay, 2004). Other politicians, such as the Information Minister Chief Dapo Sarumi, countered immediately by arguing that there are no attempts by the federal government to change the present structure of the police from a central organization to state or regional police. The minister assured that policing in Nigeria is a constitutional matter and that the only way to change the present federal structure of the police is through a constitutional amendment (Abinndu, 1999). Meanwhile, the Nigerian police have not abandoned efforts to implement and integrate community-policing principles in its operations. In 2002, the International Criminal Investigative Training Assistance Program (ICITAP) visited Nigeria to help the NPF improve its management capabilities and to develop training on basic recruit courses and a community policing program. ICITAP is developing a community policing project aimed at helping Nigeria's nascent community policing initiatives that may serve as a vehicle to help reduce ethnic violence and armed robbery in the country (Dept. of Justice, 2008).

Additionally, the CLEEN Foundation reported that between 2003 and 2004, the inspector general of police led a delegation to three cities in the United States—Houston, Atlanta, and Chicago—to learn more about their community policing programs. The goal of the visits was not to follow rigidly the practice of community policing in America, but to adopt community-policing principles that will work well with the Nigerian model. Nigerian investigators were informed that community policing in the various cities they visited has contributed immensely to crime reduction, improved community relations, and diminution in disorder and fear of crime (CLEEN, 2008a). According to CLEEN, other police teams from Nigeria also visited Great Britain to learn about their police systems, and both delegations, with the backing of the Inspector General, are now considering developing a community policing program for the NPF.

The uniqueness of the Nigerian situation requires that any development of CP by the NPF, that is, top-down CP in Nigeria, ought to be adapted to fit the Nigerian character. The new initiative in CP philosophy in the Nigerian context must be tailored to incorporate the customary bottom-up IPS that has been historically part of regional police systems in the country. This plural law enforcement formation recognizes the benefits of IPS and their establishments in various districts of the federation. This could be accomplished through state and federal legislations that will empower state governments to formally recognize the guard activities of the IPS groups. Strictly borrowing the CP modalities from Europe and America may not provide the solutions in policing as the Nigerian delegates experienced in their investigative missions abroad. What works in Europe and America may not necessarily work in Nigeria.

If the NPF administrators adopt such a framework, legitimized by federal and state statutes that incorporate the partnership of informal police organizations in the NPF vision, citizens of Nigeria will be better protected from crime. Legalized IPS groups will make a formidable partnership to accomplish the goals and objectives of top-down policing in Nigeria. The official certification of IPS may be determined by licensures that are renewable each year by the NPF operators. This will assuage fears by Nigerian citizens that are a consequence of the historical misuse of the police by native authorities. Such a model would recognize and stimulate civil and traditional society initiatives. The national police will remain specialized and professional in the fight against crime, the apprehension of criminals, and the maintenance of law and order. Depending on its policing needs, each local area of the federation will decide if it will embrace this framework. Where no civil society inventiveness is in place, the NPF may initiate its own community policing program. The originality of African policing styles lies in the strength of informal policing as well as in the traditional justice systems (Okereaforezeke 2002; Elechi 2006), which should be stimulated rather than repressed and replaced by an imported CP brand that may be less efficient.

Conclusion

A reading of the Nigerian policing experts and their works (Tamuno, 1970; Marenin, 1985; Kayode, 1976; Ekpenyong, 1987; Iwarimie-Jaja, 1988; Ekeh, 1997) indicates evidence of police decentralization prior to colonial oppression, during colonial regime, and after political independence. Each region of the federation practiced its style of official and nonofficial styles of community policing. These scholars also observed that even the colonial government established different forms of its own police structures in order to control local leaders and divide them under the existing Nigerian federal government (Tamuno, 1970). The greatest blow to the continued advent of community policing existence was the invasion of military regimes into the Nigerian political life. For survival purposes, it was to the advantage of the military to suppress regional police formations so as to control the military armory. The fear that local areas would control police arsenals posed a significant threat to the dictatorial regimes in Nigeria. While other federal systems of government may practice community policing successfully, the uniqueness of Nigeria dictates that CP can better function under a decentralized federal system.

Furthermore, the Nigerian society is calling for a return to police decentralization due to rising crime rates, insecurity, and threats posed by the criminal underworld to the citizens and their local authorities. In Nigeria, the new reemergence of IPS groups, such as the Bakassi Boys, is primarily the result of feelings of insecurity at homes, towns, markets, and public squares in various communities. It is argued that by decentralizing the Nigerian police, the police will be closer to the people that they police. The police will be friendlier with the people, closer to the IPS groups, and familiar with IPS operations, and work as a team with local citizens.

References

Abinndu, C. (1999). *Government denies plan for state squads.* http:// File://\decentralizationli9.htm (accessed September 21, 1999).

Adebayo, D.O. (2005). Ethical attitudes and prosocial behavior in the Nigerian police: Moderator effects of perceived organizational support and public recognition. *Policing: An International Journal of Police Strategies and Management, 28*, 169–189.

Aderemi, S.J. (2006). Cultural nationalism, democratization, and conflict in Yoruba. Perspectives: Focus on O'odua Peoples Congress (OPC) in Nigerian politics. *Studies Tribes Tribals, 4*, 131–144.

Alemika, E.O. & Chukwuma, I.C. (2000). *Police community violence in Nigeria, Lagos. Center for Law Enforcement Education and National Human Rights Commission.* Lagos: CLEEN.

Alemika, E.E.O. & Chukwuma, I.C. (2004). *The Poor and Informal Policing in Nigeria. A Report on the Peoples' Perceptions and Priorities on Safety, Security and Informal Policing in A2J Focal States in Nigeria*, Lagos: CLEEN Foundation.

Anambra State Vigilante Services Law, No. 9. (2000, August 4). *Anambra State Official Gazette*, Awka.

Bailey, D.H. (1991). Community policing: A report from the devil's advocate. In J.R. Reene & S.D. Mastrofski (Eds.), *Community policing: Rhetoric or reality* (pp. 225–337). New York: Praeger.

Black, D. (1983). Crime as social control. *American Sociological Review, 48*, 34–45.

Broeck, T.V.D. (2002). Keeping up appearances? A community's perspective on community policing and the local governance of crime. *Policing: An International Journal of Police Strategies and Management, 25*, 169–189.

Cheurprakobkit, S. (2002). Community policing: Training, definitions and policy implications. *Policing: An International Journal of Police Strategies and Management, 25*, 709–725.

Chukwuma, I. (2000, July–September). Vigilantes and policing in Nigeria. *Law Enforcement Review.*

Chukwuma, I. (2002). Responding to vigilantism. *Human Rights Dialogue, Series 2*(8).

Constitution of the Federal Republic of Nigeria. (1989).

CLEEN Foundation. (2008a). *Community policing takes chief of police to United States.* http:/wwww.cleen.org (accessed March 31, 2008).

CLEEN Foundation. (2008b). *The poor and informal policing in Nigeria: A report on poor people's perceptions and priorities on safety, security and informal policing in A2J focal states in Nigeria.* Report written by E.O. Alemika & I.C. Chukwuma at the Center for Law Enforcement Education (CLEEN), Lagos. http:/wwww.cleen.org (accessed March 10, 2008).

Cordner, G.W. (1997). *Community policing: Elements and effects.* In R.G. Dunham & G.P. Alpert (Eds.), *Critical issues in policing: Contemporary readings* (pp. 45–468). Prospect Heights, IL: Waveland.

Dent, M.J. (1978). Corrective government: Military rule in perspective. In K. Panter-Brick (Ed.), *Soldiers and oil* (pp. 101–137). London: FrankCass.

Department of Justice (DoJ). (2008). International Criminal Investigative Training Assistance Program (ICITAP): Nigeria Project Overviews. http/www.usdoj.gov/criminal/icitap/textnigeria.html (accessed March 19, 2008).

Eck, J.E. & Spelman, W. (1989). Problem-solving: Problem-oriented policing in Newport News. In R.G. Dunham & Alpert, G.P. (Eds.), *Critical issues in policing: Contemporary readings* (pp. 489–503). Prospect Heights, IL: Waveland.

Ekeh, P.P. (1997). *Wilberforce conference on Nigerian federalism: Introduction, Association of Nigerian Scholars for Dialogue,* No. 1. Buffalo, NY: University of Buffalo.

Ekpenyong, R.A. (1987). Nigeria. In G.F. Cole, S.J. Frankowwki, & M.G. Gertz (Eds.) *Major criminal justice systems: A comparative view* (pp. 71–103). Newbury Park, CA: Sage.

Elechi, O.O. (2003). *Extra-judicial killings in Nigeria: The case of Afikpo town.* Paper presented at the 17th International Conference of the International Society for the Reform of Criminal Law, The Hague, The Netherlands.

Elechi, O.O. (2006). *Doing justice without the state: The Afikpo (Ehugbo) Nigeria model.* New York: Routledge.

French, P. (2001). *The Virtues of vengeance.* Lawrence: University Press of Kansas.

Gaines, L.K., Kappeler, V.E., & Vaughn, J.B. (1994). *Policing in America.* Cincinnati, OH: Anderson Publishing Company.

Goldstein, H. (1979). Improving policing: A problem-oriented approach. *Crime and Delinquency, 25,* 236–258.

Goldstein, H. (1990). *Problem-oriented policing.* New York: McGraw-Hill.

Greene, J.R. & Pelfrey, W.V. (1997). Shifting the balance of power between police and community: Responsibility for crime control. In R.G. Dunham & G.P. Alpert (Eds.), *Critical issues in policing: Contemporary readings* (pp. 393–423). Prospect Heights, IL: Waveland.

Heald, S. (2007). Controlling Crime and Corruption from Below: Sungusungu in Kenya. *International Relations* 21(2): 183–199.

Human Rights Watch. (2007). *Bakassi Boys.* http://hrwpubs.stores.yahoo.net/nigbakboy.html (accessed February 20, 2008).

Iwariniie-Jaja, D. (1988). The police system in Nigeria. *Criminal Justice International, 4,* 5–7.

Johnston, L. (1996). What is vigilantism? *British Journal of Criminology, 36,* 220–236.

Kayode, O. (1976). Public expectations and police role concepts: Nigeria. *Police Chief, 43,* 56–59.

Kolajo, A.A. (2000). *Customary law in Nigeria through the cases.* Ibadan, Nigeria: Spectrum Books.

Marenin, O. (1985). Policing Nigeria: Control and autonomy in the exercise of coercion. *African Studies Review, 28,* 73–93.

Newman, G.R. (2006). *Office of community oriented policing services: Problem guides series,* No. 38. Washington, D.C.: U.S. Department of Justice.

Nolte, I. (2007). Ethnic vigilantes and the state: The o'odua peoples congress in southwestern Nigeria. *International Relations, 21,* 217–235.

Norwegian Directorate of Immigration. (2004, February 23–28). Report from a fact-finding trip to Nigeria (Abuja, Kaduna, and Lagos). http://www.laninfo.no/asset/162/1/162_1.pdf (accessed March 20, 2008).

Ogugbuaja, C. (2002). *Imo chief judge deplore killings by Bakassi Boys.* http://www.nigeriannews.com/ (accessed February 27, 2002).

Okereaforezeke (Okafor), N. (2002). *Law and justice in post-British Nigeria: Conflicts and interactions between native and foreign systems of social control in Igbo.* Westport, CT: Greenwood Press.

Okereaforezeke (Okafor), N. (2007). Traditional social control in an ethnic society: Law enforcement in a Nigerian community 1. *Police Practice and Research: An International Journal, 4*, 21–33.

Onwudiwe, I.D. (2000). Decentralization of the Nigerian Police Force. *The International Journal of African Studies, 2*, 95–114.

Onwudiwe, I.D. (2001). Policing democracy. In D. Livinson (Ed.), *Encyclopedia of crime and punishment* (pp. 1200–1203). Thousand Oaks, CA: Sage.

Peak, K.J. (2009). *Policing America: Challenges and Best Practices*. Upper Saddle River, NJ: Prentice Hall.

Scharf, W. (2000). *Community justice and community policing in post-apartheid South Africa. How appropriate are justice systems in Africa?* Workshop on the rule of law and development, Institute for Development Studies, University of Sussex, U.K.

Shaw, M. (2000). *Crime and policing in transitions: Comparative perspectives*. Johannesburg: SAIIA.

Simonsen, C.E. & Spindlove, J.R. (2004). *Terrorism today: The past, the players, the future*. Upper Saddle River, NJ: Prentice Hall.

Tamuno, T.N. (1970). *The police in modern Nigeria, 1861-1965*. Ibadan, Nigeria: University Press.

Tertsakian, C. (2003). *The O'odua Peoples Congress: Fighting violence with violence*, New York, Human Rights Watch.

ThisDay. (2004). *Nigeria: Legislation on community policing soon*. http://www.nigeriannews.com/ (accessed November 9, 2004).

Trojanowicz, R. & Bucquerroux, B. (1990). *Community policing*. Cincinnati, OH: Anderson Publishing Company.

Walker, S. (1997). *"Broken windows" and fractured history: The use and misuse of history in recent police patrol analysis*. In R.G. Dunham & G.P. Alpert (Eds.), *Critical issues in policing: Contemporary readings* (pp. 451–468). Prospect Heights, IL: Waveland.

Wisler, D. & Onwudiwe, I.D. (in press). Community policing in comparison. *Police Quarterly*.

Wilson, J.Q. & Kelling, G.L. (1997). *Broken windows*. In R.G. Dunham & G.P. Alpert (Eds.), *Critical issues in policing: Contemporary readings* (pp. 424–437). Prospect Heights, IL: Waveland.

The French Centralized Model of Policing
Control of the Citizens

5

CHRISTIAN MOUHANNA

Contents

Introduction

From a theoretical point of view, the French system of policing seems to be one of the more rational and one of the more efficient of Western democracies. The national police forces, which represent the main part of the police forces, are organized in a very hierarchical and centralized way. All rules governing these forces are produced in a top-down logic, supervised by the *Ministère de l'Intérieur* (Home Office) in Paris. This centralization is supposed to offer the best way to use the police officers and the materials.

Actually, this kind of management is related to a more global paradigm, which explains the functioning of the French state and the French society. First, it has to be said that the police force is not the only organization following this model. Schools and energy supplies—and also essential parts of the French economy—were until the end of the 1990s organized in a national and centralized system. Every public service, in the French sense, was supposed to be delivered by the state and its administrations. Of course, security and safety were also provided by the national government.

In this system, there is no place for any intermediary like communities, churches, or other kinds of organization between the state and the people: the citizens are directly confronted to the national level and the state officials (Zauberman & Levy, 2003). Even local governments were evaluated on their ability to obtain credits and facilities from the central government. Until the 1980s and the first laws on "*décentralisation,*" local authorities were not allowed to take part in any policy dealing with economic or social matters and were totally excluded from policy management in the field of safety and security. The main goal of the centralized state was to maintain the direct link with the citizen. That is why the idea of community policing was totally unthinkable in the French politicians and high-level civil servants' mind. Firstly, there is no recognition of any community, and, secondly, it is irrelevant to have a police force depending on any other power than the national state.

That explains why the security has for a long time been a national topic more in France than in other countries. The national government is solely responsible for the service given to the citizen. The presidential election in 2002 has shown how important the question of public safety is in France as illustrated by the candidacy of Jean-Marie Le Pen, a leader of the extreme right for the second round of the election. The question of security was one pillar of his campaign. It was also a very popular topic in the media before the election, and certainly the socialist leader lost the election in 2002 because he was not able to present a program in order to face the growing concern about public security. Present President Nicholas Sarkozy, one of the qualified candidates before being elected in 2007, built his public security reputation during his tenure as *Ministre de l'Intérieur* (2002–2004, 2005–2007).

Even if there is a direct link between the state and the citizen, it must be emphasized that the situation is far from being enviable for the latter, i.e., the citizen. In France, security concerns are national in nature; they cannot be delegated to local authorities, citizens, or communities. The national government wants to be the one who decides. That is why the centralization of the national police forces has always been the main rule. The history of the diverse form of community policing in France will illustrate how every reform trying to change this rule has no chance of succeeding. This is not only a question of police officers' culture, as it is often underlined in the French case; the police organization has been unable to build a real proximity to the population because they are answerable to the central police command that wields power. Many examples could show how some police officers who wanted to be more open to the society have been rejected by their organization. We will examine the main reforms of the police and their implementation on the field. We will also discuss the differences between the two French police forces: the

French *Police Nationale* and the French *Gendarmerie Nationale.* Although these two forces are centralized, they are very different in their practices.

A System Not Focused on Public Service

Consequences of Centralization

Before looking at the reforms that have tried to modify the policy of policing in France, it is useful to state what centralization exactly means inside the police forces. The first point is that the police officers are expected to follow national policies. In this top-down system, their priority is to act as if everything was planned, not to answer to the demand of the public. To illustrate how heavy and precise this system was, one may recall that until the beginning of the 1990s, police officers from the whole of France, from Marseille to Lille, were supposed to change their winter uniforms for the summer ones simultaneously as dictated by the central police HQ.

As far as the human resources policy is concerned, it has to be underlined that the recruitment of the police officers—as well as the gendarmes—is made at a national level. Most of them are coming from small cities in the quietest parts of France, and are sent to urban centers for their first assignments. There are two causes that explain this movement. One is the officers' career. After one or two years, they are allowed to ask for a new position and they have the use of this possibility. Indeed, all of these young officers prefer to quit the most dangerous districts where they know nobody and to go to another place closer to their home region. And after two or three years in this second place, they change again. They continue to do the same until they arrive in the city that they prefer. The global result is a movement that affects the entire country. Young police officers always take the position of the older colleague who has left the place, and are waiting for a position available near their home city. Another consequence is that many police officers are working in districts where they are not involved in the local life, and where they often reject the population because they have no association with them.

But the other reason that explains this movement is not the consequence of individual choices. It refers to national policy. The national administration of the police forces has for some time established rules that put the stress on mobility. Like in all French centralized administrations, the main idea is that the civil servants' changes help to prevent them from getting too close and personal with the population. This rule was historically adopted in order to fight against regionalism and in order to create a nation with civil servants more attached to the central government than to the local society. Their mission is to enforce national laws, not to adapt them. Of course, the managers also believe that the preservation of a gap between the civil servants and the population could prevent the latter from corruption. Following this tradition, the national police administration frequently reminds its troops that the movement is the rule, and that every officer, including the high-level officer, is not to stay more than two or three years in the same place.

As a result, the police officers are very reluctant to be involved in the local life and to work in order to solve the problems of the citizens because they know that they will not stay long enough in the same place to see the result of their prospective involvement. Actually, a large number have their families remain in their home region. They spend four or five days in the city where they work and then drive or take a train to live with a "real" life among their family and their friends far away from the workplace for a couple of days. During the week, the vast majority of these officers have only to relate to the people they arrest. They refuse to hear about the local problems and often look at the population of their districts with prejudice.

However, this way of functioning also has another fundamental consequence, which is dealing with the question of intelligence. Because they act as if they are strangers in the city where they work—and, in fact, they are—it is almost impossible for them to build a network. Therefore, it is a difficult challenge for them to investigate a crime. The development of technologies for identification or of diverse kind of files is supposed to replace the direct knowledge, but nobody has yet to prove this. Without information and local relationships, the police officers enter main areas with a lot of uncertainty: Is the place quiet or not, are the police accepted or not, who are the good guys and the bad ones, etc.? The result is that the risk of being trapped is high and unpredictable. The lack of support among the population increases this risk. That is why a number of police officers stress the fear they feel when they enter one of these sensitive suburbs that has became world known after the riots of November 2005. One of the major concerns in the police stations is to protect the police building and to preserve the troops from being injured. As a result, many observers say that the police are more interested in their own protection than in the public one.

Facing this central organization, the local police chiefs have little power because they are also committed at the national level. They are not allowed to manage their staff like they want. For example, the organizational rules, the officers' functions, and the methods of punishment against offenders are controlled by the decisions of the top echelon of the national police command. The police officers' unions represent another limit to the chiefs' power. While France is a country with a weak rate of unionization (5% for the private sector, 15% for the civil servants in 2005), 75% of the police officers belong to unions. It is important for the union members because all the movements that we have described before and all the changes in the structures are controlled by special commissions in which these unions have a great place. These organizations defend equity and prevent the chiefs from using any discretionary power. And, these unions follow the centralized model. Every decision in the commission is adopted for the whole of France and must be implemented in every district. For example, if one chief of district wants to assign some officers to another unit, he will have to face not only the unions, but also the top-level management who is responsible for the entire organization.

In order to lead such a centralized organization, a system of reporting is needed. Many police officers spend all of their time creating statistics and developing analyses for the hierarchy. Headquarters can be found at different levels. Indeed, all police officers, including those who belong to patrol units or to criminal investigation groups, have to produce many reports in order to justify their activities. The national police force is surely one of the biggest French bureaucracies. Therefore, the national police force is an organization hard to reform and more interested in its own problems than in the society and its problems. Even if reporting has always been a big task, the introduction of the New Public Management in this organization is likely to have increased the part of paperwork. As I will stress later, instead of creating a new kind of management more open to the service due to the citizens, the reforms have led to reinforcement of the central administration and of the bureaucratic way of functioning.

The Public Order: Protect the State

I would like to shed some light on one other consequence of police centralization. Because the security problems are treated at a national level, the French government is very sensitive to this question. The government always wants to show that it is the only one that holds the power on the police. This notion means that it is the state (i.e., the central government) in France that exercises the legal monopoly of force. However, the state is not only the provider of security, it is also the first beneficiary of the police services (Monjardet, 1996).

What does it mean? As it was outlined before, security is a pillar of the French republic. In a country well known for its tradition of revolution and demonstration, the government not only wants to control the police forces, but also wants to use them in order to be protected. That means that a large portion of police staff is mobilized to protect the state, its buildings, and its services. The most important priority for the police forces is to prevent public movements that could create a danger for the institutions. Around 17,000 *gendarmes mobiles* out of 84,000 gendarmes, and 14,000 police officers out of 119,000 serve in "riot police forces" whose purpose is to maintain public order. These troops are not attached to a territory for the reasons that have been evoked before; they are needed to keep a gap with the population in order to better control it. Actually, the *compagnies de gendarmerie mobile* and the *compagnies républicaines de sécurité* are deployed all over the French territory, but they rarely or never intervene where they live. Though they are barracked in the city of their posting, they are on the road half the year or more. Their placement varies constantly across the French territory, depending on which neighborhoods are thought to be facing potential trouble. They always work in groups, never alone. Trained and equipped to deal with demonstration and riots, they are not supposed to negotiate or to speak with the public (Bruneteau, 1993). These forces do nothing but seek to prevent riots, contain demonstrations, and patrol in at-risk sectors.

These units, which stay as a reserve in case of troubles, are not the only ones involved in public order. Among other local police forces—who do not belong to the former group—a number of officers serve in "intervention squads," whose role is very similar to that of riot police forces. All police officers, even those who are supposed to answer emergency calls, have to deal with public order, and patrol police officers are especially trained to "handle" riots and demonstrations. Although the French government has tried to limit their involvement in these matters, many police officers guard public buildings or protect official visits. As far as the police chiefs are concerned, they are very sensitive to orders from the central hierarchy because their career depends more on their result in the field than on their satisfactory relationship with the citizens.

The French police force has a longstanding tradition of riot control. It has developed specific skills and strategies designed to ensure that these situations are properly handled. One of the main concepts is to prevent riots and violence before they happen through a balance of power that swings toward state forces. This requires that the state has enough police officers on the field to be sure that the demonstrators cannot control the streets. Such a tradition leads to a strategy of containment, not to cooperation. Therefore, many police officers avoid building a relationship with the inhabitants of the territories; their interests do not lie in this direction. The result of this lack of commitment is a problem of intelligence: it makes it hard for these police officers to gather information.

Because the government does not want to get involved in local problems and because it is not able to face all of these local situations, it manages the police organization through national top-down guidelines that are not always adapted to the territories. The police officer is not supposed to think by himself and to adapt his strategy to his environment; he must follow the national priorities.

Governing the Police through Figures

The lack of information in each district, the inability to deal with all specific cases, and the need to face the issues of policing at a national level lead the government to a management style based on figures. Every centralized bureaucracy uses quantitative indicators to assess their actions. But, inside the police forces, this concern has become more and more significant, and especially during the past 10 years. Because they have to evaluate and to provide means to more than 400 police departments and almost 100 *gendarmeries*' forces spread over 3,600 locations, central civil servants prefer to have simple tools in order to measure the activity of each unit. Therefore, statistics, in this case, are the best way to manage a centralized and complex organization.

However, statistics are not only a tool implying rational choices. Because they appear to provide synthetic information, they have always tended to take a growing place inside the police forces at different levels. As stated above, the national administration of the police forces is very fond of these figures, and especially of the crime and clearance rates that are required monthly. And, for all the hierarchy, the production of these statistics has for a long time become a main concern. The police at local levels are subjected to a double constraint. On the one hand, they are reluctant to display dreadful figures because they could be regarded as inefficient. On the other hand, they are also careful not to overrate the statistics because the central administration could use this argument to make cuts in staff. This explains why local chiefs spend a lot of their time trying to arrange the presentation of their figures. Some cases are stored or forgotten, some others are regarded as out of the range of official statistics (Matelly & Mouhanna, 2007).

As far as the clearance rate is concerned, there are many strategies on how to increase the figures. Police officers focus on the type of crime that produces rates equal to 100%. For example, the fight against drug users or prostitution leads to situations where the crimes are discovered and the perpetrator of the crime is identified at the same time. In that case, clearance rates are equal to 100%, or even more than 100%. By contrast, clearance rates for other type of crimes, like burglaries, are less than 10%. If the police districts want to present statistics that would appear less bad, they have to put the stress on the first type of crime in order to reach a presentable average between bad and good statistics no matter what the public thinks about this priority. Another strategy is voluntarily "to forget" to register the complaints, or to invite the victim to submit the complaints to other police stations. Doing so, the police officers try to avoid facing the less easily solved crimes that lead to bad figures. Here can be found an advantage for the police officers belonging to a national administration: accountability is not their business. Even if the public is not satisfied with the reception at the police station, there are few ways of filing complaints. There is neither an ombudsman nor a local representative available to answer their complaints. Also, if somebody wants to protest, he is likely to be charged with "*outrage*" (i.e., insult to a police officer, which is a crime in France). In that sense, we can argue that the figures are not a tool that helps to produce a better service to the citizens, but a tool that is mainly devoted to internal management.

However, the statistics also have an impact on citizens. We have to remember that the fear of crime has been for a while a major issue during the diverse elections in France, both local and presidential. Paradoxically, the mayors have been held responsible for the question of security and policing, although they are not allowed to take part in the command of the police forces. Therefore, the mayors worry about the statistics published for their own cities. Bad figures can be used as an argument by their opponents. But, the mayors are powerless in this regard and can only rely on the goodwill of the police unit in their cities, as the mayors do not possess the power to direct the police. The situation is quite different at the national level. In centralized organization, the government is able to put pressure on the police services in order to obtain "good statistics." When he was *Ministre de l'Intérieur*, the current French president clearly stressed this point. He was very convincing to the heads of police services. At the beginning of his mandate, every month, the chiefs of the districts that had the worst results were invited to the *Ministère* and were required to justify their bad figures. And, nobody wanted to be there twice!

The pressure has consistently been passed from the top chiefs to the lowest ranks. Each level has tried to present his superior statistics that reflect his expectations. The pressure varies considerably from one period to another, and most chiefs are sensitive to this because their careers can be speeded up or slowed down due to these figures. Sometimes, they prefer rearranging the figures rather than relaying the true numbers. For example, they usually are not ready to accept an increase of complaints if the government has ordered an improvement in security. Also, they encourage their troops to suppress the demands that are not acceptable from a national point of view. Even if all chiefs are more or less involved in this system, from the top echelon to the street-level commanders, this causes several problems. A management system that emphasizes the measurement of activity without any concern for accountability becomes a prisoner of its own figures. Statistics prevent the police officers from being evaluated on anything else than internal topics. The focus on statistics and the gap between reality and the actual reports lead to a loss of a chief's credibility. When the street-level police officer solves a problem, it doesn't appear in the statistics. Many police officers do not accept this logic and feel uncomfortable, but they are not able to change the organization because the cost of individual investment is high and not enough to produce collective change.

Looking at these main elements that characterize the French system of policing, one could argue that this Weberian bureaucratic model does not need to develop any kind of community policing strategy. The public is not considered as a community, the top-down centralized control and command organization is far from accepting the demands from the street-level police officers, and even the system of information is not built in a way that offers enough elements to answer to the public demand. The main task for the police forces is to control and contain the population, and especially the ones who seem to be the most dangerous for the state. The consequence is a politicization of the debate about security matters. Because he is not allowed to get into a community in order to criticize the policy of policing, because he has no other way to protest or to be heard, and because the local politicians do not have the power to answer to their wills, the citizen expresses his concern on security through national debates or through his vote. The nationalization of security concerns leads to a vicious circle because it reinforces the need to control the police forces from the center and keeps the problems from being solved when they are only local ones. When these problems become national issues, the answers are harder to find and they can be more or less inappropriate.

The result of this policy is a costly organization and a growing dissatisfaction among the citizens, especially in the poor suburbs. In this context, a vast communication offensive is often the best answer from the government's view. During the past 30 years, both law and order and more smooth policies have alternatively been announced in the media. Each time, the government promotes the reform that be will an answer to all problems, without looking at the past experiences. From this point of view, the story of community policing in France is more a question of communication than a real change in the policy of policing. Moreover, these reforms are likely to have widened the gap between the police and the population.

Police Practices: Between Bureaucracy and Hidden Way of Acting

Before looking at the impact of these reforms, let us examine the police officer's concrete practices. For a long time in France, sociologists have described the consequences of a centralized and top-down organization on the civil servants who are working face-to-face with the public (Dupuy & Thoenig, 1983). One of them is a lack of rigor in applying the rules. Dealing with concrete problems that are not always prescribed by the official rules, the civil servants have often tried to adapt them to the situation that they have to face. Sometimes, they do not hesitate to cheat or to forget to apply all the rules because they are involved in a human relationship, far from the general, inappropriate, and abstract laws. The street level bureaucrats (Lipsky, 1980) always detained a part of discretion that can be used in favor of the citizens, even if it can also be used against the citizen. Of course, the local police officers belong to this street level bureaucracy (Ericson, 1982). This concrete remark leads us to examine the police officer practices not only through a global and institutional point of view, but also through his position inside his environment. Although police officers are involved in very centralized and hierarchical organizations, they are able to interpret the rules because they are also involved in interactions with the public and because they live among people.

The Police Officer and the Rules

We have already described how the national system of recruitment does not help the police officers to build close relationships with the citizens. We also have underlined how the hierarchy is important in building the priorities. However, looking at several police stations and making a comparison between *Police Nationale* and *Gendarmerie Nationale*, it is easy to find a number of differences in the practices. Although the structures are almost identical, the involvement in the local society differs from one place to another. We want to point out three elements that explain these differences.

The first one is linked to the age of the police officers. If they have to begin their career in a city far from their home region, after a while it is possible that they could reach a city that suits them. Some do prefer to go to small cities with fewer problems. The oldest police officers often work in areas where they develop better relationships with the citizens and know a number of people in their district. Thus, they want to stay in that same place for many years. They are more concerned, however, with what the citizens think about their actions. These older police officers have also learned that they do not have to respect all the rules. They try to avoid punishing people, especially when these people belong to the middle and upper classes. Even in poorest areas, they sometimes try to build better contacts in order to prevent disorders and to ensure their own security. Although they could use the rules to punish all the offenders, they choose to put the stress on negotiation (Mouhanna, 2002). They ignore some offences, but keep an eye on the offender. When threats are not always implemented, they become a tool to prevent these abuses from ever occurring again. People are grateful to the police because they have given them a chance. That explains why in some cities, the *Police Nationale* have a better image than those in the poor suburbs of big cities, where young police officers strictly adhere to all the rules.

A second element that explains the differences deals with the function of the police officers. A police officer working in the *Compagnies Républicaines de Sécurité* is more likely to be more severe than a patrol officer who spends a lot of time in the same area. A foot patroller alone in the street is less able to follow the rules than a group of four police officers in one car because he has not enough means or backup to implement the rules. Beyond these obvious elements, it has to be emphasized that the police officer's goal structures his relations with the public (Shearing and Ericson, 1991). For example, a juvenile squad whose main mission is to protect the children against abuses is more likely to try to understand why these children are involved in crime than a unit specialized in fighting against street crime, whose main "clients" are the victims of these children. Or, a drug squad often chooses to ignore small drug dealers' offenses in order to obtain from them information about bigger dealers. Each unit inside the police develops its own culture and builds its own priorities. It means that they have to choose between many different tasks that are not compatible with each other. It is impossible for the police officers to answer to all priorities for which they are asked. If they want to get help and information from the citizens, they have to be flexible; otherwise, they are not accepted in the community.

A third element important in understanding how the police officers really act combines organization and environment. The comparison between *Police Nationale* and *Gendarmerie Nationale* illustrates this idea, which is fundamental to explaining why the reforms of the police in France have failed, or even have worsened the former situation.

Two Models of Policing in France

If the two forces are organized on the same ground, with a top-down management and a strong hierarchical principle of command and control, they are very different in their practices. The French *Police Nationale* is a civil force, with civil servants who can belong to unions. This police force is in charge of urban areas. There are 424 police districts *(circonscriptions)* in France. All the police officers working in a city and its suburbs are dependent on one chief, the *commissaire central de police*, who is responsible for the whole district. Even if this *commissaire* has to answer to the dictates of the central direction of the police in Paris, he has also to take into account local demands emerging from the city's mayor or from the citizens. It should be noted that the modernization of the police forces during the 1970s has led to the reorganization of all the troops into one large police station in the city, in which are located the *commissaire* and his/her headquarters, the switchboard where all emergency calls are directed, and all units. A lot of small police stations located in different parts of the cities were closed during the 1970s and 1980s because it was considered too costly and because the chiefs did not control the police officers there. The principle was to build large organizations with specialized units.

The French *Gendarmerie* is a military force with military traditions. This status produces a lot of constraints for the gendarmes. They are not allowed to belong to unions and they have to live in barracks with their families. They are supposed to be on duty 24 hours a day. The *Gendarmerie* is mainly the police force of the rural areas, which still represents one half of the French population. More than 3,000 *brigades de gendarmerie* (the smallest unit) are distributed throughout French territory. Most of them have less than 10 gendarmes. There are specialized units, but they are located in big cities, far from the brigades. Therefore, the local forces have to face all the problems with their own staff. Of course, there is a strong hierarchy, with four different levels of command and control between the brigades and the general direction of the *Gendarmerie* in Paris (Dieu, 2002). But, it is impossible to have a tough control on all the brigades because they are a far distance from the chiefs.

An outside observer could argue that a military police force is likely to be more authoritarian and less democratic. Military regimes are the opposite of an open and peaceful democracy. However, as far as the practices are concerned in France, it has to be admitted that the *Gendarmerie* was more a model of community policing than the *Police Nationale*, at least until the beginning of the twenty-first century. There are many reasons that can explain this fact. One refers to the military tradition of the French army. Following the example of the French colonial army and French military administrators of the former colonies, such as Louis H. B. Lyautey,* the French soldiers have developed a myth of closeness with the people. Although we are far from idealizing the French colonial past, there is still a tradition inside the army—the idea is that the general rules have to be adapted to the local situation and customs. This tradition persists in the *Gendarmerie* and, to be exact, it endured until the beginning of the 2000s.

Some of the practical explanations of this trend stems from the fact that the gendarmes mostly live in small villages where everybody is well known. Because of their military status, they are not allowed, like the *policiers*, to have their home far away from the place where they work. Therefore, there is little gap between their personal and their professional life. The *gendarmes* are supposed to be on duty 24 hours a day, which reinforces the idea that they are always present to solve problems. Traditionally, the *gendarmes* have been involved in the local social life. They were doing their shopping in the villages under their jurisdictions. Their children went to school in the village where the barracks were located. Paradoxically, their obligations to live in the place where they work led them to be closer to the population they watched over than the police officers (Mouhanna, 2001). They were a key element of the local society, acting as judges and sometimes as welfare workers. Of course, the rural culture is also quite different from the urban culture, as it was underlined a long time ago (Tonnies, 1887). The socialization of the young gendarmes with their oldest colleague has been also very important. The gendarmes were bound to maintain good relationships with the local society because they depended on the public in order to have information and even resources. The Central Direction has never been able to provide

* Louis Hubert Gonzalve Lyautey (1854–1934), general and colonial administrator, especially in occupied Morocco (Lyautey, 1900).

enough resources to allow the *gendarmes* to be efficient without help from outside. Although the *policiers* were civil officers, they rarely succeeded in building a deep relationship with the public, as did the gendarmes.

Our main concern here is to put the stress on the gap between official and formal organization and the concrete practices (Terrill & Mastrofski, 2004). As we will argue, all the reforms that have tried to improve or to impose different kinds of community policing in France have failed because of the lack of relevant analysis of this gap. Whenever they announced a change of structures in order to create a new form of policing, the police heads and the politicians in charge of these policies produced a more centralized organization.

Reform and Police Officers' Practices: Reinforcing the Command and Control System

Our description of the French centralized police forces, designed in order to protect the state more than the citizens, prompts us to imagine that community policing is far from being a natural movement inside these organizations. We have stressed the involvement of some police officers and of many gendarmes in a close partnership with the population. However, this involvement is not an official strategy, but rather a practice often hidden, that most of the heads of the police forces prefer to ignore. Some of them are even ready to criticize this kind of strategy, by denouncing it as corrupt or lacking in respect for the laws. Apart from the question of policing, one of the basic principles of the French Republic is that there is no intermediary between the citizen and the state. Therefore, it is not possible to recognize any community as a partner for public policies. That is why there has officially never been any community policing in France. The French government spoke about *îlotage*, coming from the French word *îlot* (i.e., block) and later about *police de proximité* (neighborhood policing). The main idea was to create a police force closer to the population, but without a real involvement of the public in the police strategy (Monjardet, 1999).

A First Attempt without Benefit of Instruction

The history of the French modern police reforms began in the late 1970s with the conservative *Ministre* Alain Peyrefitte who organized a commission charged to find a solution to what was called "*a growing violence in the society*" (Peyrefitte, 1977). One of the results of this diagnosis was the lack of confidence in the police forces and a need to build a better relationship between the population and these forces. The problem was particularly relevant for the *Police Nationale* and less for the *Gendarmerie*. However, the government never applied the results of this work and preferred to pass law enforcement measures. When the socialist François Mitterrand became president in 1981, the government tried to implement this idea of a new policing because they thought that police forces had to stop being a tool for repression directed to lower classes and leftist movements (Belorgey, 1991). Beyond the question of the relationship between the national police forces and the citizens, it must be noted that the government also wanted to limit the need for vigilantism or for local police forces that emerged in various communities. Although they were far from being as developed as today, they were perceived as competitors and dangers for the government's monopoly of policing. In that sense, the creation of a police force closer to the population was also a means used to preserve the centralized system.

In order to improve the contacts between the police and the different parts of the society without upsetting the police officers, they decided to promote an old practice: the *îlotage*. The main principles of this old fashioned way of policing were undoubtedly simple: foot patrols were created, with the same police officers always working in the same area. This visible action aimed to reassure the citizens whose fear was to diminish with this permanent presence. Unlike their colleagues, these patrol officers were allowed to speak with the citizens, and especially with the youngsters, who were said to represent the greatest danger for the citizenry. The patrol officers were encouraged to spend their time speaking with shopkeepers, janitors, and the elderly in order to allay their concerns. Although some of the police officers were enthusiastic and were very much involved in this work, such as playing football (soccer) with young males in poor suburbs and organizing meetings with the inhabitants in order to provide them with solutions to their problem of safety and security, many of the officers were very reluctant to do what was not considered a "real police job." For these men and women, the main goal of a police force was not to keep the peace in the streets or to reassure people, but to arrest bad guys; they did everything they could to avoid serving on foot patrol units. They found this way of patrolling both dangerous and tiring because they were called to solve all sorts of problems at any given moment. They felt more "protected" in their cars, protected from any aggression, and also from public demands.

However, the street-level police officers were not the only ones who slowed down the development of a different police force. The police chiefs were not ready to abandon the hierarchical and centralized organization. For these chiefs, the new form of policing was perceived as a loss of power because the priorities were determined by citizens' demands. They didn't have any idea of their staff's work and were not able to evaluate it through statistics. The chiefs were not ready to recognize the police officers' autonomy, even if it was only an official recognition of the police discretion. They resisted reforming to the new system by failing to apply the reforms. If the official policy was to transform 6,000 police officers in *îlotiers*, only a few of them were really involved in a real strategy following the basic principles of a police force that serve the needs of the citizens. The others were only part-time *îlotiers*; in a reverse of the new policy, they changed from one place to another each day, or transported prisoners to court.

In the few places where the experiment was really implemented, *îlotage* generated a real satisfaction among the public and the practitioners. *Ilotage's* practices also led to the reduction of fear of crime among many communities (Weisburd & Eck, 2004). Without official support, this concrete and pragmatic problem-solving policing strategy (Goldstein, 1990) met with certain success in many places, but stayed isolated inside the police organizations. *Ilotiers*, considered by their peers to be weak, were excluded from corporatist networks. *Ilotage* was never recognized as a successful reform at a national scale because of the reluctance of the chiefs, who transmitted many criticisms about this new idea of policing to the upper levels of command and control. Additionally, there was evidence of little enthusiasm as exhibited by the vast majority of the police officers who were afraid of the development of this nonmasculine style of policing, coupled with the fear of many politicians who saw the danger of a police force that no longer served the interest of the government. The centralized organization was frightened by the development of autonomy among police officers, which threatened to undermine one pillar of the centralized French Republic. Despite the citizens' enthusiasm for this new form of policing in the places where the police chiefs and the police officers played the game, the government acceded to the gradual demise of *îlotage*. The police officers involved in local networks had to prove that they were able to arrest people and that they could produce good statistics. The increase of bad figures concerning crime rates was a good justification for ending this experiment of *îlotage*. The excesses of some *îlotiers*, who spoke with young offenders instead of taking them to court, it was argued, have demonstrated the consequences of unregulated police activity.

The Second Attempt: Law and Order Proximity

In 1997, surprisingly coming back into power, the newly elected socialist government tried once more to reinvent policing. They had to cope with a dilemma. Although many socialists were still in favor of a police force closer to the population, they were not allowed to go back to *îlotage* because the so-called weakness of this strategy had led to a rising crime rate. The solution they found was to create *la police de proximité*, a police force still close to the population, but with a main goal: to use their involvement in the population solely to catch offenders. Even if the new *police de proximité* seems to look like the former *îlotage*, it was quite different. The methods were strictly defined by the heads of the police force, following a top-down model. Instead of being free of setting their own priorities, the police officers who belonged to the new force were bound to produce measurable results. In fact, the police heads decided to open small police stations in every district of the cities and especially in the poorest suburbs. Between 6 and 10 police officers were assigned to a police station in one district. It was ironic to see that the police forces reopened this type of police stations that have been closed 15 years earlier because they were costly and old-fashioned. It was also surprising to note that although the new organization was a replica of the traditional *Gendarmerie,* indeed, both organizations and forces were in competition with each other.

Like the *îlotiers* or the *gendarmes*, the new *policiers de proximité* had to improve contacts with the local population, but only in order to take complaints and to arrest offenders. The main issue was not only to solve security problems, but to "produce" cases that could be sent to the courts. This explains why, unlike the *îlotiers* (who were not allowed to take complaints), the new police officers *de proximité* are encouraged to do so. This difference sheds light on a very important point. With this second reform, the French government wanted to create a police force closer to the population, but also one better able to control the citizens by learning more about crimes and offenses, and by moving them through the judicial system. Undeniably, this new strategy was expected to agree more with the police officers' views about safety and security matters because they no longer were asked to be social workers or to play football (soccer) with youngsters. They were supposed to use their judicial powers and to use it to conduct law and order enforcement strategies.

Many of these police officers embraced their law enforcement functions, but instead of spending their time in the streets, they stayed in the police stations and registered citizen complaints that they were often unable to solve. The courts were totally overwhelmed by the number of cases for which they had to deal. As a result, there was a dramatic increase in official crimes and offenses and decrease in clearance rates. In the districts where the police officers succeeded in creating better relationships with the citizens, the figures were worse because the people were content with participating in the process, interacted with the police, and believed that finding solutions to the problem of crime is a common problem shared by the police and the citizens, the former put to the police cases that they would not have if the relationship were not so good. The new *police de proximité* helped to reveal a pattern of dark figures of crime because citizens filed many official complaints in order to solve crimes. For example, young pupils with belligerent behaviors in the playgrounds and the problem of noise in the neighborhoods were brought to the attention of the police in the form of official complaints. The search for judicial cases encouraged police officers to treat all these hidden problems in an official manner, instead of trying to find pragmatic solutions or to issue warnings to potential violators (Mouhanna, 2002). Whatever the real increase of crime, this strategy has led France to a vicious circle with a growing concern about crime. Our purpose is not to say that the *police de proximité* generated the growing fear of crime, but it is obvious that this strategy, developed to give an answer to this concern, by contrast has promoted an increasing fear because it increased the numbers of crime revealed, and because it participated in transforming social problems or problems of relationship between people into crime and offenses.

This theme takes us back to the question of politics. During local and national elections that followed the reform of *police de proximité*, the socialists were unable to defend this innovation or provide plausible answer to the attacks that described the police as lazy, weak, and inefficient. The paradox was cruel. Although the socialist government insisted on the repressive character of the *police de proximité*, denying the police officers' right to work in prevention or in problem-solving strategies, the same government was accused of favoring the rise of crime. Refusing to assume an innovative policy, and declining to believe in a different way of policing, which is looking for equilibrium between the social part and the repressive part of the police action, the leftist government lost the elections.

Counterrevolution of Policing

The conservative party wanted first and foremost to give a definitive answer to the question of crime that had favored the rise of an extreme right party for more than 15 years. Although local police forces and private security companies had increased during this period, the new government was not ready to abandon the myth of a national and centralized power of policing the society. In order to convince the police officers to work primarily for the state, the government gave a lot of money to the police officers and to their chiefs. Officers were also provided with new materials, such as police vehicles, nonlethal arms, and a new system of files. The aim was clear and was exposed in official discourses, making it difficult to criticize the police forces or to try to reform them. The strategy was designed to "win the battle against crime" by giving the police forces all the means, including new laws, in order to build a zero tolerance society. This strategy also represented a return to the old practices that was never completely abandoned. The question is no longer to improve the relationship between the public and the police forces, but to improve the centralized command and control system, which situates the government and especially the *Ministre de l'Intérieur* at the center of everything.

The idea was to limit police officers' autonomy and discretion by reinforcing the hierarchy and the weight of national rules. Two traditional ways were used to achieve this goal. Firstly, the production of good statistics was assigned to police officers with a strengthening system of control. Published every month, these figures have to prove that the situation is under control of the government. Generally, these tactics of the government put a gratuitous pressure on the police officers, making it tricky for them to have dialog about infractions and a denial of discretion in the performance of their law enforcement functions. If they want to avoid blame and earn more money, they have to be severe and to have cases sent to the courts. Clearance rates have shown unbelievable progress. The publication of crime statistics has been transformed into "good news." Secondly, the *Ministre de l'Intérieur* has repeatedly insisted on a black-and-white vision of society, which emphasizes "good" police officers that fight crime and young offenders from the poor suburbs who menace society. Apart from being an ideology, this discourse has also another utility: it prevents the police officers from being in a strategy of openness and locks them in logic of confrontation. Even the observers of this situation have no choice; they have to sustain the police forces or be suspected of encouraging disorder.

From a neutral point of view, one could ask whether these policies met success or not. There are several answers to this question. For the *Ministre* who has become president, Sarkozy obviously took advantage of these strategies, which were elaborated in short-term logic. The riots in the French suburbs at the later part of 2005 could have thwarted his career. But this point is not our main concern. As far as community policing, proximity policing, or neighborhood policing are concerned, France presents now a typical example of the refusal of any opening of the police forces to the public demand. Definitely, public demand regarding security has to be presented to the national government, who will decide which answer will be the good one. Today, the main answer is a zero tolerance policy. If some people seem to be satisfied with this kind of answer, many citizens are now deploring an overly simplified way of acting that produces a lot of unexpected effects and among them a dramatization of problems that encourages conflicts. Let us take one example from a concrete situation.* Imagine a particular district of Paris consisting of people of different social classes who are having dinner and socializing together on the terrace. At the same moment, teenagers played football (soccer) and the ball hits the restaurant guests. Anger was rising and somebody called the police. Dozen of police officers arrived and arrested the youngsters. Very surprised, the people who sat at the terrace tried to explain to the police that they did not want the youngsters to be prosecuted, but only invited the police to maintain order or quite things down. But, the police refused to hear their pleas. Some of the guests were even charged with "insult to a police officer," an offense in France. The result was a growing reluctance by citizens to call the police, raising tensions between youngsters and other citizens, and tensions between police officers and all others. This example is not isolated; many incidents of this sort take place in poor areas where the

* Lecadre, R. (2002, June 6). La partie de foot tourne à la rafle puis à l'AG, *Libération*.

youngsters are designated as "targets" for the police forces. In such an environment, nobody wins, including the population or the police officers. In the face of all these distrusts, individuals have demonstrated against this policy, and even police officers have voted for unions who were against a policy that rejects police use of discretion.

One could argue that the failure of the national police forces as a public service, i.e., able to answer to the public demand, would help the development of alternatives. And, in fact, it does. Private security companies are more and more present in the field of security and safety. They replace police patrols in many tasks. For example, they are responsible for security in shopping centers, make interventions when houses are burglarized, and provide security escort services at financial institutions. The competition with the national police forces is real. Whenever the government decides to withdraw its forces from one task, private companies are happy to replace them if there is money to be made. One socialistic main point when they have had to defend the *police de proximité* reform is to insist on the fact that poor people are not able to pay for their own security, and that was why the new police units were especially developed in the poor suburbs.

One other main point refers to local police forces. As we mentioned above, until the late 1990s, the government wanted to prevent the development of such forces by increasing a national police force closer to the population. But things have changed since different laws, passed between the mid-1990s and now, favored the increase of power for local police forces. In some cities, the local police forces are better equipped than the national police force in the same district. They have faster cars, better equipments, and are better staffed. In other cities, the local police forces are reduced to less than 10 people and they focus their attention on the problem of the car park (Malochet, 2007). However, whatever the situation, there is no competition between local police forces and the national one because they have complementary interests. When they are powerful, local police forces arrest offenders, but are bound to surrender these offenders to the national police force. The offender will be handed over to the civil servants who possess the power to detain people before sending them to courts; these rights belong only to the national police forces. The national police officers are happy to increase their clearance rates without any risk. They have all the advantages without leaving their offices.

What about proximity or community policing? Are these local forces closer to the population? In spite of the fact that they are paid by the local authorities, the cities, the local police officers are not always ready to endorse the operation of the community or neighborhood policing. Many of them entered the local police force in order to act as if they were "real" police officers. They want to arrest offenders, to fight crime, and not to be "social workers" speaking with youngsters or elderly ladies. Situation varies from one city to another (Malochet, 2007). But, even if some of them are really involved in neighborhood policing, there is a general movement suggesting that a majority of local police officers are not ready to assume this function. Borrowing some ideas from the national police command structure, they have created national schools for local policing, national unions, a unified statute all over the French territory, and a national labor market. That means that local police officers are allowed to change from one city to another. Therefore, they are involved in the same movement as the national police officers, moving from "bad" cities to "good" ones, resulting in the same consequences. The development of local police forces, at this moment, is not automatically an answer to the question of relationship between the police force and the populations, even if it could be in some places.

Generally speaking, the failures of all attempts to create a national police force closer to the population have finally resulted in a growing gap between the two. The reform, conducted in a top-down logic, produces few results because the main objective of the promoters of the reform is to reinforce the power of the central state more than really answer to the local demands of the people. They are not ready to assume the consequences of a real neighborhood or proximity policing; the priorities are set by people who want their own problem to be solved, even if these problems are not strictly entering the field of security and safety. That is why the police officers are right when they associate community policing and social work as one of the same. *Gendarmes*, who were closer to the population, merely assume this social position. A real community policing, whatever the label, leads inevitably to social policies that many governments refused to develop.

The failure of law and order policies, instead of producing a debate about their relevance, leads to an inflation of new laws, new harms, and new conflicts. This is the irony of the situation: instead of a growing control on the population that the *police de proximité* could have given to the government, the law and order policy has produced a more alienated society, less easy to control.

References

Belorgey, J.M. (1991). *La police au rapport*. Nancy, P.U. de Nancy: Ligue des Droits de L'Homme.

Bruneteaux, P. (1993). Cigaville: quand le maintien de l'ordre devient un métier d'expert. *Cultures & Conflicts 9–10*, 227–247.

Dieu, F. (2002). *La gendarmerie, secret d'un grand corps*. Paris: Complexe.

Dupuy, F. & Thoenig, J.C. (1983). *Sociologie de l'administration française*. Paris: Armand Colin.

Ericson, R.V. (1982). *Reproducing order: A study of police patrol work*. Toronto: University of Toronto Press.

Goldstein, H. (1990). *Problem-oriented policing.* New York: McGraw-Hill.

Lipsky, M. (1980). *Street-level bureaucracy: Dilemmas of the individual in public services.* New York: Basic Books.

Lyautey, H. (1900). Du rôle colonial de l'armée. Paris: *La Revue des deux mondes.*

Malochet, V. (2007). *Les polices municipales.* Paris: Partner University Fund (PUF).

Matelly, J.H. & Mouhanna, C. (2007). *Police: des chiffres et des doutes.* Paris: Michalon.

Monjardet, D. (1996). *Ce que fait la police, sociologie de la force publique.* Paris: La Découverte.

Monjardet, D. (1999, Juillet). La police de proximité, ce qu'elle n'est pas. *Revue Française d'Administration publique, 91,* 519–525.

Mouhanna, C. (2002). Faire le gendarme: De la souplesse informelle à la rigueur bureaucratique, *Revue Française de Sociologie* 42–1, 31–55, Janvier.

Mouhanna, C. (2002). Une police de proximité judiciarisée. *Déviance et société, 22,* 163–182.

Peyrefitte, A. (1977). *Réponses à la violence.* Rapport du comité d'études sur la violence, la criminalité et la délinquance. Paris: La Documentation Française.

Shearing, C.D. & Ericson, R.V. (1991). Culture as figurative action. *The British Journal of Sociology, 42*(4), 481–506.

Terrill, W. & Mastrofski, S.D. (2004). Working the street: Does community policing matter? In W.G. Skogan (Ed.) *Community Policing, Can it Work?* (pp. 109–135). Stamford, CT: Thomson/Wadworth.

Tönnies, F. (1887). *Gemeinschaft und Gesellschaft.* Leipzig: Fues's Verlag. (*Communauté et société,* Paris: Partner University Fund, 1944).

Weisburd, D. & Eck, J.E. (2004). What can police do to reduce crime, Disorder and fear? *The Annals of the American Academy of Political and Social Science, 593,* 42–65.

Zauberman, R. & Levy, R. (2003). Police, minorities, and the French republican ideal. *Criminology, 41*(4), 1065–1100.

Community Policing in Belgium

The Vicissitudes of the Development of a Police Model

SYBILLE SMEETS
CARROL TANGE

Contents

Introduction

In the past 20 years, the word police has been associated with a number of issues that have figured prominently in Belgian's news media. These include robberies, insecurity, dysfunctions, and interagency competition. To meet these issues, government bodies have reorganized the police agencies and, more importantly, tried to implement community policing. But, more than a policy, community policing has become a catchphrase for politicians, a dominant theme of the willingness to revisit the work of the police and its relationship with the community. The notion of community policing, however, is vague and is often interpreted differently by different people, including police officers themselves.

The construction of the Belgian version of community policing has been the result of two successive major reforms undertaken in a troubled political context and prompted by a series of highly publicized dramatic events. The first phase of this reform process dates back to the former Belgian police system, which, before 2001, was composed of three distinct police forces: the judicial police (*la police judiciaire près les parquets*)[*], the *gendarmerie*[†], and the municipal police (*police communale*)[‡]. The second phase begins with the new integrated police, structured on two autonomous levels—federal police and local police—and the 1998 police reform act that gave birth to this new

[*] The judicial police (PJP) performed judicial police tasks within judicial districts. The PJP was under the authority of the King's prosecutor and the general prosecutor.

[†] The *gendarmerie* performed judicial and administrative police tasks. The *gendarmerie* was composed of two main bodies: a national body (general staff, national operational, and support units) and territorial units operational in districts. In each district, there was a territorial brigade as well as surveillance and research brigade (*brigade de surveillance et de recherche*, BSR) tasked with specialized judicial missions.

[‡] Before 2001, there were 586 municipal police forces in Belgium, which were tasked with judicial and administrative police competencies within the territory of their municipality.

system*. These two reforms shaped the particular way community policing crystallized in Belgium. Community policing today in Belgium is the result of the sedimentation of these two waves of reforms that took place in the 1990s. The current version of community policing in Belgium emerged from a number of initiatives, which, sometimes were theoretically driven, sometimes induced from the practices, sometimes from both, but most of the time in a context that placed security at the center of the political agenda.

In the first part of this chapter, we will examine how the notion of community policing evolved at the policy and discourse levels during the course of these reforms with a special attention to the regulative norms issued by the successive governments. In a second section, this chapter analyzes the practical translation of these reforms on the ground, the constraints faced, and the paradoxes surfacing before and after the reforms were implemented.

The Concept of Community Policing: A Belgian Model?

The notion of "model" is misleading as it suggests implicitly the existence of a clearly identifiable policing doctrine called community policing. The rationale behind the use by federal authorities of the concept of model as well as their constant references to foreign experiences and practices was obvious. It intended to create a reassuring impression that the reforms are substantiated by a coherent and robust policing framework readily applicable to Belgium.

While the political will to implement a new philosophy of police action has manifested itself since the early 1990s, it was not until prior to 2003 that formal guidelines would be formulated and put into practice. The lack of clarity, and perhaps even confusion, over the exact meaning of the new policy is best illustrated by the burgeoning of terms designating the community policing approach: proximity police function (*police de proximité*), basic police function (*fonction de police de base*), first line police function (*police de première ligne*), full-fledged police function (*police à part entière*), and excellent police function (*fonction de police excellente*)†.

* The December 7, 1998 Act governing the integrated police, *Moniteur Belge*, January 5, 1999 (*Loi sur la police intégrée*, LPI).

† Our use of the expression *police function* is meant to emphasize that the reforms have been mostly organizational. The Belgian police structure is the product of an instrumental or state-centered approach despite a real tradition of local autonomy in the country. The notion of "policing" remains a very problematic one to translate in French because it does not limit itself to the police. Thus, Belgian police authorities and officers usually use the notion of policing as "a way of not deciding," especially when they have to find a word to qualify a model both in French and Flemish.

The First Phase: A Proximity Police Model between Political Guidance and Internal Reforms

Proximity Police, Base of Crime Prevention Policy: The Municipal Police

The main trigger of the wave of police reforms initiated during the past 20 years in Belgium was a series of dramatic events in the 1980s. These included the tragedy at the football stadium of Heysel, terrorist acts perpetrated by the *Cellules Communistes Combattantes* (Combating Communist Cells), and the Killers of the Brabant. These events led the political elite to pay attention to the functioning of the judiciary and the police apparatus. As early as 1990, the federal government put forward a number of measures aimed at improving the functioning of the services delivered by the police. These measures concentrated on municipal police agencies and aimed at integrating the police action within a framework of a policy of crime prevention by financing so-called local security contracts (*contrats de sécurité*).

With the fight against urban insecurity as cornerstone of their architecture, the security contracts were aimed at meeting the three new governmental priorities: police, crime prevention, and victim assistance. Signed by the federal government, two of the three federal regions and an increasing number of municipalities* pursued the goal of improving local security and service delivery by promoting municipal policing. In addition to the modernization of municipal police bodies (training, recruitment, organizational reform, and supply management), the government encouraged the development of the proximity police function, with the intention of improving police interaction with the population, restoring confidence in the police, and improving service delivery. In practice, "proximity police" was understood as a strategy to "put more blue on the streets" or, in other words, putting more police officers on the streets and implementing the so-called *îlotage* (beat policing) with groups of neighborhood constables stationed permanently within neighborhoods (on the model of similar practices in France and The Netherlands in the 1990s).

Community Policing as Reconquest of the Streets: The *Gendarmerie*

At the same time, but independently from any political initiative, senior officers from municipal police bodies and, especially, from the *gendarmerie* started locally developing new approaches to crime prevention at the end of the 1980s. In 1992, the *gendarmerie* launched its projects for a "basic

* In 2007, the security contracts were renamed Strategic Plans for Security and Prevention and currently exist in 103 (over 586) municipalities.

and quality police function" (*fonction de police de base et de qualité, FPB-Q*) inspired by the Neighborhood Watch programs. Additionally, the *gendarmerie* started encouraging the development of local networks of citizens tasked with the surveillance of their neighborhoods.* In theory, the concept of community policing adopted by the *gendarmerie* was intended to apply to the entire agency. But, in practice, it was mainly applied to the territorial brigades, the newly created sector officers, and the *alter ego* of the beat officer of the municipal police services. The agenda behind this development was clear: the *gendarmerie* intended to regain the local terrain that had been progressively lost to municipal agencies.

Community Policing, Police Collaboration, and Sharing of Tasks

The concepts of proximity police (municipal police) and of basic and quality police function (*gendarmerie*) converged in 1994 when the federal government decided the creation of so-called interpolice zones (ZIP). The ZIPs are territories formed by one or several municipalities and are conceived as the smallest unit of cooperation and redefinition of the distribution of the tasks between different police agencies. In the framework of the new ZIPs, a doctrine of community policing was, for the first time, formulated officially by the Belgian government.

The term *community policing* was indeed introduced and defined in 1994 in a circular of the Ministry of the Interior. The document stated: "[community policing] is a vision, a philosophy and a concept, underlying the approach and police execution of tasks that focuses in priority on citizens' problems and perceptions of insecurity in communities. This should translate into a police force that is visible and accessible and that aims to resolve insecurity problems in cooperation with the population, local authorities, and all other organizations that can contribute to this endeavor."† In this framework, community policing was understood mainly as an organizational issue involving a redistribution of tasks between police agencies. These tasks were identified as: 24/7 police presence, crime prevention, criminal investigations, local order maintenance, enforcement of traffic control and environmental legislation, contacts and interaction with local population, victim's assistance, and

* This was the first step in the implementation of the neighborhood information networks (particularly active in Flanders).

† Circular ZIP1 of the Federal Public Service Interior, December 5, 1995. The original text reads as follows: "*[Le community policing] est une vision, une philosophie et un concept, relatif à l'approche et à l'exécution policière des tâches qui est essentiellement axée sur les sentiments et les problèmes d'insécurité de la population dans un territoire donné et qui se traduit par une police visible, accessible et abordable, qui a pour but de résoudre les problèmes d'insécurité en concertation avec les autorités locales et la population ainsi qu'avec toutes les autres instances locales ou organisations qui peuvent y contribuer.*"

advice to citizens. The circular of the Ministry of the Interior insisted upon the necessity to establish a partnership with the local population involving more collaborations, availability and accessibility of the police to residents in general, a new problem-solving approach, a better accountability of police authorities, increased cooperation and collaboration with local authorities and other local organizations, greater visibility, greater flexibility, adaptability, and devolution of decision-making power. None of these objectives, however, were new; in fact, most of them were already stated in the security contracts established by the previous wave of reforms. In addition, these official publications did not help to clarify what was meant by "community policing." In fact, many practical questions were left unanswered. Due to the obvious lack of guidance from the federal authorities, the neighborhood constable, and the *îlotier* (beat officer) became naturally the focus of the attention of later reforms.

To summarize, before the 1998 reform of the police, it appears that the Belgian version of community policing had two distinct faces. The first face was a proximity police initiated by the top (the Ministry of Interior), which took the form of federal-sponsored programs of local crime prevention (the so-called security contracts). This community policing strategy affected only those municipal police forces that entered into a formal agreement with the federal level. The second face of community policing was basically a pragmatic reorganization of the distribution of tasks between municipal police and the gendarmerie.

The Second Phase: Community Policing within the Framework of an Integrated Police

This first wave of reforms was not given enough time to demonstrate its validity. Dramatic events were soon to occupy the front stage. The kidnapping and murder of children between 1996 and 1997 (the Marc Dutroux case) was one of the main reasons for the initiation of a new wave of comprehensive reforms that took place in 1998. The police structure that emerged from this reform is the current integrated police service of Belgium. The new system involves two autonomous organizational levels: the federal police and the local police. The local police*, as they emerged from this reform, are a decentralized unit that operates in 196 so-called police zones, each consisting of one or several municipalities. Local police forces perform all administrative and judicial police tasks for so-called local cases as well as a number of federal tasks

* Former municipal police bodies and former territorial brigades of the *gendarmerie* compose the local police.

delegated to them. When a case is defined as nonlocal, the federal police* take the lead and perform all associated specialized administrative and judicial tasks. Furthermore, the federal police assist the local police when necessary.

The Reform of the Police: The Organization before the Substance

The intention of the authorities was to close the definitional gap of community policing before the formal establishment of the new police (2001 for the federal police and 2002 for the local police). But massive popular mobilization following the Dutroux case and a series of obstacles (change of government, financing issues, difficulty in negotiating a new statute for the police, reluctance of the judiciary to agree on the formalization of the discretionary power of the police) changed the course of events. It is only much later (in 2003) that a document on community policing known as the "CP1" was finally drafted. This meant that the new integrated police was instituted before the formulation of a clear vision and a doctrine; such a vision, however, would have been necessary to define the action plan, the organizational structure, and the priorities of the new police. The government had missed a clear opportunity to move the reform beyond a simple organizational restructuring. In the interim period that would last until the publication of the CP1, the local police were once again designated as the main agency meant to enact the community policing philosophy.

Standardized Minimum Service and the Six Basic Functionalities of the Local Police

During the interim period that lasted until the CP1 publication in 2003, a new notion appeared, even though its substance was far from being revolutionary. The idea guaranteed minimal police services to the population. The guiding principle was indeed to offer a standardized minimal quality service throughout the territorial zones of municipal police. A regulative framework of norms was consecutively issued by the federal government and its main circular† defined six basic mandatory functionalities to be performed by the local police. These include reception, intervention, public order maintenance, neighborhood policing, local criminal investigation, victim assistance, and the minimum quality standards for each of them. While it seems quite obvious that the six basic functionalities were meant to have a positive impact on the quality of the relationship with the population, the circular

* The former judicial police, the central bodies of the *gendarmerie*, and the BSRs compose the federal police.

† Circular PLP10 of the Federal Public Service Interior, October 9, 2001 (*Moniteur Belge*, 16.X.2001).

referred explicitly to the proximity police only in the case of the neighborhood policing. The neighborhood policing was meant to be "the corner stone of the relationship of the police with the community."* It was presented as the main instrument to improve the quality of the collection of information at the neighborhood level, to disseminate relevant information to the public, to prevent crime by more street visibility and presence of the police, to respond with concrete answers to citizens' demands, to identify and solve small conflicts, and to execute police tasks that require sound knowledge of local realities or good networking within the local population. The minimum quality standard was set at 1 neighborhood constable for 4,000 inhabitants.

The Development of a Specific Norm: CP1, CP2, and Community Policing Pillars

The central philosophy of community policing in Belgium was finally formulated and presented in the CP1 circular published in 2003† as mentioned earlier. The circular had been elaborated with the technical assistance of social scientists of the University of Ghent. In the introduction of the circular, the Ministry of Interior declared that "community policing had become a conceptual framework whose content lacked precision and whose objectives were unclear. It had also become synonymous with any project that involved the participation of the population. It, therefore, was imperative to standardize its concepts and their definitions."‡ Concretely, so for the CP1, community policing includes five pillars essential for a community-oriented police:

1. *External orientation*: The police must be integrated and involved into the life of the community.
2. *Focus on problem solving*: The police must identify and analyze potential causes of criminality and conflict in communities to be able to act upon them.
3. *Partnership*: The police are not the only agency responsible for providing security. Concern for security should be conceived of as an integrated approach where various partners are part of a comprehensive and integrated approach.

* *Ibid.*

† Circular CP1 of the Federal Public Service Interior, May 27, 2003 (*Moniteur Belge*, 9.VII.2003).

‡ *Ibid.* The original text reads as follows: "*Le community policing est devenu une sorte de 'concept cadre' avec un contenu manquant de précisions et des objectifs fort confus. Il est de plus en plus devenu le réceptacle accueillant toute initiative impliquant, à quelque titre que ce soit, la population. Il apparaît donc urgent (...) de standardiser les concepts de l'interprétation à lui réserver.*"

4. *Accountability*: The police must develop mechanisms enabling them to account for the way they respond to expectations, demands, and needs of the society they serve.
5. *Empowerment*: The police and the population must jointly tackle problems of insecurity and must have the resources to do so.

To a large extent, the circular of the Ministry of Interior reiterated widely acknowledged principles of community policing; its principal novelty was the demonstrated willingness to apply these principles comprehensively at both the local and federal police levels. Despite this declaratory statement, the "explaining note" accompanying the circular focused only on local police. This circular was presented as the first of a series of subsequent publications expected to focus on the practical aspects of community policing. Unique in its kind, the circular limited itself at attempting to harmonize at a conceptual and theoretical level the police management principles and community policing.

In 2004, a second circular, the CP2, was issued and complemented the CP1.* The CP2 aimed at providing management tools† and frameworks of reference for the implementation of community policing at the local police level. The framework of reference was designed to achieve the objectives of an integrated police strategy, sound financial planning at the local level, a systematic sharing of experience and practice across police forces, an increase and improvement of operational availability (partly achieved by transferring administrative tasks to other actors and focusing on police priorities), and increasing minimal norms of quality and standards based "on experiences in the field." While more practice-oriented, the CP2 remained as its twin CP1, very general, offering little operational or organizational guidance. Concrete guidance, it was stated in these circulars, should emerge from the sharing of experiences and good practices inside the police organization as well as the implementation of pilot community policing projects in pilot test zones.

The Excellent Police Function: An Encompassing Notion?

The final layer of the Belgian model of community policing is provided by the notion of "excellent police function"‡ defined as: "In order to carry out his/her missions, every staff member of the integrated police has to observe the principles of community policing, information-led policing, and optimal

* Circular CP2 of the Federal Public Service Interior, November 3, 2004 (*Moniteur Belge*, December 29, 2004).

† These tools stem from the EFQM model of excellence, the Common Assessment Framework (CAF) model and the INK model of management.

‡ Bruggeman et al. (2007).

management (as well as an internal prevention and welfare policy) in order to strive for an excellent police function."* This notion of "excellent police function" was created to underline the willingness to provide for a general and encompassing framework for all police levels (the federal and the local) integrating into a single frame of reference management and minimum standards of policing. The new framework now included:

- Five measures of the "chain of security" (proactivity, prevention, preparation, reactivity, and follow-up), which constitute the framework of reference for policing crime and insecurity.
- Five pillars of community policing, which constitute the "normative and cultural" frameworks of the police.
- Five characteristics of intelligence-led policing as working method (proactivity and reactivity, value-added character, information-sharing, focusing on critical objectives). Intelligence-led policing needs to be "a permanent concern of the integrated police for running the organization at strategic, tactical, and operational levels, using information about insecurity, quality of life, criminality, and police operations (experience and skills)."† The five characteristics of the concept include: setting the goals, proactive and reactive work, providing added value, exchange, and goal-oriented.
- Five principles of optimal management (result-oriented, transparent, permanent improvement, professional cooperation, and forward-looking leadership) adapted to the police from models and theories of management, and which can be summarized with the catchphrase: "It is more important to do the right things than doing the things right."‡
- Five fields of the police organization (management and leadership, policies and politics, management of human resources, management of means, and management of processes).§

As its inceptors rightly noted, the notion of "excellent police function" is not a revolution in the field, but rather an evolution: "To evolve, to develop, and to grow does not mean to start from scratch, it means building on what

* http://www.polfed-fedpol.be/org/org_missionstatement_en.php.

† Bruggerman et al. (2007, p. 23).

‡ Bruggerman et al. (2007, p. 31).

§ In addition, the framework identifies five main groups of stakeholders in the policing sector (clients, service providers, contributors, society, and administration and financial backers) and five phases of the evolution of an organization (focus on activities, process, system, chain, and transformation). This resulted in an original seven by five table of characteristics.

has proven effective in the past."[*] The model that emerged is surprisingly highly complex and built on a broad conceptual web that, among other things, incorporated what had proved useful in the past, or, at least, what existed before the reform. The next section looks beyond the merits of the many individual concepts and notions of this new encompassing framework and assesses its utility at the operational level in the daily police practice of the Belgian police.

Organizational and Professional Implementation of Community Policing

The First Phase: On the Brink of the Reform, a Proximity Police Function at the Margins

Before the law on the integrated police was passed, the neighborhood constables and municipal police forces were the main actors designated by the policy framework to implement the proximity police. A study conducted in 2000 by academics analyzed the implementation of the proximity police in the region of Wallonia[†] and could demonstrate that the gap between policies and practices was wide open.[‡] While the municipal police chiefs were keen to declare that consultation with the population was the top priority, few if any had conducted effectively such consultation in the past. The priorities of municipal forces proved to be mostly defined by their chief in a top-down manner and even within the police force there was no evidence of an established formal dialog with neighborhood constables and the senior management of the police, despite a rhetoric designating these constables as the eyes and ears of municipal authorities.

While at policy level, decentralization, devolution, decompartmentalization of police services, and despecialization were key to the police reform, in reality, the autonomy of midlevel decision makers, when it existed, proved often more the result of neglect rather than of policy and a consequence of the geographical distance of the manager from his supervisor. Furthermore, no formalization or even recognition of police discretion could be documented. The versatility of the neighborhood constables was not integrated into a coherent policy at managerial level (providing a specialized training or determining selection and recruitment criteria). Geographical decentralization was found to be applied only to neighborhood departments, which encouraged the compartmentalization and a disconnect with other police departments.

[*] Bruggeman et al. (2007, p. 13).

[†] One of the three regions of Belgium.

[‡] Smeets and Strebelle (2000).

The study found that municipal forces had not promoted and advertised the role of the neighborhood constables by the necessary public campaigns.

Concrete guidelines for the incorporation of so-called "regulatory missions" (prevention, assistance, and proactivity) within the police were found to be also entirely missing. The lack of definition of these regulatory missions impacted negatively, not just on neighborhood policing, but also on any meaningful evaluation effort. Most of the time, neighborhood constables interpreted them as being the preventive patrols type of activity as well as transfers of problematic cases to social departments. For many policemen, this was nothing really new, except perhaps that the workload increased.

Another scientific study conducted in the Brussels region arrived at similar conclusions.* In spite of an official discourse emphasizing rhetoric of proximity police, the study found that priority was clearly given on the ground to centralized, motorized units that valued crime fighting rather than peacekeeping. Neighborhood policing was being pushed to the margin, in terms of image, priorities, financial means, and strength. Emergency intervention and criminal investigation tasks remained the top priorities of the police management, while neighborhood policing was conceived simply as a marketing tool to improve the general image of municipal police. Neighborhood constables were declared useful by their colleagues only when they were successful in supporting them with information for running criminal investigations or public order operations. Constables working for neighborhood policing departments were conceived by colleagues as reservists to be mobilized for emergency situations by other police departments.

Three examples of how policies enunciated at the federal level were interpreted at the local level will illustrate the disconnect between the proximity police rhetoric and the reality. A priority of proximity policing was, as mentioned earlier, a 24/7 dispatching service aimed at guaranteeing the accessibility and availability of police services to the public. In reality, however, this service responds mainly to calls for services involving complaints or urgent situations, rarely a problem as defined at the neighborhood level. Second, in blatant opposition to the aim of despecialization called for by the proximity police model, neighborhood constables are given more and more specialized judicial missions. As a matter of fact, transfer to the criminal investigation department is increasingly seen as a promotion by neighborhood constables. Third, as the volume of law and order operations has increased constantly at the municipal level, police managers prioritize their operational mobilizations according to the needs of the neighborhoods.

The reality of the new policing model as translated in practices reveals that, rather than involving more of the local population in the everyday

* Tange (2000).

running of police affairs, traditional sectors of police activity were indeed reinforced and strengthened (intervention, criminal investigation, and public order). While the national *gendarmerie* tried to (re)invest the local terrain, municipal police had to deal with a complex institutional context. On the one hand, they were an instrument of a federal political will to change "the way things were done"; on the other hand, at an organizational level, they had to compete with the *gendarmerie* and were left with little option than to adopt an inherited model of "crime fighters." Proximity policing ended up being pushed to the edge. Information gathering originally intended to help solve community problems was consequently used by police officers to support the repressive machine instead. Most police officers have a self-image as being crime fighters and the tasks associated with neighborhood policing are belittled and discredited.

Both researches concluded that the implementation of proximity police at the local level has been at best a partial failure. The main reasons for this failure stem from the difficulties of combining two highly contrasting visions within the police institution: on the one hand, a traditional view of a law and order enforcement police and, on the other hand, the new model of proximity police. The weakest of them—proximity police confined to the discredited neighborhood department—could not resist eventually the increased competition of the more traditional vision and, at times, paradoxically, reinforced the impact of the latter. The reform of the police in Belgium appears, therefore, as little more than a continuation of the past when, instead of remaining at the rhetorical level, practices are scrutinized.

The Second Phase: A New Integrated Police Trapped in Old Logics

The Problematic Location of the Police, between Structural Changes and Modeling of the Police Action

Voted with haste under the circumstance described earlier, the 1998 reform took some time to be implemented. The will of the federal government to rapidly implement structural changes led to a hasty introduction of the police reform without the necessary critical reflection and evaluation process that such a major exercise would have required. Municipal police forces, which by law were expected to come into existence in 2002, were immediately confronted with major difficulties. The municipal police had to reorganize its internal structure, comply with new operational standards, follow the dictates of new statutory norms, and operate without an increase of the budget. There were some practical issues that pushed the substantial question of the definition of community policing into the background. Even in the so-called pilot zones of community policing, daily mundane concerns resulted in police forces to select in the "community policing menu" those services that they chose to implement. [*] We will return later to this topic.

In addition, other reform components have dominated the political and police agenda, particularly the aspects of planning, organizing, and evaluating of police services. The implementation of the security planning zone (*Plans zonaux de sécurité*—PZS), which specified the approach, priorities, and goals of the municipal police every four years, became a privileged tool to marginalize further community policing. These plans stressed, for instance, that a single framework of reference (in this case, community policing) did not provide the management with sufficient flexibility to address all policing problems and called for more room of maneuver. In that regard, a document published by the Ministry of Interior stated that "even if a number of guidelines have gained prominence in recent years because of their importance for the functioning of the new police structures … this should not mean that the reform of the police should follow rigid and definitive guidelines; the reform must rather be seen as an evolutionary process."[†] The document stressed that everyone in the police force "must look in the same direction." The question left unanswered was of course: "Which direction?"

The flexibility requirement proved problematic at all levels of the hierarchy. Subject to contradictory demands, police officers were left with a Cornelian choice: insisting on their own autonomy and accountability (as stressed by the community policing philosophy) and following orders and instructions by administrative and judicial authorities (as required by a more traditional model of policing). The "flexibility" requirement prompted a wider debate in Belgium about the exact systemic position or location of the police as an institution and its essential tasks in the context of the transformation of the relationship between police and authorities, on the one hand, and police and society, on the other.

The (Non)essential Tasks

The political will to put more police on the streets has led in more recent years to review all police tasks and identify those that could be transferred to other agencies. To identify the "transferable tasks," the option chosen was to distinguish between essential and nonessential tasks using as criteria the association with the use of force. Only those tasks implying the potential use of force were identified as essential. Framed this way, the broader and essential issue of the general role of the police did not surface. Following this debate, administrative tasks and office work were transferred to municipal agencies or to civil servants hired by the police. The protection of courts and transportation of prisoners were transferred to a third public

[*] Smeets and Tange (2004, p. 240).
[†] Ponsaers and Enhus (2001, p. 4).

security agency while the surveillance of parking was transferred to private security companies.*

The *îlotage* was a further "casualty" of the methodological approach adopted in Belgium. Focusing on what the police *should not* do rather than on what the police *should* do resulted in transferring also one of the key community policing tasks (i.e., the *îlotage)* to other agencies. The surveillance tasks of public space by foot were indeed progressively transferred to peacekeepers (parks and public space wardens and urban stewards). The guiding idea that proximity police should be implemented by versatile and generalist practitioners had, in this case, been wrongfully interpreted as meaning that it did not require any particular qualification and, therefore, could be implemented by anyone wearing a police uniform. The main unintended consequence of this decision was that the cooperation between police officers and the wardens deteriorated, which further contributed to discredit the *îlotage*.†

Two-Speed Partnerships: Police between Citizens and Authorities

The joint production of security approach has blurred the borderlines between public and private actors (citizens and civil society organizations). New actors, from the individual citizens to organizations, emerge on a daily basis and old ones see their role changing. This evolution has itself raised a set of issues. During a recent series of police workshops and retreats (2006), the issue of the limits, if any, of citizen involvement emerged as one main concern of the police:‡

- Should citizens be viewed as passive and the social demand be interpreted by the police or, on the contrary, should citizens actively contribute to the police agenda?
- How should the citizens be represented in the phase of problem definition?
- Who should initiate police action?

Concerns over the respective role of institutional players were also expressed during these workshops:

* Smeets (2006).

† Smeets (2006).

‡ The following questions are taken from workshops organized by the *Centre d'études sur la police* (Seron et al., 2004). See also publications from the *Centrum voor politiestudies*, expressing the Flemish approach of many topics: the police reform (Enhus et al., 2001); public private partnerships (Ponsaers et al., 2002); or the orientation of police work (Van Erck, 2003).

- If citizen participation is necessary for the police, it cannot be an end in itself.
- The sharing of responsibilities can, in practice, dilute responsibilities and lead to uncontrolled transfers of charges from one actor to another.
- The aims of security are not shared similarly by all actors involved.

The conflict of norms, in particular in the framework of the relations between the police and the judiciary, stressed recurrently by participants of the workshops, was a symbol of the difficulty of reconciling the two visions of "the police as instrument of authority" and "the police as partner of authority."

The Split between the Local Police Policies and Crime Prevention Policies

The police reform was not limited to an internal reorganization; it revisited also the political steering mechanism of policing and transformed the relationship with other groups theoretically associated with this steering in the framework of the community policing philosophy. In this regard, some paradoxes emerged.

While the primary intention of the reform was to initiate a rapprochement between the police and the people, it also established new geographical entities larger than before: the so-called police zone (*zone de police*) composed of one or more municipalities. The municipality has a political and social coherence entirely missing in the larger police zone. In fact, the police zone is an artificial entity that serves rather a pragmatic goal: rationalize means, so as to offer equal police services to citizens throughout the country. Even if one assumes that the planners were careful when designing these zones, the larger territories to be covered by the local police had a negative impact on the ties between the police and the population.

In addition, within the police zones consisting of more than one municipality, there is a structural disconnect between various institutional bodies: those in charge of the development of a crime prevention policy (the municipal council and a local council for the prevention of delinquency*), those in charge of the organization of the local police (the police council and the

* Local councils for prevention of delinquency are mandatory for those municipalities with a local "security contract." In general, members of these councils are the mayor or city administrator, a judicial magistrate, the chief of local police, or other representatives of the police, the local official responsible for crime prevention, the project manager, the internal evaluator, and municipality and civil society organizations representatives.

police "college"*), and those in charge of the definition of police priorities (zones security council). This disconnect has a negative impact on the coherence and harmony of security policies and community policing.

Moreover, the introduction of the so-called Security Council's zones has further exacerbated the difficulty to define coherent police priorities by multiplying the number of actors responsible for the definition and evaluation of police policy.† Despite existing provisions for mechanisms for the resolution of internal conflicts, many problems remained. Firstly, municipal magistrates rarely attend meetings and invest little time and effort into the process, either due to minimal interest or poor knowledge of the mechanisms in place. Secondly, there is also a lack of priority or, sometimes, too many priorities from the judiciary. Finally, local police chiefs continue to play a central or dominant role in the definition process of local police priorities. This, it should be stressed, does not derive from a particular insistence by police authorities, but rather from their lack of experience and skills. Consequently, strategic planning in the local police necessitates the multiplication of informal preparatory meetings between local police and federal police, and it is during these meetings that priorities are set and later simply ratified by the zone security councils. This process rather than intentions explains why police priorities rarely take into account local prevention policies promoted by municipal mayors.

Between Conceptual Theories and Organizational Realities: À la Carte or Au Menu?

As outlined above, community policing had two distinct faces before the reform and this fact accentuated the discrepancy between the discourse and practice. At first sight, it might seem that the police reform had succeeded in standardizing all the doctrines of community policing when it issued the CP1 and CP2 circulars and formulated the "excellent police function" doctrine. This theoretical coherence remained at the policy level while, in practice, police services continued to lack standardization and to show great variation in the distribution of manpower and equipments.

* There is a disconnect between the mayor as highest administrative police authority in the municipality and the new organs managing the new interzone police. This is now the responsibility of the "police college" (composed of all mayors of a police zone). Within the college, the number of votes of each member is proportional to the amount of money invested by the municipality in the police zone, a mechanism that has created a lot of tensions and difficulties.

† See Henin and Smeets (2008); see also Devroe, Matthijs, Keulenaer, and Thomaes (2006).

While the conceptual model of community policing has never been completely put into practice, a number of initiatives derived from this model have been implemented with the assistance of the federal police. But, again, in practice, only a handful of police zones (the test zones*) were involved and the way community policing was implemented varied considerably from one zone to another. In practice, only selected projects or services were experimented at a time (the *à la carte* option). Committees were established to oversee these projects, but the real enthusiasm displayed at the beginning progressively faded away as it was not matched by a strong political support at the top.

This should not be interpreted as if nothing has been done in the various police zones of Belgium during this period. Evidence of successful implementations is rare even though it may be stressed that empirical researches on the topic during that period are widely missing. However, there is good reason to believe that the first wave of reforms remained mainly a "paper reform" or, in other words, that it did not result in a radical departure from the past and the reform proved unsuccessful in upgrading the marginal status of the community policing officer in the local police forces. As mentioned earlier, this first reform wave had emphasized on organizational matters, management and planning tools for emergency intervention, criminal investigation, and, last but not least, road safety.†

Specialization, Support, and Complexity: What Role for Community Policing?

At the heart of the police work environment today, relations between actors are conceptualized from a perspective of partnership. This is a key factor for an improved communication and better management of human resources. Inside the police agencies, as well as in their relationship maintained with others, an optimal flow of information has now become essential for the successful operation of the police in general and the decision-making process in particular.‡

An empirical research studying the organization in the local police in the territorial zones found substantial evidence that police departments continue to work in "hermetic silos" with minimal communication between them.§ The report of the evaluation commission of the reform summarized this finding by stressing that "a common observation in many police zones is that the

* There are six Flemish zones, three Walloon zones, and one Brussels zone for a total of 196 police zones.

† Commission d'accompagnement de la réforme des polices au niveau local (2007).

‡ Commission d'accompagnement de la réforme des polices au niveau local (2007, p. 241).

§ Dieu et al. (2002).

former war of police forces has given way to a war of police departments."*
The reasons for this compartmentalization are similar to those encountered in the previous analyses: variations in prestige of various departments and differences in human resources and equipments. This research further highlighted specific problems of the reform itself. For instance, neighborhood constables have shed light on constraints imposed on their work by the integrated data processing system of complaints used by the local police: "... given existing categories, all complainants are automatically considered 'victims' and all accused automatically considered 'suspects' even when complaints are unfounded."†

As far as the internal organization of the local police is concerned, two types of organizations have been implemented. In some police municipalities, so-called proximity departments have been established and specialized in administering the basic function of neighborhood policing. In others, a direction of the proximity police was created and tasked with the internal promotion of values and philosophies associated with community policing in all departments and services of the police. Nevertheless, in general, what has predominated is a mentality that values the traditional tasks of police and marginalizes those associated with the neighborhood.

This highlights once again the tension between a "new" model of policing and an organizational structure that is not readily adaptable to this model. The authors of the research suggested that it is the cohabitation of two incompatible cultural models—the traditional and the new community police models—which impedes the creation of a radically new organization. This cohabitation is at the origin of tensions and conflicts.

This being said, police forces tend today to be less hierarchical, less militarized, and to favor the function rather than the rank. These tendencies existed before the police reform, in particular in the *gendarmerie*, but their significance has increased since. In parallel, however, the organizational structure of the local police has grown in complexity and size and this development has been accompanied by a massive proliferation of norms, instructions, and directives, from the federal ones to the local ones.

Which Policeman? What Sort of Community Policing?

While scientific evidence is scarce on the matter, various indicators tend to suggest that local police practices have not changed significantly. Even if new specialized competences have emerged in recent years (in particular those associated with civilian specialists hired by the police), these are often not related to community policing.

* Dieu et al. (2002, p. 35).
† Dieu et al. (2002, p. 34).

In the context of the multiplication of support and specialized services in the police, the two recurrent issues are: (1) the lack of resources (in particular the insufficient local staff) and (2) the growing load of administrative tasks. While these two issues are often presented as the main reason behind the lack of police officers on the street and as a major obstacle to a broad-based community policing approach, the working methods of police officers, in particular, their "street work," are also frequently identified as necessitating a fundamental transformation.*

The main challenges of community policing and neighborhood policing of the future were highlighted during a conference on local police tasks (2002).† Participants to the conference raised a series of issues and proposed principles and practices including: building an "organizational culture of proximity" for the entire police body and not just for selected departments, revisiting the selection and recruitment processes, developing continuous training and time management programs, establishing links with the community through neighborhood constables, decentralizing police zones, coordinating weekly meetings with local authorities, police reception office within local community centers, and an organization that is more versatile. During the conference, the debates focused on the consequences of the steady increase in the size of police forces since the creation of the police zones, the shut down of neighborhood police stations, the centralization of the organization of local police, the disappearance of rural police officers, and the central role played by intervention tasks (motorized police). These trends are antithetic to the philosophy of community policing.

Training as an Impetus for Change? Relations between the Support Actors and the Field Actors

In Belgium, community policing has been first and foremost the field of trainers and support officers, a specialty for a transversal direction running across operational departments. Apart from a few exceptional case studies, the general picture is that of a poor translation of community policing at operational level. The case of the Directorate of Relations with Local Police (CGL) may underline the poor status of community policing in the Belgian system today. This body, which is under the authority of the general commissioner of the federal police, experiences difficult times and their staff was recently reduced. As a hybrid institution staffed by federal and local police agents, CGL is often perceived negatively because of its support role in issues, such as community policing and excellent police function (it also includes financial management, police strategies management, and support

* Seron et al. (2004).

† Dieu et al. (2002).

to local reform). On the one hand, CGL develops indirect strategies, such as coaching and support of local trainers and, on the other hand, it offers direct support to various other training programs. These services are provided to fill the gap created by a lack of trainers in community policing in the various training departments of the Belgian police. In promoting local projects of community policing, CGL has not only tried to provide assistance at the local level, especially within the test zones, but has also served as a platform for the diffusion of best practices regarding community policing, especially practices that come from local police bodies.

Shortcomings in the Training Processes

The initiative to recruit a greater number of women and minorities into the police as a means of changing mentalities and to better reflect the diversity of the society started before the current police reforms. Since the 1980s, a number of new training programs have also been created and implemented, even though it should be stressed that they were aimed at increasing the professional level[*] of the police rather than changing the cop culture. These training programs do not challenge the traditional image of the police officer, with the exception of the "quality of intervention" courses emphasizing the nonuse of force and a new short training module (18 hours in total) for the field personnel. Community policing is sometimes taught as a separate subject within police academies, but only as part of the specialized "functional training" given to neighborhood constables—not as a core topic of basic police training program. The community policing philosophy is a marginal aspect of the overall training of the police in Belgium.[†] The organization of training reflects an understanding that community policing is associated with the neighborhood policing function and not the police *per se*. In summary, community policing is at best a specific and isolated police task and at worst window dressing to help legitimize the police institution.[‡]

Belgium initially implemented models and experiences imported from abroad, especially from Holland and Anglo-Saxon countries. However, since the publication of the CP1 and since the introduction of the notion of excellent police function, the Belgian police have begun to export their

[*] Whether this was achieved is disputed by many police chiefs. These sceptics consider that these programs resulted in a loss of competences, particularly those associated with judicial tasks. They are also critical of the focus put on management skills for senior police officers and, as consequence, the resulting loss of operational skills.

[†] The Standing Police Monitoring Committee, *Annual report 2006*, Brussels, 2007, pp. 23–24.

[‡] See, in particular, the 2003 EVA evaluation, the 2004 training day for executive officers and the 2005 training seminar for officers. These reports are available at www.police.ac.be.

own police model abroad. This suggests a significant shift in terms of national and international positioning, and reflects a dramatic change in the discourse in Belgium. The process of exportation regarding community policing takes place mainly through the European institutional networks, such as the European Police College (CEPOL), and via handbooks of best practices. And, when training programs are proposed to other countries (especially to developing countries), while the core of these programs are still constituted by classical fields of police intervention, such as crowd control operations, cultural aspects of the police reform in Belgium (for instance, the Belgian police code of ethics*) move gradually to the center as well.

Each local police body is entitled to maintain privileged relations with foreign police agencies, a possibility that has led some police forces in Belgium to initiate international exchanges of information and training programs. One illustration is the often-mentioned example of the police zone of Schaerbeek–Evere–Saint-Josse in Brussels that was innovated locally by taking inspiration from the Japanese *Koban*† and which, as most of the larger police zones in Belgium, maintains a direct relationship with a foreign police. Quebec has been a regular partner of police zones in Belgium.

Conclusion

If there is a Belgian model of community policing, known as the "excellent police function," it is particularly complex, even confusing, and considered by senior police officers as having little concrete function. The reasons for this complexity are due to the construction process of the model and the political will to quickly reform the police, regardless of organizational or cultural obstacles and of resistance from policemen.

The measures to improve the functioning of the police apparatus were always made in haste in response to dramatic events. The Belgian model of community policing, therefore, is the image of the various reforms of police services in the country. It was built piecemeal by aggregation of various models implemented since the early 1990s, vague concepts from foreign examples, some good practices, and, lately, management principles. However, these construction stages were never questioned or even subjected to a real assessment of the effects of the model on field practices. Like the 1998 reform, the model of community policing has also emphasized the answer to issues of organization and of management of human resources, including the sensitive

* In Belgium, the code of ethics of the police services became effective on May 30, 2006.

† The Japanese Kobans are small police units covering a very limited area (for instance, a street).

issue of redistribution of tasks between police agencies, while crucial issues were pushed into the background (such as the issue of the relevance of such a model, the objectives of its implementation, and the definition of the patterns of police interventions).

The lack of clarity, steadiness, and concrete examples, which characterizes the community policing model, partly explains the cool reception of the model within police agencies and the gap between policies and field practices. But this gap is also explained by the fact that it was the federal government, not the police, which initiated the model, even if some senior police officers and academics contributed to its definition. This top-down process was not accompanied by the necessary means to implement the model, neither in regards to financial means, recruitment of policemen, or training and selection policies, nor in regards to political guidance. Furthermore, the impression that the government did not know what to do with its own model was reinforced by the transfer of, in the wake of the 1998 reform, responsibility for the process of implementation of community policing to the federal police, and within it, to a department also limited by lack of adequate resources.

It has also strengthened the impression the local police already had that the federal government imposes a model that contradicts the traditional policing model and the fundamental idea of crime fighting. This perception is corroborated by the quasi-exclusive assignment of community policing of local police, while the federal police specialize more and more in judicial tasks related to organized crime.

In addition, the marginalization of community policing is supported by the limited capacity in innovation within local police combined with the absence of additional resources that lead local police to restrict the implementation of community policing to the departments of neighborhood constables. These departments are already discredited within local police, mainly because the neighborhood constables are seen as generalists (good for everything and, therefore, good for nothing), the opposite of the policemen specialized in criminal investigation and emergency intervention. Furthermore, for the neighborhood constables, the community-policing model was perceived as an additional workload that did not improve the quality of their field practices. For the specialized policemen, the implementation of the model exclusively in the neighborhood constables departments has been interpreted as evidence that the tasks associated with community policing are not "real" police work. To conclude, the loss of credit of community policing, both by police officers and by senior police officers, explains that there has been a gradual transfer of the nonessential tasks (including *îlotage*) to civilians outside the police unit. As a result of this transfer, we can say that, today in Belgium, most of the existing community-policing practices are implemented outside the police.

References

Bruggeman, W., Van Branteghem, J.-M., & Van Nuffel, D. (2007). *Vers l'excellence dans la fonction de police.* Brussels: Politeia.

Commission d'accompagnement de la réforme des polices au niveau local (2007, June). *Troisième rapport d'évaluation.* Brussels: Politeia.

Devroe, E., Matthijs, E., De Keulenaer, S., & Thomaes, St. (2006). *Les procureurs du Roi ont la parole.* Étude d'évaluation des plans zonaux de sécurité. Antwerp: Maklu/Criminal Policy Service.

Dieu, A.-M. et al. (2002). *Soutien à la réflexion managériale et à la mise en œuvre du changement dans 5 zones de police.* Final report of a research done for the Ministry of the Intérior (PGR). Liege: University of Liège, LENTIC.

Enhus, E. et al. (2001). *De politiehervorming.* Brussels: Politeia/Centrum voor politie studies.

Henin, J.-P. & Smeets, S. (2008). *Polices locales et autorités administratives. Je t'aime, moi non plus?* Brussels: Politeia/CEP.

Ponsaers, P. & Enhus, E. (2001). *Vade-mecum Plans de sécurité pour la rédaction du plan national de sécurité et des plans zonaux de sécurité.* For the Ministry of the Interior. Ghent: Ghent University.

Ponsaers, P. et al. (2002). *Partnership en politie.* Brussels: Politeia/Centrum voor politiestudies.

Seron, V., Smits, M., Smeets, S., & Tange, C. (2004). *Police de proximité. Un modèle belge entre questions et pratiques.* Bruxelles: Politeia.

Smeets, S. (2006). *'Nouveaux uniformes' et État social actif: vers une recomposition du champ de la sécurité en Belgique?* Doctoral dissertation, Brussels: Free University of Brussels.

Smeets, S. & Strebelle, C. (2000). *La police de proximité en Belgique. Vers un nouveau modèle de gestion de l'ordre,* Brussels: Bruylant.

Smeets, S. & Tange, C. (2004). Conclusions générales. In V. Seron, M. Smits, S. Smeets, & C. Tange (Eds.), *Police de proximité. Un modèle belge entre questions et pratiques* (pp. 237–251). Brussels: Politeia.

Tange, C. (2000). La police de proximité. *Courier hebdomadaire du CRISP.* Brussels, no. 1691–1692.

Van Erck, J. (2003). *Externe oriëntering van de politie. Gemeenschapgerichte politiezorg.* Brussels: Politeia/Centrum voor politiestudies.

7 Patterns of Community Policing in Britain

ANITA KALUNTA-CRUMPTON

Contents

Introduction

British Policing before Contemporary Community Policing

> It should be understood, at the outset, that the principal object to be obtained is the prevention of crime. To this great end every effort of the police is to be directed. The security of person and property, the preservation of the public tranquillity, and all the other objects of a police establishment, thus, will be better effected, than by the detection and punishment of the offender after he has succeeded in committing the crime. This should constantly be kept in mind by every member of the police force, as a guide for his own conduct (Reith, 1956, pp. 135–6).

A brief narrative of the history of modern-day British policing lays a foundation for understanding the origins of contemporary community policing in the British context. As indicated in the above quoted instructions that accompanied the Metropolitan Police Act 1829, crime prevention was seemingly the emphasized focus of the British police force following its birth in 1829. Sir Robert Peel was the key architect of the "new police" that signaled modern British policing. The "new police" was first introduced in London as the Metropolitan Police and, therefore, was the pioneer of all modern police forces in England, Wales, and Scotland. Prior to the emergence of the "new police," the "old" system of policing was marked by incompetence and, as Reiner (2000, p. 17), states, "was said to be uncertain, uncoordinated, and haphazard, relying on private and amateur effort, and prone to corruption."

The old policing system of the eighteenth and early nineteenth centuries consisted primarily of parish constables who were paid a watch rate by their respective parishes to carry out street patrols and order maintenance in their assigned parish. Their duties included making an arrest for disorderly behavior, vagrancy, prostitution, theft, and other similar misconduct.

In the midst of social disorder and fears of increasing crime that accompanied the rise of industrialization and urbanization in the eighteenth and nineteenth centuries, the call for police reform in the form of a competent and disciplined police force found justification. Whilst it has since been argued in academic works that the fundamental real reason for the creation of a "new" police system was to oversee and regulate class conflict in the interest of the ruling capitalist class (see Reiner, 2000), it is nevertheless doubtless that at the governmental level the prevention of crime was made apparent at the outset as the key object of the "new" policing system. In line with this preventative approach—which arguably guised the legitimization of an institution that represented state authority and power—emerged uniformed police officers on foot patrols; they were not to carry firearms and were only equipped with a stout truncheon. This symbolic representation of the police was meant to create a socially acceptable police force and, in sum, an image of a police officer as merely a "citizen in uniform." Yet the "new police" received a range of oppositions from different quarters. According to Reiner (2000, p. 39), working class resentment toward the new police "… was roused by police intervention in its recreational activities, and the use of the police to control industrial and political reform organization." In relation to the upper and middle classes, "… fears for traditional civil liberties, apprehension about central government encroachment in local affairs, and at the expense to ratepayers" (Reiner, 2000, p. 39) were reasons for their hostile response to the "new police."

Despite the apparent opposition from some sections, a police force was established in every county and borough in the country by the mid-1860s. Their key mission to "prevent crime" entailed regular street patrols and surveillance as a strategy for deterring thieves. In addition, they were given powers to make arrests or as Emsley (2003, p. 68) states, "… to take an individual's name and address for a future summons …." Emsley (2003, p. 68) notes that "within weeks after their first deployment, the new police were also being used in groups to clear the streets of Saturday night's hung-over human detritus, before the respectable walked to church for the Sunday morning service." Such array of duties assigned the new police signifies that from the beginning as Emsley (2003, p. 68) further states, "The new police were seen as a means to establish and to maintain a new threshold of order and respectability on the public highways" beyond their principal responsibility of crime prevention. As the new police (i.e., modern British policing system) found itself undergoing changes, developments, and refinements in policy and practice, the preventative ethos was also gradually becoming diluted amidst the changing variety of police duties that were not directly related to crime prevention as envisaged by Robert Peel.

By the late 1960s, emphasis on managerial professionalization, bureaucratization, specialization, and technology, and a focus on law enforcement have had the impact of marginalizing foot patrols in favor of motorized patrols. While the utilization of motorized patrols was aimed at affecting a speedy police response to public calls, a notable consequence of this transition was evident in diminished police community relations, which foot patrol work previously offered. In a sense, the origins of the modern British policing embraced elements of community policing, whereby foot patrol policing encouraged police community relations. The image of a British police officer as someone who could provide citizens with immediate assistance with the time, directions to streets, and so forth was quickly disappearing with increasing police powers and as policing became more technical. Subsequent police corruption scandals, increasing crime rates, and militarized-style policing of public disorders in the 1980s, among other things, culminated in a decline in public satisfaction with the nature of British policing. It was against this background that ideas relating to community policing surfaced.

Locating Community Policing in British Policing

Aside from the aforementioned instances of policing problems that gave rise to the notion of community policing in Britain, interest in community policing was influenced significantly by difficulties that were facing traditional policing in a society that was fast becoming characterized by a plurality of racial and ethnic groups. This was perhaps more apparent with the influx of black and Asian immigrants following World War II, and the subsequent series of confrontations between the British police and the new immigrants, particularly the black community. As illustrated in incidents of violent racial attacks on blacks and Asians that occurred in the 1940s and 1950s and escalated and worsened in the 1970s and 1980s, police response involved disproportionate arrests of black victims of racist attacks (Gordon, 1983; Miles and Phizaclea, 1984; Solomos, 1993). Consequent race-related riots that followed such racial attacks attracted similar police response. Despite many years of allegations against the police of high-profile policing and indiscriminate stop, search, and arrest practices in black localities, drug planting and fabrication of evidence, use of excessive physical force, and racist language (Hunte, 1966; John, 1970; Hall et al., 1978), it was in the aftermath of the 1981 Brixton (London) riots that the need to improve police–black community relations was highlighted. The riots involved violent clashes between the police and black youths. In his inquiry into the riots, Lord Scarman (a member of the House of Lords) emphasized the importance of police engagement with the communities they serve. One of Lord Scarman's recommendations to this effect related to police commitment to training provision in community relations. According to the Scarman Report (1981, p. 5.28):

> Training courses designed to develop the understanding that good community relations are not merely necessary but are essential to good policing should, I recommend, be compulsory from time to time in a police officer's career up to and including the rank of Superintendent. The theme of these courses should be the role of the police as part of the community, the operational importance of good community relations, the techniques of consultation and the moral as well as legal accountability of the police to the public.

Based on Scarman's recommendations and subsequent Home Office recommendations, there emerged Police Community Consultative Groups. While the Scarman Report assigned substantial impetus to what seemed to be a go-ahead for community policing, the idea of "community policing" is one that is not clearly defined in the United Kingdom policing policy and practice, but yet its key ethos of involving the community by way of policing *for* and *with* the community as opposed to policing *of* the community is found in narratives of contemporary British policing. In official discourses and documents, this is often mirrored in emphasized references to the need for partnership working relationships between the police and the public with the view to improving police–public relations, public confidence, the quality of public satisfaction, and police service provisions and delivery (Bennett, 1994). In theory, this understanding of community policing is captured in Alderson's *Policing Freedom* (1979, p. 199) where his framework for a "police system … in a free, permissive and participatory society" is underpinned by the following objectives:

- Contribute to liberty, equality, and fraternity.
- Help reconcile freedom with security and uphold the law.
- Uphold and protect human rights and thus help achieve human dignity.
- Dispel criminogenic social conditions, through cooperative social action.
- Help create trust in communities.
- Strengthen security and feelings of security.
- Investigate, detect, and activate the prosecution of crimes.
- Facilitate free movement along public thoroughfares.
- Curb public disorder.
- Deal with crisis and help those in distress involving other agencies where needed.

In keeping with Alderson's conceptualization of community-oriented policing in the United Kingdom and the general academic understanding of what it means in principle, community policing marginalizes emphasis on traditional law enforcement to prioritize community engagement with policing in a way that serves the benefit and interest of the quality of life of the community. Furthermore, community policing embraces some elements of problem-oriented policing, which in its broad sense seeks to adopt a strategic approach to effectively addressing issues and problems—of relevance to police crime control interests—that pose serious concerns to a community. The notion of problem-oriented policing owes its origins to the work of Goldstein (1979) whose examples of problem-oriented community concerns include "street robberies, residential burglaries, vandalism ... even fear" (p. 242). In some aspects, problem-oriented policing can require community involvement. Despite its scientific approach to crime control in terms of researching, data analyzing, understanding, and responding to the problems based on scientific interpretations, it can engage and mobilize the community in the identification and reduction of community problems that fall within the remit of the police (Anderson et al., 1994). To Skogan and Hartnett (1997), problem-oriented policing is a requirement of community policing amidst a range of other strategies through which community involvement in policing is initiated and sustained. Such strategies include police engagement in crime problem solving within communities and neighborhoods, and close working relationships between the police and the community in identifying problems and ways of responding to them.

In essence, community policing is responsive to the local community, which takes the lead role in defining community priorities and problems and policing needs; it is premised upon police organizational decentralization and community self-governance. However, the extent to which the fundamentals of community policing are illustrated in practice in the United Kingdom is questionable. The guiding principle of community policing seems straightforward, but to put it into practice throws the generic interpretation of community policing into chaos. In practice, it is interpreted and implemented in varying ways. According to Tilley (2003, p. 331), such variations are consistent with the "fluid ways in which community policing has been characterized" and, as such, "what is done in its name varies widely. Implementing it comprehensively has proved to be difficult." In spite of the lack of clarity about the specifics in practical community policing, a range of initiatives and practices have passed for an expression of community policing. Regardless of whether or not they have been effective in adhering to the philosophy of community policing, such initiatives have been bound together by their interest in partnership working between the police and the community to prevent and reduce crime and invariably improve community safety.

Community Policing in Practice

In the midst of inconsistencies as to what constitutes community policing in the British scenario, Weatheritt (1993, p. 126) draws out three features of what can be done in practice in community policing:

1. Establishment of structures and processes for consulting local communities about their policing priorities and problems.
2. Greater use of foot patrols and the posting of officers to geographic areas for which they have continuing responsibility.
3. Development of partnerships in crime prevention.

As noted above, the establishment of Police Community Consultative Groups was initiated by incidents of urban disorders and industrial disputes that characterized the 1980s, and these situations called for dramatic changes in the structure and policing style of the police force of which police engagement with the public constituted one of the changes. The Scarman Report, which laid the foundation for the formation of the Police Community Consultative Groups, partly attributed the cause of the 1981 riots to a lack of police–community consultation. Thus, Police Community Consultative Groups were viewed as a way forward for improving communication between the local police and the local community that they serve. Under Section 106 of the Police and Criminal Evidence Act 1984, the establishment of local consultative committees to effect community consultation became a statutory requirement, which was further endorsed and strengthened under the Crime and Disorder Act of 1998.

While there is evidence that police forces consider consultative committees a useful instrument for local community consultation, there is also evidence that this system faces challenges in terms of its effectiveness in establishing community participation. For one, there is the problem of community representation along the lines of who should be included in the consultation process and whose interests are being represented. As an acknowledgement of this problem, Section 6 of the Crime and Disorder Act 1998 also requires community consultation process to include "hard-to-reach" sections of the community. This would, in principle, include the views of marginalized and socially excluded groups, such as sections of minority ethnic communities and disaffected young people. To the extent that such social categories are more likely to come into contact with the criminal justice system, are more likely to attract negative media attention, and are more likely to be perceived as a "problem" within their local community, their representation has tended to be marginalized in local consultation. Another notable problematic issue relates to the extent to which local community participation in consultation informs police policy-making process. It has been claimed that such community consultation makes no significant impact on local policing policy (Commission for Racial Equality, 1991; Morgan, 1992) given that police responsiveness to community advice does not necessarily amount to police accountability. Police Community Consultative Groups have tended to amount to weak community involvement and participation because much decision-making power has rested with formal agencies. The success of community consultation mechanisms, therefore, has produced mixed findings in evidence (Jones et al., 1994).

The physical presence of community police officers in local community areas constitutes another way of bringing the police closer to the community. In one respect, this form of community policing involves foot patrols that, according to Eck and Spelman (1988, p. 32), "cast the police in the most traditional of roles. Because they are in direct contact with the public at almost all times, foot officers become informal authority figures … ." In the United Kingdom, foot patrols can help reduce people's fear of crime, and, as Shaftoe observes (2004, p. 150), ranks highest in "many surveys of the public's priorities about what they want in order to reduce crime list," even though they may not be effective in crime detection or prevention (Bennett, 1991). According to Shaftoe:

> The reason why more police patrols doesn't result in less crime lies in the nature of the crime itself. It is usually committed stealthily and not always in public places where the police are likely to be. For instance, a police officer might once every four years be within 100 metres of a place where a crime is being committed, and he or she will not necessarily see it take place. (Shaftoe, 2004, p. 149)

Furthermore, the presence of community beat officers is not necessarily a guarantee for a trusting relationship between all community members and the police. Hancock (2001) acknowledges this point in his observation that it is not often the case that community police officers relate to a community in ways that attract the trust of the community. Within communities where relations with the police are known to be relatively weak, the physical presence of police officers on foot patrols in such communities may not be received with open arms; instead it is more likely to generate suspicion rather than equip such communities with a feeling of trust in the police or even a general feeling of safety. After all, police officers on foot patrols are a part of the police service and, as such, their knowledge of neighborhoods and information gathered in the process of their community policing duties can inform police intelligence and influence policing policies. In this sense, this type of community policing can be viewed as a covert method of infiltrating communities and as an information-gathering tool for the police service with the primary objective to serve the interest of effective traditional policing (Gordon, 1984; Brake and Hale, 1992).

Notwithstanding the negatives and positives of foot patrol, it does not seem to be a significantly utilized and celebrated form of community policing for a variety of reasons, some of which Shaftoe outlines as:

> It is possibly this failure to reduce crime through patrolling that prompted the police to lose interest in putting bobbies on the beat, despite an overwhelming desire from the general public to have visible policing of the streets. It also has to be recognised that random patrolling is a boring activity for (predominantly) males who joined the police because it looked like it was going to be challenging and exciting. This restlessness may partially explain the high turnover of community police officers that undermines the building up of local intelligence and trust, but another factor is the tenure system in British police forces. Allegedly as a career progression facilitator but possibly as an anticorruption measure, police officers are systematically moved around both localities and tasks. Thus, for example, a community constable, who may just be beginning to really get to know the residents and needs of a particular neighbourhood, will be forcibly transferred to traffic duties in another area or on a city-wide drugs operation. (Shaftoe, 2004, p. 150)

Morgan and Newburn (1997) had expressed similar views a few years earlier when they stated that foot patrol is a low-status duty within the police service, and it is usually carried out by probationers who are often "the least experienced officers." Shaftoe (2004, p. 185) also observes that while public opinion in support of an increase in the number of foot patrols has had that effect in some police areas, there is a general problem of limited resources, which means that "police establishments would have to be increased many times over to make any serious impact on the visibility and accessibility of officers on the street." In like manner, Morgan and Newburn (1997) have argued that any police work that does not yield immediate or worthwhile potential dividend in terms of crime prevention, detection, and clear-up rates is less likely to be considered by the police service as an effective use of police time and resources.

Of the various forms of community policing, it seems that community involvement in crime prevention partnerships is more demonstrative of the philosophy of community policing. Without delving into the origins—located in the 1950s and 1960s—of the multiagency partnership approach in contemporary British crime prevention strategy (see, for example, Gilling, 1997, for information on origins), it is nevertheless the case that the political agenda to widen crime prevention responsibility beyond the auspices of the traditional system of policing was to involve community participation. By the late 1970s and early 1980s, the growing concerns about crime and the increasing critique of the criminal justice system for failing to effectively tackle and control crime were among crucial precipitators of the "new" approach to practical crime prevention. Findings from the first British Crime Survey in 1982 (Hough and Mayhew, 1983) and subsequent sweeps of the survey in the 1980s revealed increasing public fear of crime and uncovered notable "dark figure" of crime, which was significantly attributed to considerable rates of nonreporting of crime victimization. In both scenarios, the effectiveness of the criminal justice system in alleviating public fear of crime and in engaging public trust in the system was called into critical questions, and thus grounded justifications for informal systems of control in the fight against crime.

Herein, the "community" features as an informal control system in crime prevention in a way that mirrors a framework whereby the community polices its own community. The idea of community policing in crime prevention stems from a philosophical notion that strategies to prevent crime should be localized and invariably reflective of collective community experiences of the crime problem. In keeping with this notion of community as the starting point for policing local crime is the understanding that the community presents a site for an informal social control of crime. This interpretation, which favors a decentralized approach to tackling local crime, advocates the involvement and participation of all sections of the community in the fight against harmful and damaging consequences of crime that affect their everyday lives. The crime problem-oriented approach underpinning this thinking of the central role of the community appeals to a partnership approach, which draws interventions from the community through community groups, and a range of relevant agencies in the voluntary, private, and public sectors. A notable example of the "community" as an informal policing agent in crime prevention is the neighborhood watch (NW), an import from North America. The neighborhood watch crime prevention initiative is an apparent illustration of public concerns about crime as well as public dissatisfaction with the traditional method of policing crime.

First introduced in Britain in 1982, NW schemes are a collective endeavor involving low-level local surveillance by residents who watch out for each other's property and suspicious behavior in particular neighborhoods. Coordinators are appointed to take the lead role in liaising with the police. Neighborhood watch has been considered the most visible and successful crime prevention strategy in Britain, at least judging by its rapid growth and geographical spread during the 1980s and 1990s. Five years after its emergence, an estimated figure of 2.5 million people resided in areas with a NW scheme. By 1992, one in five households was a member of a NW scheme (Dowds and Mayhew, 1994). Following its birth, it was supported and promoted by senior police officers as a useful instrument through which community members would principally become the "eyes" and "ears" of the police and invariably work closely with the police in crime prevention. Two aims underpin the NW crime prevention initiative. The first and most important is to reduce primarily residential burglary and "opportunistic crime," and, secondly, criminal damage and vehicle crime. The second aim encompasses a range of objectives, such as promoting crime prevention awareness in local communities, reducing people's fear of crime, and facilitating and improving interactions between neighbors and between the community and the police.

In spite of the enthusiasm with which this crime prevention scheme was received, it has faced a range of challenges thereby limiting its effectiveness. One challenge that has faced many NW schemes relates to the problem of limited life expectancy as a result of their tendency to be inactive. Although this problem of NW inactiveness is evident in middle-class communities and neighborhoods where the scheme is known to have flourished, it is most apparent in deprived inner-city areas with high levels of crime, heterogeneous and transient populations, and little sense of community cohesion (Hope, 1988). Also important to the functioning and activeness of NW schemes is police involvement and participation. Police officers' responsiveness to the NW-type community policing would be welcomed in some communities and not in some others. As Laycock and Tilley (1995) note, appreciation of police support for NW policing would typically occur in relatively stable communities, usually middle-class localities, where attitudes toward the police tend to be favorable and where invariably police–community trust is established to foster support for and cooperation with the police. Such areas that are noted for their low levels of crime often have established NW schemes composed of members who are likely to be the typical "ears and eyes" of the police. Consequently, police resources will tend to be diverted to these areas.

In contrast, socially disorganized communities with high levels of socio-economic deprivation and crime, and where relationships with the police have exhibited little or no trust, are less likely to embrace police involvement in their business even though such communities tend to be most in need of NW schemes and similar forms of community policing. To illustrate this point, see Kalunta-Crumpton, 2005, on the issue of black community safety within the general framework of community–police partnership to effect crime prevention and community safety. The author notes in the 2005 article that black people have continued to be over-represented in police "stop and search" and arrest figures for crime perpetration (Home Office, 1998, 2002, 2005, 2006). Meanwhile similar police attention is not accorded the black community at the point of crime victimization. Findings from the British Crime Surveys have shown that black people's risks of criminal victimization are higher or comparable to those for whites for differing household and personal crimes, but the levels of worry about crime, in general, are higher among blacks than whites (Salisbury and Upson, 2004). However, black victims of both household and personal crimes feel a higher level of dissatisfaction with police response than their white counterparts particularly in relation to racially motivated hate crimes (Clancy et al., 2001). Other situations, which have placed huge obstacles in the way of healthy black community–police relations, relate to police brutality and deaths of blacks while in police custody. The latter instance has in the past aroused incidents of violent confrontations between the black community and the police as demonstrated in the Brixton (London) and Tottenham (London) riots of 1985 following the death of a black woman, Cynthia Jarrett, during a police search of her home, and the 1995 Brixton riots in the wake of the death of Wayne Douglas (a black man) in the Brixton police station.

I consequently argued that, given the long history of tense police–black community relations, community policing in the forms of crime prevention and community safety strategies that is meant to thrive on contacts and liaisons between the black community and the police is less likely to be successful principally because of the black community's distrust of the police. As Hall (2001, p. 8) states in his article, *From Scarman to Macpherson*, "relations between black communities and police have continued to be marked by mistrust, prejudice, and disrespect, often leading to tragedy." Related to these, fears that reporting crime in the black community could lead to further criminalization of the black community can preclude support for any police-linked community policing. In the context of this scenario, the role of the police in NW schemes can act as a deterrent rather than a favored initiative for inner-city resident participation, particularly the black community, in these schemes. This observation coincides with Tilley's (2003, p. 332) view that "those attracted to working with the police on these terms are rarely the disaffected whose relatively poor relations with the police prompted recommendations for community policing." He adds:

> Indeed, there is a risk that it might reinforce notions among the disaffected that there is too cosy a relationship between sections of the community, with their own interests and the police service (Tilley, 2003, p. 332).

That notwithstanding, there is evidence that NW schemes can attract support in neighborhoods with high risks of crime and the support is notably facilitated by resident satisfaction with their neighborhoods (Hope, 1988). However, NW schemes in such neighborhoods may also have a high attrition rate, which many NW schemes have experienced, including schemes in middle-class neighborhoods. As McConville and Shepard (1992, p. 115) note, most NW schemes have "low take-up rates, weak community penetration and limping, dormant or stillborn schemes." Herein, low-level participation in NW schemes can be demonstrated simply through street signs indicating areas covered by NW, having a neighborhood watch window sticker, and/or having a NW member's name and a number on the police crime prevention figures. To an extent, this level of activism is also linked to the level and nature of police involvement in the schemes. As a result of limited police resources, many NW schemes are under-resourced in terms of the level of police assistance that can be provided to these schemes. As another example, Shaftoe (2004) identifies quick turnover of community police officers as a crippling factor for community policing initiatives including NW schemes. He observes:

> Local residents, particularly those actively involved in community initiatives, such as neighbourhood watch, find this rapid turnover of nominated police officers particularly frustrating; a problem compounded by the tendency for those deployed at the soft end of policing to be called away at a moment's notice to react to emergencies and high-profile incidents. This instability of policing was a significant factor in the failure of an initiative that purchased extra community policing for a neighbourhood in York … . (p. 150).

In the midst of the range of challenges that have faced NW schemes, there has nevertheless been some evidence of benefits from these schemes. Although findings in relation to their effectiveness in crime reduction are mixed (Bennett, 1989, 1990; Dowds and Mayhew, 1994), they tend to have an effect on the reduction in fear of household crime and increased feeling of community cohesion.

The neighborhood watch initiative has since its birth in the early 1980s produced offshoots, which have included "street watch," "boat watch," "farm watch," "business watch," and "vehicle watch." Of the offshoots from the NW scheme, the most notable has been the street watch. This has involved the patrolling of neighborhoods by NW groups. The idea for street watches was initiated in 1994 by the then Home Secretary, Michael Howard, whose suggestion that neighborhood watch schemes should "walk with a purpose" through volunteer resident patrols, amounted to widespread operation of street watches. The use of street watch as a crime prevention and community safety measure has received criticisms particularly in relation to its potential for vigilantism. In one example of a street watch aimed at tackling drugs and prostitution in a major English city, Birmingham, there were claims that, in the process of street patrols by local residents, innocent women were mistaken for prostitutes, and prostitutes were unduly harassed and intimidated. This was despite evidence of reductions in prostitution as well as violent crimes and burglary during the period of the street watch. Its success in this respect was effected by residents gathering and transmitting information to the police (Atkinson, 1996).

Street watch by virtue of its link to neighborhood watch is in some ways bound to experience challenges that have faced the neighborhood watch scheme in its own right. For example, street watch is more likely to succeed in the relatively better organized residential areas as opposed to neighborhoods with the highest rates of crime and socio-economic deprivation, and heterogeneous and transient populations. There are also problems of sustaining active participation and interest over time, and a key problem of establishing accountability and legitimacy in support of its actions—an issue that grounded police opposition to civilian policing in the form of street watch in the wake of Michael Howard's announcement.

In Conclusion

As it stands, there is no general consensus as to what community policing illustrates in practice so that what constitutes practical community policing is equivalent to variations in its definition. Given this, the instances of community policing described above should not be viewed as representing an exhaustive list. Although these examples may illustrate practical community policing from a majority perspective, there are other forms of community or public involvement in policing that have been interpreted as community policing and these include scenarios where civilians are employed by the police force to engage in policing work in the community. Examples are found in the form of "response policing," Special Constabulary, Police Community Support Officers, and the Neighborhood Policing Program.

To some, response policing is an example of community policing; it involves emergency 24-hour response by police officers to calls from members of the public (Foster, 2003). Some others could view Special Constabulary as an example of community policing. Special constables are individual members of the public who join the police force as formal volunteers to provide support service to the police. As a move toward promoting public involvement in policing in crime prevention and community safety, Special Constabulary has been encouraged by the government notably since the 1980s. Special constables wear uniforms and possess the powers of police constables, but are hardly exposed to situations where they might have to utilize those powers.

Police Community Support Officers (or Community Support Officers—CSO) can also be seen as a form of community policing given the recruitment of civilians to "police" communities under the formal auspices of the police force and under the direction of the local police commander. These, like similar forms of civilian policing, are members of what is referred to as the accredited "extended police family." In the midst of resource pressures on the police to provide the public with its demand for patrol service, the use of Police Community Support Officers (PCSOs) as an alternative form of police patrol was facilitated by the Police Reform Act 2002. Police Community Support Officers were introduced in September 2002, despite a notable degree of opposition from the police service at the prospect of a formal civilian patrolling service. The role of PCSOs is to provide a visible presence in local communities by way of foot patrols, and in doing so "combat low-level antisocial behavior and provide reassurance" (Crawford, 2003, p. 157). As paid and uniformed officers, they "are intended to support police officers and release fully trained officers from tasks that do not require their level of skills" (Crawford, 2003, p. 157). Like the Special Constabulary and other members of the "extended police family," the powers of PCSOs are limited as Crawford indicates:

> The powers of CSOs are restricted to hand out, fixed-penalty tickets for minor disorders, to request the name and address of a person acting in an antisocial manner, to stop vehicles, direct traffic and remove vehicles. … More controversially, CSOs will be able to detain a person for up to 30 minutes pending the arrival of a constable or to accompany that person to a police station with the person's agreement. Significantly, CSOs will also have the power to use reasonable force to enforce that detention (Crawford, 2003, p. 158).

More recently, the government's agenda of communitarian police reform is illustrated in the Neighborhood Policing Program introduced in 2006. Neighborhood policing embraces key principles of (public) reassurance policing to improve "sense of security," reduce "antisocial and quality of life offenses," improve "confidence in policing," and increase "social capital/collective efficacy" (National Reassurance Policing Program, 2003). The community–police partnership framework of neighborhood policing is illustrated in the statement below:

> We want every community to benefit from dedicated, accessible and visible neighbourhood policing teams—led by police officers but involving special constables, community support officers, volunteers, neighbourhood wardens, and others too—and to know who their local police officers are and how to contact them (Home Office, 2007).

And the neighborhood policing concept of public reassurance is illustrated in the following excerpt (Home Office, 2007):

> … true neighbourhood policing means more than extra frontline resources or public reassurance. It means becoming more effective at crime reduction by working directly with and harnessing the energies of local communities. It means reconfiguring the whole relationship between the individual citizen, the local neighbourhood, and the police service so that they work in partnership to deal with crime and anti-social behavior.

> We see neighbourhood policing as key to ensuring mainstream local policing services are driven by neighbourhood and community needs. So that people who are actually affected by problems of crime, and disorder, who are often best placed to find solutions right for that area, have a say in what the priorities are.
>
> But this isn't just about responding to whoever shouts the loudest. It means taking an intelligence-led approach, with the application of NIM (Police National Intelligence Model, *author emphasis*) to neighbourhood issues, and putting in place the right resources to deal appropriately with the particular problems of different neighbourhoods.
>
> Recognize a "one-size fits all" approach will not work. Numbers, staffing mix, skills, and powers will need to be appropriate to the particular needs of the neighbourhood. This means in some areas community support officers and employees of local authorities such as wardens will be best placed to deal with local problems.
>
> But in other places—perhaps with the more acute crime problems—police officers will be doing most of the work (Home Office, 2007).

In this context of neighborhood policing, the evident multiagency partnership, in which the police seemingly take the lead role, is bound to experience conflictual situations, for instance, in relation to power and resource distribution that is often found in multiagency partnership working.

A major obstacle to an effective neighborhood policing is the role of "the community" in the partnership. This crucial feature of neighborhood policing throws in its own complexities, and this is principally because of the difficulties in making sense of what "community" illustrates in theory and practice. In reality, "community" is not a universal, collective, and stable entity, rather it is changeable, plural, and fragmented by its characterization of differing and conflicting identities and interests.

This problematic concept of "community" applies to differing forms of policing enterprises where community involvement and participation is a central feature. While the notion of "community" in the rhetoric of community policing is that which articulates an image of a community reminiscent of Emile Durkheim's "collective conscience"—exhibited, for example, in shared values, morals, and attitudes—the reality is that much of the failure of community policing is related to this misconceived idea of "community." As already described above, community policing is difficult to operate in residential areas where it is most needed: socio-economically deprived inner-city localities with high crime rates. In such areas, crime tends to be intracommunal—a scenario that itself generates a divided and an exclusive community as opposed to a united and an inclusive one. The heterogeneous nature of many urban areas renders the notion of "community" questionable in terms of what it actually signifies. In sum, I refer to Morgan and Newburn's (1997, pp. 144–145) concerns about the idealized use of the concept of "community" in the British context:

> It is one of the ironies of the late twentieth century social policy that "community" is the title designed to make acceptable so many policy initiatives—community care, community medicine, community policing, and so on—during a period when there is arguably less of a sense of community than at any point in our social history. But that, of course, is the explanation of the fashion. The promotion of "community" suggests the restoration of a world that we have lost but hanker for. It follows that we must beware that concepts, such as "community policing," will prove little more than rhetorical devices masking an implausible aspiration and a barren operation.

To date what constitutes community policing—although unclear in the British context—has taken various forms incorporating a range of community–police partnerships, some which are not described in this paper. Notwithstanding any limitations presented by the various forms of what can be interpreted as community policing, the involvement of the community in policing has continued to find favor in the British government's approaches to policing.

References

Alderson, J. (1979). *Policing freedom*. Plymouth: Macdonald and Evans.

Anderson, D., Chenery, S., & Pease, K. (1994). Biting back: Tackling repeat burglary and car crime, *Crime Detection and Prevention Series Paper* 58. London: Home Office.

Atkinson, R. (1996). *Reclaiming the streets: Building a sustainable community.* Birmingham: Phoenix.

Bennett, T. (1989). The Neighbourhood watch experience. In R. Morgan & D. Smith (Eds.), *Coming to terms with policing* (pp. 138–155). London: Routledge.

Bennett, T. (1990). *Evaluating neighbourhood watch.* Aldershot: Gower.

Bennett, T. (1991). The effectiveness of a police initiated fear reducing strategy. *British Journal of Criminology, 30*, 1–14.

Bennett, T. (1994). Community policing on the ground: Developments in Britain. In D. Rosenbaum (Ed.), *The challenge of community policing* (pp. 224–246). Thousand Oaks, CA: Sage.

Brake, M. & Hale, C. (1992). *Public order and private lines.* London: Routledge.

Clancy, A., Hough, M., Aust, R., & Kershaw, C. (2001). *Ethnic minorities' experiences of crime and policing.* Findings from the 2000 British Crime Survey, Findings 146. London: Home Office.

Commission for Racial Equality. (1991). *The point of order: A study of consultative arrangements under Section 106 of the Police and Criminal Evidence Act.* London: Commission for Racial Equality.

Crawford, A. (2003). The pattern of policing in the UK: Policing beyond the police. In T. Newburn (Ed.), *Handbook of policing* (pp. 136–168). Devon: Willan Publishing.

Dowds, L. & Mayhew, P. (1994). *Participation in neighbourhood watch: Finding from the 1992 British crime survey.* Home Office Research Findings No. 11. London: Home Office.

Eck, J.E. & Spelman, W. (1988). Who ya gonna call? The police as problem-busters. *Crime and Delinquency, 33*, 31–52.

Emsley, C. (2003). The birth and development of the police. In T. Newburn (Ed.), *Handbook of policing* (pp. 66–83). Devon: Willan Publishing.

Foster, J. (2003). Police cultures. In T. Newburn (Ed.), *Handbook of policing* (pp. 196–227). Devon: Willan Publishing.

Gilling, D. (1997). *Crime prevention: Theory, practice and politics.* London: University College London.

Goldstein, H. (1979). Improving policing: A problem-oriented approach. *Crime and Delinquency, 25*, 236–258.

Gordon, P. (1983). *White law.* London: Pluto.

Gordon, P. (1984). Community policing: Towards the local police state. *Critical Social Policy, 10*, 39–58.

Hall, S. (2001). From Scarman to Macpherson. *Society Matters, 3*, 1–12.

Hall, S., Critcher, C., Clarke, J.. Jefferson, T., & Roberts, B. (1978). *Policing the crisis.* London: Macmillan.

Hancock, L. (2001). *Community, crime and disorder: Safety and regeneration in urban neighbourhoods.* Basingstoke: Palgrave.

Home Office. (1998). *Statistics on race and the criminal justice system.* London: Home Office.

Home Office. (2002). *Statistics on race and the criminal justice system.* London: Home Office.

Home Office. (2005). *Statistics on race and the criminal justice system.* London: Home Office.

Home Office. (2006). *Statistics on race and the criminal justice system.* London: Home Office.

Home Office. (2007). *Neighbourhood policing.* http://www.homeoffice.gov.uk (accessed April 30, 2007).

Hope, T. (1988). Support for neighbourhood watch: A British crime survey analysis. In T. Hope & M. Shaw (Eds.), *Communities and crime reduction* (pp. 146–161. London: HMSO.

Hough, M. & Mayhew, P. (1983). *The British crime survey: First report*, Home Office Research Study No. 76. London: Home Office.

Hunte, J. (1966). *Nigger* hunting *in England?* London: West Indian Standing Conference.

John, G. (1970). *Race in the inner city.* London: Runnymede Trust.

Jones, T., Newburn, T., & Smith, D. (1994). *Democracy and* policing. London: Policy Studies Institute.

Kalunta-Crumpton, A. (2005). How safe is Britain's black community? *Community Safety Journal, 4*(2), 21–28.

Laycock, G. & Tilley, N. (1995). *Policing and neighbourhood watch: Strategic issues.* Crime Prevention and Detection Series Paper 60. London: Home Office.

McConville, M. & Shephard, D. (1992). *Watching police watching communities.* London: Routledge.

Miles, R. & Phizaclea, A. (1984). *White man's country.* London: Pluto.

Morgan, R. (1992). *Talking about policing.* London: Macmillan.

Morgan, R. & Newburn, T. (1997). *The future of policing.* Oxford: Oxford University Press.

National Reassurance Policing Programme. (2003). *Performance management conceptual paper.* London: Home Office.

Reiner, R. (2000). *The politics of the police.* Oxford: Oxford University Press.

Reith, C. (1956). *A new study of policy history.* Edinburgh: Oliver and Boyd.

Salisbury, H. & Upson, A. (2004). *Ethnicity, victimisation and worry about crime.* Findings from the 2001/02 and 2002/03 British crime surveys, Findings 237. London: Home Office.

Scarman, L. (1981). *The Brixton disorders 10–12 April 1981.* Report of an Inquiry by the Rt. Hon. The Lord Scarman. London: HMSO.

Shaftoe, H. (2004). *Crime prevention: Facts, fallacies and the future.* Basingstoke: Palgrave.

Skogan, W. & Hartnett, S. (1997). *Community policing Chicago style.* New York: Oxford University Press.

Solomos, J. (1993). *Race and racism in Britain.* London: Macmillan.

Tilley, N. (2003). Community policing, problem-oriented policing and intelligence-led policing. In T. Newburn (Ed.), *Handbook of Policing* (pp. 311–339). Devon: Willan Publishing.

Weatheritt, H. (1993). Community policing. In H. Butcher, A. Glen, P. Henderson, & J. Smith (Eds.), *Community and public policy* (pp. 124–138). London: Pluto Press.

Community Policing in the United States
Social Control through Image Management

8

DAVID E. BARLOW
MELISSA HICKMAN BARLOW

Contents

Introduction

Scholars and practitioners around the world have adopted the term *community policing* to describe a wide variety of policing strategies during the past 30 years. Most discussions of the history of police in the United States refer to the latest chapter in U.S. police history as the Community Era of policing, as the era was identified in Kelling and Moore's (1988) now classic work. Departing from Kelling and Moore, we have identified the past three decades of policing in the United States as "postmodern policing" (Barlow & Barlow, 1999, 2000). In this chapter, we discuss how characterizing the contemporary era in policing as *postmodern* not only captures the various initiatives that have been implemented in policing during the time period, but also has explanatory power, connecting developments in policing to developments in the political economy. We demonstrate that the changes that have occurred in policing in the past three decade and the ways in which policing has failed to change in the United States have resulted from the nearly universal adoption of community policing.

Postmodern policing refers to a variety of initiatives, including but not limited to community policing, problem-oriented policing, and quality of life policing. The terminology alone leaves little doubt that the past three decades in U.S. policing represent a historically specific paradigm that is notably distinct from the previous period, which Kelling and Moore (1988) called the Traditional Era, and we refer to as Modern Policing. It is clear that there has emerged an effective communication toward policing in the past three decades. On close examination, to say that there have been changes in rhetoric does not deny the substantive changes that have occurred in police practices during the past 30 years. However, we do reject the dichotomy of rhetoric versus reality as expressed in Greene and Mastrofski's (1988) collection of readings entitled, *Community Policing: Rhetoric Versus Reality.* Rhetoric is powerful and it is real. Words and images matter and can shape processes, policies, and strategies. On the other hand, though dramatic changes have occurred in the rhetoric of policing, the fundamental role of police in society has not changed (Barlow & Barlow, 2006). As part of the criminal justice system in the United States, the role of police is to maintain the social order. The criminal justice system is part of the social structure of accumulation in the capitalist political economy. As such, its purpose is to preserve the status quo in relations of power. For this reason, the perpetual problems faced by police scholars and practitioners in their attempts to (1) define community policing (Oliver, 2000), (2) implement the early tenets of community policing while reducing crime and the fear of crime (Williams, 1999; Scheider, Rowell, & Bezdikian, 2003), (3) transform the structure of police agencies (Maguire, 1997; Vito, Walsh, & Kunselman, 2005; Bromley & Cochran, 2000; Pelfrey, 2004), or (4) change individual police officer perspectives (Lilley & Hinduja, 2006; Giacomazzi & Smithey, 2001; Vito, Walsh, & Kunselman, 2005) are rooted in the fundamental contradictions associated with the pursuit of justice in an unjust society (Barlow & Barlow, 2000).

Explanation

The topic of community policing has dominated police literature for over two decades, but very little work has focused on explaining this paradigmatic shift. The vast majority of the literature focuses on description rather than explanation. Countless articles and books have been written on defining community policing, evaluating community policing strategies, or measuring whether things have really changed. The rhetoric of community policing is so positive and seemingly benign that few question the value of implementing community policing. Who among us would be opposed to the police being more responsive to the community or seeking to solve the problems that produce crime with proactive and innovative strategies rather than simply reacting to crime? To question the value of community policing places the critic at odds with humanity and justice. It is generally assumed that the turmoil of the 1960s and the apparent failure of the police to reduce crime and disorder led thoughtful people to "reform" the police, making police more humane, just, and effective. The police scholarship of the 1970s and 1980s clearly established the reform perspective as the foundation for the philosophy of community policing (Oliver, 2000).

Zhao (1996) is one of a few scholars who have attempted to *explain* the emergence of community policing within police departments, rather than simply to assume that community policing is merely a reflection of the march of progress. Zhao tested a number of hypotheses regarding factors influencing departments to adopt community policing and argued that the primary causal factor has been the external environment. Zhao's conclusion is consistent with our view, but we take a more macrolevel approach to the question. Rather than focusing on individual police agencies, we consider the question of what drives the broad-based community policing movement in the United States. If, as Zhao suggests, the external environment influences police departments to adopt community policing, what are the forces that shape the external environment? We argue that the mesolevel external environment central to Zhao's explanation is shaped by and gives shape to the broader political economy. In fact, Zhao's research identifies an important link between what goes on in police departments and what goes on in the broader political economy. Klockars (1991, p. 240) wrote that community policing "is best understood as the latest in a fairly long tradition of circumlocutions whose purpose is to conceal, mystify, and legitimate police distribution of nonnegotiable coercive force." Zhao's findings combined with Klockars' observation begin to suggest an explanation for the community policing movement in the United States.

Contrary to the tendency of police textbook writers to present an evolutionary perspective on police reform, community policing is one among many innovations in policing that have emerged in various periods in the history of the United States. Our ability to explain this development, or any other in police history, is lost when we assume that police reform is an inevitable and progressive march toward ever better and more enlightened policing. Police institutions, policies, and practices are forged within political, economic, and social contexts by human actors with specific intentions and motivations that are not necessarily, or even typically, altruistic or noble. Explanations must account for the ways in which the politics of gender, race, and class influence the specific formations of police because they are part of every aspect of U.S. life and history. Our explanation of community policing in the United States connects community policing to a political economy of criminal justice.

A Political Economy of Criminal Justice

Our analysis of the historical development of police in the United States (Barlow & Barlow, 1995, 2000; Barlow, Barlow, & Johnson, 1996) is part of a broader theory of criminal justice (Barlow, Barlow, & Chiricos, 1993) that we developed by linking the punishment and social structure literature, building on the work of Georg Rusche (Rusche & Kirchheimer, 1968; Rusche, 1978), with the work of Gordon, Edwards, and Reich (1982) on the social structure of accumulation. The punishment and social structure literature provides evidence of a direct relationship between economic conditions and criminal justice policy. Gordon et al.'s (1982) theory on the social structure of accumulation illustrates the interdependence of political and economic institutions within the capitalist democracy of the United States. Our theory is that crime control policy and practices are integral components of the political structure and, as such, are shaped by critical shifts in both the mode and means of production. Thus, investigating the history of police in relation to political and economic developments helps to explain the shifts that have occurred in the organization and operation of policing in the United States.

According to Gordon et al. (1982), the social structure of accumulation consists of all of the institutions that affect, directly or indirectly, the process capital accumulation. In a capitalist economy, the *process* of accumulation is characterized by a cycle of investment, production, consumption, and valorization. The *structure* of accumulation includes a number of components, including the level of technological development, the intensity of the class struggle, the organization of work, the structure of the labor market, and the form of the state. The vital role of the state is to secure and maintain the social order, thus contributing to business confidence. Business confidence, of course, is a necessary precursor for investment, which is necessary if the cycle is to continue. Through state apparatuses of social control, including the criminal justice apparatus, government officials work to preserve the peace. Social peace enhances business confidence, which facilitates economic growth. All of the relationships are multidirectional. That is, not only does social peace create business confidence leading to economic growth, economic growth is essential to the social peace in a capitalistic society.

Based on our political economic theory of criminal justice, the methods by which police seek to secure the social order are largely shaped by the particular character of the political economy in operation at any given time. For example, before the U.S. Civil War, the Southern states had a political economy based on racial slavery. Exceptionally harsh and violent methods were commonly practiced to maintain social order in the context of an openly exploitative and oppressive political economy. As northern states developed an industrial economy, based on free rather than slave labor, new and different forms of social control emerged in the context of a political economy in which the exploitation of labor was masked by the capitalist ideology of a politically free society. Violent corporal punishment was rarely necessary to secure compliance with the relations of production. Within a democratic society, those who govern must secure the consent of those who are governed in order to police them because citizens of a democratic society have freedoms and opportunities to resist being policed (Barlow et al., 1993; Barlow & Barlow, 2000). Social control is more effective when the agents of social control are viewed as legitimate by those who are controlled. Community policing is not the only strategy to have been employed by police to secure legitimacy. It is simply the most recent (Barlow & Barlow, 1999).

Our historical analysis divides the formation and development of publicly funded municipal police organizations in the United States into four distinct periods. We label the first period Preindustrial Policing because it includes police organizations that emerged before the formation of large industrial urban areas. Industrial Policing describes the second period because it includes the formation of new municipal police organizations that emerged in large cities following the first industrial revolution between the 1790s and the 1820s. The third period, Modern Policing, encompasses the radical reconstruction of public policing of public policing that occurred in conjunction with modernization, beginning in the 1870s and continuing through the first part of the twentieth century. We refer to the most recent innovations in police strategies that employed beginning in the late twentieth century in the United States as Postmodern Policing (Barlow & Barlow, 1999, 2000).

Each of these four eras represents revolutionary changes in policing strategies, organization, and technology; however, the transition from one period to another is not abrupt and distinct. Similar to revolutionary shifts in the political economy within capitalism, each period in policing has overlapping stages of exploration, consolidation, and decay (Gordon et al., 1982; Barlow & Barlow, 1995, 2000; Barlow, Barlow & Johnson, 1996). During periods of exploration, new approaches are explored and experiments are undertaken. In periods of decay, legitimacy crises arise in relation to the adopted policing strategy. Between the exploration and decay of a form of policing, there is a "consolidation" phase in which the distinctly new police strategy is institutionalized and becomes prevalent. Although a new strategy dominates during consolidation, remnants of previous stages remain and some agencies simply do not adopt the new strategy. The following analysis of developments in U.S. policing in relation to the political economy helps us to place the most recent organizational strategy of policing, community policing, into historical perspective.

Preindustrial Policing

According to Walker (1980), Southern cities, such as Charleston, South Carolina, formed the very first publicly funded municipal police departments in the United States in order to preserve the racist social order and to maintain slavery. Charleston established a mounted daytime patrol in the 1740s as part of a larger effort to control the growing slave population. By 1837, the Charleston Police Department had 100 officers and the primary function of this organization was slave patrol. Genovese (1976, p. 617–618) explained that to "curb runaways, hold down interplantation theft, and prevent the formation of insurrectionary plots, the slaveholders developed an elaborate system of patrols." These officers regulated the movements of slaves and free Blacks, checking documents, enforcing slave codes, guarding against slave revolts, and catching runaway slaves. Walker (1992b, p. 6) referred to this "distinctly American form of law enforcement," the slave patrols, as the "first modern police forces in this country." According to Genovese (1976, p. 22), the slave patrols were made up of mostly poor Whites who frequently "whipped and terrorized slaves caught without passes after curfew." In the following excerpt, Williams and Murphy (1990, p. 4) described the extensive power granted these patrols:

> "Slave patrols" had full power and authority to enter any plantation and break open Negro houses or other places where slaves were suspected of keeping arms, to punish runaways or slaves found outside their plantations without a pass, to whip any slave who should affront or abuse them in the execution of their duties, and to apprehend and take any slave suspected of stealing or other criminal offense, and bring him to the nearest magistrate. Understandably, the actions of such patrols established an indelible impression on both the whites who implemented this system and the Blacks who were the brunt of it.

The patrols were very successful in accomplishing their main purpose: "They struck terror in the slaves" (Genovese, 1976, p. 618).

African slaves and their descendants did not simply acquiesce to their predicament. Resistance took many forms, including work slowdowns, breaking tools, theft, arson, murder, and even armed rebellion. For Whites, the most frightening form of slave resistance was armed revolt. Genovese (1976, p. 615) explained that violent rebellions were frequent enough that "in every decade slaveholders in every part of the South got an occasional jolt from news that normally obedient slaves had killed a master, mistress, or overseer." It is informative to note that Stono, South Carolina, experienced a relatively large rebellion in 1739, shortly before the formation of the Charleston slave patrols. According to Zinn (1980), about 80 slaves participated in this armed revolt. As they marched to the beat of two drums and shouts of "liberty," they broke into warehouses to steal guns, burned buildings, and killed Whites. The militia responded and 50 slaves and 20 Whites were killed in the ensuing battle. Williams and Murphy (1990) argued that the primary motivation for the creation of this new form of policing was the fear that the militia was unable to adequately control slave rebellions.

Considering Charleston's critical role in the slave trade, its large slave population, and the highly unstable nature of a slave economy, it is not surprising that Charleston was the site of the first public municipal police force in the United States. According to Zinn (1980, p. 76), fear of social disorder was so prevalent that, during the American Revolution, South Carolina "could hardly fight against the British, her militia had to be used to keep slaves under control." From their inception in this country, police have played a pivotal role not just in maintaining social order, but also in preserving the status quo—a status quo that was extremely unequal, racist, and unjust. Williams and Murphy (1990, p. 2) argued that this legacy is a critical element in understanding police history, and for understanding contemporary police.

The fact that the legal order not only countenanced but sustained slavery, segregation, and discrimination for most of our nation's history—and the fact that the police were bound to uphold that order—set a pattern for police behavior and attitudes toward minority communities that has persisted until the present day. That pattern includes the idea that minorities have fewer civil rights, that the task of the police is to keep them under control, and that the police have little responsibility for protecting them from crime within their communities.

When placed in historical context, the maintenance of order cannot be viewed as a neutral function for the equal benefit of all in society. As long as the social order is an unequal order, then the maintenance of order is inherently repressive to those on the bottom and beneficial to those at the top.

Industrial Policing

By the onset of the nineteenth century, Northern states had eliminated slavery except as a condition of punishment or debt. However, just as the origin of the first public, salaried municipal police in the South was slave patrols whose job was to control the slave population, the first police departments in Northern industrial cities were charged with controlling urban poor populations comprised of free Blacks and recent immigrants. Economically, surplus populations are an asset to capitalists because they serve as an available pool of workers for business owners faced with labor disputes, strikes, or even contract negotiations (Adamson, 1984). However, because surplus populations are at the bottom of the social stratification system, they are also a liability to the system. They derive little benefit from the existing social order and, therefore, pose a potential threat to social order. For police to maintain social peace in a society with sharp class divisions, their efforts are logically directed toward economically marginalized populations.

From the 1780s into the 1820s, the United States experienced an industrial revolution with the large-scale introduction of artisan-produced machines and the steam engine into the manufacturing of goods (Wright, 1979). With accelerated growth and the formation of a world market for industrial goods, the rate of profit was high, leading to high levels of investment and production (Mandel, 1978). During this period of economic growth, industrialists needed a large supply of laborers. A massive number of immigrants were attracted to the United States. Most were poor and destitute (Gordon et al., 1982). The rapid growth of urbanization, industrialization, and immigration gave rise to a host of social problems, which the leaders of the young nation were either unable or unwilling to address (Gordon et al., 1982). Rapid population growth, increasing class distinctions, high levels of mobility, and increasingly impersonal work relationships contributed to widespread concerns about unrest and disorder. When these elements combined with a severe economic depression in the world economy, between the 1820s and the 1840s, official and organized action mobilized to create the first bureaucratically organized, public, salaried, uniformed municipal police in the Northern industrial cities of the United States (Richardson, 1980).

In the context of a declining economy, social unrest escalated to the point that it seemed to threaten the very foundation of this brand new nation. An important element of concern about social disorder was fear of and anger toward the most recent wave of immigrants. Mob violence often centered on the most recent immigrants, either as the object of attack or as participants in violence. Poor Irish and German immigrants, free Blacks, and the urban poor in general came to be viewed as "dangerous classes" who lacked discipline and required control. To wealthy industrialists, preserving the social order meant preserving a good business climate by maintaining a stable and disciplined workforce. The creation of public police departments in urban centers was an exceptional reaction by fearful political leaders in a period of crisis.

The primary role of these newly developed police agencies was to maintain the social order, including the existing system of social stratification. The greatest perceived threats to the social order were from the so-called dangerous classes. It had become increasingly clear that the earlier watch systems were unable to suppress the riots, demonstrations, and strikes that became frighteningly frequent during the 1830s, without the aid of the militia. New public police departments supplemented the policing provided by private police, such as the Coal Police, the Railroad Police, and company town police agencies hired by specific industrialists to break strikes, suppress hunger riots, and generally exercise control over immigrants in the urban seacoast slums.

Police also played a critical role in maintaining the stratification of society along racial lines, regulating and suppressing the activities of free Blacks living in urban areas. Although Northern cities did not have the large slave population with which to contend, they aggressively sought to control the free Black population (Hawkins & Thomas, 1991). A common problem was that Black residential communities were under-policed with regard to receiving police protection, while, outside of the residential areas, Blacks were over-policed and subject to arrest for such actions as congregating or breaking curfew (Hawkins & Thomas 1991). Police were responsible for enforcing racist "Jim Crow" laws, which actually began in the North and were transported to the South with the abolition of slavery. Therefore, the municipal police departments that emerged in Northern industrial cities played an important role in maintaining the status quo in relations of power by controlling the perceived dangerous classes: the poor, Irish and German immigrants, and free Blacks.

This review of preindustrial and industrial policing demonstrates that two distinctly different forms of municipal policing were operating in the United States during the first half of the nineteenth century. The slave patrols in the South served an important social control function that helped to preserve a political economy based on racial slavery. Industrial policing developed in the large cities of the North and Midwest and served a distinctly different social control function in the political economy of competitive capitalism. The slave patrols came to an abrupt official end with the end of slavery. Southern cities eventually adopted industrial styles of policing, but only after the Civil War and they often operated in ways that were reminiscent of the slave patrols. Large numbers of recently freed Blacks comprised a large problem population that was severely poor and unemployed. According to Adamson (1983, p. 558), "Crime control in the antebellum South was subordinated to race control. With the abolition of slavery, alternative forms of race control had to be found, and race control naturally became a major aim in crime control." Black Codes, a series of state and local laws passed throughout the South, legally restricted African Americans to being rural labor without property. The few political and legal rights promised to Blacks by radical Republicans were not forthcoming or were meaningless given the economic destitution of newly freed slaves. Through both formal and informal racial discrimination, African Americans were systematically forced into becoming sharecroppers or convict laborers. Blacks who refused to become sharecroppers, destined to live their entire life in severe poverty and debt to landlords, could be arrested simply for having "no visible means for support" and then sentenced to work as free labor at the same plantation (Adamson, 1983, p. 559). Even freedom of movement was eliminated by the many restrictions placed upon African Americans. The industrial police forces that emerged in the South were charged with enforcing these laws and preserving the racist social order.

Whites in the North were apprehensive about the flood of freed slaves into Northern urban areas (Hawkins & Thomas, 1991). Northern police supported many racist legal codes and social norms, although they were somewhat less extreme than the codes in the South. According to Hawkins and Thomas (1991, p. 72), as African Americans moved into Northern cities, they were "relegated to the worst jobs and housing along the red light districts teeming with vice and crime." Relentless poverty and racial oppression pushed many newly freed African Americans into crime and vice, which were then attributed to their innate character rather than to the horrible social conditions. Government officials and police departments used crime by Blacks as an excuse to create racist legal codes and to harass, arrest, and jail African Americans at a much higher rate than Whites. The industrial police of the North thus systematically preserved their own racist social order.

Kelling and Moore (1988) referred to the period we call Industrial Policing as the Political Era because local political machines dominated industrial police departments. Early nineteenth century police departments in urban America were very corrupt and brutal by today's standards. Haller (1976) found that the Chicago Police Department of the early nineteenth century was highly decentralized and under the control of local political organizations. He also noted that corruption was so rampant that the officers ran the agency as if it was a "racket" or personal income-producing activity. Operations were so informal that strong relationships developed between the police and professional criminals. In New York, police were granted a great deal of discretion, which allowed officers freedom to handle legal and extralegal issues informally (Miller, 1977). This informality offered opportunities to bargain with criminal offenders and to the exercise of immediate "justice." Police obtained greater authority to use violence, as they were issued firearms and other weapons. Police discretion, together with popular perceptions of the urban poor, recent immigrants, and free Blacks as dangerous classes, contributed to widespread use of curbside justice and police violence (Platt et al., 1982).

Despite the development of public police departments, private police agencies continued to dominate the social control function until the late nineteenth century. Harring (1983) observed that, at first, public police agencies were often fragmented, inefficient, and unreliable. Sometimes the interpersonal relationships between police officers and the public, as well as their loyalty to political machines, made public police unpredictable during periods of intense social unrest. Private police could be counted upon by industrial capitalists to be unequivocal in doing the job of breaking the power of labor (Spitzer, 1981). In the late nineteenth century, industrial police began to show signs of decay as they lost their ability "to guarantee the kind of stable, predictable, orderly environment that alone permits sophisticated forms of markets to flourish" (Spitzer & Scull, 1977, p. 276). Between 1875 and 1900, a new form of public policing was developed to fulfill the police role of preserving the social order: modern policing.

Modern Policing

Neither the public nor the private police organizations that emerged during the period of industrial policing were able to preserve social peace in the late nineteenth century, particularly during the 1870s. Beginning with the devastating depression of 1873, social unrest and discontent spread throughout the cities of the United States. With the introduction of new, labor-saving technologies by many industries, millions were left unemployed. "Public relief was usually nonexistent and private charity either insufficient or offered only on the most demeaning terms" (Dubofsky, 1975, p. 20). In New York, between 1873 and 1879, demonstrations, organized by the unemployed, often drew 10 thousand to 15 thousand people who had to be dispersed by mounted police (Piven & Cloward, 1971). In Chicago, during the same period, "mass meetings of unemployed, organized by anarchists under the slogan, 'Bread and Blood,' culminated in a march of 20,000 on the city council" (Piven & Cloward, 1971, pp. 43–44). Dubofsky (1975) identified 1877 as the most violent year in the late nineteenth century. This time period represents a critical crossroads for social stability, the labor movement, capitalism, government, and for the police. Police departments in every major city were on the front lines of a class war that ensued between industrialists and workers. Their job was to maintain the social order. In this context, a new form of policing emerged, which we call "modern policing."

Much of the violence on the part of workers was directed at the destruction of the factory because its machines were viewed as the cause of unemployment and job insecurity. However, the most recent wave of immigrants was often blamed for the violence and social unrest during this period. "The American ruling class perceived newer immigrants as particularly prone to violence" (Dubofsky, 1975, p. 8). Business owners often used African Americans and recent immigrants as scabs to break union resistance and then placed the blame on these groups for causing unemployment among union workers. Antiimmigrant rhetoric, especially against the Chinese, played upon nativism tendencies of workers, who had become angry and afraid because of the intense competition for jobs brought about by the economic depression of the 1870s. Many in the labor movement began suggesting that poor people, social radicals, African Americans, and recent immigrants were instigating the violence and economic insecurity of the time. Through the criminalization and enforcement of various victimless crimes from vagrancy to opium smoking, an assault was launched against the "dangerous classes" and it was the police officer's job to enforce these racist and class biased laws (Walker, 1980).

Possibly the most two significant events in the formation of modern policing were the Great Strike of 1877 and the Great Upheaval of the 1886. The first signified the failure of industrial police to maintain social order, and the second signaled the success of the social experiment of modern policing. Police departments in the era of industrial policing lacked the technology, organization, and sheer numbers needed to effectively handle large-scale social disorder. In addition, the familiarity between police officers and the people in their communities, as well as their extremely informal and personal approach to law enforcement, sometimes led officers to ignore certain laws as they became sympathetic with the struggle for better pay, living conditions, and job security. Most industrialists continued to use citizens organized into militia to put down strikes. The civilian militia was very prone to violence and often became more riotous than the strikers. Private police, such as Pinkertons, employed such brutal forms of repression that they often inflamed workers to even greater resistance and violence. None of the strategies of industrial policing proved sufficient for putting down the Great Strike of 1877 and, eventually, the U.S. military had to be called to maintain domestic order. According to Harring (1983), it was during the 1877 strike that industrialists first recognized the need for a more disciplined, efficient, and organized police force. As a result, a great social experiment took place as the major cities in the United States, particularly in the North and Midwest, invested in a revolutionary reorganization of policing. This reorganization is often referred to as the "professionalization" of police (Walker, 1980; Kelling & Moore, 1988).

An important aspect of this radical transformation in policing was a move from the use of private police to the use of public police as the dominant social control instrument for breaking strikes, suppressing riots, suppressing the dangerous classes, regulating the activities of the poor working class, and protecting property. The movement from the use of private police to the use of public police was not a smooth linear transformation, but rather it took place in spurts. The first sign of this was in the 1830s and 1840s, but the transformation was completed in the last three decades of the nineteenth century. According to Spitzer (1981, p. 331), "… [s]ocialized policing did not spring full-blown from the head of the capitalist class; it evolved dialectically through several imperfect and at least partially 'privatized' forms."

The expansion of the municipal police was part of an increase in an array of services provided by municipal governments. Industrialists had a vested interest in socializing the costs of reproducing the working class. That is, they wanted to distribute the expenses of education, training, housing, health and welfare, and order maintenance among a large number of people rather than bearing these costs themselves. In democratic societies, socializing the costs of reproducing labor entails shifting these costs from individual industrialists to governments through taxation. However, the shift in U.S. capitalists' approach to strike breaking and social control was not a smooth transformation. Many industrialists had to be convinced that the municipal police would be beneficial to them. Eventually, most business leaders and political officials began to realize the failure of their earlier forms of control during the Great Strike of 1877.

A critical factor that helped to convince powerful people that a strong municipal police department was superior to private police agencies, local militia, and even the military for social control was the issue of legitimacy. If a police agency does not have legitimacy, then it must operate by the use of brute force. This is untenable in a democratic society for any extended period. The private police agencies that worked directly for industrialists, business owners, railroads, wealthy citizens, or mining, lumbering, and steel companies did not have legitimacy particularly in the eyes of the workers in these organizations. Therefore, the private police had to rely heavily on brute force to maintain order. Their efficiency and effectiveness declined as more and more people resisted their efforts. As people rebelled against the blatant repression by property owners, the severe brutality of private police often triggered more violence and destruction of property than the private police prevented (Dubofsky, 1975). Public police were able to obtain legitimacy, even as they were doing essentially the same job as private police because, in a democracy, the government is conceived as a neutral entity working for the common good.

Thus, the professionalization of police can be seen as a response to declining profits, a crisis of legitimacy in policing, and the threat of a social revolution. Professionalization entailed a radical reorganization of police, including greater discipline, increased centralization, bureaucratization, and a greater division of labor, new technology, and extraordinary increases in the numbers of officers. By 1905, most urban police departments had grown from 6 to 10 times their size in 1865. This increase was not due simply to the increases in the size of cities. Many police agencies grew to twice the number of officers per capita. Kelling and Moore (1988, p. 8) referred to this stage of policing as the Reform Era, suggesting that these developments evolved solely in response to police corruption and brutality. We locate the professionalization of police within the historical context of modernity and consider the broader social forces that brought on the changes in U.S. policing in the latter nineteenth and early twentieth centuries.

The innovations indicating the shift to modern policing included not only the shift to large, centralized, and highly disciplined police forces, but also the introduction of new technologies and changes in the rights of police officers as employees. The most significant technological developments were designed to make the police department into a more socially sensitive response system. In other words, new technologies were applied to make the police capable of responding more quickly and in greater force to potential trouble spots.

The most significant innovation in the rights of police officers as employees was the introduction of civil service (Harring, 1983). Some of the major problems of earlier police departments were high turnover rates, poor working conditions, and political corruption. A movement to solve these problems and to reduce the instrumental control of the police by powerful politicians initiated civil service protections for police. Two such movements occurred almost simultaneously in Milwaukee and Brooklyn in 1884. Another move toward the professionalization of police was the first school of instruction, established in Buffalo, New York, in 1893 (Harring, 1983; Richardson, 1974). Both the rhetoric of professionalism and the reality of police being more separated from the people on the beat, and less under the direct control of local politicians, reduced the likelihood that individual police officers would falter in the performance of their duty due to personal sentiments.

During the first half of the twentieth century, modern policing consolidated under the banner of the "professional model of policing," as the accompanying "crime-fighting" rhetoric was firmly established as the dominant approach to understanding the nature of police work. According to Walker (1980), "... [b]y the late 1920s and 1930s, the crime-fighting model of policing moved to the forefront" of police departments throughout the country, and much of its technology, such as the radio patrol car, airplanes, and psychopathic laboratories, reflected the desire to make the police more efficient. Throughout the 1920s and 1930s, the police were a popular focus of reform; however, this reform was almost exclusively centered on making the police more efficient and effective. The answer to reforming the police was almost always increased professionalization, with greater training, management, technology, discipline, and autonomy from political machines. Even reformers who sought to reduce police corruption and brutality viewed professionalism as the answer. Modern policing dominated law enforcement in the major cities of the United States until the mid-1980s; however, signs of decay in modern policing emerged during the confrontations between police and the social movements of the 1960s. It was during the 1960s that experimentation began toward the stage of policing that we refer to as "postmodern policing."

Postmodern Policing

In the 1960s, police in the United States clashed with a series of major social movements seeking to change the social order. The "professional crime fighting units" of the Modern Era came under serious criticism from nearly every sector of society for being too repressive, or too ineffective, or both. The criticism of what was called "traditional" policing came from both the left and the right, from practitioners and academics, from activists and politicians, and from the inner city poor to middle-class suburbanites. Of course, criticism also came from the business community. The police themselves began to recognize the limits of modern policing and started to experiment with new forms of policing. Just as postmodern theory critiques faith in modernity as a panacea for social ills, new approaches to policing were often based on a critique of professionalism as a panacea for failures in policing. As police departments began to reject bureaucracy, advanced technology, and efficient management techniques as solutions to the complex problems of policing in an age of mass media, they transcended modern policing and began to construct something entirely new. What emerged is what we call "postmodern policing." Consistent with each previous historical transition in policing, the impetus for and the consequences of this radical change in policing have been preservation of the social order.

Charged with maintaining social order, police came into conflict with numerous, and often overlapping, social rebellions that challenged the existing social order. For example, the Civil Rights Movement exposed inequality and unfairness as it challenged the forms of social control placed on African Americans. The student movements for free speech and against the Vietnam War challenged "the Establishment." Along with the political movements, the 1960s experienced a cultural revolution in which youth rebelled against traditional forms of social restraint. Hippies espoused flagrant use of drugs, changes in sexual mores, and contempt for traditional styles and appearances. The social disorder of this period produced fear in mainstream U.S. society, as it appeared that family, church, school, and particularly the police were losing their ability to maintain control. As defenders of the social order, and as the most accessible and visible instruments of that social order, the police were an integral part of these social conflicts.

The most violent social conflicts of the period occurred in the Black ghettoes of major U.S. cities, where urban uprisings were met with a violent and reactionary response by White America. Social disorder reached unprecedented heights between 1964 and 1968, as riots engulfed every major city. Most were sparked by incidents involving the police (Piven & Cloward, 1971; Walker, 1980). Riots in Harlem (1964), San Francisco (1966), Atlanta (1966), and in several other cities were each triggered by the shooting of a black teenager by a White police officer. Riots in Philadelphia (1964), Watts (1965), and Newark (1967) escalated from routine traffic incidents. The Detroit (1967) riot developed after a police raid on an after-hours bar in the ghetto. The level of violence of the Newark and Detroit riots exceeded that of the Watts riot. In the aftermath of these urban uprisings, President Johnson established the National Advisory Commission on Civil Disorders to investigate and offer potential solutions. In the first nine months of 1967, there were 164 disorders involving "Negroes acting against local symbols of White American society, authority, and property in Negro neighborhoods" (Harris & Wicker, 1988, p. 6). Police were deeply implicated in these disturbances as they came to symbolize "White power, White racism and White oppression" (Harris & Wicker, 1988, p. 11). The police were well known for their inappropriate and frequent violent reactions that tended to escalate disorder rather than ending it. According to the Commission's investigation, the number one grievance identified by communities was "police practices."

The initial police response to the civil disorder of the 1960s was confrontation with physical force, designed to repress activities. This response was enormously problematic for many reasons, not the least of which was that it was contrary to the professional model of policing. Modern police were supposed to have transcended the use of brute force. Police reliance on brute force in the conflicts of the 1960s was criticized as unprofessional. Professionalization once again became a major goal of the police, as authority was centralized and the chain of command was tightened (Walker, 1980). In sum, the initial reaction to the failure of the police to control crime and disorder in the 1960s was to increase its professionalism. Notably, a key component of the new police professionalism was militarization. The strategy was to mobilize the police, nearly at a national level, into a better trained, educated, armed, disciplined, specialized, and technologically advanced fighting unit, capable of suppressing any insurrection. At the same time, though, an undercurrent of resistance to this approach was emerging, with a focus on the need to improve "community relations."

Community relations programs were developed beginning in the late 1960s in many U.S. police departments, and were the initial experiments into a radical revolution in policing that is being consolidated today. Police–community relation's initiatives sought to improve the relationship between police and communities by going to community locations, such as community centers and schools, to engage in dialog with community members. In some organizations, these programs grew into ride-along programs, neighborhood storefront offices, fear reduction programs, police academies for citizens, cultural diversity training, police–community athletic programs, and the Drug Abuse Resistance Education (DARE) program. Early on, staunch proponents of the professional model of policing argued that the police–community relation's movement would dismantle the necessary social distance that had been established between professional police crime fighters and average citizens. The fear was that the police were giving up some of their autonomy and professional status by opening up to citizens and asking for support, assistance, and guidance. Police–community relations programs came to be marginalized from "real" police work, and, as Walker (1992a, p. 252) notes, they became "little more than public relations efforts, designed to sell the department to the community rather than to change police operations." Thus, community relations problems established in the aftermath of the conflicts of the 1960s did not change the fundamental nature of the relationship between police and marginalized communities. They did, however, become an important component of image management, which, we argue, has become the defining characteristic of postmodern policing.

Another post-1960s experiment was the effort to decentralize police through such strategies as "team policing." The fundamental thrust of team policing was to decentralize and despecialize the police so that they could work as coordinated and relatively self-sufficient neighborhood units. One of the goals of team policing was "to improve police–community relations by assigning officers to particular neighborhoods for extended periods of time" (Walker, 1992a, p. 254). Largely due to poor planning and limited commitment by the departments, team policing experiments were not a success. However, the movement to decentralize police decision making and to localize efforts to confront problems of crime and disorder was revitalized by Goldstein's (1979) "problem-oriented policing." Goldstein (1979, 1990) critiqued the preoccupation with efficient management and the militaristic and bureaucratic organization of police departments. He argued that police departments needed to decentralize, develop a more fluid management style, and allow more creativity and innovation among the rank and file. Goldstein (1979, 1990) critiqued the modern, professional approach of distancing the police from the public, arguing that, in order to identify and solve problems in the community, police and the public must become much more connected.

The strategy, known as "community policing," emerged in the 1980s and now dominates the rhetoric of nearly every major police department in the United States. Community policing fully integrates image management as an essential component of policing. The logic of community policing is often based on a classic article by Wilson and Kelling (1982) called "Broken Windows: The Police and Neighborhood Safety," in which the authors argue that image management is not only an important crime prevention tool for the police, but it is essential for communities as well. The basic argument is that if a community presents the image that it is in a state of disrepair, disorder, and is crime-ridden, then it soon will be. As the analogy goes, if a broken window is left unrepaired, then soon all the windows in the building will be broken. Therefore, working together, the police and the community should aggressively address the signals (such as untended property and untended behaviors) that send the message that a community is in a state of disorder. Wilson and Kelling (1982) suggested that, even if this effort does not really reduce crime, it improves the quality of life among the citizens by reducing their fear of crime. Further, Wilson and Kelling (1982) strongly recommended foot patrols as an important police strategy, even as they noted that evaluations of this strategy demonstrated that it does not reduce crime.

Wilson and Kelling (1982, p. 358) acknowledged that what foot patrols do is manufacture an image:

> These findings may be taken as evidence that the skeptics were right—foot patrol has no effect on crime; it merely fools the citizens into thinking that they are safer. But in our view, and in the view of the authors of the Police Foundation [*of whom Kelling was one*], the citizens of Newark were not fooled at all. They knew what the foot patrol officers were doing, they knew it was different from what motorized officers do, and they knew that having officers walk beats did, in fact, make their neighborhoods safer.

Based on such logic, community policing blurs image and reality to the point that not only are they inseparable, distinguishing between the two is unimportant. This approach fits perfectly with the postmodern concept of "hyperreality," where media images and reality are so intertwined that our images become real and reality becomes an image (Schwartz & Friedrichs, 1994). The police become a commodity to sell to the public, much like any other product on the market.

An essential part of this sales campaign has been to promote community policing as being more responsive to the community. Police Chief Lee P. Brown (1984) was one of the first and most successful police chiefs to implement community policing in a major U.S. city. Brown promoted community policing as an alternative to the old model of policing that was ineffective in reducing crime and disorder in the 1960s. The most significant differences between modern professional policing and community policing are that the philosophy of community policing encourages the scrutiny of the police by the public, enhances the accountability of the police to the public, provides customized police service, and shares the responsibility for solving the problem of crime with the public (Brown, 1984). Trojanowicz and Bucqueroux (1990, p. 5) defined community policing as "a new philosophy of policing, based on the concept that police officers and private citizens working together in creative ways can help solve contemporary community problems related to crimes, fear of crime, social and physical disorder, and neighborhood decay." According to proponents of community policing, involvement of the community in policing is designed to ensure that the police effectively meet the needs of the community. The police now openly admit that they cannot solve crime on their own and they need the community to help them. If community members are more involved in the crime-fighting process, they will be more supportive and cooperative with the police. The idea is to convince the public that the police are in their community to help them; therefore, to interfere with the police in the performance of their duty is self-defeating and illogical.

Community policing is image-management policing. Even evaluations of community policing concentrate on the public's image of the police. The most common measurements have involved "soft direct indicators" of the public's perceptions about the police and crime (Bayley, 1994, p. 98). Police departments often use evaluations that focus on the public's satisfaction with the police. These measures of the "image of crime" have become particularly important, as most community policing strategies appear to have little effect on the "reality of crime." Thus, under the rhetoric of "improving the quality of life," postmodern policing is taking on the image of crime rather than crime itself.

Conclusion

Postmodern policing is essentially social control through image control. By convincing the public that they are going to receive a police department that is responsive to their specific needs and is an advocate for the improvement of the quality of their lives, the police hope to produce a public that will provide them with information, grant them greater flexibility in the dispensing of curbside justice, and offer less resistance to their efforts to maintain order. This is precisely what happened in Reno, Nevada, in 1992. In preparation for a riot in Reno following the acquittal of the Los Angeles police officers who beat Rodney King, the success of the Reno Police Department's community policing program was that it was able to prevent a social uprising by organizing their own protest march through the streets of Reno with the police chief leading the procession.

The image management component of community policing is a powerful mechanism of social control. Manning (1991, p. 28) referred to community policing as a "new tool in the drama of control." The power of community policing is that "[i]t wraps the police in the powerful and unquestionably good images of community, cooperation, and crime prevention" (Klockars, 1991, p. 257). In other words, community policing evokes powerful positive images that tend to insulate police from critical analysis. Who is against a more responsive police force and stronger communities, greater cooperation between the police and public, and the prevention of crime? A police department that appears to be more responsive to the community can be a more effective agent of social control. In a democratic society, the police are most effective when they do not have to rely on physical force. Effective policing in a democracy requires the police to be seen as legitimate in the eyes of the people being policed. Community policing secures legitimacy through the manipulation of public opinion. The link between early police–community relations programs and the current widespread adoption of community policing is image management. Community policing, like the police–community relations initiatives developed in response to the urban uprisings of the 1960s, seeks to convince those who have reason to believe that they are being repressed by the social order that the police are their friends. But no matter how many town meetings are held, no matter how many baseball cards are handed out, no matter how many "officer friendly" robots appear in inner city classrooms, the role of police is to preserve the social order. The role of the police is to maintain the status quo in relations of power.

References

Adamson, C. (1983). Punishment after slavery: Southern state penal systems, 1865-1890. *Social Problems, 30*(5), 555–569.

Adamson, C. (1984). Toward a Marxian penology: Captive criminal populations as economic threats and resources. *Social Problem, 31*(4), 435–458.

Barlow, D.E. & Barlow, M.H. (1995). Federal criminal justice legislation and the post-World War II social structure of accumulation in the United States. *Crime, Law and Social Change, 22*, 239–267.

Barlow, D.E. & Barlow, M.H. (1999). A political economy of community policing. *Policing: An International Journal of Police Strategies and Management, 22*(4), 646–674.

Barlow, D.E. & Barlow, M.H. (2000). *Police in a multicultural society: An American story*. Prospect Heights, IL: Waveland Press.

Barlow, D.E. & Barlow, M.H. (2006). The myth that the role of the police is to fight crime. In R.M. Bohm & J.T. Walker (Eds.), *Demystifying crime and criminal justice* (pp. 73–80). Los Angeles: Roxbury Publishing Company.

Barlow, D.E., Barlow, M.H., & Chiricos, T.G. (1993). Long economic cycles and the history of criminal justice in the U.S. *Crime, Law and Social Change, 19*, 143–169.

Barlow, D.E., Barlow, M.H., & Johnson, W. (1996). The political economy of criminal justice policy: A time series analysis of economic conditions, crime and federal criminal justice legislation, 1948-1987. *Justice Quarterly, 13*(2), 223–242.

Bayley, D.H. (1994). *Police for the future*. New York: Oxford University Press.

Bromley, M.L. & Cochran, J.K. (2000). A case study of community policing in a southern sheriff's office. *Police Quarterly, 2*(1), 36–56.

Brown, L.P. (1984, August). Community policing: A practical guide for police officers. *The Police Chief, 26*, 72–82.

Dubofsky, M. (1975). *Industrialism and the American worker, 1965-1920*. Arlington Heights, IL: Harlan Davidson, Inc.

Genovese, E.D. (1976). *Roll, Jordan, roll: The world the slaves made*. New York: Vintage Books.

Giacomazzi, A.L.J. & Smithey, M. (2001). Community policing and family violence against women: Lessons learned from a multiagency collaboration. *Police Quarterly, 4*(1), 99–122.

Goldstein, H. (1979). Improving policing: A problem-oriented approach. *Crime and Delinquency, 25*, 236–258.

Goldstein, H. (1990). *Problem-oriented policing*. New York: McGraw-Hill.

Gordon, D.M., Edwards, R., & Reich, M. (1982). *Segmented work, divided workers: The historical transformation of labor in the United States*. Cambridge, MA: Cambridge University Press.

Greene, J. & Mastrofski, S. (Eds.) (1988). *Community policing: Rhetoric or reality*. New York: Praeger.

Haller, M.H. (1976). Historical roots of police behavior: Chicago, 1890–1925. *Law and Society Review, 10*, 303–323.

Harring, S.L. (1983). *Policing a class society: The experience of American cities, 1865–1915*. New Brunswick, NJ: Rutgers University Press.

Harris, F.R. & Wicker, T. (Eds.) (1988). *The Kerner report: The 1968 report of the national advisory commission on civil disorders*. New York: Pantheon.

Hawkins, H. & Thomas, R. (1991). White policing black populations: A history of race and social control in America. In E. Cashmore & E. McLaughlin (Eds.), *Out of order: Policing black people* (pp. 65–86). New York: Routledge.

Kelling, G.L. & Moore, M.H. (1988). The evolving strategy of policing. *Perspectives on Policing, 4*, 1–15.

Klockars, C.B. (1991). The rhetoric of community policing. In J.R. Greene & S. Mastrofski (Eds.), *Community policing: Rhetoric or reality* (pp. 239–258). New York: Praeger.

Lilley, D. & Hinduja, S. (2006). Organizational values and police officer evaluation: A content comparison between traditional and community policing agencies. *Police Quarterly, 9*(4), 486–513.

Maguire, E.R. (1997). Structural change in large municipal police organizations during the community policing era. *Justice Quarterly, 14*, 547–576.

Mandel, E. (1978). *Late capitalism*. London: Unwin Brothers Press.

Manning, P. (1991). Community policing as a drama of control. In J.R. Greene & S. Mastrofski (Eds.), *Community Policing: Rhetoric or Reality* (pp. 27–45). New York: Praeger.

Miller, W. (1977). *Cops and bobbies: Police authority in New York and London, 1830–1870*. Chicago: University of Chicago Press.

Oliver, W.M. (2000). The third generation of community policing: Moving through innovation, diffusion, and institutionalization. *Police Quarterly, 3*(4), 367–388.

Pelfrey, W.V. (2004). The inchoate nature of community policing: Differences between community policing and traditional police officers. *Justice Quarterly, 2*(3), 579–601.

Platt, T., Frappier, J., & Jon, R. et al. (1982). *The Iron fist and the velvet glove: An analysis of the U.S. police* (3rd ed.). San Francisco: Synthesis Publications.

Richardson, J.F. (1974). *Urban police in the United States*. Port Washington, NY: Kennikat Press.

Richardson, J.F. (1980). Police in America: Functions and control. In J. Inciardi & C.E. Faupel (Eds.), *History and crime: Implications for criminal justice policy* (pp. 211–225). Beverly Hills: Sage Publications.

Rusche, G. (1979). Labor market and penal section: Thoughts on the sociology of criminal justice. *Crime and Social Justice, 10*, 2–8, [originally published in 1933].

Rusche, G. & Kirchheimer, O. (1968). *Punishment and Social Structure*. New York: Russell and Russell [originally published in 1939].

Scheider, M.C., Rowell, T., & Bezdikian, V. (2003). The impact of citizen perceptions of community policing on fear of crime: Findings from twelve cities. *Police Quarterly, 6*(4), 363–386.

Schwartz, M.D. & Friedrichs, D.O. (1994). Postmodern thought and criminological discontent: New metaphors for understanding violence. *Criminology, 32*(2), 221–246.

Spitzer, S. (1975). Toward a Marxian theory of deviance. *Social Problems 22,* 641–651.

Spitzer, S. (1981). The political economy of policing. In D.F. Greenberg (Ed.), *Corrections and punishment*, 265–286. Beverly Hills: Sage Publications.

Spitzer, S. & Scull, A.T. (1977). Social control in historical perspective: From private to public responses to crime. In D.F. Greenberg (Ed.), *Corrections and punishment* (pp. 265–286). Beverly Hills: Sage Publications.

Trojanowicz, R. & Bucqueroux, B. (1990). *Community policing: A contemporary perspective.* Cincinnati: Anderson Publishing Company.

Vito, G.F., Walsh, W.F., & Kunselman, J. (2005). Community policing: The middle manager's perspective. *Police Quarterly, 8*(4), 490–511.

Walker, S. (1980). *Popular justice: A history of American criminal justice.* New York: Oxford University Press.

Walker, S. (1992a). The origins of American police-community relations movement: The 1940s. In E.H. Monkkonen (Ed.), *Policing and crime control,* Part 3 (pp. 813–834). New York: K.G. Saur.

Walker, S. (1992b). *The police in America: An introduction*, 2nd ed. New York: McGraw-Hill.

Williams, B.N. (1999). Perceptions of children and teenagers on community policing: Implications for law enforcement leadership, training, and citizen evaluations. *Police Quarterly, 2*(2), 150–173.

Williams, H. & Murhpy, P.V. (1990). *The evolving strategy of police: A minority perspective.* Washington, D.C.: National Institute of Justice.

Wilson, J.Q. & Kelling, G.L. (1982). Broken windows: Police and neighborhood safety. *The Atlantic Monthly, 249,* 29–38.

Wright, E.O. (1979). *Class, crisis and the state.* London: Verso Editions.

Zhao, J. (1996). *Why organizations change: A study of community-oriented policing.* Washington, DC: Police Executive Research Forum.

Zinn, H. (1980). *A people's history of the United States.* New York: HarperCollins.

Fit for Purpose Working with the Community to Strengthen Policing in Victoria, Australia*

9

JOHN CASEY
DAVID PIKE

Contents

Introduction

Law enforcement agencies throughout the world have made "community" central to their strategies (Findlay, 2004; Skogan, 2006). Whether it is through

* The authors would like to acknowledge the contributions of Margaret Mitchell and Delaine Trofymowych for their assistance in the previous stages of this research. Sections of this paper have appeared in Casey and Trofymowych (1999), Casey and Mitchell (2007), and Mitchell and Casey 2007). This chapter is based on an earlier version that appeared in 2007 in the *Flinders Journal of Law Reform, 10*(1), 373–401.

a commitment to a catchall "community policing" approach or because they use other contemporary policing strategies that presuppose strong community links, law enforcement agencies are compelled to engage with the communities they operate in. Community engagement is the active dimension of all community policing efforts.

However, community engagement continues to operate in the context of the conundrum identified by Casey and Trofymowych (1999). Community engagement is a core element of contemporary policing, but there is also widespread dissatisfaction on the part of both police and community participants with its processes and the outcomes. In the past few years, important new initiatives in community engagement have been launched at the same time as evaluations continue to identify the weaknesses in the models used and in the implementation of existing programs (Myhill et al., 2003; Myhill, 2006; Newburn & Jones, 2002; Skogan, 2006). Given that engagement is based on a series of contested concepts, such as *community, representation,* and *participation* (Wilson, 1992), and that evaluations tend to focus primarily on subjective assessments by stakeholders, it is not surprising to find that there continues to be little consensus about the outcomes.

This chapter focuses on community engagement in the state of Victoria, Australia. Victoria is the smallest mainland state in Australia (only the island state of Tasmania is smaller). It is the most densely populated and urbanized, with a population of 5.1 million, of which 3.5 million live in the metropolitan area of Melbourne, the capital city. Victoria Police is the sole law enforcement agency for the entire state, with 11,000 uniformed officers and 2,100 civilian staff working in some 330 police stations. Victoria Police was formally established in 1853, two years after the colony of Victoria separated from New South Wales. When the former British colonies became states of the new federated nation of Australia in 1901, policing remained a state responsibility, so while there is extensive cooperation between Australian police agencies, policies and strategies continue to be decentralized.

Community engagement in Victoria follows a top-down model (see Chapter 1). In the last decades, Victoria Police has instituted an array of community policing initiatives with the goal of bridging the gap between the agency and citizens and to foster community dialog on public safety. Policing in Victoria is carried out within the context of a high level of community consent in an established industrialized democracy. Victoria Police has had its share of scandals, but there is generally a high level of community trust. According to the 2006 Australian National Survey of Community Satisfaction with Policing, 72% of Victorians indicate that they are satisfied with their police service and 89% feel safe in their community (Victoria Police, 2008).

It is important to note that the focus of the chapter is on local-level engagement processes that involve a small locality, neighborhood, or suburb, or on those processes targeted at a specific social group (immigrant communities, youth, gay and lesbian, etc.), particularly where this correlates in some way with locality (e.g., because of ethnic enclaves, or specific attempts to dialog with local youth). In Australia, where the eight state-based police agencies are relatively large organizations, there is a significant institutional distance between local-level and higher-level engagement processes, such as a Police Board or agency-wide Ethnic Affairs unit.

The chapter provides a short background section to the theory and practice of community engagement and then examines a number of recent evaluations of engagement processes in Victoria. A final section looks at current trends in the development of a new *fit for purpose* service model based on the experience of the last decades. A general disclaimer is necessary from the very beginning of this chapter: Victoria has a relatively low crime rate compared to other states in Australia, but drawing a cause–effect relationship between community engagement and crime rates is speculative at best.

Understanding Community Engagement

Community engagement refers to the processes used to promote external input into policing policy and strategy, involving individuals or organizations (Casey & Trofymowych, 1999). This is a deliberately broad definition, given that engagement can refer to a wide range of processes and activities that differ considerably in both the locus of control (i.e., by police or external stakeholders) and in the direction of the information flow. Community engagement abuts at one end to processes, such as police public relations, that merely serve to communicate a police agenda and, at the other end, to independent community or citizens' initiatives, such as protest or vigilante activities, that are clearly outside police control. The range of possible community engagement activities and structures is often represented by continuums, such as Arnstein's *ladder of participation* (Arnstein, 1969) that puts *manipulation* at the bottom of the ladder and *citizen control* at the top.

The term engagement is often used interchangeably with terms such as *liaison, relations, consultation, involvement, collaboration, participation,* and *partnership,* with the later terms suggesting more equal relationships between police and external stakeholders (Myhill, 2006). The use of any of these terms to describe external input into policing may seem to imply a deliberate choice to position activities along an engagement continuum, but the reality is somewhat more haphazard. Whichever term an agency uses to label its community-related processes, the reality is that "poor" or "thin" processes—even if they are labeled collaborations or partnerships—essentially become public relations exercises. In contrast, "rich" processes can be the basis for real partnerships and effective joint governance of ongoing projects or programs.

Moreover, it should be noted that, while community engagement implies nongovernment input from individuals, advocacy groups, and community organizations, many of the processes discussed in this chapter, in fact, include the participation of other government departments, such as social services, education, health and public safety, as well as from other tiers of government, particularly local governments. What is presented as community engagement is often, in effect, an interagency or intergovernmental coordination process and, therefore, the distinction between whole-of-government and community engagement processes may not always be clear.

There is a wide range of possible community engagement processes, but most discussions of engagement in Australia and other industrialized countries tend to focus on the single technique of consultative committees. Community consultative committees—variously called *patrol committees, customer councils, local safety committees*, etc.—are by far the most common form of engagement (Myhill et al., 2003; Skogan, 2006; Ward, 1995). Police community consultation committees vary greatly in their functioning between jurisdictions and between localities within the same jurisdiction within the following key parameters:

- *Coverage*: Committees may cover policing districts, local government areas, neighborhoods, or even a single shopping street or business precinct, or they may be focused on a specific target group, such as youth or ethnic minorities.
- *Ownership/Control*: The "ownership" of the committee (in terms of who initiates, chairs, hosts, provides administrative support, etc.) may reside with the police, other public agencies, or with nongovernment groups, such as community improvement associations. In the Australian context, local governments are taking an increasing role in crime prevention and they often initiate local liaison processes that become the primary means of engagement between police and the wider community.
- *Appointment/Selection of members*: Members of the committee may be appointed by controlling authorities or selected through a range of processes that may include elections.
- *Open versus closed participation*: Attendance, voice, and vote at the meetings may be restricted to appointed/selected members or may be open to the public.
- *Relationship to other processes*: The committee may be a standalone process or may be connected to related activities such as Neighborhood Watch and other crime prevention programs.

- *Focus of activities*: The committees may have different primary foci, such as information exchange, development of local safety strategies, or the management of public safety and crime prevention programs.

Debates about the efficacy of these committees dominate evaluations of community engagement. Whichever format a committee takes, it must demonstrate its legitimacy as a valid process through its capacity to measure the pulse of public safety and crime concerns in the community and to translate these concerns into meaningful actions to address them. In order to achieve this, committees often employ a range of other engagement processes (surveys, town meetings) to gather additional input into their deliberations, and they often sponsor or manage projects that engage the police and community in joint problem solving.

Community engagement is not, in itself, a process or practice separate from other more global policing developments, such as *community policing*, *policing by consent*, and the notion of a police *service* (as opposed to *force*), all of which imply dialog with and legitimation by the communities and citizens policed (Findlay, 2004). Community engagement is the basis of a range of strategies considered to be *social* and *preventive* responses to crime and disorder that are part of the *multilateralization* of policing (Bayley & Shearing, 2001). There has been a shift in our understanding of the governance of security, including the increased responsibility being transferred to third parties and to partnerships between a range of government and nongovernment organizations (Ransley & Mazerolle, 2007). The new understanding is conceptualized by some authors as *nodal governance* (RegNet, 2006), which recognizes the multiple *nodes* (clusters of stakeholders) that impact on crime control and prevention.

In contemporary policing, there is widespread awareness of an operational necessity to maintain an open dialog with the communities served. Crime is mostly solved by information gathered in the community from cooperative citizens and informants (Findlay, 2004; Dixon, 2005), and community engagement processes can foster the trust needed to ensure that citizens do indeed cooperate. The current move to strengthen intelligence-driven policing seeks to combine the objective data generated by centralized crime mapping with the community intelligence provided by local input, and the possible information flow from community engagement processes can be a key to achieving this input (Maguire & John, 2006). However, there are real questions about how community engagement can be reconciled with intelligence gathering. Working closely with communities while at the same time observing members of these communities as potential objects of suspicion arguably produces dissonance in frontline policing.

The rise of community engagement in policing has coincided with broader shifts in the relations between state and nonstate institutions. The crisis of faith confronting both representative democracy and the Weberian notions of efficiency in the public service have led to a legitimation gap that Western democracies have sought to bridge through government restructures that reflect both New Public Management and governance approaches (Davis & Weller, 2001). An integral part of these new approaches is the increased emphasis on the role of community, civil society, and citizens in both policy development and service delivery, which have resulted in profound changes in the way in which all public sector organizations operate. The notion of public agencies directly providing services has given way to approaches that seek greater stakeholder involvement in policy processes, more transparent accountability of public services, and stronger public–private partnerships in service delivery. Internally within government there is also an increased emphasis on collaboration between agencies and whole-of-government approaches (Bayley & Shearing, 2001; Fleming & Rhodes, 2004).

Community engagement by the police has not been without its critics. As Casey and Trofymowych (1999) noted, criticisms of community engagement can be classified as ideological, structural, or operational. Ideological critiques reject what they see as the tokenism of engagement processes, such as consultation, with progressives claiming that it mainly serves to stifle dissent, while conservatives see it as pandering to special interests and diverting police from core policing tasks. Structural criticisms focus on the difficulties of reaching the most marginalized sectors of society, on the uneven power relationships between police and those being engaged, and on internal police procedures that do not necessarily reward engagement efforts. Operational criticism is focused on performance indicators and the difficulties of documenting the direct impact of engagement.

Local Priority Policing in Victoria

While police in Australia have tended to operate at some distance from the communities they serve, they could not remain isolated from international changes in both policing and public management and so a range of community policing initiatives were begun in the mid-1980s. In 1986, Bayley noted that, although the police commissioner of the state of New South Wales, John Avery, had called for the establishment of community consultative councils in his 1981 book, *Police, Force or Service*? (published by Butterworths, Sydney, three years before he became commissioner), and a 1985 Commission of Inquiry into Victoria Police had recommended the establishment of local liaison committees, until then "nothing along those lines [had] been created anywhere in Australia" (Bayley, 1986, p. 22).

Since the mid-1980s, there has been a significant shift to community engagement throughout Australian policing, but, given that individual states continue to have sole responsibility for policing, there are differences in strategies and approaches. For example, the state of New South Wales recently instituted a network of Community Safety Precinct Committees, and has since 1990 appointed 100 gay and lesbian liaison officers who work closely with those communities; but in 2006 the state government somewhat curiously chose to rename the agency the New South Wales Police Force after having used the name Police Service for some 16 years. Victoria is the Australian police jurisdiction that has made community participation most central to its operating philosophy. In 1998, Victoria Police embarked on a major strategic realignment known as Local Priority Policing (LPP). The goal of LPP was to ensure that the local community became an active participant in shaping police service priorities. As stated by the then chief commissioner, the first two of seven key characteristics of LPP were:

- Community significantly influences which services are provided.
- Local service issues are the prime focus (Victoria Police, 1999).

LPP was implemented in three phases: Phase 1 was a statewide management model that aligned the district-level operational boundaries to coincide with local government boundaries; Phase 2 was a service delivery model that gave local managers more control over specialist services; and Phase 3 was a community consultation model (CCM) that established local community input structures (Victoria Police, 2003).

As part of the CCM, each district inspector was responsible for the establishment of a Local Safety Committee (LSC) as the key local-level component of the LLP strategy. The LSCs were established in 2000 as a means of identifying local crime and public safety issues, as a conduit for input by local agencies into policing initiatives, and as a forum for police to account for local strategies and practices. The LSCs were implemented against the background of the prior existence of an experimental Police Community Involvement Program, first established in 1981; Neighborhood Watch, established in 1983; the expansion of the rebranded Police Community/Schools Involvement Program in 1989; and Police Community Consultation Committees (PCCC) established in 1991. The PCCCs are a network of community consultation structures first launched as the primary consultation mechanism under previous Victoria government crime prevention initiatives, such as the Safer Cities and Shires program. There was also a wide array of previously established community safety committees and other community-based crime prevention programs that had been instituted by other public organizations, such as local governments, social service agencies, and nongovernment organizations.

The membership of LSCs comprises a range of appointed representatives from local government, from local offices of statewide agencies and nongovernment organizations, and some community representatives. The LSCs were not intended as forums for grassroots community representation; instead, they are seen more as local government area-level management committees for local crime prevention and community safety activities (Victoria Police, 2003, p. 17). LSCs generally seek to involve senior staff from participating agencies and focus on strategic issues and high-level interagency collaborations. A core task of the LSCs was the development of a Community Safety Plan. The aims of the LSC included:

- Identify and satisfy validated local community needs and expectations.
- Involve the public in shaping policing services and action plans.
- Develop effective partnerships with the community to prevent crime and improve community safety.
- Improve community perception of crime and public safety.
- Increase public confidence in the accountability, professionalism and integrity of police.
- Provide information on police decision making.

District inspectors were given flexibility to implement LSCs according to local conditions and local experiences with previous consultation. As a result, in some districts preexisting community engagement structures took on LSC responsibilities and a range of different linkages were created between the new LSCs and existing PCCCs and Neighborhood Watch. And, while LSCs were to be the key component of the community consultation model, district inspectors were required to institute other mechanisms for engagement and for strengthening their knowledge of the local community, including the development of community profiles that documented the demographics and the security concerns of their districts.

While Victoria Police now appears to downplay the brand aspect of Local Priority Policing, it is still very much a core philosophy and its structures are still in place. The LSCs continue to be one of the current chief commissioner's flagship initiatives under the 2003 to 2008 five-year strategic plan known as *The Way Ahead* (Victoria Police, 2003).

In recent years, four separate research projects have evaluated the LSCs, the PCCCs, and the community governance of community safety and crime prevention programs. All four were based on survey techniques and focused on assessments of the outcomes by current participants in the processes. Table 9.1 provides the details of the research projects.

The combined findings of the four evaluations give a comprehensive picture of the operation of community engagement in Victoria. The evaluations of LSCs and PCCCs are considered first, given the overlap between these

Table 9.1 Research Projects on Community Engagement

Research Project (Bibliographic Reference)	Researchers	Focus and Aim
Evaluation of Community Consultation Model of Local Priority Policing (CMRD 2004)	Victoria Police: Internal evaluation by Corporate Management Review Division (CMRD)	Evaluated the Community Consultation component of Local Priority Policing; focused on the LSCs and directly related consultation and fact-finding activities
Evaluation of Police Community Consultation Committees (PCCCs) (Bonato, M. & Associates, 2003)	Crime Prevention Victoria (a division of the State Department of Justice) contract to private consultants Martin Bonato and Associates	PCCCs and related activities
Evaluation of community governance in crime prevention and community safety (Armstrong and Rutter, 2002; Armstrong, Francis, & Totikidis, 2004; Totikidis, Armstrong, & Francis, 2005)	Crime Prevention Victoria and Victoria University, joint researchers; funded by the Australian Research Council	Ongoing evaluation that targeted a range of governance processes; some of the research has ended up focusing on LSCs, although the ownership of the four committees that are the subject of the 2005 paper are attributed more to local government than to Victoria Police
Evaluation of local government Community Safety Officers (CSOs) (Sutton, Dussuyer, & Cherney, 2003)	Crime Prevention Victoria and Melbourne University, joint researchers; funded by the Australian Research Council	Did not directly deal with the work of Victoria Police community engagement structures, but a 2003 paper from the project provided some assessment of these structures

two police-initiated structures. Subsequently, the evaluations of community governance structures are used to contrast the internal structures.

Evaluations of LSCs and PCCCs

Both evaluations highlighted that there is considerable variation in how LSCs and PCCCs operate and how they interact with other engagement mechanisms. As a result of these variations, LSCs and PCCCs were able to respond to local conditions and generally garner positive reviews. Those interviewed for the PCCC evaluation noted that when Victoria Police introduced them in 1991, they were an important and groundbreaking initiative at the forefront of a shift to a community policing philosophy. The evaluation concluded that some PCCCs have strong, committed, active, and long-term memberships that have been very productive with limited resources. The LSCs, established almost a decade after the first PCCCs, were seen as being able to fulfill a commitment to extend existing community engagement processes by building on the past experiences.

The LSC evaluation concluded that they have helped drive the wider community engagement initiatives and promote a wide range of community safety and crime prevention programs as well as assisting in attracting funding. The two reports found that both PCCCs and LSCs had significantly enhanced relationships with other government departments, local governments, and organizations within the community. The LSC evaluation found that there was majority support within police ranks for the LSC initiative as a key component of community engagement. A conflation of a number of survey questions in the report indicated that some 50 to 55% of officers considered LSCs to be very valuable or generally valuable, some 20 to 30% considered the value limited by quality, 15% considered them of little value, and no one considered them to be of no value.

However, both reports also indicated that, despite the successes, there was also widespread concern about the functioning of community engagement. The signature phrase in relation to the PCCCs was:

> The supporters of PCCCs were able to identify many useful projects and initiatives, but most PCCCs appear to have been limited by lack of sustained interest and funds or inability to increase the reach of the committee to incorporate the views of local communities with common interests or concerns. In an attempt to identify outputs and outcomes of PCCC, the reviewer found a great deal of skepticism and inability to articulate significant outcomes, even from some PCCCs regarded as model performers by their peers (Bonato, M. & Associates, 2003, p. 9).

The conclusion was that most PCCCs have not achieved sustained, effective consultation and information exchange with broad representation from local citizens. Most PCCCs had limited reach into the community due to a lack of time and resources, and the skills and knowledge on how to approach the wider community were sometimes lacking on committees. Some senior police did not believe PCCCs had a significant impact on their work; while some acknowledged the value of the interactions on committees and relationships built, the impacts were generally not considered substantial in terms of their own operational targets.

The subsequent introduction of LSCs somewhat complicated the situation for PCCCs. The evaluation of PCCCs found that their role was "severely challenged" by the implementation of LSCs as many of the stated aims and objectives of the two committees were the same or similar, despite the theoretical division between the more grassroots focus of PCCCs and the focus of the LSCs on creating interagency forums of managers. In theory, LSCs are supported at the local level by a network of PCCCs and Neighborhood Watch Groups, but it appears that, in practice, the connection is, at best, loose and there is no formal requirement for PCCCs to report to LSCs. According to the PCCC evaluation, "… there is a palpable divide between many LSCs and PCCCs leading to confusion and at times animosity and rivalry" (Bonato, M. & Associates, 2003, p. *v*). Some PCCCs have been disbanded or absorbed into LSCs or other local structures and those that remain are not necessarily complying with requirements or expectations originally laid down for PCCCs. In some instances, however, the continued existence of PCCCs allows the replication of the LSC structure at a lower level so that supervisory and frontline staff also have the opportunity to participate in community engagement structures.

There appeared to be a significant division of opinions about the relationship between the PCCCs and LSCs, with many of those surveyed seeing a complementary role, but also many considering that the PCCCs are now redundant and should be disbanded. There was consensus that PCCCs need to be realigned within the newer and broader community safety and crime prevention infrastructure.

While LSCs were more an integral part of LPP, they were still hampered by structural difficulties in the model and there were few mechanisms to link community engagement with other operational processes. The LSC evaluation found that Victoria Police internal cultures and current management processes, such as COMPSTAT (short for COMPuter STATistics or COMParative STATistics), continued to tie reward and recognition more to reactive crime-fighting approaches than to preventive approaches and to pursuing cross-agency synergies. There continued to be operational staff, particularly district inspectors, who still had not embraced community engagement and/or did not have the skills or commitment to promote successful processes. Moreover, other government agencies were not always prepared to participate in the LSC process, sometimes because their boundaries were not aligned, or because it required a single agency representative to sit on multiple committees, or because they felt their expertise was not used.

Both the LSC and PCCC evaluations identified key elements for successful engagement. For the LSCs, the most successful outcomes were observed in long established forums with mainly local government leadership, but there were also successful police-driven LSCs. Successful engagement appeared to emerge in response to pressing urban issues, such as drug problems or youth violence. Where such triggers did not exist, there appeared to be less incentive to maintain the structures. The success of community engagement was also dependent on the commitment and capacities of key individuals, usually district inspectors, and terms like *enthusiasm, leadership, skill*, and *level of expertise* were used to identify success factors for individual LSCs. The report drew a distinction between "reporting" and "action" LSCs, with committees that helped create ongoing crime-prevention activities being seen as more successful. For action-oriented LSCs, their capacity to obtain funding for initiatives was seen as the key to success. Similarly, the features of successful PCCCs included: strong leadership through a local "champion," a clear direction and a sense of purpose, representative membership and continuing attendance, effective chairing of meetings, the availability of resources to support the committees' work, and a strong sense of having achieved results.

Both reports make recommendations for strengthening the work of the LSCs and PCCCs:

- *The importance of local flexibility*: The LSC evaluation recommended that committees not necessarily be required to use the LSC name, and the PCCC evaluation recommended that they be an optional form of engagement and that any decision to create/continue or discontinue a PCCC should be made with reference to the views and needs of the relevant local community. As part of this flexibility, both reports emphasized the need for all engagement processes to define their purpose, principles, goals, objectives, and performance measures as well as the rights and responsibilities of members.
- *The need for central coordination and sufficient resources*: Both reports called for greater coordination between LSCs, PCCCs, and other community engagement processes, and the PCCC evaluation called for greater formalization of the relationship between LSCs and PCCCs.
- *The need for dissemination of information about consultative process and good practices*: Both reports called for a range of measures including regular statewide forums of staff involved in community engagement, the improvement of training materials, and greater presence on the Internet and other means of communication by Victoria Police.
- *The need for integrated performance reporting*: Both reports stressed that consultative processes should be better integrated into performance management at all levels. There was particular emphasis on the need to incorporate the outputs and outcomes of community engagement into performance processes, such as COMPSTAT.
- *The need for skills training*: The reports noted that consultative committee members, both police and external, need ongoing training and development in the role, function, focus, and process of committees and on establishing, maintaining, and achieving results from partnerships.

- *The need for varied engagement processes*: The reports recommended the use of processes, such as surveys, focus groups, inviting people to attend meetings on a short-term basis, or joining existing committees with projects initiated by other groups.

Evaluation of the Community Governance of Crime Prevention

Three preliminary reports of the joint Crime Prevention Victoria—Victoria University research project on the governance of crime prevention have been published (Armstrong & Rutter, 2002; Armstrong, Francis, & Totikidis, 2004; Totikidis, Armstrong, & Francis, 2005). The 2004 and 2005 papers focused on the work of LSCs and, while they noted that LSCs were launched by the police minister and chief commissioner in 2000, almost no other mention or analysis was made of the role of Victoria Police or of the Local Priority Policing approach. From data in the tables and the responses to survey questions about chairing, funding, and reporting of the committees, it appeared that the ownership of the LSCs was attributed more to local councils than to Victoria Police. This attribution of ownership to local councils is not inconsistent with the flexibility accorded by Victoria Police to district inspectors, which allowed them to build on existing local structures when implementing LSCs under Local Priority Policing. However, it is also a reflection of an apparent lack of clarity by the researchers about the drivers of the LSCs and, perhaps, of "turf wars" over ownership.

The 2004 report on the determinants and inhibiters of community governance focused on LSCs and indicated that:

> The conclusions are that the LSCs are very effective in generating networks of people. They had input into local government safety plans, and were able to bring diverse resources together to successfully tackle local issues. Limitations to their success were lack of leadership, infrequent meetings, lack of objectives, and lack of seniority in the members of participating partners … and data sharing was limited. (Armstrong, Francis, & Totikidis, 2004)

The results of the 2005 report were also generally positive. Almost 83% of LSC members surveyed agreed with the statement that LSCs facilitate partnerships between agencies, while 55% had a strong sense of achievement from their participation and 54% believed that the LSC was very successful in preventing crime.

Conclusions from the Evaluations of Community Engagement

From the above evaluations, it can be concluded that LSCs, PCCCs, and other community governance structures have been successful in extending and entrenching community engagement as a core strategy in Victoria Police as well as in other government entities involved in crime prevention and public safety. The implementation of LSCs and PCCCs and the development of LPP demonstrate that Victoria Police has come a long way since Bayley's declaration 20 years ago that there was no community engagement in Australia (Bayley, 1986). When implemented, LPP was a new way of doing business for Victoria Police and tipped the organization on its head, both structurally and philosophically. In restructuring the organization, LPP devolved decision making and accountability to the local level and the designers hoped it would involve the key stakeholders of local communities in solving local problems. Moreover, LPP has developed community engagement models that are used for other engagement processes, such as the Police and Community Multicultural Advisory Committee (PACMAC), and has resulted in more officers becoming interested in community liaison positions.

The evaluations highlight the importance of flexibility in implementation, with local commanders being given leeway to make arrangements according to local conditions/history. The goal is to implement processes appropriate to local conditions and, as research papers from Victoria University demonstrate, LSCs sponsored by local councils also can be successful.

Despite the successes, there continues to be an undercurrent of resistance to, and lack of skills in, community engagement, as well as more widespread confusion about the role of competing processes. While the various processes appear to have strengthened interagency connections, there still appear to be significant issues of "turf" and ownership. The recommendations of the evaluative reports focus on:

- Strengthening organizational commitment to consultation at all levels.
- Entrenching flexibility as a positive aspect of consultation.
- Clarifying the roles of diverse consultative processes and formalizing the commitment of participants.
- Identifying underperforming consultative processes and providing the support and training needed to strengthen them.
- Facilitating information sharing on successful models and providing assistance to obtain resources for crime prevention and community safety initiatives.

In considering these finding and recommendations, it should be kept in mind that the evaluations have focused on current participants in community engagement and governance activities and on the outputs of the processes. There has been little attention given to nonparticipants and to the evaluation of substantive outcomes.

Have the LPP, PCCCs, and LSCs impacted on crime rates? Victoria has the second lowest crime rate in Australia (after Tasmania), despite the fact that it is the most urbanized state. The low crime rate can be seen as a result of strong community networks, but it is, at best, speculative to conclude that these networks are a result of effective community engagement by Victoria Police. An equally plausible interpretation is that the cause–effect relationship is in the opposite direction, i.e., the successful outcomes of engagement efforts by Victoria Police, in fact, may be the result of the preexisting strength of the community networks. One of the paradoxes of community engagement is that building trust between stakeholders is a desired outcome of engagement processes, but that trust is also a necessary preexisting condition for the success of community engagement (Casey et al., 2008). If some level of trust does not already exist among stakeholders who gather at the table, then engagement processes are unlikely to result in positive outcomes (see Skogan, 2006, for an analysis of the impact of networks and trust on police community engagement in different racial–ethnic communities in Chicago).

Barriers to the Success of Local Priority Policing (LPP)

While the evaluations continue to express support for community engagement, this appears at times to be more for the theory than the practice. There are case studies of "success stories," but another common theme that emerges from the evaluative research is an apparent skepticism about the outcomes.

Those working with community engagement in Victoria Police can, at least, take heart in the fact that it appears to operate with the same contradictions as in policing overseas. Myhill et al. (2003, p. 3) found that some three-quarters of United Kingdom police authorities still ran Police Community Consultative Group meetings despite the fact that none of them considered them very effective. Some authorities had tried to reform or replace the meetings, but this also had mixed success. In the United States, Skogan (2006) found that community engagement structures had been successful with some communities in Chicago, but less successful with others.

Moreover, in other areas of the public sector, the situation is much the same. A recent review of the consultation by the ACT Planning Department concluded that it was "characterized by strengths worth retaining and building on … but also by low levels of trust and confidence among stakeholders … [and it was] not always conducted in a transparent and accountable way …

and was subject to problems in communications and the effective dissemination of information" (National Institute of Governance, 2004). The Victorian Department of Human Services, in an evaluation of its consultation process, concluded that 63% of nongovernmental agencies they dealt with were very satisfied with the processes, 20% were neutral, and 18% were dissatisfied (Ipsos, 2005). In a recent meta-analysis of evaluations of community engagement in various public sector agencies, a pattern started to emerge. While the evaluation methodologies and definitions used were different, and the issues dealt with and types of participants surveyed varied, there seemed to be a certain consensus that a small majority of those surveyed (around 60%) were supportive of the outcomes and processes, a small minority (around 20%) were dissatisfied, and the remainder (around 20%) were taking a "wait and see" attitude (Casey et al., 2008). These figures are similar to the Victoria Police figures quoted above and it appears that the police and the public sector in general share an attitude to community engagement that can be described as "skeptical goodwill" (Rawsthorne & Christian, 2004).

There are a number of structural and cultural barriers that have stopped LPP from reaching its full potential. One of the greatest problems has been the large number of policies and instructions relating to the delivery of policing services that have been centrally promulgated since the advent of LPP. These policies are very prescriptive and attempt to ensure that all regions comply with common rules and conditions. This is at odds with the principles of LPP and tends to discourage local managers from using innovative, locally developed solutions to resolve local community problems.

It is not surprising that senior managers who were brought up in a system of central control would be uncomfortable with those below them having free rein, but such attitudes, unfortunately, limit the ability of more junior members to introduce innovative local ideas. Even in response to the evaluations outlined in the previous section, which recommended more local flexibility, Victoria Police has unfortunately promulgated yet more central directives that have been not only unhelpful to LPP, but unnecessary and have led to those who were initially expected to gain autonomy being stifled.

As the summaries of the four research projects demonstrate, community engagement by Victoria Police has been the subject of extensive evaluations and these evaluations have provided specific recommendations for future directions. The question then becomes: Will Victoria Police learn from this experience, and what factors are likely to inhibit learning? In a recent round of confidential interviews with stakeholders in community engagement in Victoria Police, the following barriers to organizational learning about these issues emerged:

- The organizational culture in policing and crime prevention continues to be somewhat averse to scrutiny and possible criticism.

Evaluations—such as the LSCs and PCCC evaluations cited above—are not widely published, disseminated, or discussed. When they are published, the response is more generally defensive.
- While decentralization in Victoria Police and other government agencies has created local flexibility, it has made coordination and cross-agency learning about community engagement more complicated.
- Any institutional commitment to a particular approach continues to be tempered by individual commitments by key local leaders who must act as "champions" for engagement. The reality is that some local police commanders are not committed to community engagement.
- Programmatic "silos," both within agencies and between agencies, continue to have a negative impact. Different community engagement programs operate through separate units/agencies and there is little discussion between them. These silos have an interest in their own continuity, so are often not able to reform themselves.
- A high turnover of staff involved means changing levels of interest in the subject matter, in commitment to changes, and even doubts over ownership of material. One research organization involved in evaluations of community engagement ended up returning funds it had been granted to evaluate a specific community engagement initiative after having dealt with three different directors of the sponsoring government department during the research period.
- A change of government means significant changes in priorities and programs. When the government changed in Victoria, the former government's Safer Cities program was essentially abandoned.
- Changes cannot be implemented within a community engagement program in isolation from other agency processes that may be less amenable to change. Or conversely, related processes in the agency may be changed without taking into account the implications for community engagement.
- Interest in the implementation of an evaluation quickly wanes when another related evaluation takes place. During interviews about the LSC and PCCC evaluations, a number of people noted that any changes should wait until the completion of the new Nexus evaluative program that was just starting up (see information about Nexus below in The Professional Decision Making Model).
- In an organization the size of Victoria Police, and given the number of other stakeholders involved, there are limits to knowledge circulation. For example, the external evaluation team from a university was unaware of internal LSC and PCCC evaluations, even though they had police on their steering committee.

- Organizational learning and change have real costs that often cannot be met. Given the size of the Victoria Police, it is estimated that the cost of a single meeting to disseminate good practice is around $25,000 in terms of travel, accommodation, and staff time.
- Good practice in community engagement is often dependent on structural issues that are unlikely to change or be taken out of the hands of any single agency. Successful LSCs are often dependent on the local council having a full-time crime prevention officer and/or on being successful in obtaining funds from outside sources.
- Community engagement, particularly when it is functioning well, is not seen as a core/high priority issue for some of the agencies involved.
- The fact that successful community engagement is difficult to measure and even more difficult to link to changes in crime data continues to be a barrier.

Some 15 years ago Beyer (1992) expressed her confidence that, by building on the success of the original 1981 Police Community Involvement Program, Victoria Police would soon adopt what she referred to as "holistic community policing," which involved widespread community engagement. After all, Beyer claimed, "Once police become familiar with the new way of working, they will not want to give it up," and she called for "changes from the ground up, rather than from the top-down" (1992, p. 100). While LPP has started to move Victoria Police in that direction, the reorganization that Beyer saw as necessary is still a work in progress.

Postscript: Beyond Local Priority Policing

A review of LPP in 2005 (Victoria Police, 2005) recognized that LPP had been partially successful in moving Victoria Police from a central command and control structure to one where local managers actively involve the community in finding solutions to the problems they face. However, it found that this paradigm shift had been hindered by the three models used to implement it (the statewide management model, the service delivery model, and the community consultation model), which were seen to be overly prescriptive and so hindered the delivery of policing services that were tailored to local community needs and expectations. Added to this, the proliferation of corporate policies and procedures has limited the empowerment of local managers and front line police, which is one of the key philosophies of LPP.

The review concluded that if Victoria Police was to make the cultural change from an organization governed by centralized command and control structures to one that was more devolved in its authority and accountability and inclusive in its decision-making process, it was time to remove many of the constraints. They recommended a new *fit for purpose* service delivery model. This model was accepted in 2005 and is now being implemented across the state (Victoria Police, 2005).

While LPP started the journey towards true community policing for Victoria Police, the new model is a continuation of this journey. The architects of *fit for purpose* believe that it will assist managers and frontline police to play a key role in both building community strength and improving social outcomes through the use of community and partnership policing. It will also nurture a work environment within which all employees are included in the development of policing initiatives and programs. Such inclusion should ensure policing initiatives are creative in their conception and sensitive to the wishes of local communities. As such, they will be far more effective than programs developed centrally. Local managers and frontline police will be given increased authority in decision making, but along with the increased authority will come the accountability for achieving frontline service delivery. Local managers and frontline police will be accountable to their communities for their work performance rather than the traditional reliance upon bureaucratic rules and regulations.

The foundation stones of *fit for purpose* are three key reforms. These are (Victoria Police, 2005):

- Aligning Accountability and Authority for Achieving Frontline Service Delivery
- Adopting the Strategic Work Focus Model of Organizational Hierarchy
- The Professional Decision Making Model

These key reforms are described in the following sections.

Aligning Accountability and Authority for Achieving Frontline Service Delivery

While LPP has been successful in moving Victoria Police along the path toward true community policing it has been unsuccessful, for reasons previously discussed, in aligning accountability and authority for the delivery of frontline policing services. *Fit for purpose* aims to rectify this by allotting 24-hour accountability for the service outcomes delivered within a geographical area to the manager of that area. In doing this, it mandates that the smallest unit of service delivery become a local government area in order to ensure that local partnerships and cooperation with other government and community groups are maintained.

Under the LPP model, local government areas have been known as districts and controlled by district inspectors; however, under the new model this is to change. Local government areas will become Police Service Areas (PSAs) and the managers of such areas will become police service area managers. In doing this, it has been decided that PSA managers may vary in rank depending on the size and complexity of the area; some may require a superintendent, while others may be served by a senior sergeant. In the main though, these PSA managers will continue to be inspectors.

There is an acknowledgment that PSA managers will need the autonomy to deploy their resources in ways that are most likely to meet locally identified policing needs and priorities. The present system of fixed staffing quotas in response zones and specialist areas has led to noncooperation across areas due to the consequent silo mentalities they create. Where people are located and for how long will be the responsibility of the PSA manager rather than being determined and authorized centrally or by those above or below. To make this a reality, it has been proposed that position descriptions and the interpretation and application of industrial agreements and human resources policies need amendment.

Under the LPP structure, the existence of LSCs was mandated. This was the primary method to identify local problems and implement strategic initiatives to resolve them. The 2005 review concluded that the generic LSC model across the state with little or no consideration of local factors is not best practice. While LSCs are appropriate and work well in some areas, in others, due to factors such as culture, population mix, etc., they do not. Therefore, PSA managers are to be given the ability to choose the manner of community consultation that best fits their area. With this increased autonomy will come the accountability for the quality and effectiveness of their community consultation and building of partnerships.

Adopting the Strategic Work Focus Model of Organizational Hierarchy

It has been accepted that under LPP there was generally an absence of clearly defined roles and requisite levels of autonomy and authority. This caused further problems as higher level managers disempowered those below them by micromanaging them. This micromanagement also made the issue of accountability unclear due to the authority of lower level managers being compromised. In order to alleviate this problem, Victoria police will move from a strict line control model of management to a strategic focus model. Under this model, roles of each level will be clearly defined and management accountability will be aligned accordingly. Job functions will be allocated on the basis of complexity rather than position. This will enable managers to be held accountable for the outcomes of their particular role. In holding managers accountable, Victoria Police proposes that they be given the material and financial resources as well as the freedom of decision making required to be successful.

The Professional Decision Making Model

Fit for purpose attempts to enhance the ability of local police to institute problem-oriented approaches to their local problems by removing the high level of formalization, in terms of prescriptive rules and regulations promulgated at state, regional, and divisional levels, that exists within Victoria Police. LPP's philosophy of flexibility leading to innovative solutions was hindered by this formalization.

This formalization not only disempowers the workforce, but it also stifles true creativity and hinders the implementation of innovative solutions to local community problems. It also reinforces the notion among lower levels that the hierarchy is more interested in adherence to rules and regulations than it is in the notion of community service. To overcome this, *fit for purpose* proposes to adapt the model developed by Simmons (2000, cited in Victoria Police, 2005, p. 51), which is reproduced below (Figure 9.1).

In this model, rules are set as boundaries that cannot be changed. These are identified in the model below as government, legislative, and organizational boundaries. The lightly shaded area in the middle is the leeway in which local managers and frontline police are free to find the solutions they

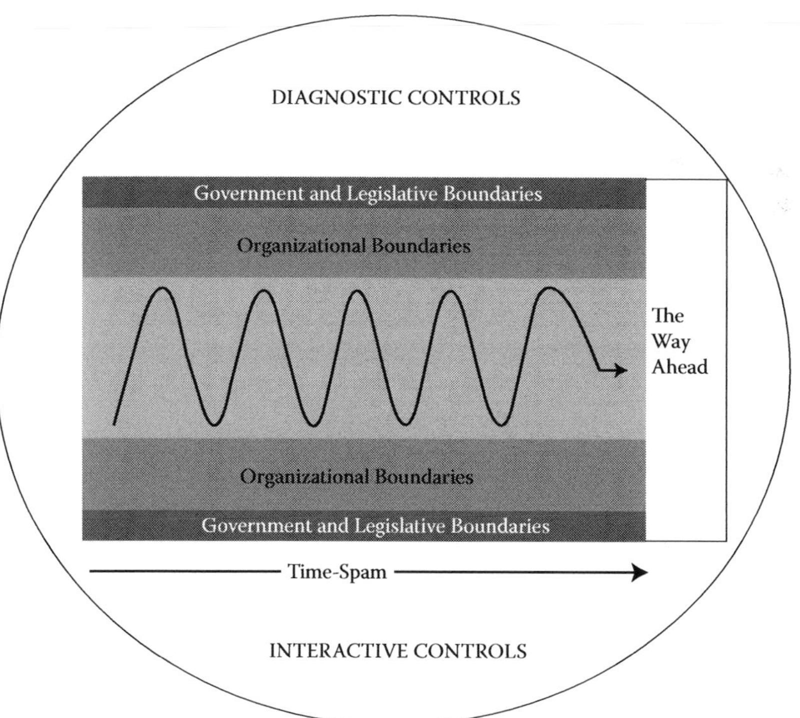

Figure 9.1 Professional Decision Making Model. *Source:* Victoria Police (2005).

need to solve local problems. In doing this, they are guided by the customs, values, culture, and practices of the organization.

In addition to these reforms, Victoria Police is undertaking a range of other programmatic changes that are likely to impact on community engagement. Victoria Police has entered into research collaborations with a number of universities to examine various aspects of its operations. Of particular interest to community engagement is the joint four-year research and innovation project with the Australian National University titled *Nexus Policing: Partnerships for Safer Communities* (Victoria Police, 2006). Nexus will work in partnership with key service providers and community groupings to address issues as diverse as indigenous, multicultural, and youth affairs; sex offender recidivism; and public transport safety. Research is mapping the ways in which Victoria Police, service providers, and community groups coordinate and integrate their knowledge, skills, and resources in addressing community safety. A particular focus of the project is to build an understanding of the diverse nodes that impact on the governance of local security concerns (RegNet, 2006).

The Nexus research will inform the development of models designed to achieve "smarter" ways of promoting safety through partnerships and networks. There are currently seven pilot sites that look at the following issues: (1) safety in public housing, (2) family violence, (3) indigenous issues, (4) youth safety, (5) youth and multicultural issues, (6) safety on public transport, and (7) sex offender recidivism.

The Nexus project will develop programs that can be applied throughout Victoria to address community safety issues. Once implemented, the ongoing sustainability of the project will be determined by local police, government service providers, and community agencies closely involved in the development of the project specific to their area.

Conclusion

From the case study of Victoria Police, it can be concluded that, despite any shortcomings, community engagement continues to have some success as a process that creates dialog and interchange on local crime and disorder issues and serves to assist police in meeting local accountability and oversight imperatives. Victoria Police is a somewhat prototypical example of a police agency in a Western democracy in search of and, to a significant extent, finding its community (see Chapter 1). The creation of consultation mechanisms, along with the structural realignment of Victoria Police has integrated a wide range of both citizens and government entities into the policy development and service delivery processes of the agency. The extension of consultation has not, however, been simply a self-initiated process by Victoria Police, but has also been a response to a clamor from a wide range of stakeholders for a greater voice in the response to crime and disorder. Whether the qualified success of engagement mechanisms has helped create stronger community networks or whether preexisting networks have been able to assure the establishment and success of community engagement will continue to be contentious.

Community engagement in Victoria Police has established legitimacy with key stakeholder communities, such as business and community elites, local activists, other government officials, and specific ethnic and racial communities, and it continues to be an integral part of the new public management and governance frameworks applied to policing. Community engagement processes can be essential for mobilizing support for police (Squires, 1998) and for responding to the consumerist rhetoric of an ethos of effective service and responsiveness to clients. While the link to crime reduction of these outcomes may be hard to measure, they are an important value in themselves. Despite its flaws, community engagement continues to reinforce the current agenda of *serving* the community and provides the basis for intelligence-led and problem-solving approaches to policing. Engagement with the community is a "lynch pin" of both operational effectiveness and public accountability; it continues to enjoy widespread support, both from within policing and from external oversight bodies, and it is an integral part of a wider movement of public sector reform and citizen participation.

As community policing strategies became more extended in Australia, Moir (1992) questioned whether it was possible for police to use engagement processes to work with communities to become co-producers of public order. Later, Sarre and Tomaino (1999) declared that it would be a "formidable task" translating community policing rhetoric into reality because expecting police to accept widespread community engagement involved a fundamental challenge to police leadership and culture. Yet, as this review of the community engagement efforts of Victoria Police indicates, there is now substantial evidence that Australian police agencies have been prepared to meet those challenges. Significant barriers remain; however, there also seems to be little doubt that police agencies have made significant strides in the move to incorporate community engagement as an institutional commitment. Under the new service and governance arrangement currently being developed, and through its research collaborations, it appears that Victoria Police is well positioned to embed this institutional commitment and to provide the local flexibility that effective community engagement requires.

References

Armstrong, A., Francis, R., & Totikidis, V. (2004). *Managing community governance: Determinants and inhibiters*. Paper presented at the 18th ANZAM Conference, Dunedin, New Zealand.

Armstrong, A. & Rutter, A. (2002). *Evaluating the success of a crime prevention strategy targeting community capacity and participation*. Paper presented to Australasian Evaluation Society International Conference, Wollongong, Australia. http://www.evaluationcanada.ca/distribution/20021030_armstrong_anona_rutter_anthea.pdf (accessed August 5, 2006).

Arnstein, S.R. (1969). A ladder of citizen participation. *Journal of the American Institute of Planners, 35*, 216–24.

Australasian Police Ministers Council. (2005). *Directions in Australasian Policing 2005-2008*. Australasian Police Ministers' Council. http://www.acpr.gov.au/pdf/Directions05-08.pdf (accessed July 18, 2006).

Bayley, D.H. (1986). *Community policing in Australia: An appraisal*. Australasian Centre for Policing Research, Report Series No. 35. http://acpr.gov.au/pdf/ACPR35.pdf (accessed August 11, 2005).

Bayley, D. & Shearing, C. (2001). *The new structure of policing: Description, conceptualisation, and research agenda*. Washington, D.C.: National Institute of Justice. http://www.ncjrs.gov/pdffiles1/nij/187083.pdf (accessed August 5, 2006).

Beyer, L. (1992). The logic possibilities of 'wholistic' community policing. In J. Vernon & S. McKillop (Eds.), *The police and the community* (pp. 89–105). Canberra: Australian Institute of Criminology.

Bonato, M. & Associates. (2003). *Report from review of police community consultative committees*. Unpublished confidential paper. Crime Prevention Victoria.

Casey, J., Dalton, B., Melville, R., & Onyx, J. (2008). An opportunity to increase positive results or "so disappointing after so much energy?" A case study on the long gestation of working together for NSW. CACOM Working Paper No. 79. Center for Australian Community Organizations and Management, University of Technology, Sydney.

Casey, J. & Mitchell, M. (2007). Police-community consultation in Australia: Working with a conundrum. In J. Ruiz, & D. Hummer (Eds.), *The handbook of police administration* (pp. 335–355). Boca Raton, FL: Taylor & Francis.

Casey, J. & Trofymowych, D. (1999, December 9–10). *Twenty years of community consultative committees: Is it possible to solve the conundrum?* Paper presented at the History of Crime, Policing and Punishment Conference Australian Institute of Criminology, Canberra. http://www.aic.gov.au/conferences/hcpp/caseytro.html (Accessed August 5, 2006).

CMRD (Corporate Management Review Division, Victoria Police) (2004). *Evaluation of local priority policing phase three: The community consultation model. Victoria Police*. (Unpublished confidential paper) Management Review Division, Melbourne.

Davis, G. & Weller, P. (2001). *Are you being served? State citizens and governance*. Sydney: Allen and Unwin.

Dixon, D. (2005). Why don't the police stop crime? *Australian and New Zealand Journal of Criminology, 38*, 4–24.

Findlay, M. (2004). *Introducing policing: Challenges for police and Australian communities*. Melbourne: Oxford University Press.

Fleming, J. & Rhodes, R. (2004). *It's situational: The dilemmas of police governance in the 21st century.* Paper presented at the Australasian Political Studies Association Conference University of Adelaide. http://www.adelaide.edu.au/apsa/docs_papers/Pub%20Pol/Fleming%20%20Rhodes.pdf (accessed February 5, 2006).

Ipsos. (2005). *DHS – Partnership survey 2005: State-wide report*. Ipsos Consulting Report for Victorian Department of Human Services. http://www.dhs.vic.gov.au/pdpd/partnership/downloads/2005_partnership_survey_report.pdf (accessed September 9, 2006).

Maguire, M. & John, T. (2006). Intelligence led policing, managerialism and community engagement competing priorities and the role of the national intelligence model in the UK. *Policing and Society, 16*, 67–85.

Mitchell, M. & Casey, J. (2007). Community-police consultation: What is it and what is it intended to do? In. M. Mitchell & J. Casey (Eds.), *Police leadership and management* (pp. 218–230). Sydney: Sydney Federation Press.

Moir, P. (1992). Community policing: Questioning some basic assumptions. In J. Vernon & S. McKillop (Eds.), *The police and the community* (pp. 59–66). Canberra: Australian Institute of Criminology.

Myhill, A. (2006). *Community engagement in policing: Lessons from the literature.* UK Home Office. http://police.homeoffice.gov.uk/news-and-publications/publication/community-policing/Community_engagement_lit_rev.pdf (accessed December 12, 2005).

Myhill, A., Yarrow, S., Dalgleish, D., & Docking, M. (2003). *The role of police authorities in public engagement*, Home Office Online Report 37/03. http://www.homeoffice.gov.uk/rds/pdfs2/rdsolr3703.pdf (accessed December 12, 2005).

National Institute of Governance. (2004). *Review of stakeholder engagement in ACT planning.* National Institute of Governance. http://www.actpla.act.gov.au/publications/reports/nig-report.pdf (accessed August 5, 2006).

Newburn, T. & Jones, T. (2002). *Consultation by crime and disorder partnerships.* Home Office Police Research Series Paper 148. http://www.homeoffice.gov.uk/rds/prgpdfs/prs148.pdf (accessed January 11, 2005).

Ransley, J. & Mazerolle, L. (2007). Third party and partnership policing. In M. Mitchell, and J. Casey (Eds.), *Police leadership and management* (pp. 37–49). Sydney: Federation Press.

Rawsthorne, M. & Christian, F. (2004). *Making it meaningful: Government-community sector relations.* Western Sydney Community Forum. http://www.communitybuilders.nsw.gov.au/download/Making_it_Meaningful.pdf (accessed January 3, 2007).

RegNet. (2006). *Regnet program review 2001–2006-impact case study: Victoria police – Security.* RegNet Program, Australian National University, Canberra. http://regnet.anu.edu.au/program/review/SupportingDocs/CaseStudy1_Security.pdf (accessed March 19, 2007).

Sarre, R. & Tomaino, J. (1999). *Exploring criminal justice: Contemporary Australian themes.* Adelaide: South Australian Institute of Justice Studies.

Skogan, W.G. (2006). *Police and community in Chicago. A tale of three cities.* New York: Oxford University Press.

Squires, P. (1998). Cops and customers: Consumerism and the demand for police services. Is the customer always right? *Policing and Society, 8*, 169–188.

Sutton, A., Dussuyer, I., & Cherney, A. (2003). Assessment of local community safety and crime prevention roles in Victoria. Crime Prevention Victoria and Department of Criminology, University of Melbourne. (Unpublished).

Totikidis, V., Armstrong, A., & Francis, R. (2005, August 15–17). Local safety committees and the community governance of crime prevention and community safety. Paper presented to the Beyond Fragmented Government: Governance in the Public Sector Conference, Victoria University, Melbourne. http://www.businessandlaw.vu.edu.au/conferences/psc_proceedings/Totikidis_VUREF.pdf (accessed August 8, 2006).

Victoria Police (1999). *Strategic development department, continuous improvement handbook*. Melbourne: Victoria Police.

Victoria Police (2003). *The way ahead: Strategic plan 2003-2008*. Melbourne: Victoria Police. http://www.police.vic.gov.au/files/documents/352_The-Way-Ahead-Strategic-Plan-2003-2008.pdf (accessed August 11, 2005).

Victoria Police (2004). *Statement of purpose for the Latrobe district youth officer*. (Unpublished confidential paper). Victoria Police.

Victoria Police (2005). *A fit for purpose service delivery model for Victoria police*. (Unpublished confidential paper). Victoria Police.

Victoria Police (2006). *Nexus policing project*. Retrieved 8/03/07 from http://www.police.vic.gov.au/content.asp?Document_ID=5524 (accessed August 3, 2007).

Victoria Police (2008). Community safety report. www.police.vic.gov.au/retrievemedia.asp?Media_ID=823 (accessed May 5, 2008).

Ward, J. (1995). *Facilitative police management*. Melbourne: Partnership Press.

Wilson, P. (1992). Avoiding the dangers and pitfalls of community policing: Ten questions that need to be addressed. In J. Vernon & S. McKillop (Eds.), *The police and the community* (pp. 1–3). Canberra: Australian Institute of Criminology.

A Chinese Theory of Community Policing

10

KAM C. WONG

Contents

> The value of criminal records for history is not so much what they uncover about a particular crime as what they reveal about otherwise invisible or opaque realms of human experience.
>
> **Muir and Ruggiero (1994)**

> The American city dweller's repertoire of methods for handling problems including one known as "calling the cops."
>
> **Bittner (1970)***

> If the people were allowed to manage their affairs for themselves, they could do that with half of the number of policeman who were now employed.
>
> **Halley Steward, MP (1888)†**

Introduction

Introduced in the 1970s (in the United States), community policing (CP) is a philosophy and strategy to involve and engage the public to fight crime and improve the quality of life in their own community. The ultimate purpose of CP is to provide for better (responsive and responsible, efficient and effective) police service. CP takes many forms, e.g., team policing, and is realized in different ways, e.g., problem-oriented policing (POP).

CP, as a democratic practice, seeks to actualize Sir Robert Peel's (United Kingdom prime minister, 1834 to 1835) principle of "police are the people, people are the police." CP requires the police to work together with the community in identifying, prioritizing, and dealing with crime, safety, and order issues.

"Mass line policing" (MLP) was a revolutionary practice introduced by Mao Zedong in 1974. As a communist ideology, MLP pursues the ideal of "from the people, to the people." MLP requires the police to listen to the people, ascertain their problems, and empowers the people to solving them.

CP and MLP share much in common. Both seek to actualize democratic (West) and people (China) policing. Both claim that police and policing should be of, for, and by the people. Both engage the public to solve community problems. Both look to the community for guidance, support, and supervision. Both are accountable to the people. CP and MLP, however, are not identical. They differ in one major respect—CP relies on the police to fight society's crime, MLP depends on the people to solve their own problems

This chapter explores the philosophy of CP–MLP in China (Qilu & Dawei, 1995), as it offers a radically different Chinese theory of community policing—police power as social resource theory (SRT)—to explain and explicate CP–MLP practices.

The SRT addresses three main questions: What is the role and function of the police? What is the relationship of the police with the people? Why

* Bittner (1970, pp. 36–47); Gaskill (2002). (It is important to investigate people's mentality about crime to gain an insight into how people think, feel, and act on crimes.)

† *Hansard*, CCCXXVII, June 19, 1888, cols. 605–606.

do people call the police? This Chinese theory of policing (re)conceptualizes police power (1) from the perspective of the people, not that of the state, and (2) as a function of problem solving, not defined solely by law. In terms of foundation, SRT is a theory of the people, a theory of democratic governance, a theory of empowerment, and a theory of self-help.

This chapter is divided into seven sections. Following this brief introduction is an overview of what is community policing as understood and practiced in the United States. The next section explores the philosophical differences in policing between the East (China) and the West. The section on constructing a Chinese theory of policing defines the basic concepts and key propositions of the SRT. The next section is on principles of mass line policing, which underscores SRT. The sixth section discusses the essential foundational elements of the theory and provides justifications thereof. In the conclusion, the author compares the salient differences between MLP and CP.

What is Community Policing?

In the United States, CP resulted from an overall failure of the police to fight crime, maintain order, and service the people (Carter, 2000). More simply, it is a reaction to the perception that in policing, nothing works (Sherman et al., 2002).

According to empirical research, random patrol does not deter crime (Kelling, 1974). Incidence-driven policing does not solve community problems. Speedy response has little success in catching criminals (Kansas City Police Department, 1977). Detectives rarely solve crimes (Sanders, 1977). Traditional policing deals with the symptoms, not roots, of crime and disorder (Gutis, 1988). Bureaucratic policing is not addressing people's real needs and concerns (Wender, 2008). Professional policing substitutes expert judgment for public opinion (Dobrin, 2006; Bobinsky, 1994). Legalistic policing prefers procedural justice to substantive justice (Wilson, 1968). Technocratic policing allows efficiency to stand in the way of effectiveness (Bevir & Krupicka, 2007). Paramilitaristic policing is too confrontational (Benson, 2001; Waddington, 1993). Profiling policing is too discriminatory (Bjerk, 2007). And, in the end, people were frustrated and dissatisfied with traditional, professional policing. They wanted changes.

At this juncture, researchers were able to show that taking care of "broken windows" thaws crime (Wilson & Kelling, 1982), well-kept neighborhoods improve quality of life (Kelling & Coles, 1998), and foot patrol reduces the fear of crime (Kelling et al., 1981). Police started to change their policing strategy (Ellison, 2006; Skogan, 2006). Instead of reacting to crime, they started to look at crime as a problem with which they had to deal with (Goldstein, 1990). The new policing paradigm was called *community policing.*

The seventh of Sir Robert Peel's nine Principles of Policing provides a solid foundation for community policing:

> To maintain at all times a relationship with the public that gives reality to the historic tradition that the police are the public and that the public are the police; the police being only members of the public who are paid to give full time attention to duties which are incumbent on every citizen, in the interest of community welfare and existence.*

There are two mainstream approaches† to defining CP, i.e., as a philosophy or as a strategy. The philosophical approach described CP as:

> A new philosophy, based on the concept that police officers and private citizens working together in creative ways can help solve contemporary community problems related to crimes, fear of crime, social and physical disorder, and neighborhood decade (Trojanowicz & Bucqueroux, 1990, p. 5).

Alternatively, Trojanowicz described CP as:

> A philosophy of full-service, personalized policing where the same officer patrols and works in the same area on a permanent basis, from a decentralized place, working in a proactive partnership with citizens to identify and solve problems (Trojanowicz et al., 1994, p. 3).

In South Africa, the "main objective of CP is to establish and maintain an active partnership between the police and the public through which crime, its causes, and other safety-related issues can jointly be determined and appropriate solutions designed and implemented" (National Ministry of Safety and Security, 1996).

Approached this way, CP is democratic governance in action, i.e., providing or promoting public participation in policing, from inputting of ideas (Bureau of Justice Assistance, 1994) to engaging with operations to monitoring the outcome.

As a strategy, CP has variously been associated with police public relations, team policing, foot patrol, and crime prevention. Whatever the strategy, it is directed at:

* The nine principles by Sir Robert Peel. http://www.magnacartaplus.org/briefings/nine_police_principles.htm#nine_principles (accessed July 30, 2008).

† There are other more marginalized accounts. Barlow and Barlow (1999) ("Community policing is image-management policing."); Bayley (1994, p. 100) ("Police must not be allowed to make performance a 'con game' of appearance management."); more generally, Greene and Mastrofski (2001).

> [T]he enhancement of human relations, a community-sensitive and user-friendly police service, consultation on the needs of communities, respect for human rights, cultural sensitivity, continuous positive contact with community members, discretion on the part of police officers when they enforce the law, and the establishment of mechanisms to enhance the accountability and transparency of the police (National Ministry of Safety and Security, 1996, p. 1).

CP has revolutionized policing* in untold ways, some by design, most by default. Thus, while there are continued and unrelenting debates over various aspects—philosophy, strategy, effectiveness†—of CP, there is little debate that community policing has changed fundamentally the way police organize and operate, i.e., decentralized organization and problem-oriented policing.

Philosophy of Community Policing in Modern China

The People's Republic of China (PRC) has taken a contrary approach, at least up until very recently, in defining police–community roles and functions in fighting crime and keeping order.

According to Luo (1994, p. 57), "Our public security work … is not to have matters monopolized by the professional state agencies. It is to be handled by the mass … . The mass line principle … is to transform public security work to be the work of the whole people … ."

Historically, social control in China was decentralized and organized around natural communal and intimate groups, e.g., family and clan, with governmental endorsement and support (Wong, 1998). Local social control was institutionalized. The emperors ruled the state by and through their officials who, in turn, governed the people by and through the family head and community leaders (Chang, 1955). Such decentralized, grassroots, social control practices were informed by Confucian teachings:

> Wishing to govern well in their states, they would first regulate their families. Wishing to regulate their families, they would first cultivate their persons. Wishing to cultivate their persons, they would first rectify their minds. Wishing to rectify their minds, they would first seek sincerity in their knowledge. Wishing for sincerity in their thoughts, they would first extend their knowledge (De Barry et al., 1960, p. 115).

* Police have always engaged in aspects of CP activities, from reaching out to the community and to engaging in problem solving. The change that is radical is that police have shifted focus, redefined missions, reorganized structure, changed culture in order to make police more community-oriented.

† See Cordner (2005, pp. 401–402). It is extremely difficult to demonstrate effectiveness of community because of its "programmatic complexity," "multiple effects," "variation in program scope," and "research design limitations."

When asked, "What is meant by 'in order rightly to govern the state, it is necessary first to regulate the family'?" Confucius answered:

> It is not possible for one to teach others while he cannot teach his own family. Therefore, the ruler, without going beyond his family, completes the lessons for the state. There is filial piety: therewith the sovereign should be served. There is fraternal submission: therewith elders and superiors should be served. There is kindness: therewith the multitude should be safe (Legge [trans], 1981, p. 23).

Thus, functional social control in China was supplied informally and extrajudicially within the family and throughout the community. This resulted from deliberate state policy, building upon existing natural communal structure of interdependence (Dutton, 1992, pp. 84-85), established cultural habits of informal social control (Williams, 1883; Chu, Tung-tsu, 1962), and entrenched customary practices of clan rule (Lui-Wang, 1959, p. 56). Hence, while in theory the local magistrate's offices (*yamen*) were supposed to be in total control on all matters large and small in rural China, in practice, broad police powers were delegated or conceded to the local community and exercised by the family and clan (Ibid, Chapter 2).

The authority of the Chinese *pater familias* was much stronger than intra-familial leadership required; and he owed his extraordinary power essentially to the backing of the despotic state. Disobedience to his orders was punished by the government. On the other hand, the local officials could have him beaten and imprisoned if he was unable to keep the members of his family from violating the law. Acting as a liturgical (semiofficial) policeman of his kin group, he can scarcely be considered the autonomous leader of an autonomous unit (Wittfogel, 1957, p. 50).

Consistent with the above Confucius ideas and ideals, crime prevention and social control in traditional China was realized through indigenous groups: starting with the family which provides the education and discipline for character building, the neighbors who provide the supervision and sanction against deviance, and the community that sets the moral tone and customary norms to guide conducts.

Finally, the state acts as the social control agency of last resort in providing economic maintenance and social welfare to anticipate civil disorder, and impose punishment on criminals to inculcate a habit of obedience. In this regard, the Chinese have taken a broad notion of control that includes the internalization of norms (by the individual), socialization and disciplinary regime (by the family), setting up custom and accountability systems (in the community), removal of criminogenic conditions (by the administration), and defining the moral and social boundary (by the state) (Gibbs, 1982, pp. 9-11). The Chinese approach comes close to Edward A. Ross's definition of social control: "The molding of the individual's feelings and desires to suit the needs of the group," including supernatural, ceremonial, public opinion, morals, art, and education, which all forms the normative structure of a society. In a very real sense, Chinese social control is a totalitarian gem (Wittfogel, 1957) and a disciplining type (Williams, 1883; Chu, 1962).

The organization and practice of decentralized and informal social control in China changes the way deviance is defined and dealt with. In a family and communal setting, with blood relations, tight bond, and enduring association, "deviance" and "disorder" are not recognized by official label as "crime" deserving punishment, but seen as problems to be "dealt with," accepted, avoided, prevented, resolved, and suppressed by varieties of means. Problems are cognizable as things that should not have happened, i.e., breach of expectation ("bugai"). The objective is to deal with "problems" to promote group welfare by returning to settled group norms and individual expectations.

Constructing a Chinese Theory of Policing

This study explores the philosophy of MLP in China (Qilu & Dawei, 1995), and offers a radically different Chinese theory of policing: "Police power as social resource theory (SRT)" to explain and explicate such MLP practices.

SRT

Proposition 1: People confront problems routinely; some of them are called crime.

Proposition 2: To the people, problems of everyday life are unmet expectations resulting from a lack of resources.

Proposition 3: All problems can be solved by redefining expectations and/or acquiring resources.*

Proposition 4: People experience crime as a personal problem not as a legal violation.

Proposition 5: People call the police because they do not have (or unwilling to spare†) the necessary resources to deal with their problems, whether it is a crime or a noncrime.

* Everyone has to come to terms with his or her problem. The ultimate solution to one's problem is to take one's life.

† For the purpose of SRT, in cases where people are unwilling to spare personal resources to deal with a problem, the people really do not have a problem. This remains to be the most controversial aspect of SRT: Should police—social resources—be made available to deal with people's nonproblems?

Proposition 6: People call the police because they are resources of legitimacy and coercion.

Proposition 7: Police power is a kind of emergency (social) resource made available to the people to solve their problems.*

Proposition 8: The more resources at the disposal of the people, the less problems the people will be confronted with.

Proposition 9: The more resources at the disposal of the people, the less they have to call on the police when a problem (crime) happens.

Proposition 10: The more (adequate and appropriate) resources at the disposal of the police, the more effective they are in solving people's problems.

Proposition 11: The less (adequate and appropriate) resources at the disposal of the police, the more likely they will resort to illegal or extralegal means in solving people's problems.†

Proposition 12: The person who is closest to the problem in interest and value (physically, emotionally, culturally) is the best person to take care of the problem.

Definitions

Police: A depository and coordinator of social resources. Police is an all purpose emergency problem solver who is authorized to use "legitimacy" and "coercive" resources to solve people's problems in a domestic situation and during peaceful times.

* The idea that police are problem-solvers is traceable to Goldstein. This is misconceived. *Police as a problem solver is misconceived* because long before Goldstein, and certainly with other cultures, police have been observed to be 24/7 problem-solvers, from helping old ladies to cross the street to repairing flat tires. There is nothing unique to this observation. What is new and refreshing, however, about Goldstein's insight is that he liberated the police from the mantel of the law, which Goldstein insightfully and rightfully observed to be constricting police's imagination and constraining their (re)actions. Goldstein preached that police should see and react to public's call for help not as legal problems, but social ills. This allows the police to venture beyond the confines of the legal definition of a problem reported to the police—rape, murder, burglary—to attend to the roots of the problem—urban plight, social disintegration, moral bankruptcy that they were first enlisted to help. Once liberated from law, as a defining and empowering device, the police are free to look at a problem in different ways and boundless manner. While liberating, Goldstein provided no clue as to how far the police should go and where the police should stop, in solving problems. This issue perplexed scholars and confused practitioners. The lawyers have long understood the pitfalls of trying to find the causes to events: proximate cause, contributing cause, ad infinitum.

† This is to make clear that the demand and supply of resources must be at an equilibrium. This can be achieved by lowering of demand through change (lowering) of expectations or change (increase) in resource. Failing that, illegality results as citizens' vigilantism or police abuses.

Problem: An unrealized expectation of wants or needs due to resource deprivation.

Resource:[*] Things of all kinds, including power, time, materials, skills, culture, ideas, knowledge, that can satisfy ones expectations of want and needs.[†]

Legitimacy: That which is endorsed, supported, and promoted by duly constituted political authority, which elicits intuitive respect and demands unquestioned obedience.

The Principles of Mass Line Policing[‡]

SRT is build upon the idea behind *renmin jingcha* (people's police) and MLP.

The PRC police was named *renmin jingcha* at the first National Public Security Meeting in October of 1949.[§] As an occupation title, *renmin jingcha* captures the basic nature and essential characteristics of police in Communist China; the police are at one with, belong to, and dependent upon the people.[¶] The imagery used to depict police versus people's relationship is "fish (police) in the water (people)" (Damin, 2001, pp. 200-205).

The revolutionary hero, Lei Feng, a People's Liberation Army (PLA) soldier who sacrificed his life in the service of the Party, people, and country, was made to personify the Chinese police. Lei Feng stands for "Love for the Communist Party and hatred of class enemies, obedience to the party,

[*] Depending on context and discipline, there are many definitions of the term *resource*. Some common ones include "a source of aid or support that may be drawn upon when needed"; "the local library is a valuable resource" (wordnet.princeton.edu/perl/webwn); "a person, thing, or action needed for living or to improve the quality of life" (www.ec.gc.ca/water/en/info/gloss/e_gloss.htm); "an aspect of the physical environment that people value and use to meet a need for fuel, food, industrial product or something else of value" (www.wasd.k12.pa.us/district/curriculum/geography/geography_glossary.htm); "something which is required to complete a task—resources are characterized by the fact that they have a limited time availability (e.g., an employee that works eight hours a day, five days a week)" (www.koffice.org/kplato/docs/glossary.html).

[†] Resource has three innate properties: First, resource *is a necessary thing*, as in: a student said, "I need a pen to write." That is to say people cannot do without it under certain set of circumstances. Second, resource is *an instrumental thing*, as in: a general said, "I need a battalion to secure the battle zone." That is to say, resource is needed to get things done. Third, resource is a *goal-oriented thing*, as in: "I cannot live without money." This is to say that recourse is of use in solving problem.

[‡] There is no MLP per se, as much as there is policing with ML philosophy and principles. See generally, Xingguo (1998).

[§] The other name for police is *gongan*, which aptly describes police functions to maintain "public security."

[¶] This recalls Sir Robert Peel's principle of policing: "The people are the police and the police are the people." See Principle 7 of "The nine principles by Sir Robert Peel." http://www.magnacartaplus.org/briefings/nine_police_principles.htm#nine_principles (accessed July 30, 2008).

selfless service to the people, thrifty living, hard work in any assignment" (Holley, 1990). Lei lived to serve the Party and make people happy. "If you are a drop of water, you have moistened an inch of soil; if you are a ray of light, you have brightened a foot of darkness."* Consistent with Chinese tradition and Confucian thought, Lei Feng was used to reeducate people to engage in virtuous conduct as officials and citizens.

The CP lesson we can learn from *renmin jingcha* is that "the people are the police and the police are the people" (Sir Robert Peel). The Chinese rendition of this venerable policing principle is that the police and the people are "blood bothers" from the same family, perfectly aligned in political ideology, class interests, and personal outlook, as a sought-after ideal state, as exemplified by the Lei Feng spirit.

The United States' rendition of Peel's policing principle above is different. It is not necessary for the police and the public to be one and the same in constitution, interest, and outlook. It is important for the police to consult and work for the people under the law.

That understood, Chinese police have no separate identity and interests beyond that of the people. They are supposed to see crime and disorder from the perspective of the people, as personal problems, and not to respond to them as legal violations. The police should and will do everything they can, including sacrificing their own well being, interests, and welfare to solve people's problems.

Mass Line Policing (MLP)

Mass line is the basic tenet of governance of the Chinese Communist Party (CCP). James R. Townsend observed:

> The theory of the mass line is probably the strongest part of the legacy [of Maoist "populism"]. It is now deeply implanted in CCP ideology, and it would be difficult to reject it without altering the ideology as a whole. The legitimation of populism means that it has been accepted as a fundamental

* Eckholm (2001). Lei has been made an icon of the CCP and suited to fight Party corruption, public anomie, and social ills. See also Eckholm (1998): "The promotion of Lei Feng comes in waves, with different focus messages and purpose. After the student-led demonstrators in Tiananmen Square in 1989, Lei Feng was used to bolster the public's confidence in the integrity of the Party. In the 1990s, Lei Feng was used to fight "spiritual pollution," to exalt people to work harder on reform ("something in Lei Feng's spirit that can help solve some of the most pressing problems in modern China, like the reform of state-owned enterprises, which has led to massive layoffs of redundant workers"), and to remind people of the need to make sacrifice in the face of market restructuring ("hope that Lei Feng's spirit of sacrifice and dedication can keep people adversely affected by reforms and restructuring in a good mood and help avoid social contradictions").

> principle of the Chinese political system—that is, it has acquired an aura of "constitutionality" (Townsend, 1977, p. 1011).

The mass line is at once an ideological postulate,[*] a revolutionary perspective,[†] a mission statement, a leadership style, an organizational method,[‡] and an operational principle for the police.[§] As such, MLP has direct application upon how the police is led, organized, and operated.

Ideologically, mass line makes the people the master of their own destiny. In all matters of political governance and social maintenance, the people's perspective, value, and interest prevails. Functionally, a mass line perspective allows the masses[¶] to see where their true and long-term interests lie. It effectively liberates the people from the straightjacket of "false consciousness" in a capitalistic society. It allows the masses to gain political consciousness by having them analyze their own social, economical, and political circumstances from their own vantage point, with their own experience, and in their own way. In so doing, the mass line recognizes that nobody understands the plight of the people more than the people themselves.

Operationally, the mass line is a method of revolutionary leadership adopted by the CCP to educate, prepare, and mobilize the people in an epic class struggle to establish a utopian communist state. It consisted of three recurring steps: (1) gathering scattered ideas of the masses, (2) processing (concentrating and systemizing) ideas of the masses, and (3) using the ideas to lead the masses to struggle against class enemies with education, propaganda, and mobilization. The method is commonly referred to as "from the mass, to the mass." "The mass line is, everything for the mass, everything depends on the mass, everything from the mass, everything to the mass."[**]

The principle of mass line as a practice in China has a long history and dates back to the earliest days of the CCP during the Yenan era (1927 to

* The Communist Party and the police are of the people, by the people, and for the people (see Damin, 2001, pp. 200–205).

† "Firm faith in the majority of the masses, and first and foremost in the majority of the basic masses, the workers and peasants—this is our fundamental point of departure" (Mao Zedong, 1957).

‡ Mass line gives us the organizational principle of democratic centralism (see Duchu, 1980, p. 29).

§ For an extensive and comprehensive study of "mass line" as a political platform and ideological principle, see Scott, H. (no date).

¶ Mao talked about "mass line" and "masses." There is one "mass line" doctrine but many masses.

** "*Qunzhong luxian, jhisi yiqie we qunzhong, yiqie yikao qunzhong, zhng qunzhnglai, dao qunzhng chu* - 群众路线，就是一切为了群众， 一切依靠群众， 从群众中来，到群众中去". (Liao Wan, 2007).

1936).[*] As a practice worldwide, it is traceable to Lenin and beyond that to Marx. The theory of mass line and associated principles was first espoused by Mao as a political ideology or revolution leadership style.

Although it is said that Mao is the chief proponent of China mass line, Li Shaoqi is the ultimate theorist and chief strategist, who explored and refined the intricacies of the mass line (see Shao-chi [Shaoqi], 1951, pp. 41-62). According to Liu, in order to carry out mass line, the Party must adopt four mass standpoints:

1. Standpoint of serving the people
2. Standpoint of total accountability to the people
3. Standpoint of having faith in the people to emancipate themselves
4. Standpoint of learning from the masses[†]

Mass line is based on the (scientific) understanding of the world that the masses create history[‡] by living the reality.[§] Marx and later Mao credited the masses with the ability to create knowledge and the right to take initiative[¶] to change the world in their own image and according to their own interests (Mao Zedong, 1963, p. 502).

In this regard Mao pointed out that the people[**] are the masters of their own destiny: "The people, and the people alone, are the moving force in the making of world history" (Mao Zedong, 1945, p. 257). The reason is a simple one, only the people have the necessary creativity and energy to get things

[*] Schram (1989, p. 9): "The ideas and methods corresponding to the 'mass line' begin to make their appearance" in Mao's work during the 1927 to 1936 period "though this concept is formulated systematically only during the ensuing decade"; mass line is a legacy of the Yenan heritage, see Schram (1989, p. 86). Others have suggested an earlier period, see Ristaino (1987, p. 2): "the earliest Communist practice of the mass line was initiated in China during the period under study" [i.e., 1927 to 1928].

[†] There were critical differences between Liu and Mao, especially when the mass line was put into *practice*. Liu tended to equal the mass line with selfless services and Mao demanded much more, learning from the mass and leadership over the mass. See MacFarquhar (1974, p. 117).

[‡] "The millions of people will never heed the advice of the Party if this advice does not coincide with what the experience their own lives teaches them" (Lenin, 1961, p. 426).

[§] This underscored with Mao and later Deng's idea of "to seek truth from facts" (*shi shi qiu shi*): "Facts are all the things that exist objectively, 'truth' means their internal relations, that is, the laws governing them, and 'to seek' means to study." Mao Zedong (1941, pp. 22–23).

[¶] "In the Great Proletarian Cultural Revolution, the only method is for the masses to liberate themselves, and any method of doing things in their stead must not be used. Trust the masses, rely on them, and respect their initiative." See Decision of the Central Committee of the Communist Party of China Concerning the Great Proletarian Cultural Revolution, in Fan (1968, p. 165).

[**] Though conceptually not identical, I have used the "people" and the "mass" interchangeably.

done in their own interest: "The masses have boundless creative power. They can organize themselves and concentrate on places and branches of work where they can give full play to their energy; they can concentrate on production in breadth and depth and create more and more undertakings for their own well-being" (Mao Zedong, 1955d, Chapter 11).

The people are also very motivated: "The masses have a potentially inexhaustible enthusiasm for socialism" (Mao Zedong, 1955c). However, there are many who do not want to get involved. They are too complacent with the present or too fearful of the future:

> Those who can only follow the old routine in a revolutionary period are utterly incapable of seeing this enthusiasm. They are blind and all is dark ahead of them. At times they go so far as to confound right and wrong and turn things upside down. Haven't we come across enough persons of this type? Those who simply follow the old routine invariably underestimate the people's enthusiasm. Let something new appear and they always disapprove and rush to oppose it. Afterwards, they have to admit defeat and do a little self-criticism. But, the next time something new appears, they go through the same process all over again. This is their pattern of behavior in regard to anything and everything new. Such people are always passive, always fail to move forward at the critical moment, and always have to be given a shove in the back before they move a step (Mao Zedong, 1955c, p. 1).

But, the masses do not always see the whole picture. Their information is scattered, partial, and unsystematic. Their understanding of matters is subjective, incomplete, and distorted. More specifically, the masses are confined and restricted by their life circumstances and thus have limited access to the true nature of class society and real appreciation of their standing in the class struggle.

As differently situated individuals, they have access to some but not all the facts. As people with different (moral) values and (material) interests, they see the world from their own class world view and interest. As proletarians class members, they are subject to constant bombardment of capitalistic propaganda. As laborers and workers, they have no time or ability to think for themselves. The views of the masses need to be "concentrated" and "reconstituted" (collected, analyzed, synthesized) to form the whole truth.*

Where do correct ideas come from? Do they drop from the skies? No. Are they innate in the mind? No. They come from social practice, and from it alone; they come from three kinds of social practice, the struggle for

* This means two things. First, it means taking individual ideas of the masses and putting them together to arrive at a bigger truth; a compiling process. Second, it means reformulating the masses' ideas to arrive at a higher truth; a transformational process.

production, the class struggle, and scientific experiment. It is man's social being that determines his thinking … . In their social practice, men engage in various kinds of struggle and gain rich experience, both from their successes and from their failures (Mao Zedong, 1963, p. 502).

The role of a revolutionary leader is to gather the disparate ideas and process—distillation and synthesis—them into concentrated truth, according to Marx's theory of historical materialism and Hegel's methods of dialectics. Mao observed this to be democracy in action:

> Without democracy, it is impossible to sum up experience correctly. Without democracy, without ideas coming from the masses, it is impossible to formulate good lines, principles, policies, or methods. As far as the formulation of lines, principles, policies, and methods is concerned, our leading organs merely play the role of a processing plant. Everyone knows that a factory cannot do any processing without raw material. It cannot produce good finished products unless the raw material is sufficient in quantity and suitable in quality (Mao Zedong, 1978, p. 9).

In seeking to distill and construct the truth, the leaders abide by certain general principles:

1. Seek the long-term interests of the masses over the short-term ones.
2. Seek the whole interests of the proletarian movement over any of its parts.
3. Seek political power through force of arms.
4. Seek compromises and establish alliances in struggle toward the revolutionary goal.
5. Seek unity with advanced workers and rely on them to overcome intermediate and backward workers.

When the "processed" ideas in "concentrated" form are ready to be acted upon by the masses, the ideas will be returned to the masses through study, education, propaganda, and mobilization processes.

From its inception and until now, the mass line informs upon everything the police do:

1. People and not the police should take care of their own problems.
2. People and not the police have a better understanding of their own problems.
3. People and not the police are more motivated to solve their own problem.
4. Police should look at crime and disorder as problems and from the people's perspective.
5. Police, as experts, can help the people to solve their problems.

Theoretical Framework

A Radical Theory of Policing

Built on MLP, SRT starts with the basic observation that in a state run by the people one must understand how the people conceive the nature of crime and role of the police.* From the perspective of the state, crime is a legal violation. From the perspective of the people, crime is a set of life experiences and a multifaceted personal problem. From the perspective of the state, police power is a political resource to secure control, maintain order (Robinson & Scaglion, 1987), and command obedience (Austin, 1995). It is defined coercively, structured legally, organized bureaucratically, and imposed unilaterally.

From the people's perspective, police power is a social resource made available by the state and drawn upon by the citizens to handle personal problems in an emergency or crisis situation. More significantly, in the eyes of the people, police power is not reconstructed in political image, structured by law, and organized with reference to police needs (Manning, 1983, p. 176), but dictated by the people and negotiated to fit the personal circumstances and whatever situational needs the problem calls to mind.

In its entirety, SRT argues that the definition and availability of police power as a political resource happens at a structural macro level, e.g., legislative process and policy debate, and the initiation, distribution, and disposition of police power as social resources happens at the personal, situational, micro level, e.g., reporting crime and preferring charges.†

Policing from the People's Perspective

The superiority (reasonableness and appropriateness) of looking at the police role and functions from the public's perspective can be justified on a number of grounds. First of all, MLP calls for looking at life course problems from the

* Conflict theorists have long observed that it is impossible to have all the people agree upon a uniform understanding of the social order. The radical theorists have challenged consensus theorists' understanding of law and order from the perspective of the dominant class, while totally ignoring the contribution of the dominated class. In constructing social reality and keeping social order, the consensus theorists have overlooked one important point, i.e., the people's perspective, experience, sense and sensitivity should be taken into account. The nature and distribution of police power takes different shape viewed from above, as it is from below.

† This theory offers a rebuttal to Marx's theory of policing. Put it simply, Marx observed that the police is a political agent of the state; SRT argues that the police, depending on mission, is variously a political or social agent. The state in using the police to put down the riot is using the police as a political resource to maintain control. The public in calling the police to put down the riot is using it as a social resource to solve a disorderly problem. This is what I called in my paper the "duality of police power concept."

people's perspective, as a matter of birth right and process of maturation. In Emanuel Kant's words:

> Enlightenment is man's emergence from his self-imposed immaturity. Immaturity is the inability to use one's understanding without guidance from another. This immaturity is self-imposed when its cause lies not in lack of understanding, but in lack of resolve and courage to use it without guidance from another (Kant, 1784, trans. 1959, p. 41).

This means empowering the people to meet their own personal needs and supplying them with the necessary resources, on demand and as required.

Secondly, MLP corrects the lopsided relationship between police and the people by returning the people to the center stage, and putting them in control,[*] thus achieving the communalization,[†] socialization,[‡] or personalization[§] of crime.

Thirdly, MLP marks a shift of focus from a state-centered community (oriented) policing to a people's oriented policing.[¶] While community-oriented policing (COP) calls for the police to listen and to serve the needs of the community as a collective in order to enhance its political legitimacy and operational efficiency, MLP asks of the police to be responsible and accountable to the people as individuals and groups.

[*] The domination of crime prevention, deterrence, detection, and punishment in the hands of criminal justice (CJ) experts, as noted by Mao, is not harmless. See Mao Zedong (1953). It creates dependence on the police and, in time, alienation of the people from crime as a personal and community problem. See Braithwaite (1989, p. 7).

[†] Communalization of crime recognizes that crime is given meaning by the community, in context of culture, custom, and morality. Crime as a problem cannot be solved without attending to normative (expectation) deficit of the people.

[‡] Socialization of crime recognizes that crime is a product of a society. Crime results from social resource deficits, e.g., poor schooling or dysfunctional families, and cannot be solved without investment in social resources.

[§] Personalization of crime recognizes that crime creates different problems with different victims, i.e., there are differences in expectation deficits.

[¶] There is an urgent need to draw a clear distinction between the "community" and the "people." They are conceptually different categories for analytical and operational purposes. Analytically, a community is a collectivity (group of people) sharing certain identifiable characteristics and relationship, i.e., "a group of people who share certain demographic and socio-economic traits and fellowship." (Fessler, 1976). The people are an unbounded group of individuals sharing few things in common other than a universal social nature (humanity) and particularistic political character (nationality). Operationally, COP means that "the police designate a community in which they will engage in problem solving, develop relationships (that hopefully become partnerships) with the population, collaborate with them to diagnose problems that have some generalized impact, prescribe and implement interventions to solve the problems, and continuously monitor the results."(Flynn, 1998). In the case of people's policing, it is the people's problem, individually or as a group, that should be of dominant concern.

Fourth, MLP gives "social" meaning and lends "emotional" content to police—people activities, which is what policing is all about, i.e., dealing with personal issues, human problems, relationship difficulties of one form or another.* In so doing, it socializes and humanizes the police—people interface, making police business a truly people's business.†

Fifth, MLP liberates the police from the sterile confine of the law and stifling restrains of the bureaucracy. It gets away from one size fits all "McDonaldization" of police (burger, cheese burger, or double cheeseburger is still a burger) strategy and practices.

Sixth, MLP recognizes that police work can be as diverse and complex as people's problems, i.e., policing changes with time, place, people, context, circumstances, and situations.

Finally, and most importantly, MLP allows the people to be heard. For all too long, the public is an object of policing when, in fact, they are, and should be, the subject of policing. Instead of being policed, people are engaged in problem solving.

The legal anthropologist has contributed much through the study of "trouble cases" to our understanding of how indigenous people of other cultures settle disputes and deal with problems. Such research relates that the problems of everyday life look and feel very differently from the inside than from an outside point of view.‡

The lesson to be drawn from such insider (people) versus outsider (police) points of view is that the legal classification of a problem, e.g., murder or rape, does not usually capture the problem as experienced by the parties involved. The nature of a problem must be deciphered by the parties involved who are anchored within a multifaceted social milieu, locked into an enduring human relationship role set, constricted by an all embracing local custom, and moved along by interactive situational dynamics and personal exchanges (Gibbs, 1969).

SRT as proposed—people solving their own problem with state resources—is consistent with the civil society movement (Madsen, 1993), privatization of police trend (Joh, 2004; O'Leary, 1994), and alternative dispute resolution initiative (Gross, 1995). The theory, if ever fully realized,

* Crime is never more than a breach of human trust, destruction of social relationship, and infringement personal rights. Breach of trust as failed expectation of predictability generates fear (of crime). Destruction of relationship as failed expectation of intimacy results in alienation (from others). Infringement of personal rights as failed expectation of entitlement causes loss (of property) or injury (to body). A reintegration strategy is much better than punishment strategy in renewing faith, building relationship, and repairing harm. In this way, my theory echoes the concerns of Braithwaite with traditional punishment (*cf.* Braithwaite, 1989).

† At its heart, all policing is a policing of relationships.

‡ Nader (1969, pp. 337–348). Law of the state is built upon the custom of the people, but never able to reproduce its richness or replicates its nuance.

allows the people to be the master of their own affairs. They have the right to dictate and control the extent and manner of the state's involvement in their life choices.

Legalization of People's Problems

When police power is exercised by state officials to enforce the law (e.g., criminal arrest) or invoked by the public to deal with a problem (e.g., call for police assistance), it automatically transforms the nature and handling of the "situation"* on hand. When the public calls the police, it gives the state the opportunity to transform a private/personal matter into a public/legal one. This amounts to the bureaucratization/legalization/professionalization of a private or personal problem, transforming/converting it into one that is recognizable by the police and actionable in court.

Legalization of people's problems results from the fact that the police as a criminal law agent will only recognize a case for investigation prosecution if the elements of a crime can be proved in a court of law beyond a reasonable doubt with competent evidence:

1. A conduct (*actus reus*)
2. A criminal intent (*mens rea*)
3. A harm
4. Causation
5. A law against it

In being captured by law, a personal problem loses much of its attributes and meaning derived from the social milieu, communal setting, interpersonal relationship, historical context, and situational dynamics of which it is an integral part, or what the "situation" *in situ* is all about.

Before the police intervene, a personal dispute in an office romance which ends in a street fight registers a rupture of a personal relationship, derailment of a marriage plan, disruption of office work, damaging of career prospects, not to mention hurt ego, tested confidence, and lost opportunities. When the police are called, the street fight becomes a public nuisance and the lovers involved are turned into complainant and defendant.

In the process of transformation/conversion, the personal problem loses much of its original meaning and natural feeling to the actors involved and

* Before the decision to call the police and police intervention, we have a "situation" waiting to be labeled. The nature and control of any situation remains in the hands of the people involved, until the police are called. Even when the police are called, there is oftentimes some negotiation between parties involved, ending, in most cases, in the question: "Do you want to file a complaint?"

others who might be affected, e.g., sons, daughters, and neighbors of the offender. More significantly, what matters most to the actors involved (emotion) and people affected (relationship) are of the least of the state's concern. For example, police care little about the children of an abusive husband but loving father when a case of spousal abuse is reported and acted upon.

For example, criminal law does not recognize "motive" as a justification or excuse for illegal actions. Intentional killing of one depraved criminal to save a million innocent people exhibits as much guilt as killing a million innocent people to satisfy one's depraved mind. It is still prosecuted and punished as one murder. Likewise, killing a person to relieve his pain is the same as the cold-blooded killing of a person for no reason at all (Wong, 2003). This is because, under criminal law, intent and not motive to kill is considered important. However, from the victim's perspective, communal custom and personal morality have always been connected with motivation, i.e., why a person kills is more important than the fact that someone was intentionally killed.* This is most clearly illustrated by Kobben's observation of conflict between local custom and government law:

> In the village of Ajumakonde, a man and a woman are caught in *flagrante delicto*. The woman's brothers want to beat her and the man, but the man fights back. In the heat of the fight, he is bitten by one of his assailants. The man goes to Mungo to lodge a complaint with the police; before going into the office, he rolls about in the mud to make himself look really [pitiful]. The police go to Ajunmakonde, where they arrest two men (not even the one who did the beating) (Kobben, 1969, p. 126).
>
> The event is the talk of the whole district. People are indignat[e] at the man's action, but equally at the police. "The one who broke the rules is put in the right and the others in the wrong. The police are stupid, they should ask what was the reason for the fight. It is just like a snake; when it is lying curling up and a person passes, it won't do anything. Only if a person treads on the snake will it bite. That is what we do; we don't just strike a man; we only strike him when there is a reason" (Ibid, p. 127).

For example, criminal law assumes that people are rational and the law is built on the foundation of utilitarianism (Bentham, 1781), denying emotions of everyday life. Thus, one who kills emotionally is no less guilty as one who intentionally kills. Likewise, jurors are instructed not to allow

* Wong (2007). Chinese jurisprudence considered Qing-Li-Fa before coming to judgment of liability. A daughter who killed an official to avenge the death of her father at the hands of an official executing a legal duty was executed for murder, but lauded by the emperor for filial piety to the father.

emotional considerations to influence the outcome of a case.* In both cases, core constitution and basic values of people as victims, defendants, and jury are denied in favor of the rational administration of the law.†

The process and effect of transformation of a private affair into a public matter of the event and people involved is best described by Manning:

> As the message moves the system, it loses the implicit, connotative meanings associated with the polysemic nature of what was reported to have happened and becomes more denotative, represented in police classification, and is treated by the organization more as something to sort out and deal with and less as a reflection of a complex, emotional, sensate event. I shall refer to this as bureaucratization of social and personal problems (Manning, 1983, p. 176).

Manning's observation was elaborated upon in concrete details by Canadian criminologist Jorgensen who examined 16 hours of police calls—820 telephone conversations, 210 dispatches, and 53 request reports—into a large suburban police station in central Canada. Jorgensen clearly observed that legal and administrative considerations come before the citizen's concern:

> We have seen that COs (communication officers) do not mechanically act on caller requests. Conversations are difficult and require the application of interpretations. Citizen explanations and concerns are not necessarily police consideration and concerns ... All trouble announced to the police may potentially involve "chargeable" matters, or prove otherwise ... The CO is concerned, our findings suggest, more with managing and negotiating caller requests than, perhaps, with satisfying caller demands. By placing calls under legal definitions, COs can achieve and maintain the most administrative control (Jorgensen, 1980, p. 276).

Legalization of a problem also shifts the ownership and arena of dealing with the problem from the public to the state. For example, once a family problem (dispute) becomes acted upon by the police as a legal violation (assault), the parties involved (husband and wife) cannot (re)claim ownership of the problem

* The American jury system has originated with the firm belief that community justice shall prevail over the black letter of the law (Abramson, 1994, pp. 22–33). This has led inevitably to the nullification of the law based on "conscience of the community" in modern time (see Granberry, 1990, and Van Dyke, 1991). In the case of Camden 28, the judge allowed the draft card-burning defendants to argue for nullification based on the fact that the FBI informants had supplied the antiwar protesters with the tools to carry out their draft raids (see Jackson, 1973). The defense lawyer in the case argued to the jury that the term "nullification" means: "power of a jury to acquit if they believe that a particular law is oppressive, or if they believe that a law is fair, but to apply it in certain circumstances would be oppressive ..." (Jeffrey, 1994, p. 59). The jury "nullification" doctrine clearly allows the jury to rise above the confines of the law in search of higher justice. In so doing, they imbue the legal process with moral and ethical considerations.

† See how the concept of "reasonable man" is made to accommodate local differences and give vent to emotional sentiments (Gluckman, 1969, pp. 367–371).

(which is theirs in the first place and affects them most) until such time as the police have determined it is no longer in their interest to proceed with the case.

Still, there are formal and informal ways the parties can influence the legal process and outcome, e.g., by refusing to testify, but they have to do so within the law, i.e., people can be forced to testify under a contempt order. The police and prosecutor have long respected the rights of the victims not to prosecute. Otherwise, the law makes it possible to mount a private prosecution if the police or state refuses to move forward.* More recently, the "victim's right movement" successfully reformed the law to allow victims to participate in the sentencing of the offenders,† and the reintegration shame theorists have made it possible for victims to play a key role in having some control over the disposition of their cases. Reintegration shame theory argues for the restoration of social order and repair of personal relationship after a crime (to social disruption) has been committed. This is achieved through active involvement (by way of conferencing) of parties (offender, victims, community, police) to settle personal/social/communal problems (apology, compensation, protection) arising from disruption (crime). This allows for a prominent role and active involvement of the public (victim) in the management of its own business and problems.

Policing as Self-Help

The theory SRT gives credence to CP in that it openly acknowledges in theoretical terms and explicates in concrete detail why and how the public can play a key role in the deployment and disposition of police power as a social resource in search of a solution to their own problems (Leadbeater, 1995, pp. 19-24; Katyal, 2005). To that extent, this is a theory about "self-help" (Black, 1968), "private ordering," and "personalized justice."‡

This theoretical approach—looking at police services from the public's perspective and as personal/community problems—is anticipated by Cumming, Cumming, and Edell (1965); Goldstein (1990); and Bittner (1980), though none of them carried their analysis far enough in addressing the central proposition of this theory: People should be empowered§ to solve their own problems.

* Klerman (2001, abstract): "Although modern societies generally entrust enforcement of the criminal law to public prosecutors, most crimes in premodern societies were prosecuted privately by the victim or a relative."

† See "Crime Victims' Rights" in Minnesota: http://www.letswrap.com/legal/victrts.htm (accessed July 30, 2008).

‡ To the extent "private ordering" as "self-help" involves police resources, "self-help" is mediated by the police in legal and bureaucratic considerations. "Within very broad limits, citizens must generally avail themselves of police services rather than resort to "self-help" in dealing with problems or property" (Reiss & Bordua, 1967, p.28).

§ I use empowering to mean giving the people the necessary social resource and helping them to use the resource in a proper, efficient, effective, and responsible manner.

Cumming and her colleagues properly discovered the "support" function of the police, but failed to discuss its theoretical and operational implications in terms of people's policing.* Goldstein properly identified the "community problem solving" functions of the police, but stopped short of recognizing that the public has an inherent right as citizens to demand police power in solving their own problems (Goldstein, 1990). Bittner properly demonstrated that the police bring with them the "capacity and authority" of using coercive force to solve situational problems of all kinds without also realizing that, in actuality, police possess a range of other resources (diverse capacity and multitude authority; the most sought after one is legitimacy), which makes them valuable to the public for problem solving.

All of these scholars contributed significantly to my thinking about people problem-oriented policing, but none of them envision a reconceptualization of the role (problem-oriented) and relationship (people-oriented) of the police to the people.

Policing as Social Services

Cumming and her colleagues were one of the very first to discover the dual roles of the police, i.e., as a control versus supportive agent. "Finally, besides latent support, the policeman often gives direct help to people in certain kinds of trouble" (Cumming et al., 1965). After analyzing 801 calls over 82 hours, Cumming and her colleagues found that over 50% of the police calls seek help of one sort or another. The research team concluded that the police, instead of enforcing law or fighting crime, were asked by the people to help solve their problems, i.e., acting as philosopher, guide, or friend to people in need. This research is important because it breaks with the traditional concept of the police (in the 1960s, the height of professional policing) in openly recognizing the social role and service nature of police work.

For our purpose, what social service the police rendered is less important than the fact that the police are not solely political controllers, law enforcers, and crime fighters. They help people solve problems of all kinds. Like so many other studies to follow, the research failed to draw upon the empirical findings to articulate a police theory calling for a renewed understanding of police role, focusing on problem solving. This task is left to Herman Goldstein.

Policing as Problem Solving

In a seminal article, Goldstein observed and lamented that there is a "tendency in policing to become preoccupied with means over ends" (Goldstein,

* Cumming et al. (1965).

1987, p. 236). By that, Goldstein means that traditionally police in America have structured their activities around law enforcement and crime control when they should be orientating themselves to the "substance" of policing, i.e., solving crime and related problems of the community.

Goldstein was one of the first to reorient the police function from reactive crime fighting to proactive problem solving in the community. He called for a shift in police strategy and activities to that of "problem-oriented policing" (POP), which has since then been the organizing principle of police reform in the 1980s.

Goldstein's problem-oriented policing concept is a comprehensive prescription for improving the way in which the police do business. It calls for the police to understand their work in a new light, to recognize that what they are called upon to do is to address a wide range of problems that threaten the safety and security of communities, including, but not limited to, what is commonly viewed as serious crime. The concept calls for the police to improve their understanding of the underlying conditions that give rise to community problems and to respond to these problems through a much wider range of methods than they have conventionally used (Scott, 2000, p. 15).

This invitation for the police to shift their role and function from dealing with crimes to solving community problems, challenges the police to look at the nature (complexity of causes), extent (diversity of manifestation), and remedy (variety of alternatives) to community problems beyond the narrow confines of the traditional role of police as law enforcers and crime fighters. In so doing, the police no longer fight crime and enforce law, but engage in community problem solving.

Social resource theory (SRT), while agreeing with Goldstein's POP approach, differs from his theory in a number of important ways.

First of all, Goldstein's POP theory is mainly a theory about solving "community problems" as revealed by patterns of calls for assistance from individuls, e.g., repeated calls about robbery in a neighborhood tells the police that this is a criminal "hot spot." Goldstein argued that the police should not be driven by law, focus on crime, and react to incidents. Instead police work should have a larger reference and more pragmatic concerns in dealing with citizens' problems. By that Goldstein means that police should not be organized only to fight crime reactively, but also take the initiative to deal proactively with community problems giving rise to crime and disorder.

While it is true that Goldstein's theory would readily accommodate the use of police to solve personal problems, this is not the original intent of the theory. This is an important distinction for five reasons. First, Goldstein is not interested in dealing with individual-level problems as much as he is concerned exclusively with resolving community-level problems. More bluntly,

Goldstein looks at individual problems reported to the police as indicators of larger problems in the community, not personal problems worth attending to.

Ultimately, an issue is raised as to what kinds of problem Goldstein is interested in—problems giving rise to crime or problems generated by or associated with crime? Should the police be dealing with the crime and disorder problem at its root, i.e., solving "community problems" that give rise to crime and disorder, such as a lack of welfare network and support for disabled veterans leading to crime? Or, should the police be dealing with the various problems associated with a "crime" or "incident" as experienced by the victims, including emotion–psychological, material–economical, relation–social, e.g., asking for compensation from robbers and providing counseling for the rape victims?

SRT argues that both are important, but from the perspective of the people (victim) it is the latter that is more important. That is why people call the police in the first instance, i.e., to seek help from crime-precipitated and related problems.

Secondly, Goldstein's theory is a "police" theory. His main contribution is in having the police look beyond the immediate to the larger picture. He asks the police to look at the problems lurking behind crime and disorder in the community. SRT is a pure "people" theory of policing. It asks the police to look at crime, disorder, and other problems from the perspective of the people. In so doing, what is a problem to the public is considered *ipso facto* a problem for the police.

There is an interesting question whether the police can ever disagree with the public over the existing and classification of a problem. They can. However, under SRT, the police as an agent cannot override the people's (as a principle) assessment of a situation, however irrational or objectionable. The police officer, of course, can offer his advice as an expert consultant as to how best to deal with a problem. This can give them the right to dissuade the citizen from using the police for what, to the police, is a nonproblem. Lastly, the police can certainly limit the availability of resources based on commonly agreed upon objective criteria written into law and policy.

Third, Goldstein expects the police to solve community problems with the help of the community. SRT wants the people to solve their own problems with or without the help of the police. More importantly, the police resource is only one of the many resources potentially available.

Fourth, Goldstein wants the police to have more expansive police power to solve the crime problems, e.g., the nuisance abatement law. SRT wants to empower citizens to learn how to deal with disputes or with the help of others (e.g., police, social worker, friends, relatives) to solve their own problems. While SRT does not object to police having more power to serve the public, such power should only be activated and used with the people's consent and at their direction and control.

Table 10.1 Goldstein's "Problem-Oriented Policing" Versus Wong's "State Police Power as Social Resource"

	Goldstein POP	Wong SRT
Definition of problem	Police in consultation with the public	People identifying their own personal or community problem
Ownership of problem	Police	People
Solution to problem	Police provide solution to problem	People draw upon the police as a resource to solve personal problem
Means to solve problem	More police resources	Varieties of community/ personal resources
Role of police	State control agent	People's problem solving agent
Role of citizen	Community participation (policy consultation) and assistance (eyes and ears)	Citizens consult, engage, or direct police to solve problem

Lastly, under Goldstein's formulation, police problem solving will lead to more police penetration into community lives. Under SRT, the police will be playing a lesser and lesser role in the community with the people getting better and better at taking care of their own business. Goldstein's theory allows the police to enter the people's lives at will in search of a solution. SRT will allow the public to control the police once they are called to one's assistance. In sum, Goldstein wants to enlarge the state role; SRT wants to create more civic society space (Table 10.1).

Police as a Coercive Resource

In an equally important and provocative article, Bittner convincingly argued that "the role of the police is to address all sorts of human problems when insofar as their solutions do or may possibly require the use of force at the point of their occurrence" (Bittner, 1980, p. 38). More specifically, police: "is best understood as a mechanism for the distribution of nonnegotiable coercive force employed in accordance with the dictates of an intuitive grasp of situational exigencies" (*Ibid.*, p. 41). He observed that the police are the only social institution empowered to use legitimate force to settle problems in our society in peacetime. For example, he gave this illustration of why police are called:

> In a tenement, patrolmen were met by a public health nurse who took them through an abysmally deteriorated apartment inhabited by four young children in the care of an elderly woman. The babysitter resisted the nurse's earlier attempts to remove the children. The patrolmen packed the children in the

> squad car and took them to Juvenile Hall, over the continuing protests of the elderly woman (Ibid, p. 109).

Bittner was quick to observed that in most cases police coercive force is not needed and never will be used, e.g., police treatment of lost children. However, this does not mean that as a last resort coercive force might not be necessary. In essence, to Bittner it is not the actuality or even probability of using force that defines the role of police, it is the possibility (no matter how slim) and potentiality of the use of force (no matter how contingent), which justifies the definition of the police role. More pertinent for our analysis, Bittner postulated that everyone expects the police to use force to solve problems when they are called:

> There is no doubt that this feature of police work is uppermost in the minds of people who solicit police aid or direct the attention to problems, that persons whom the police proceed against have this feature in mind and conduct themselves accordingly, and that every conceivable police intervention projects the message that force may be, and may have to be, used to achieve a desired objective (Bittner, 1970, p. 40).

Bittner and I agree on one thing: people call police as a resource to solve their problems. However, I do not agree with Bittner that all or even a majority people call the police because of the police's "capacity and authority" to use force. My disagreement with Bittner is based on the following arguments.

The public calls the police for a variety of reasons, not all of them require the use of force. In fact, most of the problems requiring police attention defy the use of force for a satisfactory resolution. For example, when the police are called to help locate a lost relative, to unlock a locked vehicle, or put out a fire, the public does not expect the police to use force because force is not necessary. Take the case of a fire in a rural area with no fire department nearby. People call the police because they lack the resources to deal with it—firefighter equipment (technology resource), firefighter skill (knowledge resource), and firefighter personnel (people resource). The "capacity and authority" to use force is certainly one kind of resource needed to remove anyone who obstructs and impedes with the firefighting, this is not the only or most important kind of resource sought. Coercive force, if used in such situations, is quite remote and very contingent. The people who call the police certainly do not anticipate such a far-fetched theoretical possibility. Bittner is stretching his logic in order to make a point.

According to SRT, people call the police to solve their personal problems because they do not have the resources to do so. That is to say that, if people have the necessary resources, they will not call the police. Because personal or community resources to deal with a given problem, e.g., fighting a small fire, is not evenly distributed, this means that someone will be calling the police for help while others will not. For the people who opt to take care of the fire problem themselves, they will be using whatever resources available to their disposal, such as calling upon their relatives to help. This certainly does not include the use or potential use of force. If the same problem could be solved by the citizens without force, it is far-fetched to claim that people who call the police on the same kind of problem are calling the police because the police have a "capacity and authority" to use force as a "contingency," however remote. The fact of the matter is, from the public's perspective, most problems they have to deal with defy forceful and coercive intervention, e.g., when people are depressed and want someone to talk to. In fact, for most of the time and with nearly every matter the police are called upon to deal with by the public, forceful invention is inappropriate if not counter-productive.

In some cases, people call police precisely because they do not want force to be used. For example, people may be calling a policeman as an arbitrator in a family dispute with strong-headed family members. An irate wife may call the police to affirm that her husband had a lady in the car when he crashed in the early morning. A frustrated father may call the police to tell his daughter how dangerous it would be to go out to a rowdy bar at night. The irate wife, in drawing upon the police's information power, wanted the police to show the husband that she has a right to be upset, to be vindicated. The frustrated father, on drawing upon the police's expert power, wanted to teach is daughter a lesson, to be reinforced. In either case, the parties do not want nor expect force to be used.

According to SRT, whether a citizen is calling on the police's "capacity and authority" to use force certainly depends on whether the citizen has the "capacity and authority" to use force relative to the police, thereby making the police "capacity and authority" superfluous. In those case where the citizen has the "capacity and authority" to use force, e.g., arresting and turning a thief over to the police, he has no need to invoke the police for its "capacity and authority" to use force, but only to process the person through the next stage of the criminal justice system.

Lastly, and perhaps most importantly, Bittner's formulation assumes that all people in all communities at all times on all matters look at the police (coercive) role the same. More pertinently, all people have the same expectation of the police role and relations. This presupposition runs counter to the first lesson learned about studying policing and society. How the people of a given society in a certain era conceive of the police and their relationship with society must of necessity depend on the cultural understanding of that society about the role, function, and relationship of the police with the public in that point in time. In prehistoric times, the tribes policed their members with high priests who were readily obeyed without the threat or use of force. In modern times, private security of a company is able to police without resort to force because its enforcement without force is accepted by the employees to be legitimate.

Police Power as a "Legitimacy" Resource

In theory, SRT postulates that police power is a "legitimacy resource" for the people to solve problems. Legitimacy is defined as "that which is endorsed, supported, and promoted by duly constituted political authority." In political science, legitimacy is acceptance of a governing authority and rule, while authority is the ability to influence people's action.

In fact, most people call the police to "legitimatize" what they are doing. In essence, the private citizens want the police to endorse their stance or action to a situation as legitimate, i.e., legal or just, to bless them with state authority. This is especially the case when citizens engage in disputes with each other over matters of right or wrong (Black, 1968). For example, in divorce cases, embattled spouses routinely call the police to be arbiters of property, custody, and privacy disputes.*

In practice, most people call the police because of their other "capacity and authority," e.g., the police as a legitimate state authority. For example, people see police as a moral authority representing the state, or "legitimacy resource." As such, they follow the police instructions voluntarily and instinctively, and expect others to do so as well. In this way, the police will be listened to, not because the officer has the "capacity or authority" to use force, but, as with the British rule, they are the representative agent of the people (of said state) and thus carry with them the moral authority of the people and state.

The importance of legitimacy and moral authority in securing compliance and helping people to resolve problems within relevant in groups is well established. Different groups secure legitimacy and privileged authority differently (Graftstein, 1981).

In Imperial China, the instruction of the father (delegated police authority) is instantly obeyed, less so because he can use force to exact compliance, but more so as a result of his elevated social status and established moral authority. Within the Catholic Church, the admonition of the Pope is never challenged because he possesses ultimate religious stature and moral authority. In a corporation, the security chief's order is never questioned, not because he can use physical force to enforce his will, but because he is empowered by the company to compel performance from the employee with

* The author was an experienced divorce lawyer.

economic means. Within the scientific community, the lead scientist has the final say over a scientific project because he has expert authority.

As the various examples above show, different people can draw on different capacities and authority to compel people to act. Likewise, police possess different capacities and authority to move along people as expected. Force is only one of the many resources used by the police to put things in order.

Problem as Resource Deprivation

As suggested above, when people call the police, they do so because they need help (with resources) to solve a problem. A problem arises as a result of unmet expectations or resource deficit. Deploying proper resources or lowering of expectations can meet expectations. For example, a simple theft is a problem because it breaches a number of expectations: the victim does not expect to be violated, the victim does not expect to lose money, the victim does not expect to have to walk to work, etc. For those who live in a crime-infested neighborhood, residences learn to adjust their normative expectations and prioritize their needs; a "crime" problem in the suburb might just be a nuisance in the inner city.

The victim might not need to call the police if he has resources to meet those expectations, e.g., if the victim is rich, he might be protected by security guards, and, if a motorist has AAA membership, he can call AAA to open the locked car. The most appropriate way to deal with crime as a personal or social problem is, first, define what problems are confronted by the people and, second, provide the people the necessary resources to prevent or resolve such problems.

This is exactly what imperial emperors did; they avoided crime through the enrichment (material resource) and the education (mental resource) of the people.

State (Police) as Supplier of Resources

In imperial China, problems of crime and issues with punishment are thought about philosophically and theoretically as integrated governance issues. The philosophy of good governance has one objective: How to perfect the emperor's rule approximating mandate of heaven. Good governance requires moral leadership and benevolent rule of the emperor (by and through his officials), manifested as stern discipline for the officials, ethical education for the public (especially the intellectuals), sound economic policy, and paternalistic social programs.

Guan Zhong* was appointed the prime minister of the state of Qi in 685 BCE. He was known for his enlightened reform policy in strengthening Qi state and improving the livelihood of the people. Guan Zong articulated and explained his thinking on good governance policy in 管子 Guan Zi.

Rulers who are shepherds of people (*mumin*) need to be vigilant and industrious. If the country is rich and strong, people would come from wide and far. "If the storage is full, people will know about protocol, if they are properly clothed and fed, they know about shame and glory."†

Guan Zhong's major approach to law enforcement, maintenance of order, and crime prevention is to provide for the material well being of the people. According to him, the effective governance of people starts with the provision of physical security and material well-being. In this regard, Guan Zhong made clear:

> When citizens are rich, they will settle peacefully at home and pay attention to the family (*an xiang zhong jia*), if they settle peacefully at home and pay attention to the family, they will be respectful of authority and fearful of crime (*jing shang wei zui*), if they are respectful of authority and fearful of crime, they are susceptible to rule (Guan Zi. Mumin).‡

In order to govern well, the state must inculcate the people with four dispositions,§ i.e., li,¶ yi,** lian,†† and chi.‡‡ People who know etiquettes will not transgress norms, thus people will not undermine authority. People who know honesty will not ask for more than they deserve, thus people will not act dishonestly. People who know honor will not cover up bad deeds, thus people will not indulge in illegality and immorality. People who know shame

* "Guan Zhong (Chinese: 管仲, Wade-Giles: Kuan Chung) (born 725 BCE, died in 645 BCE) was a politician in the Spring and Autumn Period. His given name was Yíwú (夷吾). Zhong was his courtesy name. Recommended by Bao Shuya, he was appointed prime minister by Duke Huan of Qi in 685 BCE." (*cf.* http://en.wikipedia.org/wiki/Guan_Zhong. (Accessed July 30, 2008).

† "倉廩實，則知禮節; 衣食足，則知榮辱" (Guan Zi. Mumin): "If the granary is full, (people) know about protocols; if (people) properly fed and clothed, (people) know glory and shame."

‡ "Guan Zi. Mumin" is a chapter on herding ("mu") the people ("min"). For the book of Guan Zi. Mumin, (管子. 牧民) see ftp://sailor.gutenberg.lib.md.us/gutenberg/etext05/8guan10.txt (accessed July 30, 2008).

§ "何謂四維? 一曰禮，二曰義，三曰廉，四曰恥 。" What are the four protocols: first is rite, second is justice, third is integrity, fourth is shame." Guan Zi. Mumin.

¶ "Li" is "etiquette, rite, protocol," according to the Pinyin Chinese-English Dictionary (PYCED). Hong Kong: Commercial Press. PYCED (2005, p. 415L).

** "Yi" is "justice, righteousness." PYCED (2005, p. 821L).

†† "Lian" is "sense of honor." PYCED (2005, p. 424L).

‡‡ "Chi" is "sense of same." PYCED (2005, p. 92L).

will not tolerate injustice. Thus, people will [not] tolerate bad deeds.* The best state policy is to remove people's anxiety, poverty, emergency, and evilness.† Conversely, the worse policy is to use punishment and coercion. Because punishment can never effectively remove desire and coercion has a tendency to court rebellion.‡

The above brief excursion into Chinese history and philosophy makes clear that the best way to fight crime and disorder is to secure the people from needs (materials resources) and educate the people to think (intellectual resource) and behave morally (moral resource). Once the people are empowered (materially, intellectually, morally), they will be less inclined to commit crimes. That is why crime rates in China have been so low in the past.

Conclusion

The whole purpose of this long chapter is to introduce a new way of thinking about CP, making policing a people's business and problem-solving exercise. This new way of CP is encapsulated in a new theory of policing: SRT.

The core principles that drive this research are extracted from China's MLP, captured by the Mao statement: "The people, and the people alone, are the moving force in the making of world history" (Mao Zedong, 1945).

In the case of Mao's policing, the political principle of "mass line" formed the basis of "people's policing"§ whereby the local people are supposed to be self-policed.¶

In the case of Communist China under Mao, MLP preached that in the context of fighting against political crimes (and later all social crimes), the

* "To follow rite is not to exceed bounds, to do justice is not to transgress norms, to have integrity is not to tolerate wrong, to know shame is not to participate in evil." ("禮不逾節，義不自進，廉不蔽惡，恥不從枉。") (Guan Zi. Mumin, note 112).

† "民惡憂勞，我佚樂之；民惡貧賤，我富貴之；民惡危墜，我存安之；民惡滅絕，我生育之". "When people are satisfied, they are worried, it is my job to make them happy; when people do not like poverty, my job is to make them rich; when people are concerned with safety, it is my job to secure them; when people do not have hope, I cultivate them." (Guan Zi. Mumin).

‡ "故刑罰不足以畏其意，殺戮不足以服其心。故刑罰繁而意不恐，則令不行矣；殺戮眾而心不服，則上位危矣。" "Thus punishment is not sufficient to deter people's minds, killing and maiming is not sufficient to pacific people's hearts. Thus, more punishment will lead to lack of fear, then government policy will not be effectively implemented. If by killing many and people are still not obedient, then rulers are at risk." (Guan Zi. Mumin).

§ It is more appropriate to refer to "mass line" policing in the earlier days of the PRC as "people's policing." The whole of "the people" as an exploited and oppressed class was mobilized to impose their political will. In the later years (since 1979), "people's policing" became "community policing," when the local people are encouraged to take part in managing their own affairs.

¶ For self-help literature, see http://www.ac.wwu.edu/~jimi/cjbib/selfhelp.htm (accessed July 30, 2008).

people's participation was deemed indispensable to win the "people's war" (Yean, 1997). Thus, in the suppression of counter-revolutionaries, the police was supposed to understand the people, trust the people, mobilize the people, and rely on the people (Luo, 1994, p. 82). The police played a supplemental, not central, and facilitating, not instigating, role.* In all, the people were considered the lifeblood and backbone of the police (Melville Lee, 1901, p. 83). The people and public security could be said to be co-producers (Rosenbaum et al., 1991) of revolutionary order and justice:

> We are following the mass line, freely mobiliz[ing] the mass, engag[ing] in broad propaganda, so that every household is informed, everybody understand[s], this can transform the suppression of counter-revolutionary movement into a joint action of the government and people, thus can obtain the mass's supervision and support. Because the mass is mobilized, the counter-revolutionary cannot hide (Luo, 1994, p. 193).

Practically and operationally, this means that the police must see things from the people's perspective, seek their support, and be amenable to their supervision (*Ibid.*, p. 189). Any policing detached and isolated from the people would not be effective in finding out local problems and detecting alien criminals.† Hence, one of the most serious mistakes that can be committed by the police is having an erroneous work style; being alienated from the mass through subjective idealism (*zhuguanzhuyi*), bureaucracy (*guanliaozhuyi*), or commandism (*minlingzhuyi*).‡

There are many reasons for engaging the people MLP:

1. The people have the right (*quanli*) as a ruling class to participate in their own governance. This is akin to the idea and ideal of localism in the United States§ wherein all the powers of the central government

* This policing philosophy conforms with Sir Robert Peel's first principles of law enforcement: "The police must secure the willing cooperation of the public in voluntary observance of the law to be able to secure and maintain public respect ... The police ... are the public and that the public are the police; the police are the only member of the public who are paid to give full-time attention to duties that are incumbent on every citizen in the interest of the community welfare ..." From "The nine principles by Sir Robert Peel" (Peel).

† For a statement of the problems during the revolutionary years, see Luo (1994, p. 213). For an analysis of the problem during the economy opening, see Yanhu (1966, p. 9). Police officers suffered from erroneous work style (*buzheng feng*)—from not being dedicated to playing with politics and *guanxi* to being cold, detached, and authoritative, see also Daohua and Jiangping (1996, p. 3).

‡ See Luo (1994, pp. 174–193). Public security has failed to adopt the masses' viewpoint and look down upon the people. It failed to elicit their support and subject to their supervision.

§ For a comprehensive treatment (law and theory) of localism in the United States, see Briffault (1990a, 1990b). For a brief history on the development of localism, see Eaton (1900).

come from the people. While federalism envisions a government from the top-down, localism conceives of a government from the bottom-up. The legal status and relationship of local associations to central authority (state) is best captured by the U.S. Supreme Court in *Avery v. Midland County*.* "Legislators enact many laws, but do not attempt to reach those countless matters of local concern necessarily left wholly or partly to those who govern at the local level."†

2. The people have the responsibility (*yiwu* as a citizen) to fight crime. In the PRC, people's rights and responsibilities are complementary. PRC Constitution (1982) Article 33 provides that "citizens enjoy rights guaranteed by the Constitution and law, but they must also fulfill their constitutional and legal responsibility."‡ This is akin to the notion of "communitarism" in the United States that is defined as "a mindset that says the whole community needs to take responsibility for itself. People need to actively participate, not just give their opinions … but instead give time, energy, and money" (Gurwit, 1933).
3. The people are in the best position to see that "people's justice" is done, including making decisions on who to police, what to police, and how to police. Mao supplied the rationale to MLP in his "Report on an Investigation of the Peasant Movement in Hunan": "The peasants are clear sighted. Who is bad and who is not quite vicious, who deserves severe punishment and who deserves to be let off lightly—the peasants keep clear accounts and very seldom has the punishment exceeded the crime."§ This is akin to the idea in the United States that the community notion of order and justice prevails over the rule of law (Wilson, 1968, p. 287).
4. The people were deemed to be more motivated, thus more vigilant, as an oppressed class to detect the counter-revolutionaries (Luo, 1994, p. 57). This is akin to the idea that citizens of a state, as with employees of an organization, naturally seek responsibility if they are allowed

* *Avery v. Midland County* 390 U.S. 474, 481 (1961). Challenge to the apportionment of the Midland County Commissioners Court—the county legislature—which gave a tiny rural minority a majority of the legislative seats. The apportionment was pursuant to the Texas Constitution, which did not require districts to have equal population.

† *Ibid.* 390 U.S. 474, 482. Local inhabitants have a personal stake in local government. Their self-determination is not to be interfered with by the state.

‡ The CCP has interpreted this to mean that the concept of right (*quanli*) and duty (*yiwu*) is unitary in nature (*tongyixin*): "People can enjoy rights, but also have to fulfill their duty, just enjoying rights and not fulfilling duties is not allowed; nor should the assumption of duty without the enjoyment of right be tolerated." (Zhonggong Zhongyang Dangxiao, 1993, p. 89) This is to say that right and duty are supplementary to and complementary of each other ("*xiangfu-xiangcheng*").

§ Mao Zedong (1975, p. 23). Under communism, citizens have reciprocal rights and responsibilities.

to "own" a problem. "The average human being learns, under proper conditions, not only to accept but to seek responsibility."*

5. The people are in the best position, being more able, efficient, and effective in conducting the people's business. Criminals and counter-revolutionaries lived in the mass. They cannot long survive within the mass without being exposed. For example, a Zheng zhou *zhian baowei* (security defense committee member) noticed that his opposite neighbors have seven people in the house without old people or children. They were supposed to make a living by weaving socks, but seldom worked. They have no income, but live very well. This aroused his suspicion in reporting the case to the authority. Further investigation showed they belong to "guangdao" gang (Luo, 1994. pp. 317-322, 319). This is akin to the notion in the United States that the public is the best source of intelligence for the police (Sparrow, 1993, p. 4).
6. The police could not be everywhere at the same time and in any one place all the time. This is especially the case in the sparsely populated areas, e.g., border and rural areas (Luo, 1994, pp. 317-322). It is unlikely that the police could be informed of illegal activities unless informed by the people (*Ibid.*, pp. 347-352).

Before we end, we need to compare and contrast CP versus MLP. There are substantial differences between these two approaches, in theory and practice.

MLP is the embodiment of a political ideology, i.e. communism. The ultimate objective of communism is to transform the society from a capitalistic to communist one, through raising the consciousness of the "mass." As such, MLP is an end unto itself. Practice of MLP is practicing communism.†

CP is a policing philosophy. Its ultimate objective is to improve the efficiency and effectiveness of the police by working with the people. As such, it is a means to an end. The practice of CP improves policing.

The tougher debate is whether MLP and CP are conceptually distinguishable, when CP also serves the people in a democratic society (Peel, 1829: "The people are the police, the police are the people.") More significantly, in practical terms, a clear distinction between MLP and CP cannot be drawn when for all intent and purposes policing cannot be effective without the volunteer participation and active engagement of the people, in reporting crime, supplying intelligence, and giving evidence. Viewed in this light, the conceptual discussion may be too academic to be of relevance and too refined to make a difference. However, the distinction is a very important one. When it is said

* This is the famous "Theory Y" (McGregor, 1960, p. 48). Theory Y calls for involving the employee in making and implementing decisions.

† The better analogy is that of being a "practicing" Catholic.

that MLP is an inseparable part of a larger and all-encompassing ideological framework of communism, it means a number of things:

1. MLP is not a stand-alone philosophy, theory, concept, strategy, policy, or practice; all of which have been attributable to CP. In fact, separate from its roots and cut away from its cloth, MLP has no meaning. MLP is the embodiment of communism. The suggestion that because MLP is communism in action just as CP is democracy in action and, thus, there is no discernible difference between the two, both a political–ideological practice fails to capture the essence of MLP and its relationship with communism. MLP is not something a police officer thinks (philosophy) or does (practice), though invariably communists think and act consistent with ML.
2. MLP is a dynamic process, just as communist is. Communism is a never-ending process of regeneration, renewal, refinement, always arriving, but never arrived (Starr, 1971). This is particularly so when the society is in the process of moving toward communism, a stage where China is now called "primary stage of socialism." During the primary stage, MLP takes on different missions, objects, and measures. In the early days of the revolution, MLP sought to protect the Party from domestic counter-revolutionaries and externals enemies. It called for mass mobilization for struggles against class enemies of all kinds with violent means. In the primary stage of socialism, the MLP focused on securing democratic dictatorship of the people with rule by law under established process. MLP is concerned with dealing with contradictions among friends more so than struggles with class enemies.

   The CP principle is a static philosophy capable of generating many strategies and creative applications. However, the core principle, policing works best when the community is engaged and involved, does not change. In this regard, CP is capable of applying in a democratic as well as a communist country, urban city as well as small town, with uniform policing as well as detective investigation.
3. With the arrival of communism, the "mass" is to be the master of its own destiny. There is no need for a separate organized police organs to provide for policing in a communist state. Before that, MLP was policing by the mass, from setting priorities, to implementing policies, to conducting operations. During the revolutionary stages, the police played a supplementary role. The communist helps the mass to realize its true identity as master of its own destiny and encourages the people to take the matter into their own hands, obviating the need to go to bureaucratic agencies, such as the police (Table 10.2).

Table 10.2 Comparing Traditional CP Theoretical Orientation Versus Proposed SRT Theoretical Orientation

Dimension of Police Power	Traditional CP Orientation	Theoretical Premise	Proposed SRT Orientation	Theoretical Premise
Ideological base	State	Power as instrumentality of state	Democratic	Power as a resource of the people
Whose perspective	Police	Police professional perspective	Public	Public personal perspective
Vantage point	Top-down	Power is created and imposed from a center	Bottom-up	Power is developed and shared by the people
Orientation	Past	Mechanical solidarity Punitive law Public justice Defendant's rights	Future	Organic solidarity Restitution Law Private justice Victim's rights
Method	Consensus	People are more alike than different	Critical	People are more different than alike
Dimension	Unitary	Power as control	Dualistic	Power as control and serve
Defined by	Law	Power justified by legal rule	Problem	Power justified by situational needs
Structured by	Bureaucracy	Rational rule	Culture	Historical: customary norms
Function	Coercion	Noncontingent and nonnegotiable force to suppress	Resource	Contingent and negotiable resource to resolve
Purpose	Control	Monopolistic Central Political Ideological	Empowerment	Pluralistic Local Social Personal
Availability	Supply	Determined by interests	Demand	Determined by morality
Application	Executed	Imposed by police	Self-help	Seek out by the public

Epilogue

Mao's MLP was espoused some 50 years ago. Since then, China has undergone substantial changes, especially in the reform era (1979 to the present). This is especially the case with communism as an ideology.* With the demise of communism, what will happen to MLP? This theory serves to keep MLP alive, long after the disappearance of communism as an ideology, for one good reason. Mao's MLP is a more scientific way of looking at state (police versus people [community]) business.

References

Austin, J. (1995). *The province of jurisprudence determined.* Cambridge: Cambridge University Press (first published in 1832).

Barlow, D.E. & Barlow, M.H. (1999). A political economy of community policing. *Policing: An International Journal of Police Strategies and Management, 22,* 642–647.

Bayley, D. (1994). *Police for the future.* New York: Oxford University Press.

Benson, R.W. (2001). Changing police culture: The *sine qua non* of reform. *Loyola of Los Angeles Law Review, 34,* 681–690.

Bentham, J. (1781). *An introduction to the principles of morals and legislation.* London: Athlone P.

Bevir, M. & Krupicka, B. (2007). Police reform, governance, and democracy. In M. O'Neill, M. Marks, & A.-M. Singh (Eds.), *Police occupational culture: New debates and directions* (pp. 153–180). Bingley, U.K.: Emerald Group Publishing.

Bittner, E. (1970). *The functions of police in modern society.* National Institute of Mental Health (pp. 36–47). Reprinted in R.J. Lundman (Ed.), *Police behavior* (pp. 28–43). Oxford. Oxford University Press.

Bittner, E. (1980). *The functions of police in modern society.* Washington, D.C.: National Institute of Mental Health.

Bjerk, D. (2007). Racial profiling, statistical discrimination, and the effect of a colorblind policy on the crime rate. *Journal of Public Economic Theory, 9*(3), 521–545.

Black, D. (1968). *The social structure of right and wrong* (revised ed.). San Diego: Academic Press.

Bobinsky, R. (1994, March). Reflections on community-oriented policing. *The FBI Law Enforcement Bulletin*, 15–19.

Braithwaite, J. (1989). *Crime, shame and reintegration.* Cambridge: Cambridge University Press.

Briffault, R. (1990a). Our localism: Part I—The structure of local government law. *Columbia Law Review, 90,* 1–115.

* On a recent visit to China (November 2007), I visited with five Chinese People's Public Security graduate students at their dorm. I asked them about the teachings of Mao. They frankly admitted to me that they have little knowledge and little interest in studying Mao.

Briffault, R. (1990b). Our localism: Part II—Localism and legal theory. *Columbia Law Review,* 90, 346–456.

Bureau of Justice Assistance (1994). *A police guide to surveying citizens and their environment.* Washington, D.C.: Government Printing Office.

Carter, D.L. (2000). *Reflections on the move to community policing.* (Policy Paper) Regional Community Policing Institute at Wichita State University, Kansas.

Chang, C. (1955). *The Chinese gentry: Studies on their role in nineteenth century Chinese society.* Seattle: University of Washington Press.

Chu, T. (1962). *Local government under the C'hing.* Cambridge: Harvard University Press.

Cordner, G.W. (2005). Community policing: Elements and effects. In R.G. Dunham & G.P. Alpert (Eds.), *Critical issues in policing,* 5th ed. (pp. 401–419). Long Grove, IL: Waveland Press.

Cumming, E., Cumming, I., & Edell, L. (1965). Policeman as philosopher, guide and friend. *Social Problems, 12*(3), 276–286.

Damin, K. (2001). *Treatise on the broad definition of public security* (Guangyi gongan lun). Beijing: Qunzhong chubanshe.

De Barry, W., Chan, W.-T., & Watson, B. (1960). *Sources of Chinese tradition.* New York: Columbia University Press.

Dobrin, A. (2006). Professional and community oriented policing: The Mayberry model. *Journal of Criminal Justice and Popular Culture, 13*(1), 19–28.

Duchu, Y. (1980, October 27). Liu Shaoqi's theoretical legacy, *Beijing Review, 43.*

Dutton, M. (1992). *Policing and punishment in China.* Cambridge: Cambridge University Press.

Eaton, A.M. (1900). The right to local self-government. *Harvard Law Review, 13*(6), 441–454.

Eckholm, E. (1998, April 16). Beijing journal: At a trying time, China revives Mao's model man. *The New York Times,* p. 4.

Eckholm, E. (2001, May 30). Beijing journal: A Maoist hero's ghost tilts with falun gong. *New York Times.* http://query.nytimes.com/gst/fullpage.html?res=9A05E2D8123CF933A05756C0A9679C8B63 (Accessed February 20, 2009).

Ellison, J. (2006, April). Community policing: Implementation issues. *FBI Law Enforcement Bulletin,* 12–16.

Fan, K.H. (1968). *The Chinese cultural revolution: Selected documents.* New York: Grove Press.

Fessler, D.R. (1976). *Facilitating community change: A basic guide.* San Diego: San Diego University Associate.

Flynn, D.W. (1998). Defining the community in community policing. Washington, D.C.: United States Department of Justice, Community Policing Consortium.

Gaskill, D.M. (2002). *Crime and mentalities in early modern England.* Cambridge: Cambridge University Press.

Gibbs, J. (1982). Notion of control. In J.P. Gibbs (Ed.), *Social control* (pp. 9–11). Beverly Hills, CA: Sage.

Gibbs, J.L. (1969). Law and personality: Signpost for a new direction. In L. Nader (Ed.), *Law in culture and society* (pp. 337–348). Berkeley, CA: University of California Press.

Gluckman, M. (1969). Concepts in the comparative study of tribal law. In L. Nader (Ed.), *Law in culture and society* (pp. 349–373). Berkeley, CA: University of California Press.

Goldstein, H. (1987). Improving policing: A problem-oriented approach. *Crime and Delinquency, 25*(2), 236–258.

Goldstein, H. (1990). *Problem-oriented policing.* New York: McGraw-Hill.

Graftstein, R. (1981). The failure of Weber's conception of legitimacy: Its causes and implications. *The Journal of Politics, 43*(2), 456–472.

Granberry, M. (1990, January 27). Abortion protest juries told to ignore nullification ad. *L.A. Times* (San Diego County edition).

Greene, J. & Mastrofski, S. (2001). *Community policing: Rhetoric or reality.* New York: Praeger.

Gross, J. (1995). Introduction to alternative dispute resolution. *Alberta Law Review, 1,* 1–33.

Gurwit, R. (1933). Communitarianism: You can try it at home. *Governing, 6,* 33–39.

Gutis, Ph. (1988, April 10). Daniel P. Guido: New head of police speaks out, *New York Times,* Long Island interview.

Holley, D. (1990, May 8). The foolish old man and other heroes: Although some sneer at the stories, all Chinese are fed an endless diet of role models. The government uses these folk sagas to educate, entertain—and control. *Los Angeles Times,* Part H; Page 4; Column 1; Foreign Desk.

Jackson, D. (1973, May 18). Judge instructs "Camden 28" jury. *New York Times,* p. 13.

Jeffrey, A. (1994). *We, the jury.* New York: Basic Books.

Joh, E. (2004). The paradox of private policing. *Journal of Criminal Law and Criminology, 95*(1), 49–131.

Jorgensen, B. (1980). Transferring trouble: The initiation of reactive policing. *Canadian Journal of Criminology, 20,* 257–279.

Kansas City, Missouri, Police Department. (1977). *Response time analysis: Executive summary.* Kansas City, MO.

Kant, E. (1784, 1959). *Foundations of metaphysics of morals and what is enlightenment.* (trans., L.W. Beck). New York: Macmillan.

Katyal, N. (2005). Community self-help. *Journal of Law, Economics, & Policy 33,* 49–68.

Kelling, G.L. (1974). *The Kansas City preventive patrol experiment: Tactical report.* Washington, D.C.: Government Printing Office.

Kelling, G.L. & Coles, C. (1998). *Fixing broken windows: Restoring order and reducing crime in our communities.* New York: Touchstone.

Kelling, G.L., Pate, A., Ferrara, A, Utne, M., & Brown, Ch.E. (1981). *The Newark foot patrol experiment. research brief.* Washington, D.C.: Police Foundation.

Klerman, D. (2000, January). *Settlement and the decline of private prosecution in thirteenth-century England.* Independent Institute Working Paper 19. Washington, D.C.: The Independent Institute.

Kobben, A.J.F. (1969). Law at the village level: The Cottica Djuka of Surinam. In L. Nader (Ed.), *Law in culture and society* (pp. 117–146). Berkeley, CA: University of California Press.

Leadbeater, Ch. (1996). *The self-policing society.* New York: Demos.

Legge, J. (1981). *The four books.* (trans.) Hong Kong: Culture Book.

Lenin, V.I. (1961). *Fundamentals of Marxism-Leninism: A manual.* Moscow: Foreign Languages Publishing House.

Liao, W. (2007). *From the mass.* October 15, 2007. http://zt.nynews.gov.cn/17da/Article/Zhpl/1368.html (accessed July 30, 2008).

Liu-Wang, H. (1959). *Traditional Chinese clan rules.* Locust Valley, NY: J.J. Augustin Publisher.

Luo, R.Q. (1994). *On people's public security work [Lun Renmin gong'an gongzuo].* Beijing: Qunzhong chubanshe.

MacFarquhar, R. (1974). *The origins of the cultural revolution: Contradictions among the people 1956–1957,* Vol. 1. New York: Columbia University Press.

Madsen, R. (1993). The public sphere, civil society and moral community: A research agenda for contemporary China studies. *Modern China, 19*(2), 183–198.

Manning, P.K. (1983). Organizational constrains and semiotics. In M. Punch (Ed.), *Control in the police organization* (pp. 169–194). Cambridge, MA: MIT Press.

McGregor, D. (1960). *The human side of enterprise.* New York: McGraw-Hill.

Melville Lee, W.L. (1901). *A history of police in England.* London: Methuen, (Kessinger Publishing edition, 2007).

Miller, L.L. (2004). Rethinking bureaucrats in the policy process: Criminal justice agents and the national crime agenda. *Policy Studies Journal, 32,* 569–588.

Muir, E. & Ruggiero, G. (1994). *History from crime.* Baltimore: John Hopkins University Press.

Nader, L. (1969). *Law in culture and society.* Berkeley, CA: University of California Press.

National Ministry of Safety and Security. (1996). *Draft policy document on the philosophy of community policing.* Washington, D.C.: Government Printing Office.

O'Leary, D. (1994). Reflections on police privatization. *FBI Law Enforcement Bulletin, 63*(9), 21–26.

Peel, Sir R. (1829). *The nine principles.* http://www.magnacartaplus.org/briefings/nine_police_principles.htm#nine_principles (accessed October 15, 2008).

Qilu, Z. & Dawei, W. (1995). A comparison between Western community policing and China social security comprehensive management (Sifang shequ jingwu yu zhongguo de shehuo zhian zonghe zhilu zhi bijiao). *Journal of Chinese Public Security University, 57,* 10–14.

Reiss, A. & Bordua, D.J. (1967). Environment and organization: A perspective on the police. In D.J. Bordua (Ed.), *The police: Six sociological essays* (pp. 25–55). New York: John Wiley & Sons.

Ristaino, M.R. (1987). *China's art of revolution: The mobilization of discontent, 1927 and 1928.* Durham: Duke University Press.

Robinson, C.D. & Scaglion, E. (1987). The origin and evolution of the police function in society: Notes toward a theory. *Law & Society, 21*(1), 109–153.

Rosenbaum, D.P. et al. (1991). Crime prevention, fear reduction, and the community. In W.A. Geller (Ed.), *Local government police management,* 3rd ed. (pp. 96–130). Washington, D.C.: International City Management Association.

Sanders, W.B. (1977). *Detective work: A study of criminal investigations.* New York: The Free Press.

Schram, St. 1989. *The Thought of Mao Tse-Tung.* Cambridge: Cambridge University Press.

Scott, H. (n.d.). *The mass line and the American revolutionary movement*. http://members.aol.com/TheMassLine/MLms.htm (accessed July 30, 2008).

Scott, M.S. (2000). *Problem-oriented policing: Reflections on the first 20 years*. Washington, D.C.: Department of Justice.

Shao-chi [Shaoqi], Liu. (1951). *On the party*, 3rd ed. Peking: FLP.

Sherman L.W., Gottfredson, D., MacKenzie, D., Eck, J., Reuter, P., & Bushway, S. (2002). *Preventing crime: What works, what doesn't, what's promising*. Report to the United States Congress. Prepared for the National Institute of Justice, Department of Criminology and Criminal Justice, University of Maryland, College Park.

Skogan, W.G. (2006). *Police and community in Chicago. A tale of three cities*. New York and Oxford, U.K.: Oxford University Press.

Sparrow, M.K. (1993). *Information systems and the development of policing. Perspectives on policing*. Washington, D.C.: U.S. Department of Justice, National Institute of Justice.

Townsend, J.R. (1977). Chinese populism and the legacy of Mao Tse-tung. *Asian Survey, 17*(11), 1011.

Trojanowicz, R. et al. (1994). *Community policing: A survey of police departments in the United States*. Washington, D.C.: U.S. Department of Justice.

Trojanowicz, R. & Bucqueroux, B. (1990). *Community policing: A contemporary perspective*. Cincinnati, OH: Anderson Publishing.

Van Dyke, J.M. (1991). Merciful juries: The resilience of jury nullification. *Washington and Lee Law Review, 48*, 165–183.

Waddington P.A.J. (1993). Dying in a ditch: The use of police powers in public order. *International Journal of the Sociology of Law, 21*(4), 335–353.

Wender, J. (2008, June 27). *The bureaucratic paradox: A philosopher-cop's thoughts on the role and limits of the police*. Paper presented at the annual meeting of the American Society of Criminology, Royal York, Toronto. http://www.allacademic.com/meta/p32214_index.html (accessed July 18, 2008).

Williams, S.W. (1883). *The middle kingdom*, Vol. 1. New York: Scribner.

Wilson, J.Q. & Kelling, G.L. (1982, March). Broken windows. The police and neighborhood safety. *The Atlantic Monthly*, 29–37.

Wilson, J.Q. (1968). *Varieties of police behavior*. Cambridge, MA: Harvard University Press.

Wittfogel, K. (1957). *Oriental despotism: A comparative study of total power*. New Haven: Yale University Press.

Wong, K.C. (1998). Black's theory on the behavior of law revisited II: A restatement of Black's concept of law. *International Journal of the Sociology of Law, 26*(1), 75–119.

Wong, K.C. (2003). A matter of life and death: A very personal discourse. *Georgetown Journal of Law and Public Policy, 1*(2), 339–361.

Wong, K.C. (2007, June 25–27). *A preliminary assessment of Hong Kong interception of communications and surveillance ordinance: For whom the bell toll. Hong Kong's basic law: The first ten years and its future*. Paper delivered at a conference at City University of Hong Kong.

Xingguo, G. (高 兴 国) (1998). Reflection over implementing public security mass line work (- 对公安工作贯彻群众路线的思考). *Public Security Studies, 5*, 7–10.

Yanhu, J. (1966). Shilun tigao renmin jingcha suji (Improving upon the basic qualities of the people's police). *Gongan Yanjiu* (Public Security Study) 6, 9.

Yean, S. (1997). Shehui zhian de zhengzhi bixu da remin zanzheng (The reorganization of public security must be through the waging of a people's war). *Gongan Lilun yu Shijian* (*Theory and Practice of Public Security*), 6(3), 1–4.

Zedong, M. (1941). *Gaizao womende xuexi [Reform our study]*. Selected works of Mao Tse-tung, Vol. III: 22–23.

Zedong, M. (1945). *On coalition government (April 24, 1945*). Selected works of Mao Tse-tung. Vol. III: 315–316. http://www.marxists.org/reference/archive/mao/works/red-book/ch11.htm (accessed July 30, 2008).

Zedong, M. (1951, May 10–15). *Baozheng zhengfan yundong jiangkang fazhan (Guaranteeing the healthy progression of movement to suppress counter-revolutionaries*). Third National Public Security Meeting, Beijing.

Zedong, M. (1953, January 5). *Combat bureaucracy, commandism, and violations of the law and discipline*. http://www.etext.org/Politics/MIM/classics/mao/sw5/mswv5_24.html (accessed July 30, 2008).

Zedong, M. (1955a). *The socialist upsurge in China's countryside*. Selected Work of Mao Tse-tung. Vol. II. http://www.marxists.org/reference/archive/mao/works/red-book/ch11.htm (accessed July 30, 2008).

Zedong, M. (1955b). *Surplus labour has found a way out. The socialist upsurge in China's countryside*, introductory note. Selected Work of Mao Tse-tung. Vol. II. http://www.marxists.org/reference/archive/mao/works/red-book/ch11.htm (accessed July 30, 2008).

Zedong, M. (1955c). *This township went co-operative in two years*, introductory note. http://books.google.com/ (accessed July 30, 2008).

Zedong, M. (1955d). Chairman Mao Zedong Quotes: Some Selected Quotes from Mao's Little Red Book. http://www.paulnoll.com/China/Mao/Mao-11-Mass-Line.html (Accessed February 22, 2009).

Zedong, M. (1957). *The situation in the summer of 1957*. Selected Works of Mao Tse-tung. Volume V, Beijing: Foreign Languages Press. http://www.marxists.org/reference/archive/mao/selected-works/volume-5/mswv5_66.htm (accessed August 30, 2008).

Zedong, M. (1963). Where do correct ideas come from? In Mao Zedong (Au.) *Four essays on philosophy*. Peking: Foreign Languages Press Edition. *http://www.etext.org/Politics/MIM/wim/oncorrect.html. (Accessed July 30*, 2008)

Zedong, M. (1975). Talk at an Enlarged Central Work Conference (Trans) in Stuart Schram, (Ed.), January 30, 1960, *Chairman Mao talks to the people* (p. 168). New York: Macmillan.

Zedong, M. (1978). Talk at an Enlarged Working Conference Convened by the Central Committee of the Communist Party of China" (Jan. 30, 1962), Peking Review, #27 (July 7, 1978), 9.

Zhonggong Zhongyang Dangxiao. (1993). (Communist Party School), *Zhonghua renmin gongheguo xianfa tongshi (Comprehensive interpretation of the PRC Constitution*). Zhonggong Zhongyang Dangxiao Chubanshe.

The Police, Community, and Community Justice Institutions in India

11

S. GEORGE VINCENTNATHAN
LYNN VINCENTNATHAN

Contents

Introduction*

India is in transition between tradition and modernity, impacted by its colonial history, which has consequences for its social order and social control efforts. Community policing, considered to be a new mode of social control, has actually been an important role of village *panchayats* since ancient times. These community councils of five or more elders also served as courts in settling disputes and as governmental bodies in administration of village affairs (Basham, 1954, pp. 105–107). When conflicts arose or crimes occurred, panchayat members or village heads, who lived in the same

* This study is based on fieldwork supported by the National Science Foundation under Grant No. SES-8721483, and subsequent recent visits to India.

close-knit community, would either witness them first-hand or hear about them through gossip, complaints, or night watchmen under their command, and could address matters swiftly to prevent escalation into more serious conflicts and crimes. Usually village elders were selected from the community's various kin groups and castes, among whom they lived, or from major streets of the community, with an orientation to prevent conflicts or settle disputes at their onset. When more serious conflicts did arise, the panchayat, functioning as a court, would process the dispute with a focus on reestablishing village harmony and peace.

Community policing programs, transplanted from the West, have been introduced in some Indian urban communities in recent times under the auspices and authority of the official police stations, and some have been tried in rural areas as well (Mukerjee, 2008; Brogden, 2005; Karpurthala Police, 2008). For example, in some regions of Tamil Nadu, a Friends of the Police program has been instituted by the police with a primary focus on improving perceptions of the police, and gaining help from citizens in solving crimes (Prateep, 1996). In Andhra Pradesh, the police select citizens to form Maithri Committees to help maintain law and order, and even to settle disputes (Andhra Pradesh Police, 2008). The success of these community-policing programs is mixed, as some members of these citizen groups have abused their positions for personal gains and vendettas (Rajeswar, 2003), and to promote their group interests in divided communities. Some scholars suggest the programs have for the most part failed because they are under police rather than community control, and the police continue to present images characteristic of colonial policing, which involve show of authority, practice of torture and brutality, and evocation of fear, with their community policing focus more on eliciting information to solve crimes, not on listening to the people and their concerns (Brogden, 2005). Such police qualities have created fear and suspicion on the part of the public, which led to people distancing themselves from the police and from members of citizen police groups, and not to genuinely cooperating with them. Additionally, the authoritarian police mode is not a proper fit for the democratic environment of the times. On the other hand, the informal policing and supervision by village or panchayat elders, who are themselves fellow villagers interested in the welfare of the disputants and peace in the village at large, seem to have worked better than official policing, or the new attempts at community policing.

However, in recent times panchayat elders in many villages are unable to exercise these order maintenance and social control functions, as traditional panchayats have weakened or disappeared altogether due to the impact of modernization (Vincentnathan, S.G., 1992; Baxi & Galanter,

1979), especially with the expansion of the official police and court systems. This chapter focuses on the current state of village social control through panchayats and official police administration by focusing on several cases involving panchayats and police.

The Police and Panchayat in Modern India

India has been restructuring its political and economic systems based on modern democratic and capitalistic ideologies, as have many traditional societies with past colonial and autocratic regimes. This transition includes a mix of traditional and modern values, which are affecting notions of justice and the panchayats. Some villages in India have used traditions to preserve their panchayats, in spite of challenges posed by modernization. The Indian government has also instituted a modern version of the panchayat under its Nyaya (Justice) Panchayat, to strengthen local self-governance and control, based on democratic and inclusive representation. As with experiments in community policing, these do not function well, as their decisions are often forged in favor of upper caste and class interests, and many have become defunct. Traditional panchayats, the focus of this study, have not fared well either. The expansion of police authority into rural communities, especially those closer to urban centers, has also served to weaken panchayats' social control and judicial functions. What has been happening in India is somewhat similar to the changes in Zapotec villages in Oaxaca, Mexico (Parnell, 1978); their village courts are weakened by modernization and expansion of district-level criminal justice organizations, and local individuals who have connections with influential people outside of their communities obtain judgments in their favor. In such societies, there are many patterns of adjustments: sometimes peaceful transition to modern institutions and sometimes unsettling conflicts between traditional and modern institutions. The changes in societies vary and take unique directions according to their particular cultural histories.

In India the traditional hierarchical values, which still hold some sway, are in contradiction to the budding individualistic and egalitarian ideas, and the desire for an affluent and personally pleasing and dignified life. Traditional castes were bound together by their different and interdependent occupations, in a hierarchy of unequal statuses and rewards. Individuals were expected to perform caste roles without expectation of rewards or improvement in life. The village and caste panchayats ensured through their social control function that castes and persons fulfilled their duties and remained in their place (Berreman, 1966a, 1966b).*

Industrialization, urbanization, capitalism, and democracy have greatly weakened this caste form of stratification, which bound individuals and groups together in the fulfillment of collective goals. These pressures of modernization have also led to intercaste and interpersonal competition and conflicts (Galanter, 1984; Kolenda, 1978). Moreover, modern values have negatively impacted the panchayats' ability and authority to enforce social control and resolve these conflicts. The role of the police as an arm of the state has thus become increasingly important, and has been expanding into villages, overtaking the traditional law enforcement roles of the already weakening panchayat, resulting in a variety of consequences.

The police sometimes lend support to the panchayat by referring cases brought to them to the panchayat, and other times they accept cases, thereby minimizing the power of the panchayat. In such situations, the panchayat elders feel their power and traditional rights to hear cases first are violated. When individuals upset with panchayat decisions make complaints to the police, the police sometimes chastise the panchayat for making wrong decisions. It is noted that the police may also warn or blame the panchayats for not referring more serious cases or crimes to them, which the panchayat dealt with in historical times. Sometimes the police blame the panchayat so as to make themselves more powerful over panchayat elders, especially when they favor persons opposed to the elders. As for community policing in India, the panchayat elders or village headmen (who are panchayat members in some villages) have traditionally served in that role, and today are often held responsible by the police for disciplining people and reporting unruly persons to them for the maintenance of peace and order.

The police themselves may take on different postures. Sometimes they work informally with the panchayats and the people to resolve problems, not unlike community policing elsewhere. Most villages in India do not have police stations of their own; an outside police station usually controls several villages. In this regard, cooperation between the police and the panchayat

* The original castes included Brahmins (priests) at the top, Kshatriyas (rulers, warriors), Vaishyas (merchants), and Shudras (craftsmen and laborers) at the bottom. Outside of this caste structure were the untouchables (*dalits*), who lived outside the village and performed menial work as well as tasks considered polluting to the upper castes. In Hinduism, it is believed that God created this hierarchy of castes, each with different and unequal intrinsic qualities. Intercaste marriage was forbidden. One was born into a caste, and could not change castes, except, it was believed, after death, when one would be born into a higher or lower caste, depending on the person's good or bad deeds. Over more than 2000 years of caste history, these five castes split into thousands of subcastes or *jatis*, each acting as a separate caste. Higher castes controlled lower castes and expected them to behave within their allowed boundaries. In modern India, caste-based discrimination is illegal, but social traditions persist, conflicting with modern, egalitarian ideas.

elders and headmen is necessary to maintain order. Other times, the police maintain an official persona and oppress people with their authority; they are noted for corruption and use of excessive force, a holdover from the paramilitary police function during the colonial period (Bajpai, 2000; Cole, 1999, pp. 96–97, 101).

The police, like the panchayat elders and the people, are influenced by traditional and modern notions of justice, which lead them to make various and contradictory decisions. Sometimes both the panchayat and the police may cooperate and abide by modern standards of justice. Or the panchayat may uphold the modern legal tradition, while the police impose social traditions that go against modern laws. As the police are largely concerned about maintaining order, they sometimes sacrifice the modern sense of justice by reinforcing hierarchical values to settle disputes. The police may cooperate with the panchayat and require a minority religious group to contribute funds to the majority group's religious celebration, without recognizing their individual rights. On the other hand, the police may support modern laws, while the panchayat may uphold traditional practices; e.g., a panchayat approved a child marriage, and individuals opposed to it called in the police, who prevented it from happening (*The Hindu*, 2002). The police also seek expedient methods to resolve issues, such as intercaste conflicts and violence, by arresting individuals whom they think might escalate conflicts. In certain situations, the police take extralegal and illegal measures to enrich themselves. For instance, they may make peace between disputants, or encourage them to pursue their cases in court, if there are opportunities for receiving bribes. These confluences and contradictions occur within a uniquely Indian "modernity of tradition" (Rudolph & Rudolph, 1967), in which social traditions, modern legal traditions, and extralegal behavior sometimes support and sometimes oppose each other in myriad forms. These situations of mixed notions of justice are aspects of strain occurring in the modernization process, some of which are elaborated in the case studies included below.

The modernization process in India began with British rule and gained momentum after independence in 1947. The Constitution of India became a major instrument of revolutionary change for developing a democratic society (Galanter, 1968, p. 86; Kidder, 1977; Beteille, 1986). In addition to democratization, the forces of industrialization, urbanization, and economic development have increasingly changed the country, even its remote villages, and have altered people's thinking and lifestyles (Vincentnathan, S.G., 1996, pp. 495–502). Two conceptual constructs of modernization, "social" and "political," help illuminate this transition period in India. Social modernization refers to the people's ideational and psychological changes that call for "political modernization." In India, four dimensions of social modernization can be noted, according to people's caste, class, and individual propensities. First there is an orientation to be free from the domination of higher castes and classes in community life, and at the same time gain superior status for one's own caste or groups from which one can draw personal importance (Berreman, 1966b, p. 313; Srinivas, 1996, pp. 79–82). This is more explicit in lower castes striving to use all opportunities, including government-sponsored affirmative action programs, to improve their caste image and improve their economic statuses. Second is an evolving orientation to have personal autonomy and to be equal with everyone within one's family, caste, and kin group, without regard for age, gender, and other social distinctions (Shah, 1998, pp. 12–13; *Chandigarh Tribune,* 2004; Roland, 1988, p. 101; Sinha et al., 2002). Third is an orientation to live an economically prosperous life, without the constrictions of poverty and anxieties over economic insufficiency (Joshi, 1986; Mendelsohn & Vicziany, 1998, pp. 251–271). And, fourth, there is a desire to live a dignified life, which includes feeling good about one's caste and group affiliations, one's relationships with members of one's own groups, and one's economic condition (Rudolph & Rudolph, 1967, pp. 62–63; Vincentnathan, S.G., 1996).

These expectations, as part of social modernization, call for the political system to act, which necessitates "political" modernization, the introduction of new strategies and structures in governance to address social expectations. Of relevance here are governmental programs to uplift the poor and oppressed, protect individual rights, and protect minorities from domination and victimization. The resistance to these goals among those clinging to social traditions often calls for police intervention. However, such intervention generates negative attitudes toward the police. In order to counteract this and develop positive attitudes, as well as elicit community help so as to enhance police effectiveness in controlling crime, police–community programs are created, as a ramification of political modernization. The state, apart from responding to social and political expectations in different ways, introduces various programs like these to foster public opinion toward its own image of a good society and what should be done to achieve it. The good intentions of the state, however, are sometimes not realized due to the officials' prejudices against caste and religious minorities, which impede the development of a modern, secular, and democratic society.

Protests and disputes continue to surface in relation to intercaste, interreligious, and interclass differences, and are often exacerbated by factional politics (Jacobsohn, 2003; Burger, 1993, pp. 79–84). While panchayats have difficulties in solving ordinary village conflicts, they find it nearly impossible to contain those incited by regional politics and caste and religious conflicts. Under these circumstances, police intervention becomes necessary and inevitable. The numerical strength of the police and their presence in remote areas of the country has been increasing. From 1982 to 2006, the number of police per every 100 square kilometers in India increased 58%, from 28.1 to 44.4 police (Ministry of Home Affairs, 1987, p. 143; 2007, p. 95).

Communities, Panchayats, and the Caste System

In the past, people relied heavily on the panchayat because official institutions of justice were far away, and were corrupt and oriented toward physical punishment, while local justice was more personal and directed toward peace-making (Dubois & Beauchamp, 1906, pp. 655–667). Their roles were comprehensive, the functional equivalents of policing, prosecuting, judging, and correcting. Other functions included general village administration, making decisions affecting village life, working in cooperation with officials from outside the village, and collecting contributions for the maintenance of the village temple, water tanks, and roads. If police officers came to the village and wanted to contact or arrest a person, first they would approach the panchayat head, who would take them to the appropriate residence. This empowered panchayat heads in the eyes of the community, as the police respected them and panchayat heads had control over the police.

Two types of traditional panchayats are noted: caste panchayats and village panchayats. Elders of caste panchayats police their own people and decide issues and disputes internal to their caste and, in the past, enforced caste rules and etiquette. In multicaste communities, castes are held together under the authority of the village panchayat, which consists of higher caste landowners. In communities with a numerically strong, dominant caste, the dominant caste panchayat settles its own disputes and those of other castes. As the caste system and intercaste cooperation break down, panchayats in multicaste communities are rapidly disappearing. The *dalits* (untouchables), considered to be the most "polluting" and inferior caste under the caste system and forced to live at the outskirts of the village in separate hamlets, have their own panchayats. In general, as panchayat decisions are largely oriented toward making peace and reestablishing relationships between disputants, justice may be sacrificed for peace. Elders, males, and higher caste persons may receive more favorable consideration than young persons, females, and lower caste persons, who are expected to accommodate to such decisions (Cohn, 1959; Meschievitz & Galanter, 1982).

Panchayat meetings would call for assemblage of married men from all households to meet in front of the village elders and disputants for deliberating the dispute. Women, children, and unmarried men are not included, unless they are connected to the disputes. The decisions of the panchayat are usually based on public discussion of the issues in the open forum, with the panchayat elders leading the discussion. These discussions often become noisy, as individuals try to press their points of view (Hayden, 1999, pp. 82–109). The elders, however, usually have skills to navigate between their own sense of justice and the opinions expressed to strike an amicable decision.

Both criminal and civil cases or disputes come to the panchayat. Until a few decades ago, panchayats dealt with serious criminal cases, even though under British rule and, subsequently, after Indian independence it was required that these crimes be reported to the police for official action. Even now in a few villages the panchayat may decide serious crimes, though mainly minor forms of injury, insults, and fights are brought before the panchayat, as well as civil cases related to division of family property, encroachment of property boundaries, failures to repay loans, and dissolution of marriages (Moore, 1985; Vincentnathan, S.G., 1992; Mandelbaum, 1970, pp. 367–373). The concerns of the panchayat elders are to bring people together in such a way that disputes do not impair community sentiment and order.

Adverse decisions of the panchayat would involve imposition of fines, restitution, and sometimes excommunication. The excommunicated person is allowed to live in his residence, but cannot communicate with others and must comply with other panchayat orders. Those who communicate with excommunicated individuals, including their parents, could be fined, and, in situations of repeated violation, they could also be excommunicated. Persons who do not comply with and go against panchayat orders face other consequences. Panchayat elders may not visit their homes during important occasions, such as child naming, puberty rites, bride-seeing (part of arranging marriage), and marriage ceremonies for their children, or funerals for their family members. When persons from other villages come for contracting a marriage alliance in the excommunicated person's family, and they find out about the person's disobedient behavior or see that the panchayat elders are not present, they likely would not make the alliance. The excommunicated person, who failed to obey the panchayat's order or pay the fine, would likely do so just before these occasions and make peace with the panchayat elders. These elders have to be present to establish legitimacy for the family (Vincentnathan, S.G., 1992).

Disputes, Panchayats, and Police Expansion

The Indian Constitution, founded on secular and democratic principles, to which the Indian government is committed, is an instrument of revolutionary social change, stimulating equal rights, irrespective of people's caste, gender, class, and religious differences, and rights for individuals to make personal choices. This is an important instrument of social modernization. Yet, these ideas cannot be achieved easily because of the historical caste structure that continues even today, and the intergroup and interreligious prejudices that often surge up. Further, individuals have neither developed strong separate identities of their own away from their group memberships nor are they completely free from group authority and influences. Caste distinctions and group controls on individuals conflict with people's needs for independence, equality, and self-dignity. These conflicts are causing extensive frustrations. Consequently, conflicts and disputes arise based on differences in group and individual expectations, some trying to be equal and others trying to maintain superiority. These differences are manifest in many different ways throughout India: development of upper caste organizations, lower caste organizations, Hindu fundamentalist groups, Muslim and Christian interest groups, and political groups formed along these lines. Conflicts arising from these can be noted throughout India, in rural and urban communities (Das, 1990; Ganguly, 2003).

Caste hierarchy and oppressive servitude are now disputed. A contractual system, in which people enter into temporary work relationships by choice, has supplanted the traditional system of birth-ascribed caste obligations and rights that tied landlord, workers, and artisans together in permanent unequal relationships (Kolenda, 1978; Srinivas, 1996, pp. 121–135; Maine, 1861). Caste divisions, animosities, and intracaste factions have increased, and often follow class lines; that is, upper caste persons are often upper class, and lower caste persons are often lower class. Cohn (1965, p. 105) notes from his study of Senapur in North India that sometimes disputes within a caste, between castes, or between individuals are not taken to village panchayats, but to official courts for harassing, shaming, and dominating one's adversaries, to gain status and power. It has been noted that, when caste factions arise within an upper caste, the dalits take sides with their respective high caste landlords, but when issues develop between the dalits and the higher castes, the higher castes usually join together against the dalits (Srinivas, 1996, pp. 102–120).

As a matter of maintaining caste hierarchy and keeping lower castes in submission, brutal actions sometimes are taken against lower castes, especially dalits. For instance, murder, rape, and assault of dalits, and burning of their huts have become rampant. For the year 2000, there were 25,455 reported crimes committed against dalits (Ministry of Home Affairs, 2002, p. 223). In turn, the dalits sometimes become violent in reaction to these crimes and atrocities. Activist groups, such as the Dalit Panthers, have arisen and have stimulated militant responses (Joshi, 1986, pp. 140–153). Such conflicts also parallel atrocities of Hindu supremacy groups against Muslim and Christian minorities.

While there is a growing realization that people should be able to take their disputes to the official criminal justice system, that system, like traditional justice, is also plagued with corruption, and caste and religious biases. A few rich and influential persons may take their grievances to the police and court, and others may grudgingly go along with panchayat decisions. In communities without panchayats—as mentioned, many have disappeared or are disappearing—people not wishing to go to the police, usually out of fear, may not be able to resolve their conflicts; they may "lump it" or engage in "self-help" out of desperation, resulting in fights, injuries, and killings, which do lead to police intervention. Unfulfilled modern desires and expectations at both the individual and group levels sometimes result in large-scale protests, disputes, riots, terrorism, and violence. Such incidents have become common, undermining national, regional, and village order, and overwhelming the panchayats' ability to function.

Riots in the country vary greatly year to year, but in general have increased substantially. In 1953, there were 20,529 reported riots, which rose to a high of 92,831 in 1996. In 2000, there were 80,456 reported riots, and, in 2006, there were 56,641 such incidents (Ministry of Home Affairs, 2002, p. 15; 2007, p. 22). In the rural areas, where nearly 73% of India's population are located, the riot rate per 100,000 population is higher than in urban areas, 8.0 and 5.6, respectively (Ministry of Home Affairs, 2002, p. 54). In response to this and other crime-related issues, the number of police officers has also increased. In 1963, the number of police officers in India was 536,185 (Ministry of Home Affairs, 1967, p. 30), while in 2000 it grew to 1,296,763 (Ministry of Home Affairs, 2002, p. 406), an increase of 142%.

In the state of Tamil Nadu, where this study of panchayats and police was conducted, there were 3,270 riots in 1965, which increased 53% to 5,005 in 2000, and fluctuated up to more than double this latter figure in some years in the 1980s and 1990s (Ministry of Home Affairs, 1967, p. 100; 1987, p. 30; 2002, p. 65). During the same period, the number of policemen per 100,000 population in Tamil Nadu increased from 90 to 134, an increase of 49%. The number of police stations increased about 20% from 1,115 in 1983 to 1,333 in 2001 (Department of Statistics, 1985, pp. 357–358; Department of Economics and Statistics, 2002, pp. 517–518). Disputes are increasing, and the panchayats are waning. Consequently, police expansion and intervention have increased.

In relation to these disputes, conflicts, and riots, which are happening in both rural and urban communities, the police intervention in them, often entailing harsh methods, has produced antagonistic relations between the public and the police. The police in this context realize the importance of forming citizen groups to gain a supportive attitude toward the police, and also to help control disputes and crime through gaining information. However, it seems the supportive attitudes for the police have not been adequately achieved and, therefore, the members of the citizen groups are used mainly as informants for police action. A member of one such group in the village of Mathapuram* near Chidambaram confided in us that he had been appointed to inform police about any emerging or serious problems and miscreants, and that all villages had several community members such as him.

* Fictitious names were used for all villages and persons studied.

Research Methods

We conducted this study on panchayats in Tamil Nadu between 1989 and 1992, updating the information from more recent trips. The larger study was on how a village's social structure, such as caste composition, would impact the effectiveness of the panchayat. We used an ethnographic method, which included both an emic approach (people's understanding and perception of events) and an etic approach (our interpretations in the context of local and related broader trends, our knowledge of panchayats elsewhere in India, and our general knowledge of India over decades of study). We also followed an extended case method, not only in delving into what people say, their actions, issues, and factors leading up to incidents that triggered disputes and panchayat cases, and their eventual outcomes and repercussions, sometimes over years, but also in terms of locating these disputes within larger social and cultural contexts (see Burawoy, 1998).

As we knew persons who were residents or connected with these village communities, we were able to gain quick access. We interviewed villagers and village leaders, attended some panchayat sessions when possible, and interviewed the various parties separately before and/or after panchayat sessions. When attendance at panchayat sessions was not possible (because they had already occurred), we interviewed parties involved in cases as well as panchayat elders. The focus was on how panchayats functioned in resolving conflicts and maintaining village order, and what social and cultural conditions and forces contributed to their strength or made them ineffective. Therefore, in most villages we also collected general information about social life and culture. We studied in depth the dalit hamlet of Anbur near Chidambaram over a 14-month period in 1984 and 1985 for Lynn Vincentnathan's (1987) dissertation on dalit subculture. This gave us valuable immersion and insight into village life, and also the impetus for this later panchayat study. A snowball technique was used for the other villages studied. We put the word out to the people of Anbur, and to friends and some relatives in the vicinity of Chidambaram, Mayilathurai, and Kumbakonam in the Cuddalore and Thanjavur districts of Tamil Nadu that we were interested in panchayats and panchayat cases. They would accompany us, or arrange for someone to accompany us, to give us entry into the villages and their panchayat forums. We frequently took assistants of the same caste of the people to be interviewed to gain trust and acceptance.

From our ethnographic information on panchayats and dispute settlements, it became apparent that various outside forces significantly affected panchayat effectiveness, such as the impact of nearby towns and cities; regional and national politics; national cultural trends, especially aspects of modernization, as discussed above; and various levels and types of state involvement, such as police actions. For this particular study on the police and community justice, we culled our field notes for incidents and cases, which included police involvement in village and panchayat affairs. In subsequent trips to India, we also contacted previous informants to learn about new incidents of police involvement in village affairs and outcomes of ongoing cases. We found a variety of relationships between the villages and the police, including cooperation, conflict, power struggle, and accommodation. Villagers and the police also exhibited evidence of the complex array and repertoire of both traditional and modern values and themes that guided their actions.

Communities and Case Studies

The cases under investigation here come from eight villages, which have been given pseudonyms, within a range of 60 miles in the Cuddalore and Thanjavur Districts. The two numerically dominant castes of these districts are the dalits (untouchables) and Vanniyars, a low caste, but above the dalits in caste rank. A third caste, Kallar, is much fewer in numbers in the villages studied, but some are notorious in the region for their crime and violence, and Kallars are generally feared. Kallars are considered similar in caste rank to the Vanniyars. Most of the villages also have a few other castes of various rankings. Panchayats and the police handle the various conflicts and crimes sometimes separately, sometimes together in cooperation, and sometimes differently and antagonistically. We included here disparate enough cases to provide understanding of panchayats in general, their functions and dysfunctions, and the cooperation and conflict between panchayats and the police, and to give grounded insight into changes taking place in India.

Anbur

Anbur is a dalit hamlet about a quarter of a mile from the town of Chidambaram. It has a viable panchayat. Community members generally respect the panchayat elders and the headman, who for the most part handle conflicts with deftness to elicit community unanimity, and make decisions that reestablish harmony. The elders usually find some fault with both sides, even the aggrieved victim, as well as positive traits, which helps heal relationships, rather than polarizing people, and they not only admonish and punish miscreants of petty crimes, but also encourage them to reform (Vincentnathan, S.G., 1992). The village headman (in this community, a different person from the panchayat headman, which is unusual) would in the past beat miscreants and patrol the community, and the people greatly respect him, while fearing him a bit. They are mindful that they all live close to each other, and the headman or panchayat head could easily and quickly come to know of their misbehavior either directly or through gossip and complaints.

Anbur community respect of and obedience to the panchayat is vital for its ability to maintain social control and restore community peace and order after disturbances. However, modern conditions, such as employment in the modern economy and outside influences, are impacting Anbur and its panchayat's authority, as exemplified in this following case. A young Anbur man went away to North India and worked there for many years, then returned to Anbur. He always behaved in an equal and presumptuous manner to others, including the village elders. Differences developed between him and the panchayat head. They both became critical of each other's activities. One day the young man insulted him with abusive words for unnecessarily holding grudges against him. The panchayat head assembled the members and excommunicated the young man. He was allowed to live in the village, but not talk to or interact with anyone outside of his family. He continued to be contemptuous and violated panchayat orders. Later, after violation of an order, the panchayat head lost patience and beat him severely.

The young man went to the police station and showed the injury, and also made a false complaint that the panchayat head's two sons were touching his wife and misbehaving. The police, seeing the serious nature of his injuries and hearing the false accusation, came to the village. The panchayat head told them that the young man was a menace to village order and had insulted him many times. He added that the panchayat had excommunicated him and wanted him to be punished. The policemen, thinking that the young man had been unjustly and cruelly treated for supposedly defending his wife's honor, told the panchayat head, "What kind of justice is this? Is this justice?" The police insulted him and the panchayat, and warned them to be careful in what they do. To insult a panchayat head is extremely demeaning, even though the police did contribute to a consciousness that the panchayat should be fair and just, and not inflict severe punishments. The policemen then themselves crossed that line, and used their baton to hit the panchayat head's sons, telling them to stay away from the complainant's wife. They did this without even investigating whether the complaint was true or not. Here the police acted as judge and executioner of punishment, instead of following official procedures and taking appropriate official action against the panchayat head and his sons. Even though this type of police action is illegal and uncalled for, it is a part of regular police operations to which people in India are accustomed.

This young troublemaker became proud of what he did, and continued to cause problems to his wife, the neighborhood, and the panchayat head. His heavy drinking contributed to his disorderly behavior. Over the following years, the panchayat head, unable to control this man, filed several complaints against him with the police. Time and again the young man was able to circumvent police action by using the influence of some high caste individuals for whom he worked as an electrician. One day he battered his wife severely, and a case was filed with the police. Immediately after this, he absconded from Anbur to another state, and lived there incognito for two years. Then he returned to Anbur and continued to be disorderly and abusive to his wife. This time, the wife with the support of the panchayat head went to the police and filed a complaint. The police registered a false charge of drug use against the young man, for which he could get a very long jail sentence. After he came to know this was going to happen, he committed suicide.

The police had been confounded about what to do regarding this man, who was a continuous and serious menace to his wife, the villagers, the headman, the panchayat, and the police themselves, so they engaged in the illegal action of filing a false case to send him away for a long time, an unprofessional way of addressing the issue to create peace in the village. It is not unheard of for police in India to falsely charge people, and to harass and arrest people without investigating the facts of cases (Bajpai, 2000; National Human Rights Commission, 1997).

Valavu

In Valavu, near the city of Mayilathurai, a fight was brewing between Vanniyars and dalits. A higher caste landlord, who was the trustee of a small Hindu temple, appointed a dalit as watchman. A Vanniyar, who also wanted the job, was upset. A few days later someone set the shed located at the entrance of the temple on fire. A case was filed with the police. The dalits thought the aggrieved Vanniyar who wanted the watchman job did it. This Vanniyar swore in the name of God that he did not do it, and other Vanniyars knowing his character believed him. Hostilities between the two castes increased. The Vanniyar panchayat and the dalit panchayat met a few times and could not come up with a peaceful solution. The landlord and the trustee of the temple created an ad hoc panchayat, consisting of the leading landlords for whom the Vanniyars and dalits were working. A high-ranking police official also planned to be a member, but had to go out of town and could not come. (When police officials take part in panchayats, they may not wear their uniforms.) During the panchayat, dalits and Vanniyars presented heated arguments, and some men were questioned. A Vanniyar opened up and said that he was in a liquor shop drinking and vaguely remembered seeing a dalit man there who had a kerosene bottle tied around his waist. That man was identified, and, with the threat of severe beating, he confessed that he burned the shed, and asked for forgiveness. He said he did it because he disliked the dalit watchman and wanted him to lose his job. The dalits themselves insulted and beat the man, and the panchayat subsequently felt there was no need to punish him again. A couple of days later the culprit left the village for fear of further possible actions against him by dalits and

Vanniyars. The police officers thanked the panchayat men and dismissed the case upon their request.

The police in India are—as are the prosecutors, judges, and attorneys—affected by the peacemaking social traditions of the society, and sometimes allow peaceful, informal resolutions involving community participation, along the lines of community policing (Kidder, 1973, p. 123). Peacemaking efforts are often preferred when there are possibilities for peaceful resolution of intergroup conflicts. The police take informal or formal actions depending on the seriousness of the conflict, their abilities to handle it, the help they can receive to solve the problem, the expectations of police authorities, legal requirements, and the power base of individuals seeking a particular recourse. In this case of Valavu, unlike most other cases noted here, the police allowed for an informal resolution and were accommodating to the peacemaking efforts and expectations of the landlords. The police might have taken legal action against the dalit who set the fire, except that these influential men did not want that.

Natham

Community policing-type efforts in a transitional society could result in violation of modern legal requirements and the constitutional rights of individuals and minorities. The police could lend support to the majority position, right or wrong, and the larger the group, the higher its power and influence. The reasoning is that minorities should comply with expectations of the majority. In Natham, an entirely dalit village near the city of Kumbakonam, three-fourths are Hindu and one-fourth are Catholic Christian. A conflict arose in regard to a Hindu festival. The Hindus required the Catholics to contribute money for the Hindu village festival, but the Catholics refused to pay. They said if the Hindus were willing to contribute to their Catholic celebrations, they would contribute to the Hindu celebrations. The Hindus refused to follow this suggestion, and continued to demand contributions. There were arguments in the panchayat, and the panchayat sided with the majority, but these arguments continued, resulting in fights and infliction of injuries. The Catholics registered a case with the police. Some men from both the Hindu and Catholic sides were called to the police station. The police officer in charge at that time was a Muslim, a member of a minority religion himself. He advised the Catholics that being a minority, they should learn to go along with the Hindu majority and abide by the panchayat's decision. While the two groups were returning to their village from the police station, an argument and fight erupted again.

Subsequently, the Catholics brought the matter to a leading Catholic of a higher caste in a nearby city, who took the matter to the police official there, and helped to resolve the problem. The high-ranking police official instructed the Muslim police officer that he should be conscious of minority rights, and follow fair practices, as required by the law. The leading Catholic person also went to Natham and talked to the Hindus and Catholics. He stressed their commonalities as members of the same caste, and encouraged them to be accommodating and progressive in their thoughts. He also said that he would talk to the Catholic bishop and ask him to give some money to clean up the village water tank they all used. The two sides then reconciled, and the Catholics were not required to contribute to the Hindu festival.

As Durkheim (1915, pp. 59, 63) suggested, religion is "an eminently collective thing" that makes up a group's unity. In the past, even though part of the community was Christian, they all contributed to the village Hindu festival, as the idea of individual rights over group needs for unity was not well formed. In modern times, however, there is a new awareness that religion is not only a group matter, but also a personal matter, and that the individual should not be required to support a different religion. In the Catholics' view, submitting to the Hindus' demands had become sacrilegious and degrading, and therefore, they felt they should stand up for their rights, even if it meant dissension in the village. The initial police response, perhaps in the mode of more traditional community policing, was to go along with the panchayat decision and follow social traditions that the modern law does not now permit. As Diaz (1994, pp. 207–210) suggests, until the police are trained to accept and enforce the legal traditions, they will continue to waver between social traditions and modern legal requirements.

Medu, Pallam, and Kandam

While making a delivery in Medu, a dalit milk deliveryman stared at a high caste young woman in a public place and made some remarks about her looks. A few Vanniyar men from the village of Pallam saw this and became angry. They beat him and damaged the milk cans and bicycle. The dalit man reported the incident to the owner of the milk depot, who was a Vanniyar himself, but from another nearby village, Kandam. The Vanniyar owner became angry, gathered a few Medu and Kandam Vanniyar men of his own, and beat up the Pallam men who had beaten his worker. In response, they fought back.

Medu, Pallam, and Kandam no longer had traditional panchayats to address this problem, so it escalated until some were seriously injured. The police arrested and jailed a few men. However, the fighting and violence continued and participation of others from the three villages increased. Finally the police warned that if they continued to fight, serious actions would be taken against them. The elders in one village, with the cooperation of the police, arranged for the prominent young men who were involved in the fight to go to a town 50 miles away and live there for two months under police supervision. During this time, the anger and animosities subsided. In the meantime, the elders from these Vanniyar villages formed an ad hoc panchayat, talked together, and appealed to their general kinship and caste affinities to find a solution to the matter. One elder stressed that it is better to "fall on each other's feet" as caste men and reconcile than to fight, especially in regard to a problem created by a dalit.

The owner of the milk depot had become angry with other Vanniyars because they beat his worker and ruined his milk can and bicycle. He felt that his claim, as an individual with dignity, was affected when his property and worker were harmed. However, his adversaries felt that the incident was a simple matter and he should not have taken it seriously, especially since the victim was only dalit. Even in modern times, Vanniyars try to maintain their traditional superiority over the dalits. In this incident, the dalit man behaved inappropriately toward a higher caste women. The onlookers often tolerate this, but, because the person was a dalit, the Vanniyars disciplined him. Dalits are closely scrutinized and criticized both for their social and economic improvements and for their inappropriate behavior. Their improvements bring jealousy and anger; their inappropriate behavior is magnified, and they are subjected to severe discipline. More and more challenges to dalit behavior emerge, bringing friction and conflicts, increasing the role of the police in the society.

While all of this was going on, the police were themselves interested in settling the problem informally, as there were many conflicts between dalits and Vanniyars throughout Tamil Nadu at that time. The police agreed to the compromise developed by the panchayat that they would not fight and would live in peace. The police warned both groups in the conflict that they would take severe punitive actions if they misbehaved. Thus, the police maintained a close watch on these young men. The police also took this opportunity to receive bribes from both sides for not taking official action. Peacemaking without resorting to legal sanctions is generally an accepted practice among criminal justice officials, but it can contribute to police corruption. The poor and powerless fear the police might treat them brutally; such brutality has become the norm in India (Amnesty International, 1992). One way people try to protect themselves from this is by bribing the police. It is a common aspect of Indian life for public officials, including police officials, to receive bribes for their services and favors (Verma, 1999).

Moore (1985), from her study of village panchayats near Delhi, noted an incident that is pertinent here. When the panchayat recessed to make a decision about a dispute, two policemen happened to pass by and saw the parties to the dispute arguing and fighting. They went to the panchayat elders and blamed them for not maintaining control over the people, and threatened to take actions against them and the others. Moore (1985, p. 96) reported, "The young policemen in their clean uniforms, with sticks in their hands, reminded the villagers that the power of the state reinforced their will. Finally, the police compromised and agreed to work with *Panches* [panchayat elders] to settle the dispute." This they did, after it was agreed that the police would receive a small amount of money, and leave the matter to the villagers to settle. Whether the police response results in informal community-based solutions, formal actions, or advantageous concessions, the police often ask for bribes and the people often give them unsolicited.

Pudur

Pudur, near Anbur, is mainly comprised of dalit families that were once somewhat scattered and under Anbur's panchayat rule. However, they were forced to relocate to a small area very close to Chidambaram. They later split from Anbur authority and formed their own panchayat. These villagers from early times were highly individualistic and egalitarian, and did not abide by panchayat authority. Lacking strong collective support, the panchayat became dysfunctional during our research period, and ceased to process disputes, which were then referred to the police. In addition to dalits, Pudur includes a small number of Vanniyar and Kallar families and individuals. These nondalits also contribute to community disintegration. They maintain connections with their own caste members outside of the village, and sometimes use their power to threaten, discipline, and keep the dalits in the village in submission. Some dalit men, associated with the nondalits for aid and jobs, sometimes assert their power over other dalits on behalf of their higher caste supporters.

In this context of community divisions and atomization, the panchayat (a dalit caste panchayat serving as the village panchayat) could not be powerful enough to solve serious developing problems. Panchayat meetings were announced, but usually only a small number of people turned up. Consequently, panchayat meetings were frequently canceled. In addition, the panchayat elders were afraid of the nondalits and the dalits associated with them. Because of the village divisions and factions, when disputes arose, the panchayat elders failed to intervene. Like the community, the elders themselves did not have a strong inclination to create a community with collective interests. They expected people to be self-regulating and behave with public sense and responsibility, but did not help to develop these traits among the people. These conditions allowed minor incidents to become serious, and eventually led to dangerous outcomes and police intervention.

Three incidents deserve mention. The first started as a dispute over an elderly Vanniyar man extending his thorn fence and narrowing a pathway. A thorn on the fence severely scratched a young dalit man on his back and tore his good shirt. Instead of taking the matter to the panchayat, which is the expected procedure, the dalit man became angry and shouted at the Vanniyar, telling him to move his fence back to the original place. The Vanniyar pulled the dalit by his moustache and said, “You pariah (a highly derogatory reference to the dalits)! You have so much audacity to get angry at me.” In response, the young man hit the Vanniyar on his chest. The Vanniyar became very angry and complained to the village headman. The headman advised the young man to apologize, which he did. The panchayat did not meet, even though the incident had the potential to increase animosities.

A couple of days later, the Vanniyar sought the help of a Kallar who lived in a nearby town and ran an illicit liquor shop in Pudur (with the informal approval of the police). The Vanniyar wanted to teach the dalit a lesson that he should treat his caste superiors with respect. One evening the Kallar, with dalit workers from his liquor shop, stopped the young dalit man on his way home, and severely beat him. Upon hearing about this, fellow villagers rushed to the spot and were also beaten, some seriously. The matter was reported to the police, and the police came, arrested, and jailed several of the dalit workers from the liquor shop who had taken part in the beating. A case was filed. In the meantime, the Kallar approached the village headman (head of the panchayat) and wanted the matter to be resolved peacefully. He politely asked the headman to instruct the victims to withdraw the case filed with the police. The village headman told the Kallar to approach the victims directly, and said that he himself could not do much about it. A few months later the case was withdrawn. The Kallar had bribed the police and resolved the differences with the victims by treating them nicely in the liquor shop.

The second incident involved a dalit man who let a Kallar man live in his house as a paying guest. Later he allowed him to cohabit with his wife in return for financial help. The villagers feared the Kallar because of his caste. The panchayat did not intervene to inquire into the matter and correct it. Subsequently, the man’s son, affected by shame from village gossip, enlisted the help of a relative and a friend, and killed the Kallar man. These three young men fled the area. The police seized their fathers and jailed them, hoping that they would tell where their sons were, or that the sons would surrender upon hearing about their fathers’ predicament. It is common throughout India for police, in violation of law and procedure, to punish, harass, or detain innocent family members (Bajpai, 2000, p. 84). These practices emerge from Indian social traditions that hold the group responsible for individual behavior. The police have this same view, and also use it to accomplish their ends.

One of these fathers was the head of the panchayat. He did not know where his son was. He felt that the police action was inappropriate because he was not responsible for his adult son’s action. He experienced extreme shame, as he was the panchayat head, a retired teacher, and was generally respected in the community. In our private conversation with him, he also mentioned that the police always, until recently, gave respect to the panchayat elders, and consulted with them before taking action against any villager. He said this practice has greatly changed, and the police now enter the village without reporting to the panchayat elders.

Two weeks later the sons surrendered to the police, their fathers were released, and the case was registered with the court. The sons were held in jail for a few days, and were released, pending their court appearance. Soon after, the aggrieved son, unable to bear the public disapproval of his crime and the fear of the serious penalty that could result, committed suicide. The other two accomplices maintained that they did not intend to kill the man, but simply rough him up, and they tried to stop their friend from killing him. After this, the case was closed, and the two young men were warned and asked to report to the police periodically for a year. The police were forgiving, especially when it was discovered that the murdered Kallar man was wanted for many crimes in a distant town. After these two major incidents, the panchayat elders decided not to receive cases, and directed the people to take their problems straight to the police.

Pudur's problems were brought about by modernization exacerbating the individualistic notions they had developed by earlier living in scattered locations, further atomizing the people. The egalitarian views went against caste and age hierarchies, and created tensions. Additionally, the villagers' poverty led some, such as those dalits who worked in the liquor shop owned by the Kallar, to follow their own individual strategies for survival and go against their caste members. Pudur had developed anomic democracy (Vincentnathan, S.G., 1992), where the needs of individuals to live a dignified life—without age-based and caste-based controls, and economic barriers—were not realized. The people became frustrated and angry, and engaged in intimidating and dangerous behavior. Heavy drinking in Pudur magnified these problems. In this environment, neither the people nor their leaders had the ability to make the panchayat a viable institution. Disputes that arose could not be resolved by the panchayat. This created a situation for the police to ignore the panchayat and its elders, and freely and aggressively extend their authority.

After a year, a third incident also involved intercaste conflict and inadequate panchayat and police response. A Vanniyar father asked a young dalit man in the neighborhood to help his daughter learn mathematics so that she could pass her high school examination. The young man did help her and, in the process, they fell in love and wanted to marry. Under traditional caste system rules, intercaste marriages are not allowed. The father became angry, beat his daughter, and tied her up in the house. The young man was also seriously warned and threatened. He approached the panchayat head, but because the panchayat no longer processed disputes, the panchayat head directed the young man to go to the police, which he did. The officer in charge of the police station told him that it was improper for a dalit man to fall in love with a higher caste Vanniyar woman, and he proceeded to beat him up with a cane, telling him to stay away from the woman. The young man then met with another dalit man, an elected representative to the state assembly, and narrated the treatment he had received from the woman's father and the police officer. Upon hearing this, the politician phoned the police officer and warned him about his prejudicial and illegal behavior and advice, pointing to the constitutional right of individuals to choose their spouses regardless of caste differences. The next day, the young man went to see the police officer, upon the direction of the politician. The officer this time was cordial, and told the young man that he should have mentioned his connection with the politician. He said he would talk to the woman's father, and see what he could do to help him.

This case again indicates that some police are drawn toward social traditions that the law is trying to eliminate, and that obstruct the expression of individual rights. And yet, when this traditional thinking is challenged, especially by powerful individuals, they switch to modern legal traditions. This oscillation between traditional and modern values is situational, and depends on individual police biases, their relative commitments to traditions and modern legal requirements, and whether powerful citizens and officials pose challenges to their authority. However, people, especially dalits, are becoming conscious of their rights in the modern era, and rise against arbitrary and unfair practices. Abiding by traditional expectations is demeaning by modern standards. The elders, the panchayat, and the police trying to uphold such traditions may be disobeyed, if a person can amass enough power to override them.

Ennakulam

Another village, Ennakulam, near the city of Cuddalore, is a predominantly Vanniyar caste community with a large dalit section, and a few other castes of status similar to Vanniyar. Over the years, hostilities developed between the Vanniyars and dalits. The dalits lived in a separate area situated in the center of the village, a very unusual location, as most dalit hamlets are located outside the main village. The Ennakulam Vanniyars became jealous of the improvements they saw the dalits making and of their good clothes, watches, bicycles, radios, and TVs. They were upset because the dalits were acting as equals and in a presumptuous manner with the Vanniyars. One informant told us they felt that if they did not keep pace with the dalits, they would themselves become "dalits" to the dalits.

The Vanniyars in Ennakulam and elsewhere viewed the dalit improvements as resulting from government-sponsored affirmative action programs, which were not equally accorded to Vanniyars. Tensions between Vanniyars and dalits throughout Tamil Nadu were increasing in the late 1980s. Vanniyars formed a statewide association and claimed they should receive government benefits equal to dalits' benefits, but the Tamil Nadu government initially refused. The Vanniyars then mounted protests against the Tamil Nadu government, and terrorized dalits. They also damaged buses and trains. All of these actions were to force the Tamil Nadu government to grant them greater benefits. In order to gain control over the problem, the district government established local level committees, not unlike the Friends of the Police or Maithri Committees mentioned earlier, to inform the police of emerging troubles and to help prevent violence. Similarly, the panchayat elders in villages were asked to cooperate and help maintain peace and order.

In the context of tensions in the vicinity and in the village, by 1988 violence erupted between the Ennakulam Vanniyars and dalits. A few individual episodes of arguments and interpersonal conflict opened up traditional animosities, which led to a young dalit man killing a Vanniyar. The Vanniyar and dalit panchayats in Ennakulam met separately and together to defuse the escalating problem and appeal to the people for creating peace, but they could not do much. The police officers warned the elders of both panchayats that if they failed to maintain peace, 10 persons from each caste would be arrested and jailed, including some panchayat elders. As mentioned, the police sometimes use these types of threats and practices, including preventive detention, when they find it difficult to control intergroup tensions and conflicts. Sensing the possibilities of serious danger, a few policemen were stationed in the vicinity of Ennakulam.

Following the murder, in spite of these precautionary measures, the Vanniyars raided the dalit community, injuring many and killing two dalits. They burned the huts and routed all dalits, who fled and found refuge in nearby dalit communities. Many additional policemen rushed to the area to help stop the violence. They opened fire, injuring some and killing two Vanniyars, one a young girl. The police registered cases against many individuals for court processing. The district administrator promised dalits an allotment of land for the development of a new community. In the meantime, the police kept watch on troublesome Vanniyars. They strongly instructed the Vanniyar panchayat elders to maintain control over their people and to inform them of anyone becoming unruly or defiant.

The people of Ennakulam in these modern times follow their own personal inclinations, which contradict panchayat and panchayat elders' authority and expectations for peace in the community. This happens especially in critical situations when the needs for equality and dignity are affected in interpersonal and intergroup relational contexts. Dalits want to live in equality with Vanniyars to gain personal and communal dignity, but Vanniyars, who believe themselves superior, feel their own sense of dignity eroded by dalit bids for equality, and try to block dalit progress. These and similar situations often bring about intense anger and violent outbursts, sometimes fueled by regional politics. The panchayat cannot be effective in such situations, nor can the police, even when they pursue more community-based strategies involving dialog with and participation of community members, because tensions and violence may extend beyond one village, causing large-scale problems for peace and order. The police in such desperate situations resort to extralegal practices, force, and violence to create order.

Conclusion

Modernization has progressively altered traditional practices, community power structures, and panchayat authority, greatly reducing the effectiveness of both traditional and modern forms of community policing. The modernization efforts of the British during the nineteenth and twentieth centuries and those of independent India, including economic changes, have weakened caste group solidarity and interdependent caste hierarchical relationships (Kidder, 1977, p. 171; Galanter, 1968, p. 86). These have been further undermined by evolving notions of individualism and equality, through which individuals build their sense of worth and dignity, denied earlier especially to the lower castes (Rudolph & Rudolph, 1967, pp. 62–63; Berreman, 1979, p. 167; Vincentnathan, S.G., 1996, pp. 497–499). Panchayats in their social control functions are weakened by lack of cooperation and beset by intracaste and intercaste factions. The interests of oppressed groups and privileged groups, in the general race to obtain pleasing lives for themselves, come into conflict. The privileged groups try to maintain and enhance their traditional statuses and power, and do not want to allow the underprivileged to become equal to or surpass them. The political platforms and divisions that originate from these diverse interests strengthen group affinities and intensify intergroup hostilities and conflicts at the local community level, and sometimes inflame communities throughout a region or state. Consequently, police involvement becomes necessary with the decline of panchayat authority, which further erodes that very panchayat authority.

The Hindu belief in the divine origin of the caste system, the upper caste and upper class status correlation and power nexus, the economic interdependence of castes, and the respect held for the elders all helped to keep community members conforming and compliant. When disputes, rule violations, or crimes arose, they were handled in terms of customary rules founded on caste, class, and age hierarchical distinctions (Dubois & Beauchamp, 1906, pp. 654–667). Even though justice done and punishments rendered were unequal, there was not much large-scale discontent as there is today.

In addition to our own studies in Tamil Nadu, other studies in various parts of India reveal deterioration of traditional panchayats under modern conditions: in the Karnataka villages of Dalena (Epstein, 1962) and Rampura (Srinivas, 1959); in the Madhya Pradesh village of Ramkheri (Mayer, 1960);

and in the Uttar Pradesh villages of Senapur (Opler, 1959; Cohn, 1959), Khalapur (Hitchcock, 1963), and Haripur (Mendelsohn, 1981). The government-organized Nyaya Panchayats have also largely failed; from the study of these panchayats in Bharatpur and surrounding areas in Uttar Pradesh, Meschievitz and Galanter (1982, p. 68) wrote, "What was to be a neutral, unbiased body of local leaders helping to negotiate and mediate petty disputes has either become a stronghold of landed elites and dominant castes, or in other localities, been stillborn."

Single caste communities and caste panchayats also experience similar problems. Kinship ties have weakened, and elders in the panchayat find it difficult to settle disputes and make peace. Attachment to one's group and obedience to the elders' authority have declined, and individuals act out independently in avenging hate and indignities brought on them by their adversaries in interpersonal relations, which sometimes results into group conflicts, as happened in Ennakulam, Pudur, and other places. An individual in Anbur who was more modernized, independent, self-dignified, and disrespectful of authority than many in the village posed challenges to the panchayat elders. Similarly, there were no panchayats to handle the conflict among the Vanniyars of Pallam, Medu, and Kandam. These Vanniyars had a heightened sense of independence, lacking the collective attitudes needed to sustain a panchayat and its social control function. When the fight broke out, with great difficulty an ad hoc panchayat was created, which temporarily helped to make kinship and caste ties important in order to restore peace.

Social modernization comes into conflict with traditional beliefs and practices and stimulates disputes, and political modernization tries to contain these disputes and strife. The government is making efforts to promote individual rights and equality by uplifting underprivileged groups, and secular orientations for equal treatment of persons of all religions. However, many police and government officials affected by social traditions hinder these democratic developments (Ganguly, 2003). As Tambiah (1998) suggests, until "substantive equality" (people treating each other equally, fairly, and justly) is achieved, "formal equality" (based on the Constitution and laws of the country) will not be achieved. These types of social and political issues will continue until significant strides are made in achieving social and political modernization.

In the meantime the social order of many Indian communities will be disrupted, conflicts will increase, panchayats will be dysfunctional, police presence will increase, and police–community relations will be strained. The police have increased in number, and have extended their areas of operation. However, the police alone cannot maintain the peace without the cooperation of the panchayat or community, as the police are usually outside the community, often exercising control over many communities from one police station or post. The police, by requesting and threatening, try to gain the panchayats' cooperation. They also try to help change informal justice to modern lines of justice administration, and sometimes block that change. When panchayats act unfairly, the police question their propriety and discourage their involvement in handling cases. Affected by legal traditions, social customs, and personal considerations, the police intervene. Sometimes they adhere to legal traditions or take fair and socially redeeming actions, while other times they follow antithetical social customs, or take extralegal actions. Panchayat elders also oscillate between social traditions and modern legal expectations, which brings questions and criticisms about their decisions.

The several cases presented here shed light at the microlevel on the traditional and modern forces operating in India that bring cooperation and conflict between the informal policing system of traditional panchayat control and formal system of modern police control. The panchayat's inability to contain conflict when traditional cultural and structural impediments thwart the modern needs for equality, independence, and dignity may then lead to police involvement. Additionally, in a spiraling fashion, police criticisms of panchayats, increasing police power, and police interventions further decrease the panchayat's authority in the eyes of the villagers and hasten the demise of this informal institution of social control. Consequently, there is built-in tension between panchayat elders and the police, making difficult the creation of a formal police system that works in conjunction with the informal community policing system of the panchayat, apart from the modernizing influences weakening panchayat power.

Similar repercussions and processes noted in India can be seen in many developing and modernizing countries, although under different cultural and social contexts. The underprivileged almost everywhere seek to be free from traditional authority, social constrictions, and structured inequalities. They oppose the barriers created by the rich and powerful, and resent the inabilities of the state to quickly and fairly respond to their needs. The shift in emphasis in China from communistic control under Mao to economic development beginning in 1976 has caused growing economic desires, and many poor from the rural areas flocked into cities, breaking away from residence requirements and local registration to improve their lot. Local and informal systems of social control have given way to official processing. Crimes and riots have markedly increased as a result of capitalistic development and economic inequalities. Public security forces have expanded to confront disturbances and crime, and facilitate economic development (Wong, 2002; Dammer et al., 2006, pp. 115–117).

Similarly, forces of modernization in Russia, influenced by Western Europe, increased the desires of people to be free and rich (Krygier, 1990, pp. 633–663), which the communist regime tried to nullify, but could not. Controversies and frictions developed between supporters of the old and new regimes, as in China, regarding how to run the country and reduce social problems. The political differences and social discontent have resulted in protests and violence. As in China, the Russian informal and local methods of social control have given way to formal and external police intervention, engendering negative and hateful attitudes toward the police. Political and police control have increased, and have become more organized (Gilinskiy, 2003).

The Sinhalese oppression of the Tamils with state support in Sri Lanka has led to frequent and extensive violence and crime. Local community institutions of justice and peacemaking became weaker as conflict and strife increased. As a result, resources have been diverted to expanding the police, military, and security forces away from economic development. In the context of these developments, state and police control increased greatly to maintain public order, often with the state and police working in support of the Sinhalese majority (Vincentnathan, S.G., 2005).

Today's economically developed countries seem to have gone through similar trends in their history. Weisser (1979) notes that economic and social changes occurring during preindustrial and feudal Europe (thirteenth and fourteenth centuries) have also brought forth discontent and crime problems in communities leading to continuous changes in the political systems to maintain order. In England, public prosecution replaced private justice. By the eighteenth and nineteenth centuries, forces of modernization engendered widespread social disruption due to unfulfilled desires, especially in the lower classes. Exploding crime and violence were noted in Western Europe and particularly in England. The ineffectiveness of traditional methods of local community policing led to the development of more organized and coordinated public policing systems, which first emerged in London (Jones, 1985; Critchley, 1975; Bayley, 1999).

These processes of change lead to a common theme, that people in modern societies and cultures strive to rise above the stumbling blocks and barriers imposed by traditional hierarchical and authoritarian regimes in order to be equal with others, move ahead from controls that obstruct pursuit of their desires and dreams, and live a rich and dignified life. These needs seem to be similarly experienced throughout the modern world, but they are unequally and inadequately fulfilled because of unique and different historical, cultural, and political experiences of societies.

Social changes and modernization engender conditions for disputes and conflicts, and the police as an organ of state control intervene to create public order, reducing local autonomy. The policing and judicial functions of panchayats still continue in many Indian communities. Eventually, however, they may wane, and the role of the police and other criminal justice institutions will increase to fill the void. In the meantime, cooperation and conflict between the panchayat and the police will continue in their mutual general orientation to maintain peace and order, whether it is done by the panchayats or the police using traditional, legal, or extralegal practices.

Community policing and police–community relation programs, initiated as aspects of regular, official policing, do not seem to work well because of the historical fear of the police, who came from outside the community and could cause problems for the people, such as beating or torturing them. This happened especially during the British colonial administration in India. The police at that time, being attached to colonial rule, were cruel to the people, especially those who were unruly. Consequently, people depended on panchayats for resolving their interpersonal problems. Even today Indian parents tell unruly or crying children that the policeman is coming in order to create fear and control their behavior. Because the police continue to act in colonial, paramilitary style, using various torturous means to elicit information or control people, and often demanding bribes, the people try to keep away from them as much as possible. Therefore, police–community relation programs to promote trust and confidence in the police as helpers and to control crime through people's cooperation is difficult to achieve in India.

It is possible that the informal methods of policing by the panchayat elders to prevent and contain disputes and crime, and create peace, can be restructured and revitalized. For this to happen, democratic principles and relations should become more deeply rooted, along with altruistic and strong community sentiments. The Nyaya Panchayat, as mentioned earlier, is one of those community institutions of policing and justice administration, but perhaps it was introduced too early at a time of social structural divisions and disorders. Also, the new community policing programs, such as Friends of the Police and Maithri Councils, could become successful under more conducive conditions. Japan, for instance, has almost given up its attachment to its traditional caste system in an effort to democratize the country, yet still maintains its communitarian values and respect for authority. The police tend to be honest and helpful to citizens, sometimes excusing minor infractions. In Japanese communities, there is mutual respect and trust between the police and the public, which allows for close cooperation in controlling crime and maintaining public order, and their community policing programs have been noted as models of success (Ames, 1981). It is possible Indian communities could also become more democratic and communitarian, if necessary steps are taken as part of the national agenda for building communities. Panchayats and community policing in such a setting may work. Formal policing, with the supports of informal community policing by the panchayat and other community policing programs, could be really useful, not only to promote positive attitudes toward the official police, but also to reduce crime and maintain peace and order. However, this seems improbable at this time based on the divisive politics and developing individualism that shatter community sentiments, which weakens the panchayat's authority and forcibly calls for police intervention and control.

References

Ames, W.L. (1981). *Police and community in Japan*. Berkeley: University of California Press.

Amnesty International (1992). *India: Torture, rape, and deaths in custody*. New York: Amnesty International.

Andhra Pradesh Police (2008). *Andhra Pradesh Police Manual*, Chap. 35. http://www.apstatepolice.org/html/appm/manch/c35.htm (accessed October 15, 2008).

Bajpai, G.S. (2000). Informal arrests and human rights violations. *Indian Journal of Criminology, 28*(2), 79–87.

Basham, A.L. (1954). *The wonder that was India: A survey of the culture of the Indian sub-continent before the coming of the Muslims*. New York: Macmillan.

Baxi, U. & Galanter, M. (1979). Panchayat justice: An Indian experiment in legal access. In M. Cappelletti & B. Barth (Eds.), *Access to justice: Emerging issues and perspectives*, Vol. 3 (pp. 341–386). Milan: Sijthoff and Noordhoff-Alphenaandenrijn.

Bayley, D.H. (1999). The development of modern police. In L.K. Gaines & G.W. Cordner (Eds.), *Policing perspectives: An anthology* (pp. 59–78). Los Angeles: Roxbury Publishing Company.

Berreman, G.D. (1966a). Structure and function of caste systems. In G. DeVos & H. Wagatsuma (Eds.), *Japan's invisible race* (pp. 277–307). Berkeley: University of California Press.

Berreman, G.D. (1966b). Concomitants of caste organization. In G. DeVos & H. Wagatsuma (Eds.), *Japan's invisible race* (pp. 308–324). Berkeley: University of California Press.

Berreman, G.D. (1979). *Caste and other inequalities: Essays on inequality*. Meerut, India: Folklore Institute.

Beteille, A. (1986). Individualism and equality. *Current Anthropology, 27*(2), 121–134.

Brogden, M. (2005). "Horses for courses" and "thin blue lines": Community policing in transitional society. *Police Quarterly, 8*(1), 64–98.

Burawoy, M. (1998). The extended case method. *Sociological Theory,* 16(1), 4–34.

Burger, A.S. (1993). Ethnicity and the security forces of the state: The South Asian experience. In J.D. Toland (Ed.), *Ethnicity and the state, Political and legal anthropology*, Vol. 9 (pp. 79–102). New Brunswick, NJ: Transaction Publishers.

Chandigarh Tribune (February 15, 2004). Individualism taking sheen off family ties, says expert. http://www.tribuneindia.com/2004/20040215/cth.1.htm

Cohn, B.S. (1959). Some notes on law and change in North India. *Economic Development and Cultural Change, 8*, 79–93.

Cohn, B.S. (1965). Anthropological notes on disputes and law in India. In L Nader (Ed.), The ethnography of law. *American Anthropologist*, special ed., Part 2, *67*(6), 82–122.

Cole, B.A. (1999). Post-colonial systems. In R.I. Mawby (Ed.), *Policing across the world: Issues for the twenty-first century* (pp. 88–108). London: Routledge.

Critchley, T.A. (1975). The new police in London, 1975–1830. In J.H. Skolnick & Th.C. Gray (Eds.), *Police in America* (pp. 6–15). Boston: Little, Brown and Company.

Dammer, H.R., Fairchild, F., & Albanese, J.S. (2006). *Comparative criminal justice systems*, 3rd ed. Belmont, CA: Thomson Wadsworth.

Das, V. 1990. Introduction: Communities, riots, survivors—the South Asian experience. In V. Das (Ed.), *Mirrors of violence: Communities, riots, and survivors in South Asia* (pp. 1–36). Delhi: Oxford University Press.

Department of Economics and Statistics (2002). *Statistical handbook of Tamil Nadu, 2001*. Chennai: Government Central Press.

Department of Statistics (1985). *Statistical handbook of Tamil Nadu, 1984*. Madras: Government Press.

Diaz, S.M. (1994). Police in India. In D.K. Das (Ed.), *Police practices: An international review* (pp. 181–283). Metuchen, NJ: The Scarecrow Press.

Dubois, A.J.A. & Beauchamp, H.K. (1906). *Hindu manners, customs and ceremonies*. 3rd ed. New Delhi: Oxford University Press.

Durkheim, E. (1915). *The elementary forms of religious life*, J. W. Swain (Trans.). New York: The Free Press.

Epstein, T.S. (1962). *Economic development and social change in South India*. Manchester: Manchester University Press.

Galanter, M. (1968). The displacement of traditional law in modern India. *Journal of Social Issues, 24*(4), 65–91.

Galanter, M. (1984). *Competing equalities: Law and the backward classes in India*. Berkeley: University of California Press.

Ganguly, S. (2003). The crisis of Indian secularism. *Journal of Democracy, 14*(4), 11–26.

Gilinskiy, Y. (2003). Organized crime: A perspective from Russia. In J.S. Albanese, D. Das, & A. Verma (Eds.), *Organized crime: World perspectives* (pp. 146–164). Upper Saddle River, NJ: Prentice Hall.

Hayden, R.M. (1999). *Disputes and arguments amongst nomads: A caste council in India*. New Delhi: Oxford University Press.

Hindu, The (2002, June 6). Govt. urged to take step agains child marriage. Souhern States: Karnataka. http://www.hinduonnet.com/2002/06/06/stories/2002060603610600.htm

Hitchcock, J.T. (1963). *The Rajputs of Khalapur, India*. New York: John Wiley & Sons.

Jacobsohn, G.J. (2003). *The wheel of law: India's secularism in comparative perspective*. Princeton, NJ: Princeton University Press.

Jones, T.A. (1985). The evolution of crime in industrial and preindustrial societies. In R.F. Thomasson (Ed.), *Comparative social research: Deviance* (pp. 1–15). Greenwich, CT: JAI Press.

Joshi, B.R. (1986). *Untouchable: Voices of the Dalit liberation movement*. London: Zed Books.

Karpurthala Police (2008). *Community policing*. http://www.kapurthalapolice.net/communitypolicing.htm (accessed October 15, 2008).

Kidder, R.L. (1973). Courts and conflict in an Indian city: A study in legal impact. *Journal of Commonwealth Political Studies, 11*, 121–139.

Kidder, R.L. (1977). Western law in India: External law and local response. *Sociological Inquiry, 46*, 155–179.

Kolenda, P. (1978). *Caste in contemporary India: Beyond organic solidarity*. Menlo Park, CA: Benjamin/Cummings.

Krygier, M. (1990). Marxism and the rule of law: Reflections after the collapse of communism. *Law and Social Inquiry, 15*(4), 633–663.

Maine, H.J.S. (1861). *Ancient law: Its connection with the early history of society, and its relation to modern ideas*. London: John Murray.

Mandelbaum, D.G. (1970). *Society in India: Volume two, change and continuity*. Berkeley: University of California Press.

Mayer, A.C. (1960). *Caste and kinship in Central India: A village and its region*. Berkeley and Los Angeles: University of California Press.

Mendelsohn, O. (1981). The pathology of the Indian legal system. *Modern Asian Studies, 15*(4), 823–63.

Mendelsohn, O. & Vicziany, M. (1998). *The untouchables: Subordination, poverty and the state in modern India*. Cambridge: Cambridge University Press.

Meschievitz, C.S. & Galanter, M. (1982). In search of Nyaya Panchayats: The politics of a moribund institution. In R.L. Abel (Ed.), *The politics of informal justice*, Vol. 2 (pp. 47–77). New York: Academic Press.

Ministry of Home Affairs (1967). *Crime in India, 1965*. New Delhi: Government of India, Central Bureau of Investigation.

Ministry of Home Affairs (1987). *Crime in India, 1982*. New Delhi: Government of India, Bureau of Police Research and Development.

Ministry of Home Affairs (2002). *Crime in India, 2000*. New Delhi: Government of India, National Crime Records Bureau.

Ministry of Home Affairs (2007). *Crime in India, 2006*. New Delhi: Government of India, National Crime Records Bureau.

Moore, E. (1985). *Conflict and compromise: Justice in an Indian village*. [Monograph Series No. 26.] Lanham, MD: University Press of America.

Mukerjee, D. (2008). *Community policing experiments/outreach programmes in India*. Commonwealth Human Rights Initiative, http://www.humanrightsinitiative.org/new/community_policing_experiments_in_india.pdf (accessed October 15, 2008).

National Human Rights Commission (India) (1997). *The Annual report*. New Delhi: Government of India.

Opler, M.E. (1959). Factor of tradition and change in a local election in rural India. In R.L. Park & I. Tinker (Eds.), *Leadership and political institutions in India* (pp. 137–150). Princeton, NJ: Princeton University Press.

Parnell, Ph.C. (1978). Village or state? Comparative legal systems in a Mexicon judicial district. In L. Nader & H.F. Todd (Eds.), *The disputing process—Law in ten societies* (pp. 315–354). New York: Columbia University Press.

Prateep, P.V. (1996). Friends of police movement. In M. Pagon (Ed.), *Policing in central and eastern Europe*. Ljubljana, Slovenia: College of Police and Security Studies.

Rajeswar, B.G. (2003, June 19). "Unfriendly" Maithris lose identity. *Times of India*, retrieved from http://timesofindia.indiatimes.com/articleshow/30258.cms (accessed October 15, 2008).

Roland, A. (1988). *In search of self in India and Japan: Toward a cross-cultural psychology*. Princeton, NJ: Princeton University Press.

Rudolph, L.I. & Rudolph, S.H. (1967). *The modernity of tradition: Political development in India*. Chicago: University of Chicago Press.

Shah, A.M. (1998). *The family in India: Critical essays*. Hyderabad: Orient Longman Limited.

Sinha, J.B.J., Neharika Vohra, S., Sinha, R.B.N., & Ushashree, S. (2002). Normative predictions of collectivistic-individualistic intentions and behavior of Indians. *International Journal of Psychology, 37*(5), 309–319.

Srinivas, M.N. (1959). The dominant caste in Rampura. *American Anthropologist, 7*, 149–168.

Srinivas, M.N. (1996). *Village, caste, gender and method: Essays in Indian social anthropology*. New Delhi: Oxford University Press.

Tambiah, S. (1998). The crisis of secularism in India. In R. Bhargava (Ed.), *Secularism and its critics*. New Delhi: Oxford University Press.

Verma, A. (1999). Cultural roots of police corruption in India. *Policing: An International Journal of Police Strategies and Management, 22*(3), 264–279.

Vincentnathan, L. (1987). *Harijan subculture and self-esteem management in a South Indian community*. Doctoral dissertation, University of Wisconsin, Madison.

Vincentnathan, S.G. (1992). Social construction of order and disorder and their outcomes in two South Indian communities. *Journal of Legal Pluralism, 32*, 65–102.

Vincentnathan, S.G. (1996). Caste politics, violence, and the *panchayat* in a South Indian community. *Comparative Studies in Society and History, 38*(3), 484–509.

Vincentnathan, S.G. (2005). Sri Lanka. In D.K. Das & M.J. Palmiotto (Eds.), *World police encyclopedia* (pp. 780–786). London: Routledge.

Weisser, M.R. (1979). *Crime and punishment in early modern Europe*. Hassocks, Sussex, U.K.: Harvester Press.

Wong, K.C. (2002). Policing in the People's Republic of China: The road to reform in the 1990s. *The British Journal of Criminology, 42*(2), 281–316.

Community Policing and Police Reform in Latin America[*]

12

HUGO FRÜHLING

Contents

Introduction

The peace agreements reached in 1991 and 1996, respectively, between the governments of El Salvador and Guatemala and representatives of the armed opposition in those countries, led to two of the more recent and comprehensive efforts to advance toward police reform in Latin America. In both cases, the respective agreements stipulated the creation of new civil forces to replace police institutions controlled by the military, and which had a reputation for repressive, politicized actions incompatible with a democratic system. These reforms involved a variety of international actors and arose parallel to

[*] This chapter is based on "The Impact of International Models of Policing in Latin America. The Case of Community Policing," published in *Police Practice & Research, 8*(2), 125–144.

criminal justice reforms that consisted of the introduction of oral trials and accusatory systems (Stanley, 1999, pp. 113–134; see also Neild, 2002).

Subsequently, intents at police reform expanded throughout the region. The community policing model developed in North America and Europe during the prior decade played an influential part in these processes. The Inter-American Development Bank has strongly supported the implantation of this model as a suitable path for progress toward more democratic policing (Frühling, 2004). During the 1990s, the military police of several Brazilian states began community policing programs with the stated goal of improving relations with the community, reducing police abuse, and increasing community acceptance of the police. The first experiment was carried out in Copacabana, Rio de Janeiro, in 1994.

Given the differing levels of professionalism among the police forces involved in these reform processes and the varied political and social contexts in which they work, it makes sense to question whether these national reforms can be analyzed as if they were similar. In that respect, they can be said to have the same origin: i.e., the process of democratization that the region has experienced in recent years and which has intensified demands for a reduction in the levels of police violence and corruption, and for the police to develop better relations with the community; the rise in crime that has, in turn, increased the pressure for more professional police personnel and policing strategies; and, finally, the diffusion of public management models that put an emphasis on greater flexibility in the responses of public institutions and results rather than in the mere observance of laws and regulations, and consideration for users of police services.

On the other hand, a significant number of Latin American police forces share certain common characteristics. From a historical point of view, the police in Latin America have tended to be the object of political instrumentality, which has led to their lack of impartiality and the predominance of subjective criteria in personnel recruitment and promotion processes. Second, the police in Latin American have adhered to a hierarchical organizational model, which is centralized and military-like in character. This characteristic is more visible in certain Latin American police forces, but is generally present in almost all of them. The content of police training reinforces this organizational type, emphasizing obedience and discipline. In general, it is more theoretical than practical and lacks incentives for promoting creativity among police officials.

Widely known surveys indicate that with the possible exceptions of Chile and Colombia, the traditional policing model is not highly regarded by citizens. This is manifested in low rates of crime reporting due to the sense that the police will do little with any crime reports they receive.

Among the efforts to address the aforementioned problems, the best known are those that contain a strong element of improving relations with the community. This chapter will show the potential of the community policing strategy for making progress toward more democratic forms of police action, as well as those aspects that have limited the experiences with the model in Latin America, and which must be considered part of any comprehensive police reform process.

The Origin of the Police Reform Process

The attempts at police reform, which are described in this chapter, are influenced by three factors that determine both the characteristics and the content of those reforms. The first factor is the democratization process that occurred during the 1980s and 1990s in many countries in the region. This process made evident the incompatibility between democratic and human rights norms and the actions of Latin American police forces. The second factor is the significant increase in common crime in almost all Latin American countries. Faced with such insecurity, citizens demanded an improvement to inefficient or corrupt police forces. Finally, the debate over police reform arises within the context of government transformations taking place around the world and in Latin America in particular. These changes include limiting the size of government, the privatization of public enterprises, and the decentralization of functions to local or regional governments. The goal of these changes is to establish mechanisms for the accountability of public organisms in terms of their efficiency and efficacy (Bresser, 1999, pp. 1–13). The ideas guiding these government reforms contrast starkly with the serious deficiencies affecting the police.

The confluence of the three historical factors described above explains why recent police reform programs bear little relation to prior efforts produced in different circumstances as well as the difficulties and challenges that this institutional change has confronted. First, significant sectors of the population occasionally perceive simultaneous demands for crime control and a drastic reduction in police abuse as contradictory, minimizing the continuity of many reform initiatives. Secondly, the rise in crime and fear puts pressure on the police to show results in the short term, when the circumstances would be better served by broader reforms. Finally, the necessary police modernization process often meets with strong internal resistance because it conflicts with the prevailing model, which is hierarchical, centralized, and repressive.

Some recent approaches to policing in Latin America emphasize the need to create citizen participation channels to stimulate police accountability to the public regarding the effectiveness of their actions. In the following section, we will describe some characteristics of the community policing model as it has been put into practice in Canada and the United States, as well as some of the potential benefits for Latin America.

The Community Policing Model in Western Europe and North America

The community policing model that has dominated the debate on policing in recent decades includes certain essential elements:

1. It emphasizes preventive police actions focused on a specific geographic area: the neighborhood.
2. It promotes the establishment of close ties with the community to facilitate constant feedback from community members and ensure that the police take their perceptions into consideration (Sherman, 1995, pp. 327–348).
3. It involves police efforts to mobilize the community to carry out preventive actions.
4. It seeks to ensure that police actions reflect knowledge about the conditions and circumstances that are conducive to crime and minor infractions that disrupt people's lives.

Other elements of this model that are frequently underscored, and which are related to the components described above, include:

1. A focus on resolving concrete security problems that affect residents of a neighborhood rather than merely reacting to citizen demands.
2. An emphasis on actions designed to address the fears of citizens.
3. External review of police priorities and recognition that the community, however defined, plays a central role in resolving neighborhood problems.
4. The recognition also that police forces need to be decentralized in order to meet the requirements of the community policing strategy (Rosenbaum, 1998, p. 7).

The role of the community is critical not only for providing useful information to the police, but also to strengthen the mechanisms for police accountability for their actions. In the community policing model, police consult with the community on an ongoing basis, which serves three functions: (1) it enables the police to learn about local interests and needs, which don't always coincide with perceptions; (2) it provides an opportunity for the police to educate the citizenry about crime prevention behavior; and (3) it creates a venue for citizens to directly express complaints, which serves as a kind of instant public evaluation (Bayley, 1994, pp. 105–120).

The organizational changes associated with community policing seek to promote officials who are willing to take risks, act in innovative ways, and provide police officers with incentives for professional development. All members of the institution must act professionally, with initiative, and be prepared to confront security problems from a broad perspective, which implies resolving social problems that may impact crime and employing strategies that go beyond the mere application of the law in a specific case.

A particular emphasis of the community policing model is the possibility of creating new police performance oversight mechanisms directed by citizen groups. Numerous citizens groups have formed in European countries in order to monitor police actions and provide the police with a civilian perspective on their activities. The objective of these committees is to increase oversight of the police as well as to build confidence in the police.

One of the factors that led to the development of the community policing model, particularly in the United States, was the sense among minorities and marginalized groups that the police are prone to using excessive force and discriminating against them. Although we are not aware of any studies that have credibly demonstrated this, there are good reasons to believe that the community policing model could lead to a reduction in police abuse. In effect, a police force that fundamentally values public opinion will carefully control the use of force. At the same time, a police force that defines itself as a public service is going to be less disposed to use force than a police force that defines itself primarily as a crime-fighting organization.

For the reasons mentioned, the community policing model offers significant promise for countries affected by police violence in recent years. The recent practical experiences in Latin America demonstrate that these programs significantly improve the image of the police, and that they can constitute an interesting contribution to reducing the public's fear. However, implementing community projects does encounter management problems and tends to be more difficult in places where there are very low levels of police professionalism and significant problems with administrative management.

From this perspective, there is no doubt that police institutions with greater levels of professionalism will be more likely to move toward the new paradigm of police organization that has been presented here.

On the basis of this assessment concerning the community model in Latin America and the institutional changes and training processes that are needed, below is an analysis of some experiences in the region.

Community Policing in Latin America

The police reform processes being carried out in Latin America today are varied in nature. Some seek to establish closer relations with the community, but are not called community policing because apparently the institutions involved do not accept all the premises that the model promotes. On the other extreme, there are those that seek to transform an entire police force using community-oriented programs as a basis.

The first experiment in Latin America was implemented in Copacabana, Rio de Janeiro, in 1994. Although the program did not last long, it was followed by similar attempts in other Brazilian cities (Muniz et al., 1997, pp. 197–214). In the following section, we will discuss four community policing projects from which we can extract useful conclusions with respect to the design and execution of these kinds of projects, to determine their impact on police institutions. The evaluation took place during 2001 and 2002, and was conducted by five researchers who are experts in police matters, and who focused their work on four community policing projects that were of a sufficient duration and provided enough information to enable an evaluation of the impact of the experience (Frühling, 2004). The respective reports were written by researchers María Victoria Llorente (2004), Laura M. Chinchilla (2004), Paulo de Mesquita Neto (2004), and Claudio C. Beato (2004).

Many of the conclusions are derived from the studies, which are summarized in the following section.

The Case of São Paulo, Brazil

Between 1980 and 1990, the state of São Paulo, like the rest of Brazil, experienced a sharp rise in crime. According to Ministry of Health data (de Mesquita Neto & Affonso, 1998), the number of deaths from homicide or battery rose from 3,452 in 1980 to 12,350 in 1996, that is, 36.2 homicides per 100,000 inhabitants. The robbery rate also rose dramatically. Police response to this situation was seriously lacking, and the public's confidence in the police was correspondingly low. On December 10, 1997, the commanding general of the Military Police officially adopted community policing as the force's philosophy and operational strategy.

In São Paulo, the main entity responsible for analysis and discussion of the implementation of the community policing program is the Advisory Commission for the Implementation of Community Policing. The commission's membership varies in number and individuals over time; as of August 1998, it included representatives of human rights organizations, community councils, the State Federation of Industries, business councils, the Paulist Association of the Public Prosecutor's Office, the Lawyers' Guild of Brazil, and the United Nations Latin American Institute for the Prevention of Crime and Treatment of Offenders (ILANUD), among others.

The commission discussed the population's security problems, set priorities, and determined solutions to be applied. A set of goals and objectives for the police was defined, including the teaching of democratic values and respect for human rights—concerns never previously part of Military Police doctrine. Among these goals were instituting the community policing model as the organizational strategy of the Military Police, improving police education and training, improving the recruitment and promotion system, integrating the police force with other public bodies, and enhancing the reputation and rights of the police (de Mesquita Neto & Affonso, 1998, pp. 40–50).

The police chose 41 areas in which to begin the project, with policy in place to govern patrols, women police officers, traffic police, railroad police, forest police, and fire fighters. Company commanders chose the neighborhoods where the project was to be implemented. The community policing program was implemented between December 1997 and July 2001 in 199 of the 386 companies that make up the state Military Police force; thus, over half of the companies implemented community policing (de Mesquita Neto, 2004). From September 1997 to May 2000, 239 community-based substations were created, and close to 16,000 police officers received training in community policing (Kahn, 2003, p. 2). The new program meant increased preventive patrols in selected areas, the establishment of mobile stations in certain neighborhoods, efforts to increase school security, and drug prevention programs.

Maintaining communications with the police, the Advisory Commission for the Implementation of Community Policing monitored and evaluated the problems that emerged during the implementation of the new model. Although the implementation does represent an achievement, the relationship between the community and the police was a troubled one. In meetings with citizens, the police took note of problems, but there was rarely any rigorous follow-up of the measures adopted to solve them.

On another front, a decree by the state government created Community Security Councils, each composed of individuals from a given police district to meet to discuss problems of public security and work with the police to propose solutions. The councils are to meet monthly and send minutes of the meetings to the coordinator of Public Security Councils, an organ of the state's Secretariat of Security. The dialog in these councils between police and citizens does not appear to have been productive, and they seem to have functioned more as a forum for complaints concerning, and demands from, the police than as a forum to organize collective civil solutions (de Mesquita Neto, 2004, p. 125).

The Case of Villa Nueva, Guatemala

Several community policing programs were developed as part of Citizen Security in Central America, an international project run by the Inter-American Institute of Human Rights. The program, a pilot experiment that did not involve changes in the overall organization of the police, took place in Belize, Costa Rica, El Salvador, Guatemala, Honduras, and Nicaragua, and sought to promote an approach that focused on community policing and problem solving. The fact that the organizations involved were financed by international cooperation gave the international funders influence over the program; at the same time, however, it was clear that once the cooperation period was over, the program would face the real test of sustainability. By 2004, the community policing project in Villa Nueva had ended.

At the beginning there were meetings with representatives of state entities and civil society to determine where the program would be implemented and which individuals would be responsible for the process. The location was selected by political staff at the Ministry of Government, not by the police. Villa Nueva was a municipality with 192,000 inhabitants in the area of Guatemala that included the nation's capital. Despite the lack of a system of reliable and uniform crime statistics, certain limited data recorded by the National Civil Police of Villa Nueva indicated that the most common crimes before the project began in 1998 were robbery, battery, homicide, and auto theft (Chinchilla, 2004, p. 42).

The project focused on the National Civil Police, which grew out of the peace agreements between the government and guerrilla forces. Although the old security forces were dissolved and replaced by the new police, the composition and level of training of the new force fell far short of expectations. The army continued to play a role in domestic security, and the great majority of the new force came from the ranks of the old security forces, after a period of retraining.

The National Civil Police had already made some efforts to mobilize civilians to be active in security. It had encouraged the creation of local Citizen Security Councils to provide information and support for the police and to bring together the police and the community. The councils, coordinated by the head of the force's Public Relations and Information Office, were supported by station and substation chiefs. They included representatives of the different sectors of the local population (government, fire fighters, educational institutions, professional and community associations, neighborhood committees, merchants, businesspeople, the judiciary, and the public prosecutor's office). According to one study, the councils had worked well in middle- and upper-class communities; however, in more economically depressed areas, where crime is a more serious problem or where paramilitary groups were present during the armed conflict, the model failed, due to longstanding distrust between the police and the citizenry (IEPADES, 2000).

The Villa Nueva project created a Municipal Citizen Security Council with representatives from all of the institutions and entities involved or interested in the subject. The council's objective was to coordinate the different activities that were to be carried out in Villa Nueva concerning crime prevention and control. Because of the size of the council, the members created an executive committee responsible for carrying out the actions agreed upon. The activities of the police were to emphasize patrols in high-crime areas and reduce the illegal sale of alcoholic beverages by monitoring and penalizing businesses that sold alcohol near schools and parks. Meetings were also organized among police, prosecutors, judges, and defense lawyers in order to coordinate their activities and increase the efficiency of their institutions. Contact with youth gangs was pursued, with the participation of community leaders, teachers, and members of the National Civil Police, in order to promote the social rehabilitation of gang members involved in criminal activity.

The Case of Bogotá, Colombia

In contrast to Villa Nueva, community policing in Bogotá was the result of an internal decision by the police force, although the model adopted and the training provided had a strong international component. The police force suffered greatly from the violence created by drug trafficking and guerrilla activity. In the late 1980s, the attempt to combat drug trafficking seriously affected ethical standards within the organization. Police were involved in human rights violations (Llorente, 2004, p. 67). In the early 1990s, they came under serious questioning because of their ineffectiveness and their participation in the killing of criminals, prostitutes, and mentally ill persons in various cities. Cases of corruption were also a source of concern.

In response to criticism, a two-phase reform process was begun in 1993. The first phase sought to accentuate the civil nature of the police, even though the force continued to report to the Ministry of Defense. In 1995, an internal purge was initiated. It was driven by the command structure itself, and affected senior officials as well as the rank and file. The results of this type of transformation of police culture can be seen in surveys, such as the one carried out in Bogotá in 1996, dealing with public expectations of the police (Centro Nacional de Consultoría, 1996). The survey suggested that community policing was capable of responding to citizens' demands; however, it was not until 1998 that the commander of the city's police department adopted community policing as the jurisdiction's most important program.

The initiative has been supported by the police hierarchy, and has enjoyed the collaboration of the Bogotá Chamber of Commerce, which initially proposed creating the Urban Guard to be funded by the municipal administration under the mayor's control (Llorente, 2004, p. 72). The national government, in turn, made community policing throughout the country one of the central tenets of its security policy.

One thousand police officers were chosen and trained for the community policing program. Candidates were chosen on the basis of a profile representing qualities considered relevant to the objectives. These officers form a special branch of the patrol service, which also includes employees carrying out traditional police work. The community police are assigned to work in specific permanent patrol areas.

The main manifestation of community work has been police support for the Local Security Fronts and Citizen Security Schools. The fronts serve as support networks for the police. Organized by blocks or sections of neighborhoods, they conduct informal patrols and work with neighbors when suspicious situations arise. Neighbors exchange telephone numbers and install neighborhood alarm systems. Although there are nearly 5,400 fronts in Bogotá, they cover only 13% of the city's blocks (Llorente, 2004, pp. 87–90). The Citizen Security Schools focus on local leaders and attempt to produce citizens knowledgeable about security to serve as disseminators. The police provide training on legal issues as well as information on preventive measures that citizens can take. Since their creation in 1996, these schools have trained 21,000 citizens to become members of the security fronts.

Although the driving force behind the program has principally come from within the country, there has been international support for training the officers who constituted the initial nucleus of the project. Twenty-one Bogotá police officers attended a four-week seminar at the University of Barcelona in 1998 run by specialists in community policing and by Urban Guards. In 1999, 10 additional officers participated in a similar course in Toledo, Spain.

The Case of Belo Horizonte, Brazil

In Belo Horizonte, capital of the state of Minas Gerais, the immediate predecessor of the current program was a project carried out in some of the city's neighborhoods beginning in 1993. A recent evaluation of the experiment judged it a failure because the police lacked the necessary training, the program had no indicators that would have made it possible to evaluate its effectiveness, and the program was perceived as a tool for the police to obtain funding from the community for its own projects (Souza, 1999).

In 1999, the Minas Gerais Military Police command implemented a broader program, based on results-based policing. This involved deploying police according to geographic information on crime, and the creation of Community Security Councils whose objective was to formulate, with the police, preventive strategies in response to the area's needs. The driving force behind this program is primarily the Military Police, which has received support from the Federal University of Minas Gerais to develop training, both for the members of the community councils and for the police. As in the case of São Paulo, there is little coordination between civil and military police, and the former, whose role is crime investigation, hardly participates in the program (Beato, 2004).

The central objective of the councils is to develop preventive programs with community participation. There is one council for each of the 25 companies of the police force. The members of the councils are the company commanders, and representatives of the mayor's office and other entities and associations. According to their charters, the councils are to train police for community action, attract new members, disseminate programs that help communities to protect themselves, and gather periodic information on the police services provided to citizens (Beato, 2004, pp. 142–143).

Emerging from these community councils are anecdotal examples of joint efforts with the police, designed to address acute public security problems, but their activity and the influence they exert on police action vary widely. There is also an inverse relation between the level of functioning of the councils and the level of violent crime, thus, where there is more violent crime, the functioning of these community organizations is relatively poor (Beato, 2004, p. 167).

Problems of Implementation

Institutional Obstacles to Change

As explained above, community policing programs in Latin America are trying to confront profound internal and external challenges. Consequently, their impact must be measured not only in terms of their ability to reduce fear and actual crime levels, but also in terms of their ability to produce significant change within the police itself. The comparative literature consistently shows that successful community policing programs create a problem-solving orientation among a majority of the police officers, and they require a decentralization of police functioning, emphasizing close relationships with the community and establishing a more flexible system of shifts and schedules to allow employees time to contact community members during nonworking hours when they are able to attend meetings. Studies in the United States also stress the need for a new management system that supports employee participation and views those at the command level as facilitators rather than as authorities in a hierarchically centralized system (Wyckoff and Skogan, 1994).

A central aspect of any community policing program, by definition, is the emphasis on the officers on the street, who are in direct contact with the public. It is imperative that there be more foot patrols, or some other form of ongoing presence and interaction with the public, such as occurs at small neighborhood police stations. To ensure that the police establish frequent contact and close relationships with the community, officers assigned to a given patrol area must be required to remain there for a fixed, and significant, period of time (Frühling, 2000).

However, although community policing demands a major use of personnel in order to create significant relationships with residents, funding for personnel is often not available to the extent necessary to meet the requirements of the model. The Villa Nueva substation, for example, had only 117 officers at the beginning of the project—far from sufficient (Chinchilla, 2004, p. 46). Although 80 officers from the old National Police were added, the police–resident ratio remained lower than in the rest of the country. The lack and instability of staffing led to extending the workday to as much as 12 hours. This, added to the need for more foot patrols, provoked complaints from the police officers (Ibid., p. 49). Moreover, despite the changes, the traditional features of a police organization remained in place, and the structure remained rigid and authoritarian in its treatment of subordinate personnel.

The cost of the Bogotá community policing program represented only 5.7% of all investment made in the Metropolitan Police by the national government and municipal administration in the period of time covered by the program (Llorente, 2004, p. 74). Only 6% of the police officers in the Bogotá Police Department are assigned to community policing; this is 15% of the number of officers involved in preventive patrol activity. It is clear, then, that nontargeted preventive patrolling and reactive response to incidents are still the prevailing modalities. As in the case of Villa Nueva, community service covers a significant proportion of the city—blocks containing 3 million inhabitants, or 42% of Bogotá's population. However, the ratio between officers and residents is excessively low, and the result is that, according to surveys, only 13% of households and 16% of the city's commercial establishments say that their neighborhood is served by the community police (Ibid., p. 82).

Unlike the Villa Nueva experiment, which was a pilot case, and the Bogotá program, which was not intended for immediate implementation by the police as a whole, the São Paulo program was an attempt to produce profound change in the police organization. The mission and values of the Military Police were redefined, the police participating in the program received special training, specific companies were selected to carry out the program, small stations were established in neighborhoods, and mobile stations were acquired as a way of establishing closer ties with residents (de Mesquita Neto, 2004, pp. 119–123). In 2001, a total of 7,305 police worked in mobile stations and neighborhood stations. However, both the number of police involved and the funding levels were low. In 1998 and 1999, the Military Police had no officers exclusively assigned to the implementation of community policing at either the state or local level. As a result, officers had to attend meetings or establish contacts with neighborhood residents in their assigned areas on their own time—generally after the end of their shifts. Only in 2000 did the Military Police create a Department of Community Policing and Human Rights, designed to plan and coordinate the program. Although much of its budget has been devoted to training police and neighborhood leaders, a large majority of police personnel still have not participated in the community program at all (de Mesquita Neto, 2004, p. 124). In Belo Horizonte, surveys of police indicate that only 24.7% performed foot patrols during the past five years (Beato, 2004, p. 161).

Related to these constraints is the difficulty that police management has in ensuring the stability of the force in the neighborhoods they patrol. This is due in part to demands for police in other areas, in part to requests from police themselves who wish to be transferred elsewhere, and in part to the process of promotion and transfer, which involves the constant movement of personnel. In Villa Nueva, those interviewed frequently referred to the project's high turnover rates, which required constant training of new community police officers (Chinchilla, 2004). Turnover in commanders was also identified as a problem in the Belo Horizonte program (Beato, 2004, p. 146).

Yet another institutional difficulty that affects community policing programs is the very culture of police institutions, which is skeptical that programs of this type can adequately deal with crime. As a result, the principles of community policing are not applied wholeheartedly. Although such resistance has been seen in similar programs in the United States, it can be assumed that resistance will be greater in centralized and very hierarchical institutions in societies where democratic beliefs are weak. The idea that strict enforcement of the law, alone, is enough to control crime can easily prevail in such a context.

For example, in a survey of 1,200 police officers in the city of Belo Horizonte, conducted by the Research Center on Public Security (Centro de Investigacão em Seguridade Pública [CRISP], at the Federal University of Minas Gerais), 46.1% of respondents thought that the most important measures for controlling crime were increasing material and human police resources and increasing police salaries; 58.7% agreed totally or partially with the statement that "the people equipped to evaluate what the police do are their colleagues," which raises questions about the principle of community accountability underlying community policing programs; and 44.7% of police pointed to human rights organizations in explaining why the public had difficulty understanding the work that the police do (Beato, 2004).

An ILANUD (Instituto Latinoamericano de la Organización de las Naciones Unidas para la Prevención del Delito y el Tratamiento del Delincuente) survey of a sample of military police officers in São Paulo indicates that they had a generally positive view of community policing; only

16% of respondents thought that the project should be discontinued (Kahn, 2003, p. 18). Comparing community policing with traditional police work, 46.7% of community police officers surveyed considered community policing more satisfactory from a personal perspective, and 50.6% stated that community policing did a better job of serving the community. However, only 21.4% thought community policing was more efficient in dealing with crime (Ibid., p. 25).

One final and serious obstacle to implementing community policing programs is the lack of identification that low-ranking officers feel with such programs, as well as the insufficient training officers receive in regard to problem solving. In Belo Horizonte, the street police, unlike senior officers, showed little knowledge about the community program. Evaluations show a vast difference between senior and subordinate personnel in their knowledge of and degree of preparation for participating in the program. Specifically, there is little appreciation for the role of citizen councils; only 10% of personnel below the rank of sergeant had a high level of knowledge in this respect (Beato, 2004, pp. 162–163).

The ILANUD survey of the São Paulo Military Police indicates that the concept of community policing is appreciated at the rank of sergeant and above, while officers at the corporal and private levels show resistance: 34.4% of the sample of ranking officers considered community policing more efficient as a means of fighting crime, but only 17.8% of the rank and file agreed (Kahn, 2003, p. 25). Indeed, 66.6% of the rank and file considered community policing a public relations tactic to improve the image of the police, an opinion shared by 43.5% of ranking officers as well. How does one explain this phenomenon?

First, there has almost surely been a failure in the attempts to train and involve subordinate personnel in the program. As Beato notes (2004, p. 163), a high degree of obedience by subordinates is a basic element of centralized, hierarchical organizations; hence, little effort is typically made to creatively involve lower-ranking personnel in institutional changes. Another factor is that such efforts by senior officers may evoke little enthusiasm from subordinates, who prefer to simply meet standards and carry out orders, and who resist more autonomy because it would mean having personal accountability for results.

These institutional difficulties may partially explain the information suggesting that the bulk of police activity continues to be reactive in nature, rather than utilizing the type of problem solving involved in community policing models (Beato, 2004).

The Relationship between Police and Community

Given a history of conflict between the police and the public, it is hardly surprising that difficulties should arise in implementing community policing programs in Latin America, where citizen participation has not succeeded in defining priorities for police action, and citizens are ill-prepared to interact with the police or to take courses of action designed to solve the security problems affecting them. When the Villa Nueva program project began, the Municipal Citizen Security Council was formed, incorporating representatives of all institutions and organizations involved or interested in the issues. The objective of the council was to coordinate crime prevention and control activities. It formed an executive committee to carry out the actions agreed upon. The executive committee was initially composed of a chair (a trial court judge), a woman representing education directors, and a substation chief of the National Civil Police. Shortly thereafter, it was expanded to include representatives of other sectors (religious, business, media, and municipal government). The executive committee met at least once a week through 2000; its members also dedicated time to the activities outlined in the action plan. The executive committee contributed to the process of cooperation among police, governmental institutions, and private enterprises (Chinchilla, 2004, p. 50).

In Minas Gerais, no central advisory commission was created; from the beginning, an effort was made to decentralize police activity and community relations. In each of the areas covered by the 25 companies that make up the police force, community security councils were created to work with the police to plan patrols and other preventive activity. The councils' charters state that they are responsible for bringing in new members, training police for community action, gathering and systematizing information on police services in order to assess them, carrying out informational campaigns to help communities protect themselves, and providing programs to address social problems that carry implications for citizen security (Beato, 2004, p. 143).

Training for the people participating in the local committees is indispensable if citizen participation is to go beyond voicing complaints about police inaction and actually contribute to designing measures to solve security problems. In the case of Bogotá, the Community Policing Office of the National Police has reported two types of community relations. On the one hand, mechanisms for relationship and participation are created according to the local context, with police and citizens taking flexible roles in determining the mechanisms. On the other hand, more formal programs involve neighborhood organizations in patrol activity. The most important of these are the Citizen Security Schools and Local Security Fronts, which had been developing in the city since 1996 as a National Police initiative (see preceding discussion).

The only evaluation of the community councils known to the author was carried out by CRISP. It examined a number of dimensions of the councils' functioning. The different values for the variables (participation, for example) were nonexistent, low, moderate, and high. According to the evaluation, all of the councils were functioning a year after their creation, the majority at the medium level, and a minority at a high level. The vast majority had low or medium levels of representativeness, despite efforts to attract new members. Councils were less fully representative in locales with high levels of violence, or characterized by great social diversity. The oversight capacity of councils, vis-à-vis the police, is generally low. Although there is some attendance at meetings, participation is moderate or low in most cases. Meetings are generally held on a weekly or monthly basis, with 10 to 30 people attending. In the community policing model, participation should become independent of the police command structure, so as to provide oversight of police conduct and effectively promote public priorities; however, the evaluation found that autonomy, vis-à-vis local police commands, was low or nonexistent in 11 cases, moderate in 8, and high in only 1 case. This presents a dilemma: What methods should be implemented to make the councils, created by the police, independent? In Belo Horizonte, as in São Paulo, a minority of the social organizations involved in preventive programs apparently uses strategic action planning and problem-solving methods to address crime. The level of training among the civilian leadership of the councils seems to have been generally low, although, in a minority of cases, the opposite was true. Finally, police of officer rank participating in the councils evinced a high level of support for community participation programs, while police of lower rank showed little familiarity with the programs.

One of the main factors affecting the councils' functioning seems to be the crime rate in the particular area; this is understandable because in areas with high crime rates, the readiness to cooperate with police is, by definition, less pronounced. Moreover, police officials are more supportive of community policing where the crime rates are low, while favoring more coercive methods in areas where there is more violence.

Working with Other Public Entities

The objective and subjective security of the population does not depend solely on police action. The community policing model assumes that the police will coordinate effectively with other public entities to solve security problems.

In the Villa Nueva project, the creation of the Municipal Citizen Security Council led to a series of initiatives that required coordination among police, municipal government, prosecutors, judges, and public defenders. The presence of the council helped solve specific problems, such as lighting in public places. As a result of institutional cooperation with judges, the judicial system adopted more expeditious procedures for taking statements from people arrested by the police, overcrowding in police lockups was reduced, and pressure on police finances was diminished (Chinchilla, 2004, pp. 30, 57). However, the regularity of meetings with various governmental institutions fell off notably when international participation in the project ceased.

In Bogotá, there was an effort by the police and the municipal administration to cooperate in the framework of the Mission Bogotá program, which was one of the pillars of citizen security policy under Mayor Enrique Peñalosa's administration (1998 to 2000). The program sought to recover public spaces by involving the affected public in assessing the problems and devising solutions. Joint action involving the community police was required. In these cases, however, cooperation failed as a result of institutional jealousies between the staff of Mission Bogotá and the police, competition for leadership in creating security schools and fronts, and the inherent difficulty involved in coordinating highly visible public and political entities with no direct hierarchical relationship (Llorente, 2004, pp. 86–87).

The pressure of the public security problem has impelled municipalities in Minas Gerais to provide funds for the police. In one election year, the prefect (mayor) of Belo Horizonte announced that he would provide $2 million for the purchase of police vehicles and arms, and for organizing databases for security councils. However, because of weak organizational coordination between the police and the local government, the funds were used simply to support traditional reactive police strategies (Beato, 2004, p. 165). This outcome, probably due to police preferences, also reflects the fact that organizational coordination would require that local government have explicit authority for security matters, and that the police be required to take municipal government's priorities into account when planning activities. The lack of explicit authority for municipal government makes it difficult to coordinate government and police agendas.

In North America, closer relations with the community and with local government agencies are easier for community policing programs because security policy is local and fully decentralized. This is not the case in most countries in Latin America where police report to central or regional governments and collaboration suffers accordingly. However, the fact that institutional collaboration between police and other public agencies is less systematic than might be hoped is also due to the fact that the police are resistant to assuming responsibility for social demands, which they view as lying beyond their area of authority. At the same time, local government feels that community-based programs, while they solve some problems, create new demands for investment that are difficult to satisfy.

Results of the Community Policing Programs

Measurement of the effect of these community policing programs on levels of fear among the population and crime rates is not entirely reliable, given that none of the cases compares what occurred in the areas where community policing programs were operating with areas where traditional patrols were operating. Surveys on victimization before and after the implementation of the program were only carried out in Villa Nueva. As a result, in three of the cases, police crime report figures are used.

In the case of Villa Nueva, two victimization surveys were conducted: one prior to the beginning of the project in 1998 and another in 2000. The latter survey indicates a 10-point reduction in the percentage of people who reported having been a crime victim in recent months, from 34% to 23.8%. According to testimonies collected by the researcher, the increase in police patrols and police supervision of businesses illegally selling alcohol may have contributed to that result.

It is also important to note that the interviews conducted in March 2000 showed a positive evaluation of the community policing project as well as the desire that it continue. In fact, people interviewed in August 2001 were unanimously critical of the suspension of community policing, which ended once the funding from the project sponsor, the Inter-American Institute of Human Rights, had run out.

The positive evaluation of the community policing programs by the public was also evident, with nuances, in São Paulo. The evaluation of the program's impact has been measured through public opinion surveys carried out at the state level and through studies conducted in certain local areas. The first surveys demonstrate that the public's opinion of the police tended to improve overall in the state in the years immediately following the application of the community strategy. However, because of the size of the state, and the lack of sufficiently disaggregated data, it is impossible to determine if the improvement in public opinion was due solely to the community policing program.

As a result, we believe that the only way to determine if implementation of the community model is responsible for changes in public opinion regarding police matters and levels of fear is to focus the surveys on those areas where such programs are effectively being implemented. Two studies have been conducted with that goal. The first was carried out in Jardim Ângela, one of the most violent districts of the city, by the Fórum em Defesa da Vida (Forum in Defense of Life). The Forum conducted a survey of 945 residents and merchants to determine their perceptions of community policing. Residents and people who worked less than one kilometer from the small neighborhood police stations had a better perception of community policing, its effect on citizen insecurity, and treatment of citizens than those who lived or worked farther away from the stations. This suggests that the community model has a positive effect on the opinion of those who are familiar with it, but that diffusion of the model's effects does not reach all citizens in the area.

A study carried out by the United Nations Latin American Institute for the Prevention of Crime and the Treatment of Offenders (Instituto Latinoamericano de las Naciones Unidas para la Prevención del Delito y el

Tratamiento del Delincuente, or ILANUD) in 2000 focused on 23 neighborhoods of São Paulo with community policing stations and 23 neighborhoods without them. The results suggest some similarities with the previously mentioned study. In those areas where a community policing program was in place and residents were aware of it, there were lower levels of fear, better opinions of the police, and greater support for community policing than in those areas where there was a community policing program, but no awareness of it, or where community policing was not implemented (Kahn, 2000).

The results of both surveys seem to suggest that the impact of community policing on feelings of insecurity requires a combination of methods for establishing closer personal contact and communication for promoting awareness of the program and its advantages. But it also suggests that the effects of the program are very dependent on physical proximity to the police presence. Whether because of the lack of personnel or the lack of initiatives to build closer community relations, the presence of the community policing program is not obvious to all residents.

The Jardim Ângela survey indicates that a majority of the population continues to believe that the police do very little about drug trafficking and they view the police as often collaborating with drug traffickers. The ILANUD survey, meanwhile, demonstrates that the presence of small community police stations does not have an effect on victimization levels.

The preliminary results observed indicate that community policing provides, to an important degree, a response to the need to increase public confidence in the police and that it constitutes a path toward building a police force that is guided by problem-solving methods and which acts in a scientific manner. The success of programs that have been implemented is a serious challenge for the police, which must undertake significant institutional reforms to accompany the development of closer community relations.

Conclusion

The implementation of community policing programs is expanding in Latin America, in response to a variety of factors. First, the lack of public confidence in the police; second, the need to change strategies for confronting rising rates in violent crime; and finally, the need to modernize the police as an institution.

The available information permits the assertion that community policing programs receive strong public support, which favors their continuation. They improve the public's perception of the police while at the same time reducing the public's fear, when there is effective awareness that such programs are being implemented. This indicates that community activities by themselves do not generate a reduction in citizen fears, but also require an intense and publicized police presence, regular interaction patterns, and adequate communication to the public. In general, in this relationship with the community, there should be concern for building closer relations with the lowest-income sectors, to avoid the possibility that such a strategy favors the more affluent sectors, which already have access to private security services. With respect to crime, the impact of these programs is not totally conclusive.

A crucial aspect of these reforms is the impact that they can have with respect to an overall decrease in police abuse. It is widely known that such reforms are a step in the right direction that must be accompanied by retraining programs for police who have shown a tendency to abuse, and the establishment of an early alarm system to address continual violations by certain police officers, among other measures (Frühling, 2002, p. 35).

Community policing appears to be a first step in transforming the police into a truly modern, democratic organization. The information presented here suggests that skepticism exists as to whether this goal is actually being achieved in the countries whose programs have been described—or, indeed, whether such change is even possible. In developed democratic countries where scientific assessments of community policing are available, profound transformations have been achieved. Community policing has led to new internal values systems, reduced hierarchical distance within police organizations, and produced a drive for innovation and individual responsibility that transcends disciplinary systems and other controls by the command structure. The paradigm behind the community policing model implies that the police, as professionals responsible for public order, must design strategic solutions to the demands of citizens, addressing patterns and trends in crime. It is clear that the human, material, and organizational resources in Latin American police forces, and their organizational paradigms, are very different. A skepticism regarding these programs among subordinate police personnel is part of the reality that must be taken into account, as are the lack of training for strategic problem solving and the financial and logistical problems that limit the expansion of these programs beyond mere pilot experiments.

References

Bayley, D. (1994). *Police for the future*. New York: Oxford University Press.

Beato, C.C. (2004). Reinventar la polícia: La experiencia de Belo Horizonte (Reinventing the police: The experience of Belo Horizonte). In H. Frühling (Ed.), *Calles más seguras. Estudios de policía comunitaria en América Latina (Safer streets: Studies of community policing in Latin America)* (pp. 139–175). Washington D.C.: Inter-American Development Bank.

Bresser, C.P. (1999). Managerial public administration: Strategy and structure for a new state. In L.C.B. Pereira & P. Spink (Eds.), *Managerial public administration in Latin America* (pp. 1–13). Boulder, CO: Lynne Rienner Publishers.

Centro Nacional de Consultoria (1996). La consulta ciudadana en Santa Fe de Bogota. Informe No36 entregado a la Policía Nacional. Bogotá: mimeo (Citizen consultation carried out in Santa Fe of Bogotá. Report No 36 delivered to the National Police: mimeo.

Chinchilla, M.L. (2004). El caso del municipio de Villa Nueva, Guatemala (The case of the municipality of Villa Nueva, Guatemala). In H. Frühling (Ed.), *Calles más seguras. Estudios de policía comunitaria en América Latina* (*Safer streets: Studies of community policing in Latin America*) (pp. 39–64). Washington D.C.: Inter-American Development Bank.

de Mesquita Neto, P. (2004). La policía comunitaria en Sao Paulo: Problemas de implementación y consolidaci (Community policing in Sao Paulo: Implementation and consolidation problems). In H. Fruhling (Ed.), *Calles más seguras. Estudios de policía comunitaria en América Latina* (*Safer streets: Studies of community policing in Latin America*) (pp. 109–137). Washington D.C.: Inter-American Development Bank.

de Mesquita Neto P. & Affonso, B.S. (1998). *Policiamento comunitário: A experiência en São Paulo*. São Paulo: Núcleo de Estudos da Violencia da Universidade de São Paulo.

Frühling, H. (2000). La nodernización de la policía en América Latina. In J. Sapoznikow & F.C. Flórez (Eds.), *Convivencia y seguridad: un reto a la gobernabilidad: trabajos presentados en el foro "Convivencia y seguridad ciudadana"* (pp. 207–238). San Salvador, El Salvador: Banco Interamericano de Desarrollo.

Frühling, H. (2002). Policía y sociedad. Tres experiencias Sudamericanas (Police and society: Three South American experiences). *Renglones, 51*, 23–35.

Frühling, H. (Ed.) (2004). *Calles más seguras. Estudios de policía comunitaria en América Latina* (*Safer streets: Studies of community policing in Latin America*). Washington D.C.: Inter-American Development Bank.

Instituto de Enseñanza para el Desarrollo Sostenible (IEPADES) (2000). Informe de avance sobre la investigación relaciones policía—Comunidad en Guatemala. In *Proyecto sociedad civil y seguridad ciudadana: Un estudio comparativo de la reforma a la seguridad pública en Centroamérica*. Washington, D.C.: Washington Office on Latin America.

Kahn, T. (2000). Policia comunitária: Avaliando a experiencia (Community policing: Evaluating the experience). Report on a study carried out by ILANUD, Costa Rica, and financed by the Ford Foundation, New York City, NY.

Kahn, T. (2003). *Policía comunitaria: Evaluando la experiencia*. Santiago de Chile: Centro de Estudios para el Desarrollo.

Llorente, M.V. (2004). La experiencia de Bogotá: contexto y balance (The Bogotá experience: Context and outcome). In H. Fruhling (Ed.), *Calles más seguras. Estudios de policía comunitaria en América Latina* (*Safer streets: Studies of community policing in Latin America*) (pp. 65–108). Washington D.C.: Inter-American Development Bank.

Muniz, J.S.P., Larvie, L., Musumeci, L., & Freire, B. (1997). Resistencias e dificuldades de um programa de policiamento comunitário (Resistance and difficulties of a community policing program). *Tempo Social, 9*, 197–214.

Neild, R. (2002). Reform: Democratic policing in Central America. Washington D.C.: WOLA.

Rosenbaum, D.P. (1998). The changing role of the police: Assessing the current transition to community policing. In Jean-Paul Brodeur (Ed.), *How to recognize good policing: Problems and issues* (pp. 3–29). Washington, D.C.: Police Executive Research Forum.

Sherman, L.W. (1995). The police. In J.Q. Wilson & J. Petersilia (Eds.), *Crime* (pp. 327–348). San Francisco: Center for Self-Governance.

Souza, E. (1999). *Avaliação do policiamento comunitário em Belo Horizonte.* Master's thesis, Universidade Federal de Minas Gerais, Brazil.

Stanley, W. (1999). Building new police forces in El Salvador and Guatemala: Learning and counter-learning. *International Peacekeeping, 6*, 113–134.

Wycoff, M.A. & Skogan, W.G. (1994). Community policing in Madison. An analysis of implementation and impact. In D.P. Rosenbaum (Ed.), *The challenge of community policing* (pp. 75–91). Thousand Oaks, CA: Sage Publications.

Authors

David E. Barlow is a professor and dean of the College of Arts and Sciences at Fayetteville State University in North Carolina. Dr. Barlow is also presently a member of the North Carolina Sentencing and Policy Advisory Commission. His research interests include multicultural issues in policing, white collar crime, and the history, ideology, and political economy of crime control in the United States. He has worked in the criminal justice field as a correctional officer, deputy sheriff, and university police officer in South Carolina and Florida. Dr. Barlow is the author of numerous articles in professional journals, co-editor of two books, *Classics in Policing* (Anderson, 1996) and *Police in America: Classical and Contemporary Readings* (Wadsworth, 2004), and co-author of the book, *Police in a Multicultural Society: An American Story* (Waveland, 2000).

Melissa Hickman Barlow is a professor in the Department of Criminal Justice and director of the Institute for Community Justice at Fayetteville State University, Fayetteville, North Carolina. She is co-author of *Police in a Multicultural Society: An American Story* (Waveland, 2000) and has published articles on the history and political economy of crime control policy, crime and justice in the news media, and race and class issues in criminal justice. Her article, "La Natura Ideologica delle Notizie Sul Crimine," appears in Gabrio Forti and Marta Bertolini's (2005) *La Televisione del Crimine.* Professor Barlow is interested in the race and class politics of criminal justice policy, critical resistance to mass incarceration, and grassroots efforts to reduce incarceration through community justice initiatives. She was elected second vice president of the Academy of Criminal Justice Sciences in 2009 and will serve as president in 2011.

John Casey is an associate professor in the School of Public Affairs, Baruch College, City University of New York. From 1999 to 2007, he was a senior lecturer at the Australian Graduate School of Policing, Charles Sturt University, Sydney. Previous to his academic career, he was the executive officer of the Master's in Public Management program at a three university consortium in Barcelona, Spain; the director of the Mayor's Office of Adult Literacy for the City of New York; and a social services manager in Sydney, Australia. He is co-editor of the book *Police Leadership and Management,* which was published by Federation Press in 2007.

Hugo Frühling is a professor at the Institute of Public Affairs of the University of Chile and the director of its Center for the Study of Citizen Security. He has a doctorate and a master's degree in law from Harvard Law School, and a license in Juridical and Social Sciences from the University of Chile. He has written extensively on police and criminal justice reform in Latin America, human rights, and public security policies. His latest book focused on police accountability. He has been a consultant for the Inter-American Development Bank, for the World Bank, and for the United Nations Development Program in several countries in Latin America.

Suzette Heald is a senior research fellow at the Crisis States Research Centre at the London School of Economics. As a social anthropologist, she has extensive research experience in Eastern and Southern Africa and is currently working on the *sungusungu* vigilante movement in Tanzania and Kenya, with special reference to the Kuria. She obtained her Ph.D. from University College London, completing an ethnographic study of the Gisu of Uganda, and has held academic posts at Lancaster University (U.K.), the University of Botswana, and Brunel University (U.K.) working as a professor of Social Anthropology. Her books include *Controlling Anger: The Anthropology of Gisu Violence; Manhood and Morality: Sex, Ritual and Violence in Gisu Society*; *Anthropology and Psychoanalysis* (co-editor); and *Good Deaths/Bad Deaths: Dilemmas of Death in Comparative Perspective* (co-editor); as well as *Praise Poems of the Kuria.*

Anita Kalunta-Crumpton is an associate professor at Texas Southern University in Houston. She has published extensively, particularly in the areas of race and criminal justice, and drug trafficking and drug use. Her most recent book is entitled *Drugs, Victims and Race: The Politics of Drug Control* (Waterside Press, 2006).

Otwin Marenin is a professor in the Political Science Department/Criminal Justice at Washington State University, Pullman. He received his B.S. degree from Northern Arizona University (Flagstaff) and his master's and Ph.D. degrees (in Comparative Politics) from UCLA. He has taught at Ahmadu Bello University and the University of Benin in Nigeria, and the Universities of Baltimore, California, Colorado, and Alaska-Fairbanks in the United States. His research and publications have focused on policing systems in Native American communities in the United States and on the origins and practices of policing in Africa, especially in Nigeria. More recently, he has done research and written on developments in international policing, transnational police assistance programs, and efforts to reform the policing systems in failed, transitional, and developing states. Recent publications include *Policing Change, Changing Police: International Perspectives* (editor), *Challenges of Policing Democracies* (co-editor with Dilip Das), and *Transforming the Police in Central and Eastern Europe* (co-editor with Marina Caparini).

Anthony Minnaar is a professor of Criminal Justice Studies in the Department of Security Risk Management at the School of Criminal Justice, College of Law, University of South Africa. He is the postgraduate coordinator for the department's master's degree program and acting head of the department. His research interests currently are in the broad field of criminal justice dealing with the specific issues of corruption prevention, border controls and undocumented migrants, use of firearms in violent crime, civilian oversight of public and private policing, and private security industry issues (specifically, crime prevention and private policing and security at ports-of-entry, security measures at "security villages" and gated neighborhoods) and CCTV open-street surveillance. His most recent research project looks at the function and role of the Private Security Industry Regulatory Authority in regulating and monitoring the Private Security Industry in South Africa.

Christian Mouhanna has a Ph.D. in sociology and is a permanent researcher at the Centre for Research in the Sociology of Criminal Law (CESDIP, CNRS) in Paris, France. He was head of the Research Division at the National Institute of High Studies for Security–French *Ministère de l'Intérieur* (INHES). He worked for 12 years on the relationship between police and population and on the strategies of policing. His main publications are related to the French police, the French gendarmerie, the French justice, and also to the policy of security and criminal justice.

David Pike is an inspector with Victoria Police in Australia and a doctoral student at Charles Sturt University, Sydney. He has been involved in community crime prevention initiatives in Frankston, Dandenong, and Springvale in Victoria and has been a member of a number of community committees including the Frankston Community Safety Management Team, Dandenong Local Safety Committee, and Springvale Drug Action Committee.

Sybille Smeets is a researcher at the Centre of Criminological Researches and an assistant professor at the School of Criminology (Free University of Brussels). She has a doctorate in criminology and a master's degree in Political Sciences. Her main research topics include police function, policing, local prevention policies in Belgium and Europe, and the links between security policies and the welfare state.

Carrol Tange is a researcher at the Centre of Criminological Researches of the Free University of Brussels, a professor at the University of Mons-Hainaut, and an assistant at the University Faculties of Saint-Louis. He has a master's degree in philosophy and in criminology. He is finishing a Ph.D. on the development of managerialism in Belgian police organizations. Former president of the Centre for Police Studies, his main research topics include police work and security policies at local level, and knowledge productions by and about police services.

Lynn Vincentnathan has joint appointments as an assistant professor in the Department of Criminal Justice and the Department of Psychology and Anthropology at the University of Texas–Pan American, Edinburg. She has a doctorate in anthropology from the University of Wisconsin–Madison, and a master's degree in sociology from Northern Illinois University, DeKalb. Her teaching and research areas include South Asia, the untouchables of India, research methods, anthropological theory, and environmental crime and justice.

S. George Vincentnathan is a professor and chair of the Department of Criminal Justice, University of Texas–Pan American, Edinburg. He has a doctorate in criminology and a master's degree in anthropology from the University of California, Berkeley, and a master's degree in sociology from Annamalai University in India. His teaching and research areas include criminological theory; comparative criminology and justice, especially in relation to the United States, Japan, and India; juvenile delinquency and justice; and corrections.

Kam C. Wong is an associate professor at Xavier University, Cincinnati, Ohio. He received a J.D. from Indiana University, a diploma (N.I.T.A.) from Northwestern, and a master's degree and Ph.D. from SUNY, Albany. Dr. Wong has been the vice-chair of the Hong Kong Society of Criminology (1999 to 2002); vice-president (1999 to 2002); associate fellow at the Center of Criminology, University of Hong Kong; and vice-president (2001 to 2002) and president (2002 to 2003) of the AAPS (Asian Association of Police Studies). He has published 80 articles/chapters. His latest books include: *The Impact of USA Patriot Act on American Society: An Evidence Based Assessment* (Nova Publishers, 2007) and *The Making of USA Patriot Act: Legislation, Implementation, Impact* (China Law Press, 2008; in Chinese). He is working on two new books: *Policing with Chinese Characteristics* (forthcoming) and *Cyberspace Governance in China* (in progress).

Index

A

B

C

J

K

L

M

N

Q

R

S